Truman Capote: Conversations

Literary Conversations Series

Peggy Whitman Prenshaw
General Editor

Photo: William S. Paley / Library of Congress

Truman Capote: Conversations

Edited by
M. Thomas Inge

University Press of Mississippi
Jackson and London

Copyright © 1987 by the University Press of Mississippi
All rights reserved
Print-on-Demand Edition
89 88 87   3   2 1

The paper in this book meets the guidelines for permanence and durability
of the Committee on Production Guidelines for Book Longevity
of the Council on Library Resources.

Library of Congress Cataloging-in-Publication Data
Capote, Truman, 1924-
   Truman Capote : conversations.

   (Literary conversations series)
   Includes index.
   1. Capote, Truman, 1924-   —Interviews.
2. Authors, American—20th century—Interviews.
I. Inge, M. Thomas.   II. Series.
PS3505.A59Z475   1987   813'.54 [B]   86-19116
ISBN 0-87805-274-7 (alk. paper)
ISBN 0-87805-275-5 (pbk. : alk. paper)
British Library Cataloguing in Publication Data is available.

Books by Truman Capote

Other Voices, Other Rooms. New York: Random House, 1948.
A Tree of Night and Other Stories. New York: Random House, 1949.
Local Color. New York: Random House, 1950.
The Grass Harp. New York: Random House, 1951
The Grass Harp: A Play. New York: Random House, 1952.
The Grass Harp and A Tree of Night and Other Stories. New York: New American Library (Signet), 1956.
The Muses Are Heard: An Account. New York: Random House, 1956.
Breakfast at Tiffany's: A Short Novel and Three Stories. New York: Random House, 1958.
Observations: Photographs by Richard Avedon, Comments by Truman Capote. New York: Simon and Schuster, 1959.
Selected Writings of Truman Capote. New York: Random House, 1963.
In Cold Blood: A True Account of a Multiple Murder and Its Consequences. New York: Random House, 1966.
A Christmas Memory. New York: Random House, 1966.
The Thanksgiving Visitor. New York: Random House, 1968.
House of Flowers. New York: Random House, 1968.
Trilogy: An Experiment in Multimedia. With Eleanor Perry and Frank Perry. New York: Macmillan, 1969.
The Dogs Bark: Public People and Private Places. New York: Random House, 1973.
Music for Chameleons. New York: Random House, 1980.
One Christmas. New York: Random House, 1983.
Three by Truman Capote. New York: Random House, 1985.
Answered Prayers: The Unfinished Novel. New York: Random House, 1986.

Contents

Introduction *M. Thomas Inge* ix
Chronology xiii
The Legend of "Little T" *Selma Robinson* 3
Talk with Truman Capote *Harvey Breit* 17
The Art of Fiction XVII: Truman Capote *Pati Hill* 20
A Rainy Afternoon with Truman Capote *Eugene Walter* 33
Truman Capote *Roy Newquist* 38
The Story Behind a Nonfiction Novel *George Plimpton* 47
The Author *Haskell Frankel* 69
A Visit with Truman Capote *Gloria Steinem* 73
Truman Capote Swings in the Sun *Alice Albright Hoge* 82
"Go Right Ahead and Ask Me Anything." (And So She Did)
 Gloria Steinem 86
Truman Capote, Man About Town *Jerry Tallmer* 105
Playboy Interview: Truman Capote *Eric Norden* 110
Truman Capote Talks, Talks, Talks *C. Robert Jennings* 164
We Talk To . . . Truman Capote *Barbara Packer, Laurie Deutsch, Barbara Bussmann, Ann Beattie, and Judi Silverman* 171
When Does a Writer Become a Star? Truman Capote
 David Frost 173
Truman Capote on Christmas, Places, Memories
 Mary Cantwell 179
Self-Portrait *Truman Capote* 185

Checking in with Truman Capote   *Gerald Clarke*   196
Truman Capote   *Denis Brian*   210
Sunday with Mr. C.: An Audio-Documentary by Andy Warhol
   Starring Truman Capote   *Andy Warhol*   236
Coda: Another Round with Mister C.   *Jann Wenner*   296
Truman Capote Talks About His Crowd   *Richard Zoerink*   308
The Literary Aquarium of Truman Capote   *Beverly Grunwald*   320
Truman Capote, the Movie Star?   *Josh Greenfeld*   324
Tiny Yes, but a Terror? Do Not Be Fooled by Truman Capote
   in Repose   *Patricia Burstein*   330
After Hours: Books   *Beverly Gary Kempton*   335
Truman Capote: An Interview   *Cathleen Medwick*   339
20 Questions: Truman Capote   *Nancy Collins*   346
Nocturnal Turnings, or How Siamese Twins Have Sex
   Truman Capote   351
Index   366

Introduction

"Of course the truth of it is," Truman Capote once told interviewer Gloria Steinem, "that the thing I like to do most in the whole world is *talk*. . . . If I had to choose between writing and talking—well, I just don't know *what* I'd do!" In a certain sense, there was no disjunction between the two for Capote. The persona he created in the public eye, by the way of interviews in the media and the press, was as much a fictional creation as Holly Golightly, Joel Knox Sansom, Dolly Talbo, or any of the other eccentric characters who populate his fiction. As he told Ms. Steinem in the same interview, "I invented myself, and then I invented a world to fit me."

Rather than accept his tendency to strike outlandish poses, his high-pitched voice, and his taste for the bizarre as disabilities, and seclude himself from society, Capote turned these to an advantage. Using the media, which twentieth-century technology had made available, in a calculated fashion, as did Elvis Presley, Marilyn Monroe, and other popular icons of his time, Capote created a shocking figure for the world stage—the writer as pop cult figure, sensitive but aggressive, devoted to aesthetics but deeply engaged in the world at large, concerned over his literary reputation but willing to hustle his books for increased sales and profits.

The critical establishment seems to admire the reclusive writers, the Faulkners and Salingers, who maintained their privacy and rejected courting the media. The Hemingways and Fitzgeralds they abide because they represent writers who bartered their bright talents away by pursuing public heroism, fame, and money. They seem to demonstrate and justify the myth that the writers who seek profit or popularity inevitably prostitute their art. Capote offended the critics who think this way because he insisted that one could have it both ways, that the writer could devote himself to craftsmanship and high literary values at the same time that he courted the public and created a following through audacity and outrageous public behavior.

Now that the petulant, overweight, and feisty figure is no longer among us, and the critic can no longer condescend to the Capote image, what we have left are his words, his exquisitely crafted stories and essays, his brilliantly realized characters, his sensitivity to the most delicate nuances of the English language. In the line of highly refined prose fiction, only Katherine Anne Porter and Eudora Welty, both of whom he admired, are his equals. Also among his literary remains, however, are the interviews he gave, often almost as carefully controlled in their word choice and turn of phrase as his writing but highly revealing as a reflection of the public personality. The Capote the larger public came to know and admire is partially preserved here, but we also find the side he seldom showed on television, the author as craftsman, fiercely devoted to his art, and keenly aware of his place in the world of letters.

Reading these interviews given over the space of thirty years is to witness Capote in the process of developing a public image, both in the way he exaggerated the facts and created untrue stories about himself. The extent of the exaggeration was sometimes a reflection of the way he responded to the interviewers and their gullibility. An uninformed or stupid question would bring out an amused hostility which resulted in outlandish statements, but someone adept at reading his moods could elicit serious and honest answers. Of course, Capote himself was an expert interviewer, a talent he used in researching his factual writings, even interviewing himself on several occasions, so he knew how to manipulate the questions to his own advantage. Each interview, then, appears to be one more portion of a composite portrait he developed over a lifetime. This collection gives us that portrait in full for the first time.

The interviews collected in this volume range from the first a young Truman Capote granted in 1948 shortly after the appearance of his first novel through the highly-personal self-interview published in 1980 at the conclusion of *Music for Chameleons*, the last major work he would see through the press. They appear as originally published without editorial change or abbreviation. This means that many questions have been repeated from interview to interview, but it is of interest to witness how Capote changed his answers over the course of his career, in accordance with his developing public image. In addition, the archival values of reprinting the entire interviews would

Introduction

seem to outweigh any disadvantage in the repetition. The reader will, in any case, find them both entertaining and informative, given Capote's skill as a subject. The editor wishes to express his appreciation to Peggy Prenshaw and Seetha Srinivasan for the opportunity to prepare this book and to John Baldwin for his faithful and expert assistance. This book is for Tonette, who constantly amazes.

MTI
April 1986

Chronology

1924 Truman Streckfus Persons, son of Nina Faulk Persons and Joseph Persons, born in New Orleans on 30 September. Parents would be divorced a few years later.

1927 Sent to live in rural Alabama with three elderly women and an elderly uncle, including Miss Sook Faulk, later portrayed in his fiction.

1934 Wrote a story "Old Mr. Busybody" for a children's contest sponsored by the *Mobile Press and Reporter*, but only the first installment was published when the editors realized that it was based on local personalities and gossip. Lived with a family in Pass Christian, Mississippi, which inspired the situation and scene in *Other Voices, Other Rooms*.

1939 Mother remarried Joseph Garcia Capote, who legally adopted Truman and changed his name. Began to attend a series of boarding schools including Trinity School and St. John's Academy in New York, finally to be enrolled in Greenwich High School in Millbrook, Connecticut, where he was encouraged by English teacher Catherine Wood. Began sending stories to literary journals.

1942 Employed by *The New Yorker*.

1943 First short story, "The Walls are Cold," published in *Decade of Short Stories*.

1945 "Miriam" published in June *Mademoiselle* and given an O. Henry Memorial Award in 1946.

1946 Signed a contract for a novel in progress with Random House, Capote's publisher throughout his career. "The Headless Hawk" published in November *Harper's Bazaar* and selected for inclusion in *The Best American Short Stories 1947*.

1947 "Shut a Final Door" published in August *Atlantic* and given an O. Henry Award in 1948.

1948 *Other Voices, Other Rooms* published in January.

1949 *Tree of Night and Other Stories* published in February.

1950 *Local Color* published in September.

1951 *The Grass Harp* published in September.

1952 Stage version of *The Grass Harp* opened March 27 on Broadway at Martin Beck Theater.

1953 Mother committed suicide.

1954 John Huston's film *Beat the Devil* released, for which Capote wrote the script. Musical version of short story "House of Flowers" opened December 30 on Broadway at Alvin Theater.

1956 *The Muses are Heard: An Account*, based on his travels in the Soviet Union with the American cast of *Porgy and Bess*, published in November.

1957 "The Duke in His Domain," an interview with Marlon Brando, published in *The New Yorker* of November 9.

1958 *Breakfast at Tiffany's* published in November.

1959 Richard Avedon's book of photographs *Observations*, with text by Capote, appeared. Began research on the murder of the Clutter family for his next book after reading an account of the crime in Holcomb, Kansas, in the *New York Times* of November 16.

1963   *The Selected Writings of Truman Capote* published in February.

1966   *In Cold Blood* published in January after having been serialized in *The New Yorker* on 25 September, 2, 9, and 16 October 1965. *A Christmas Memory* published in November. Hosts "The Party of the Decade" in December at the Hotel Plaza in New York.

1967   Film version of *In Cold Blood* by Richard Brooks released.

1968   *The Thanksgiving Visitor* published in September.

1971   Had operation for cancer.

1972   *Truman Capote Behind Prison Walls*, a ninety-minute documentary presented on ABC television 7 December.

1973   *Crimewatch*, a two-part interview with legal experts on crime, televised on "ABC Wide World of Entertainment" 8 May and 21 June. *The Dogs Bark: Public People and Private Places* published in August.

1975   First excerpt from the unfinished "Answered Prayers" manuscript, "Mojave," published in June *Esquire*, to be followed in the same magazine by "La Côte Basque, 1965" in November, "Unspoiled Monsters" in May 1976, and "Kate McCloud" in December 1976.

1976   Plays role of Lionel Twain in Neil Simon's film *Murder by Death*.

1980   *Music for Chameleons* published.

1984   Died 25 August in Los Angeles.

Truman Capote: Conversations

The Legend of "Little T"
Selma Robinson/1948

From *PM's Picture News*, Sunday Magazine Section, 8 (14 March 1948), 6-8.

The most discussed writer in New York literary circles today is a young novelist with the face and figure of a schoolboy. His name is Truman Capote and his first novel, *Other Voices, Other Rooms*, published January 19 by Random House, has been thrusting forward steadily on the best-seller lists until now nearly 30,000 copies have been sold.

"You can't go to any party these days but what people will line up pro and con on the subject of Truman Capote," a young woman remarked to me recently. "Some take one side, some t'other and not necessarily those who have read his book."

Since the publication of his first short story, "Miriam," in 1945, legend and speculation have clung to his name. Not only the tabloid columnists but the New York *Times Book Review* have printed fantastic "news" about him from time to time.

Last year, Cyril Connolly, writing in the British literary publication, *Horizon*, said:

> "Get Capote—at this minute the words are resounding on many a 60th floor and 'get him' of course means make him and break him, smother him with laurels and then vent on him the obscure hatred which is inherent in the notion of another's superiority."

His publishers, apart from their own enthusiasm for the book, recognized the enormous curiosity concerning the author and ordered an unusually large first printing: 10,000 copies. Six months ago, long before the publishers' West Coast salesman called to peddle the book, a bookseller in San Francisco reported that he had 23 individual orders for it. In other cities, too, booksellers and book buyers seemed to be waiting for it.

What makes its success particularly remarkable is that this book has none of the mediocrity characteristic of most best-selling fiction: its story is the sensitive story of a troubled child; the quality of its writing is subtle, fresh, poetic. Most of the reviews were highly laudatory.

The *Herald Tribune* called it "the most exciting first novel by a young American."

Who is this Truman Capote everybody's talking about? I asked his publishers, his friends, his agents, editors to whom he has sold his stories.

The blurb on the book jacket was too flip to shed much light: "Truman Capote was born in New Orleans; he is 23. He has: written speeches for a third-rate politician, danced on a river boat, made a small fortune painting flowers on glass, read scripts for a movie company, studied fortune telling with the celebrated Mrs. Acey Jones, worked on *The New Yorker* and selected anecdotes for a digest magazine."

To his publishers he is, understandably, "a dream child, a prestige author who makes money."

To his old high school teacher he is a genius with a loyalty to old friends that is unusual and touching.

His close friend Mary Lou Aswell, fiction editor of *Harper's Bazaar*, says that "Little T can be absolutely adorable or such a pain in the neck that you want to take a swift kick at him."

One who signed himself simply "A Critic" sent this on a penny post card to Random House:

> Sirs: Anent your newly found marvel, "Truman Capote" sic, it is downright foolish for you to believe this nincompoop is going anywhere, especially by his stupid poses. . . . Your ad depicts this unsuspecting fool as an inmate of the Buchenwald Camp just released in a starving condition or a flophouse bum reclining on a Bowery chair after an all-night bout with a bottle of "smoke."

The picture that irritated the post card writer is the one that appears on the jacket of the book and most of its advertisements. It shows a child with a hood of bright hair, a stubborn sensitive mouth and wide, watchful eyes, reclining on a Victorian sofa in a checked weskit and white shirt. It has excited adjectives like *haunting, appealing, predatory, sensational*, but, say the publishers, it undeniably sells books.

Truman Capote, I thought when I first met him in his stepfather's apartment on Park Avenue, seemed less frail, less wistfully innocent than his disputed photograph. He looked no more than 17: his blond straight hair fell in boyish bangs over his high forehead. He had a young boy's small body, compact and graceful, and he was dressed, without elegance, in sloppy brown corduroys and a sleeveless tan sweater. His large glasses, framed in butterscotch-colored shell, gave his face a youthful owlishness, like a young Alexander Woollcott.

In that short, stiff period when two strangers who have never met before search for a common ground of talk, Capote apologized in a high childlike voice, for the untidiness of the apartment: his mother was ill in a hospital; he and his stepfather were occupying it until he could find an apartment of his own; he would be taking a trip to Haiti presently; the maid would be in later to straighten up this mess.

It was a pleasant living room with green leaves growing and bric-a-brac on the mantel. We sat down at opposite ends of the long beige sofa. He leaned back against the arm and took off his taffy-colored specs.

How true was the biography on the book jacket, I wanted to know. He laughed. He'd put that in for a joke, he said, like the picture of himself in the weskit. . . . "I have a weird sense of humor." But part of it was true: he *did* dance on a river boat that ran between New Orleans and Monroe; he *did* paint flowers on glass but they did not bring a "small fortune," $25 or $30, perhaps; he worked on *The New Yorker* as a glorified office boy "or less" in the Art Department, opening drawings, sorting them, repacking them.

"I didn't *select* aneceotes for that digest magazine, I made them up," he laughed. "You know the kind, 'In Tacoma, Wash., a housewife rose one morning—' They paid me $75 a column. And Mrs. Acey Jones? She was a fabulous fortune teller who lived around the corner from me in New Orleans when I was 17. The first time I laid eyes on her, it was like two people who immediately knew all about each other. People came from all over to see her. She holds someone's hands tight and says whatever comes out. You get a very intense consciousness about each other. . . . I was her prize protege."

How did he feel about the reception of his book? Was he pleased, surprised, thrilled? The smile left his face abruptly and he looked a hurt, puzzled boy:

"I did not expect it to be the way it was. Some of the reviews seemed to be so blind. They call it a fantasy—decadent—they say I've written a book about homosexuality. I did not, nor did I intend to and I ought to know what I wanted it to be—I wrote the book.

"Or they call me a 'Southern writer.' I have lived in many places besides the South and I don't like to be called a Southern writer. In this book the Southern setting is very important to the story.

Some of the reviews (he rose to get a handful) had a quality of personal attack that surprised him. He fingered them with an expression that was almost fear and for a swift moment his eyes were helpless, disturbed, bright, like the eyes of some small creature—a jack-rabbit, or a chipmunk, darting into a hedge. He began to talk:

"I'm terribly paranoid about the whole thing. Four years ago I had a certainty about everything. I have a curious lack of personal certainty now. See this review? It says my book is destructive, that part about Randolph."

(Randolph, the effeminate uncle, who masquerades in powdered wig and mask to perpetuate the one happy moment of an unhappy love affair, has been confiding his strange passion for the vanished Pepe to 13-year-old Joel, his nephew, in a scene that is terrible and compassionate. Randolph appears as a sad, distorted misfit, forever restless, forever frustrated.)

Capote snatched his book as it lay in my lap, and turned the pages.

"This is Randolph speaking, you remember: 'What we most want is only to be held . . . and told . . . that everything (everything is a funny thing, is baby milk and Papa's eyes, is roaring logs on a cold morning, is hoot-owls and the boy who makes you cry after school, is Mama's long hair, is being afraid and twisted faces on the bedroom wall) . . . everything is going to be all right.' "

He skipped several pages impatiently: "This is the part where Joel wants to know what has happened to Pepe Alvarez, and Randolph says, 'If I knew . . . But, my dear, so few things are fulfilled: what are most lives but a series of incompleted episodes? . . . It is wanting to know the end that makes us believe in God, or witchcraft, believe in something.'

"Joel still wanted to know: 'Didn't you even try to find out where they got off to?'

" 'Over there,' said Randolph with a tired smile, 'is a five-pound volume listing every town and hamlet on the globe; it is what I believe in, this almanac; day by day I've gone through it writing Pepe always in care of the postmaster. . . . Oh, I know that I shall never have an answer. But it gives me something to believe in and that is peace.' Then in a voice as urgent as a bell he added . . . 'Tell me what I want to hear.'

"Joel remembered. 'Everything,' he said gently, 'everything is going to be all right.' "

Capote laid the book down flatly. "Now, what about that is destructive?" he asked.

How would he, I wondered, describe his book then. He examined the question and then his own answer: "It's this bright moment," hesitantly, "this ghostly moment of a completely lost child. A moment in his life, the moment when he gives up his boyhood." His hand snaked through the air to show the movement of Joel's life through the tangled adult world that is incomprehensible to a child. "I can see a certain pattern to Joel's summer at Skully's Landing, though I don't know what his life will be when he grows up."

One of the questions people usually like to have answered about authors is: Is the book autobiographical? It was not a question I asked Truman Capote, for I assumed that whatever the facts of time or geography, the *emotions* could have been autobiographical. The *facts* of his life are:

He was born in New Orleans, Sept. 30, 1924. His early childhood was broken by the divorce of his parents, by periods of illness, and by a series of uprootings when he went to live with one aunt or another. His earliest home was New Orleans. The "Skully's Landing" of his book was Placquemine, about 70 miles from there.

He spent part of his childhood in Louisiana and Alabama, part of his adolescence in Greenwich, Conn., and New York; he has been in every state of the union, he says, but most of his time has been spent in New Orleans and New York.

"I had the most insecure childhood I know of. It was really ghastly. I felt isolated from other people. I had few friends of my own age—most of them were much older than I. He swung his glasses by one stem and looked off across the room. "But then I suppose a great many people feel that way about their childhood."

He had a constant series of disappointments as a child, enormous hopes that children build on the casually forgotten promises of grownups. His father promised him a little dog and the boy made an important place for it in his life but it never came.

His father promised him books—books were hard to get, and he would make out elaborate, painful lists that took a long time, but no books arrived.

What other part his father and his aunts played in his life must be guessed at. He seemed unhappily reluctant to discuss it.

In his book he makes Mr. Sansom, Joel's father, a hopeless paralytic who must roll a tennis ball down the stairs to signal when he needs something; only his eyes move. Later, a cotton-mouth moccasin coils up in front of Joel: "How did Mr. Sansom's eyes come to be in a moccasin's head? . . . And why was Mr. Sansom staring at him. . . ."

Two women appear in a short story, "My Side of the Matter," which Truman read me from *Story* magazine of May, 1945, his head buried behind the orange covers. It was the story of a dull-witted boy, written in first person and he read it with hilarious dramatics until it seemed a farce played upon a stage. In the story is a devastating description of the boy's aunts:

> "I swear I wish you could get a look at these two. Honest, you'd die! Eunice is this big fat old thing with a behind that must weigh a tenth of a ton. She troops around the house, rain or shine, in this real old fashioned nighty. . . . Now Olivia-Ann's worse and that's the truth. . . . She's a natural born half-wit and ought really to be kept in somebody's attic. She's real pale and skinny and has a mustache. . . ."

Truman lived with his aunts for years, from the time he was four to about 10 or 11.

He wrote all the time: when he was a small boy staying with his aunts in Alabama he entered a story contest staged by a Mobile newspaper for school children. Most of the contestants turned in stories like "My First Day in School" and "A Picnic by the Lake." Truman's story was nothing like that. He used to trot all about the little town by himself and he got to know its people very well. His story ("it was absolutely awful") was about four people who lived in the town:

"It was a sort of *Roman a clef*—or however you say it—about a short-order cook who lived in a boardinghouse, a very fat woman who sat on her porch all day long and wrote in a horrid diary—she tried to murder her own child; a town bachelor who hated everyone and especially dogs because they kept him up all night with their howling (there was such a man who used to go out with his colored servant to help him hurl stones at the baying dogs), and I forget who the fourth was."

Truman had it stamped by a notary public for some strange reason he's forgotten, swore that it was an original manuscript thought up by him, and sent it with a note saying that it was to be printed in instalments. For weeks he haunted the post office and finally the paper arrived with the first instalment. The whole town recognized the four characters, and there was a furore: certainly the Children's Page had never known anything like it. There was just that first instalment and then everything stopped with a bang.

Everything, that is, except Truman's ambitions. He kept right on writing stories, right on sending them to newspaper contests mostly in the hope of winning the Shetland pony that was forever the first prize in such contests.

"I'm convinced there never was a Shetland pony prize," he said, his face suddenly the face of a small cynical boy. "I won second or third prize in those contests, but never first. I used to write letters to the winners but they were never answered and never returned. After a while it occurred to me that there never was a first prize won and that nobody got the pony."

He laughed aloud remembering another incident in his childhood: it was in Monroeville, a town in Alabama where he lived when he was 11 or so. He wanted always to be with older people, so he spent part of every day in a cafe patronized by men from the lumber mill and turpentine works. He was a great favorite with them because he drew their portraits or wrote poems that they would send to their girls. They fed him endless bottles of beer.

On his birthday that year the men chipped in and bought him a bicycle made like an airplane. Presently Truman convinced himself that it would sure-enough fly. He told the kids that he was preparing for a round-trip flight to China. ("Some of them believed me and most certainly I believed myself.") They came on a Saturday to see him off with little presents—an orange, chocolate kisses, pennies, a broken compass. Truman, helmeted, slid a pair of dime-store goggles over his eyes, and got into his plane.

"Then there was that awful, frightened moment when I knew it was just a dream, and the plane would sit there on the ground. Pretty soon everyone else realized it, too, but only a few of them got mad. The rest were only sorry and sad in the way that I was sorry and sad: here was simply more proof that the world is not a magic place and that we must expect no magic from it. . . . I don't know why I should remember it now."

From Alabama, Truman went to New York to live. Here he attended a private school for a year or two, until his family moved to 76 Orchard Drive in Millbrook, Conn., and he enrolled in the Greenwich High School. He was a bad student—hardly attended classes; he was poor in all subjects, even English. He did not get along well with the other students, and his teachers thought him stupid, all except his English teacher.

Her name was Catharine R. Wood. She is a beautiful, silver-haired woman who has been teaching English there for 29 years. I visited her recently in the charming, neat little house she occupies with Miss Marjorie Pierce, another teacher, in Old Greenwich.

Her dignified face grew pink and warm with pleasure as she talked about Truman. The day she first met him she had been discussing Sigrid Undset with another instructor in the school library when this young, carelessly dressed boy ("he wore sneakers, not shoes") broke in with his evaluation of Undset.

"He seemed such a child yet his opinions were so sound, so mature and he seemed so serious," she recalled. "From that time on I saw Truman all the time. He was in my classroom every day. I always recognized Truman's genius and felt we should make allowances for it. Writing was the only subject he was interested in. Other subjects simply did not exist for him, and sometimes even in my class he would seem to disappear. "But when he wanted to, he could write a composition in two minutes and it would be good."

She tried to work out a special program that would give his talents full play, tried to get him teachers who would be sympathetic to him, that would give his talents full play. Some of the faculty were quite concerned because he did not follow the orthodox line.

"I always said 'Some day you'll be proud of that boy. He'll be famous and you'll be glad to claim credit for him.' Well, the less said about *that* the better. But they're proud of him now, and last week our local paper had a big write-up about him." She leaned back triumphantly in her brown calico-covered armchair.

Truman had few friends in high school. One of them was Phoebe Pierce, a young poet now living in New York, and there were a couple of boys he knew.

"I haven't any doubt that some of the students laughed at him," Miss Wood said, rising to lead the way into a gray and yellow dining room.

She brought out a souffle, a tarragon-scented salad, and wonderful, thinly sliced bread, home-baked with herbs in it. Truman, I remarked, must like her cooking. She smiled indulgently. Her cookies, particularly, she said; he ducked to the cooky box as soon as he came in. He could eat a whole plateful, and "if we need them we hide them where he won't find them."

She returned to his school days: "Truman dressed rather queerly in anything that took his fancy. But no one ever teased him. I don't think they would have dared. They really respected him even if they didn't understand him. He was always carrying a book—he must have read a book a day. Would you like to see a snapshot of him? I have one upstairs."

The boy in the picture was blond and smiling and not too different from Truman grown up, except that he looked unclouded. There was little change in his appearance, she agreed, but suddenly this year, he seemed more mature, mellower.

She gave me old copies of the high school paper, *The Green Witch*, containing Truman's stories and poems, and one manuscript of an early short story to read. Even as a boy he was preoccupied with the problems of not quite "normal" people. One story, "Hilda," was about a young kleptomaniac; one, "Swamp Terror," was about an escaped convict in a Louisiana swamp and one, "Miss Belle Rankin," concerned the death of an ancient Southern woman.

"They were awful," today's Truman says, but I found them quite extraordinary for an adolescent boy. He spoke of seapale eyes, of a thin face topped with a great spray of red hair, of a day that was cold and gray with gusts of hungry wind eating at the gray leafless limbs, and of a rattlesnake that was the tip of a tail and a long cord of singing buttons crawling into the undergrowth.

"I couldn't have gotten into college," Truman explained to me when I saw him again. "I had no grades at all. But I do think people ought to go to college, especially writers; it tempers the mind, it gives intellectual discipline and it creates taste.

"This brings up a point, and that's about writers. I don't think most writers read enough. Young writers—some of them, I mean—are among the most illiterate people I have ever known. Mention book after book to them—they have never read them. And when they are working apparently they don't read at all.

"I read all the time. Would you like to know the authors I admire? Flaubert, Katherine Anne Porter, E. M. Forster. Virginia Woolf I love, some of Edith Wharton (particularly *Custom of the Country*). Chekhov, some of Proust. I like but do not especially admire Faulkner. I'm afraid of Faulkner, squeamish, really—I see him as a personal threat. Any writer who might have some kind of influence on me I skitter away from. I like *As I Lay Dying* and *Light in August* very much."

He reads every day, and he writes every day, even if it is only a note in his journal. He rises about noon, reads the newspapers, his mail and a book until supper time. After supper he takes a nap until midnight and then he begins to write in the tight, tiny hand that poets write. He never works more than four hours at a sitting and as he finishes piece after piece he polishes it over and over until he can do nothing more for it. Then it is done and he never goes back to it. Magazine editors and his publishers commented to me on the clean look of his final manuscript.

Other Voices, Other Rooms, a small book, took him more than two and a half years to write.

"This little book," he patted its cover, "was 150 pages of manuscript but I wrote a stack of pages this high," his hand hovered about 20 inches over the book, "by the time I was satisfied. I'm a fanatic on rhythm and language. The critics were wrong when they spoke about my style. I don't have one style or one rhythm. I shift the rhythm and style to the way the characters are, the way they talk. Randolph—everything about him is baroque and highly ornamental.

Zoo, the Negress, has a hymnal, incantationlike, regional rhythm. If you're tone deaf, you don't hear it.

"Each short story I've ever written has its own style. "Headless Hawk" had one kind of rhythm; "Shut a Final Door" had another, totally different kind. I'm not trying to find a style of my own at all, but merely fitting it to characters and situations. They are people, with rights.

"The reason *Other Voices, Other Rooms* took so long to write is that it represents the vary essence of a situation. Each word is a special problem.

"What I wanted to get into the book was the feeling of someone sitting in a room with the firelight playing, someone reading aloud. I want my writing to be very vocal; you know—as vocal as a story teller, but with dimensions no storyteller could put into it.

He laid the book aside. He was hungry, he said. How about lunch. He would make a wonderful lunch of things he had just bought at the delicatessen across the street: a can of tomato soup, an avocado pear, eggs and milk.

We went into the little kitchen and Truman poured us each a small glass of sherry. He emptied the soup into a pan, stirred it absently and then beat up six eggs, talking all the while.

"People to whom I first showed my writing said I couldn't write, shouldn't write, but I did not fear them too much, because I feel that if you are a writer you are going to be one and nothing, absolutely nothing in the world will interfere. As a matter of fact, people who attack my work don't annoy me as a writer. I know exactly what I want to do and have every intention of doing it. As to the merits of the work, that's not my concern."

The thing he wanted to do next was to write a New York novel about a woman who became a catalytic agent for four people trying to find freedom. That, and he was also preparing eight or nine of his short stories for a collected volume which he would name for one of them, *A Tree of Night*. The title of his novel would be *Monday's Folly*, he thought.

"Do you like the title *Monday's Folly*? I love titles. I'm crazy about them and always think about them," looking over his shoulder while he carried the food into the dining room. "I keep an enormous journal and I put into it things about people I've met, things I think about and hundreds and hundreds of titles."

I was curious to know more about his journal. He heaped up from his chair—he didn't want to eat, he said, the lunch was for me, anyway—and got some of its pages. They were written in his precise infinitesimal script. One concerned his thoughts on Sartre and Gide. Another was about New Orleans and formed the basis of an article published in *Harper's Bazaar.*

I read:

> New Orleans streets have long, lonesome perspectives: in empty hours their atmosphere is like Chirico and things innocent ordinarily (a face behind a slanted light of shutters, nuns moving in the distance, a fat dark arm lolling lopsidedly out some window) acquire qualities of violence . . . N.O., like every Southern town is a city of soft-drink signs. The streets of forlorn neighborhoods are paved with Coca-Cola caps and after rain they glint in the dust like lost dimes. Posters peel away, lie mangled until storm winds blow them along a street, like desert sage. Signs everywhee, chalked, printed, painted, MME. ORTEGA, READING, LOVE POTIONS, MAGIC LITERATURE, C-ME . . . IF YOU HAVEN'T ANYTHING TO DO, DON'T DO IT HERE . . . ARE YOU READY TO MEET YOUR MAKER? . . .

Truman Capote began to publish when he was about 17. He sent his short stories around to the "little" magazines, any place he thought might print them. When he was 18, *Mademoiselle* magazine bought his "Miriam" (subsequently honored by the O. Henry Memorial Award), the strange story of a disturbing child who adopts an unwilling woman as her victim. The fiction editor, Marguarita Smith, sister of novelist Carson McCullers, telephoned Marion Ives, a literary agent and formerly on the *Mademoiselle* staff: "I want you to meet a very talented young writer."

She became his agent and placed several of his short stories with *Harper's Bazaar, Junior Bazaar* and *Atlantic Monthly.*

When "Miriam" appeared in *Mademoiselle* in the spring of 1945, book publishers all over town took abrupt notice of this new, apparently significant talent. Eight of them got in touch with Miss Ives but it was the tall, Lincolnian-looking editor of Random House, Robert Linscott, who hooked the prize wth a comparatively small bait. Publishers were paying fat advances in those feverish, end-of-the-war days. Linscott paid Truman only $1500, at the rate of $100 a month. "He did not seem to need it," Linscott said. Perhaps he needed more the paternal warmth and encouragement which Linscott was able to shed on him.

Truman told Linscott the story of *Other Voices, Other Rooms* with a great, astounding multiplicity of details. (It is how he tells any story, so complete with sound, color and mood that he might be reading it.) He described weather, costumes, houses, he knew chapter for chapter how the book would go though not a line was written.

"I'll write a chapter at a time and send it to you," he said, and each chapter arrived as he had promised, polished, finished, clean.

He knew exactly the effects he wanted. There were no changes in his copy and he did not make any of the changes Linscott suggested unless they appealed to him. I saw a letter from Truman to Linscott:

1. About separating chaingang and littleone, yes, I think you are right.
2. No, I don't agree with you about the gunshot at the end of Part 1. It is rather a trick, I know. Still there is no similarity between this and the end of Chapter 2.

"Truman is rather Protean," Linscott said. "He's completely adaptable to a situation and he responds warmly to people. I took him down to meet 25 of our salesmen and he was completely at ease with them and very happy. They thought he was odd but they liked him. He knows everybody. His engagement book is always filled. He is a shrewd young man when it comes to publishing." Linscott laughed. "I thought the book would go to 10,000; he said 25,000 or more.

"As an artist, a craftsman, he is completely sure of himself. As a human being he has a great need to be loved and to be reassured of that love. Like other sensitive people, he finds the world hostile and frightening. Truman has all the stigmata of genius. I am convinced that genius must have stigmata. It must be wounded."

But Mary Lou Aswell, a sympathetic and sad-eyed woman, believes that he is not unprotected and that his look of helplessness is deceptive. "Little T" seemed uncannily to choose those people who would understand him and help him, and she felt that "it's in his stars, or his destiny, or his health-line or whatever you want to call it, that he travel in the right direction."

She pointed to these as proof: "That teacher who recognized his genius. Meeting a sympathetic, intelligent girl like Phoebe Pierce in that wasteland of Greenwich when he might have met almost anyone else—that's what I mean. His instinct leads him to the people who are on his side. To them he is outgoing and devoted.

"We love him up here. He is in and out of here all the time. He is fun to be with, and to hear his adventures is an incredible experience. It's hard to tell with him where truth ends and fiction begins because he is a terrific improvisor who gets carried away by the details.

"And Truman telling a story that he is going to write from the endless material he has stored up in himself is simply amazing. You know, with some writers you don't like to have them tell their stories before they're written because it expends so much creative energy that sometimes they never do get written. But Truman seems to develop his material that way. He can tell a story in all its complex dimensions, then sit down and write it."

A few weeks ago, I lunched again with Truman. He had just returned from his trip to Haiti. He had been deathly sick there. It was carnival time, and native drums and chants tore the nights apart.

The doctors on the island offered him little relief from his frightening temperatures and headaches.

"But at least I learned one thing," he said, "and that is that I want to live, that I do believe in life, that I do have something to say about life. When I thought I was going to die, and I did for a while, I wept—not for myself but for the stories I knew, the poetry that belonged to me."

Talk with Truman Capote
Harvey Breit/1952

From *New York Times Book Review*, 24 February 1952, 29. Copyright © 1952 by The New York Times Company. Reprinted by permission.

One crisp noontime this writer was walking in a most unlikely neighborhood and came upon Truman Capote. "What're you doing around here?" he asked Mr. Capote. "Oh, I'm going to have lunch with the Olivers," replied the 27-year-old author. "Who under earth's heaven are the Olivers?" "You know," Mr. Capote answered, dealing his words quite slowly, "Sir Laurence and Vivian."

That's one thing about Truman Capote—his affection for pronouncing his friends' names a bit differently. The other thing about him—that is, that one notices right off—is that he looks a little like a toy. That's what some people say, anyway. If he is a toy, he nevertheless has a mind that would turn those big thinking cybernetic machines green with envy. As a matter of fact, his mind has enough good steel in it to turn too many human beings the same violent color—and it has, no doubt about it. Mr. Capote's appearance is lamblike but all intellectual bullies are warned not to be deceived.

Though there are indications of description above, this writer thought it the better part of valor to have Mr. Capote describe himself. Mr. Capote, in his turn, thought it an amusing game. "Well," he said in that deceptively innocent voice, "I'm about as tall as a shotgun—and just as noisy. I think I have rather heated eyes." What on heaven's earth were heated eyes? "I don't quite know," he laughed, "but I didn't mean it complimentary." Mr. Capote worried the problem. "Let's see," he said. "I have a very sassy voice. I like my nose but you can't see it because I wear these thick glasses. If you looked at my face from both sides you'd see they were completely different. [Mr. Capote demonstrated.] It's sort of a changeling face."

Well that sort of did it, didn't it? Mr. Capote offered a footnote. "Do you want to know the real reason why I push my hair down on my forehead? Because I have two cowlicks. If I didn't push my hair forward it would make me look as though I had two feathery horns."

What about writing now? Mr. Capote was the author of four books, the most recent *The Grass Harp*, which was already in rehearsal as a Broadway play. How had Mr. Capote found the task of transposing the novel into drama? "You don't transpose," Mr. Capote said decisively and, as it turned out, illuminatively. "Playwriting has very little to do with literary talent. The theatre is so extraordinarily visual, and in order to write for it I had to forget the novel. It's as though someone asked you to take painting and make a statue of it. It's impossible. You can make the statue carry the same feeling and motivation as the painting, but it's a totally different thing. I actually looked at my book twice."

Mr. Capote's work had been unusually controversial. How did he look at his criticism? "I think it's very seldom that criticism is pertinent. The point for a writer is to have somebody help him. That's hard for anybody to do, even for the critic. The most fortunate thing for a writer is to get criticism that helps him."

Was there something in criticism that Mr. Capote liked or disliked *personally*? "I've had some very decent things written about me. That doesn't mean I like them best. What I personally dislike is when critics refer to my work as fantasy. I don't mean to attack fantasy; it's really one of the most difficult things to do. I just don't write it, that's all. I'm trying to do something that's psychologically and emotionally true. If it is true, it just isn't fantasy." Who was writing fantasy? "Walter de la Mare," Mr. Capote sad. "It's wonderfully good fantasy and it's terribly difficult to do well."

Now, to take a good jump, what about this problem of decadence in fiction today? "If what some young writers are writing today is decadence, then let's have more of it," Mr. Capote said stingingly. "I think what people mean is extravagance. Any extravagant imagination seems to run into this criticism. People imagine it's immoral. And immorality is related in people's minds to political issues. Perhaps fear of Russian propaganda is back of it. The Russians seize on this kind of thing. The perfect example is Gide. Until he disavowed communism the left press sang his praises. When he broke away, the left press turned on him like a pack of hornets and called him decadent. It has *nothing* to do with morality."

Mr. Capote faltered a little, out of earnestness rather than out of any lapse. "All writing," he said, "all art, is an act of faith. If one tries to contribute to human understanding, how can that be called decadent? It's like saying a declaration of love is an act of decadence. Any work of art, provided it springs from a sincere motivation to further understanding between people, is an act of faith and therefore is an act of love."

The Art of Fiction XVII: Truman Capote
Pati Hill/1957

From *Paris Review*, No. 16 (Spring-Summer 1957), 35-51. Reprinted in *Writers at Work: The Paris Review Interviews, 1st Series*, edited by Malcolm Cowley. Copyright © 1957, 1958 by The Paris Review, Inc. Reprinted by permission of Viking Penguin, Inc.

Truman Capote lives in a big yellow house in Brooklyn Heights which he has recently restored with the taste and elegance that is generally characteristic of his undertakings. As I entered he was head and shoulders inside a newly arrived crate containing a wooden lion.

"There!" he cried as he tugged it out to a fine birth amid a welter of sawdust and shavings. "Did you ever see anything so splendid? Well, that's that. I saw him and I bought him. Now he's all mine."

"He's large," I said. "Where are you going to put him?"

"Why in the fireplace, of course," said Capote. "Now come along into the parlor while I get someone to clear away this mess..."

The parlor is Victorian in character and contains Capote's most intimate collection of art objects and personal treasures which, for all their orderly arrangement on polished tables and bamboo bookcases, somehow remind you of the contents of a very astute little boy's pockets. There is, for instance, a golden easter egg brought back from Russia, an iron dog, somewhat the worse for wear, a Fabergé pillbox, some marbles, blue ceramic fruit, paperweights, Battersea boxes, picture postcards and old photographs. In short everything that might seem useful or handy in a day's adventuring around the world.

Capote himself fits in very well with this impression at first glance. He is small and blond with a forelock that persists in falling down into his eyes and his smile is sudden and sunny. His approach to anyone new is one of open curiosity and friendliness. He might be taken in by anything and, in fact, seems only too ready to be. There is something about him though that makes you feel that for all his willingness it would be hard to pull any wool over his eyes and maybe better not to try to.

There was a sound of scuffling in the hall and Capote came in, preceded by a large bulldog with a white face.

"This is Bunky," he said.

Bunky sniffed me over and we sat down.

Interviewer: When did you first start writing?

Capote: When I was a child of about ten or eleven and lived near Mobile. I had to go into town on Saturdays to the dentist and I joined the Sunshine Club that was organized by the Mobile Press Register. There was a children's page with contests for writing and for coloring pictures and then every Saturday afternoon they had a party with free Nehi and Coca Cola. The prize for the short story writing contest was either a pony or a dog, I've forgotten which, but I wanted it badly. I had been noticing the activities of some neighbors who were up to no good, so I wrote a kind of *roman à clef* called "Old Mr. Busybody" and entered it in the contest. The first installment appeared one Sunday, under my real name of Truman Streckfus Persons. Only somebody suddenly realized that I was serving up a local scandal as fiction, and the second installment never appeared. Naturally, I didn't win a thing.

I: Were you sure then that you wanted to be a writer?

C: I realized that I *wanted* to be a writer. But I wasn't sure I *would* be until I was fifteen or so. At that time I had immodestly started sending stories to magazines and literary quarterlies. Of course no writer ever forgets their first acceptance; but one fine day when I was seventeen, I had my first, my second and third, all in the same morning's mail. Oh, I'm here to tell you, dizzy with excitement is no mere phrase!

I: What did you first write?

C: Short stories. And my more unswerving ambitions still revolve around this form. When seriously explored, the short story seems to me the most difficult and disciplining form of prose writing extant. Whatever control and technique I may have I owe entirely to my training in this medium.

I: What do you mean exactly by 'control'?

C: I mean maintaining a stylistic and emotional upper hand over your material. Call it precious and go to hell, but I believe a story can be wrecked by a faulty rhythm in a sentence (especially if it occurs toward the end) or a mistake in paragraphing, even punctuation. Henry James is the maestro of the semi-colon. Hemingway is a first rate paragrapher. From the point of view of ear, Virginia Woolf never wrote a bad sentence. I don't mean to imply that I successfully practice what I preach . . . I try that's all.

I: How does one arrive at short story technique?

C: Since each Story presents its own technical problems, obviously one can't generalize about them on a $2 \times 2 = 4$ basis. Finding the right form for your story is simply to realize the most *natural* way of telling the story. The test of whether or not a writer has devined the natural shape of his story is just this: after reading it, can you imagine it differently, or does it silence your imagination and seem to you absolute and final? As an orange is final. As an orange is something nature has made just right.

I: Are there devices one can use in improving one's technique?

C: Work is the only device I know of. Writing has laws of perspective, of light and shade, just as painting does, or music. If you are born knowing them, fine. If not, learn them. Then rearrange the rules to suit yourself. Even Joyce, our most extreme disregarder, was a superb craftsman; he could write Ulysses *because* he could write Dubliners. Too many writers seem to consider the writing of short stories as a kind of finger exercise. Well, in such cases, it is certainly only their fingers they are exercising.

I: Did you have much encouragement in those early days and by whom?

C: Good Lord! I'm afraid you've let yourself in for quite a saga. The answer is a snake's nest of no's and a few yesses. You see, not altogether but by and large my childhood was spent in parts of the country and among peoples unprovided with any semblance of a cultural attitude. Which was probably not a bad thing, in the long view. It toughened rather too soon to swim against the current . . .

indeed, in some areas I developed the muscles of a veritable barracuda, especially in the art of dealing with one's enemies, an art no less necessary than knowing how to appreciate one's friends.

But to go back. Naturally in the milieu aforesaid, I was thought somewhat *eccentric*, which was fair enough, and *stupid*, which I suitably resented. Still, I despised school . . . or schools, for I was always changing from one to another . . . and year after year failed the simplest subjects out of loathing and boredom. I played hooky at least twice a week and was always running away from home. Once I ran away with a friend who lived across the street . . . a girl much older than myself who in later life achieved a certain fame. Because she murdered a half-dozen people and was electrocuted at Sing Sing. Someone wrote a book about her. They called her the Lonely Hearts Killer. But there, I'm wandering again. Well, finally, I guess I was around twelve, the principal at the school I was attending paid a call on my family, and told them that in his opinion, and in the opinion of the faculty, I was "subnormal." He thought it would be the sensible, the humane action to send me to some special school equipped to handle backward brats. Whatever they may have privately felt, my family as a whole took official umbrage, and in an effort to prove I wasn't subnormal pronto packed me off to a psychiatric study clinic at a university in the east where I had my I.Q. inspected. I enjoyed it thoroughly and—guess what?—came home a genius, so proclaimed by science. I don't know who was the more appalled: my former teachers, who refused to believe it, or my family, who didn't want to believe it—they'd just hoped to be told I was a nice normal boy. Ha ha! But as for me, I was exceedingly pleased—went around staring at myself in mirrors and sucking in my cheeks and thinking over in my mind, my lad, you and Flaubert . . . or de Maupassant or Mansfield or Proust or Chekov or Wolfe, whoever was the idol of the moment.

I began writing in fearful earnest . . . my mind zoomed all night every night, and I don't think I really slept for several years. Not until I discovered that whiskey could relax me. I was too young, fifteen, to buy it myself, but I had a few older friends who were most obliging in this respect and I soon accumulated a suitcase full of bottles, everything from blackberry brandy to bourbon. I kept the suitcase hidden in a closet. Most of my drinking was done in the late afternoon, then I'd chew a handful of Sensen and go down to dinner where my behavior, my glazed silences, gradually grew into a source of general consternation. One of my relatives used to say: "Really, if I didn't know better, I'd swear he was dead drunk." Well, of course, this little comedy, if such it was, ended in discovery and some disaster, and it was many a moon before I touched another drop. But I seem to be off the track again. You asked about encouragement. The first person who ever really helped me was, strangely, a teacher. An English teacher I had in high school, Catharine Wood, who backed my ambitions in every way, and to whom I shall always be grateful. Later on, from the time I first began to publish, I had all the encouragement anyone could ever want, notably from Margarita Smith, fiction editor of *Mademoiselle*, Mary Louise Aswell of *Harper's Bazaar*, and Robert Linscott of Random House. You would have to be a glutton indeed to ask for more good luck and fortune than I had at the beginning of my career.

I: Did the three editors you mention encourage you simply by buying your work, or did they offer criticism, too?

C: Well, I can't imagine anything *more* encouraging than having someone buy your work. I never . . . indeed, am physically incapable . . . of writing anything that I don't think will be paid for. But, as a matter of fact, the persons mentioned, and some others as well, were all very generous with advice.

I: Do you like anything you wrote long ago as well as what you write now?

C: Yes. For instance, last summer I read my novel *Other Voices, Other Rooms* for the first time since it was published eight years ago, and it was quite as though I were reading something by a stranger. The truth is, I am a stranger to that book; the person who wrote it seems to have so little in common with my present self. Our mentalities, our interior temperatures are entirely different. Despite awkwardnesses, it has an amazing intensity, a real voltage . . . I am very pleased I was able to write the book when I did, otherwise it would never have been written. I like *The Grass Harp* too and several of my short stories, though not "Miriam" which is a good stunt but nothing more. No, I prefer "Children on Their Birthdays" and "Shut A Final Door," and oh, some others, especially a story not too many people seemed to care for, "Master Misery," which was in my collection *A Tree of Night*.

I: You recently published a book about the *Porgy and Bess* trip to Russia. One of the most interesting things about the style was its unusual detachment even by comparison to the reportings of journalists who have spent many years recording events in an impartial way. One had the impression that this version must have been as close to the truth as it is possible to get through another person's eyes, which is surprising when you consider that most of your work has been characterized by its very personal quality.

C: Actually, I don't consider the style of this book, *The Muses Are Heard*, as markedly different from my fictional style. Perhaps, the content, the fact that it is about real events, makes it seem so. After all, *Muses* is straight reporting, and in reporting one is occupied with literalness and surfaces, with implication without comment—one can't achieve immediate depths the way one may in fiction. However, one of the reasons I've wanted to do reportage was to prove that I could apply my style to the realities of journalism. But I believe my fictional method is equally detached—emotionality makes me lose writing control: I have to exhaust the emotion before I feel clinical enough to analyze and project it, and as far as I'm concerned that's one of the laws of achieving true technique. If my fiction seems more personal it is because it depends on the artist's most personal and revealing area: his imagination.

I: How do you exhaust the emotion? Is it only a matter of thinking about the story over a certain length of time, or are there other considerations?

C: No, I don't think it is merely a matter of time. Suppose you ate nothing but apples for a week. Unquestionably you would exhaust your appetite for apples and most certainly know what they taste like. By the time I write a story I may no longer have any hunger for it, but I feel that I thoroughly know its flavor. The *Porgy and Bess* articles are not relevant to this issue. That was reporting and "emotions" were not much involved. At least not the difficult and personal territories of feeling that I mean. I seem to remember reading that Dickens, as he wrote, choked with laughter over his own humour and dripped tears all over the page when one of his characters died. My own theory is that the writer should have considered his wit and dried his tears long, long before setting out to evoke similar reactions in a reader. In other words, I believe the greatest intensity in art in all its shapes is achieved with a deliberate, hard and cool head. For example, Flaubert's "A Simple Heart." A warm story, warmly written; but it could only be the work of an artist muchly aware of true techniques, i.e. necessities. I'm sure, at some point, Flaubert must have felt the story very deeply . . . but *not* when he wrote it. Or, for a more contemporary example, take that marvelous short novel of Katherine Anne Porter's, *Noon Wine*. It has such intensity, such a sense of happening-how, yet the writing is so controlled, the inner rhythms of the story so immaculate, that I feel fairly certain Miss Porter was at some distance FROM her material.

I: Have your best stories or books been written at a comparatively tranquil moment in your life or do you work better because or in spite of emotional stress?

C: I feel slightly as though I've never lived a tranquil moment, unless you count what an occasional nembutal induces. Though, come to think of it, I spent two years in a very romantic house on top of a mountain in Sicily, and I guess this period could be called tranquil. God knows, it was quiet. That where I wrote *The Grass Harp*. But I must say an iota of stress, striving toward deadlines, does me good.

I: You have lived abroad for the last eight years. Why did you decide to return to America?

C: Because I'm an American, and never could be, and have no desire to be, anything else. Besides, I like cities, and New York is the only real city-city. Except for a two-year stretch, I came back to America every one of those eight years, and I never entertained expatriate notions. For me, Europe was a method of acquiring perspective and an education, a stepstone toward maturity. But there is the law of diminishing returns, and about two years ago it began to set in: Europe had given me an enormous lot, but suddenly I felt as though the process were reversing itself . . . there seemed to be a taking away. So I came home, feeling quite grown up and able to settle down where I belong. Which doesn't mean I've bought a rocking chair and turned to stone. No indeed. I intend to have footloose escapades as long as frontiers stay open.

I: Do you read a great deal?

C: Too much. And anything, including labels and recipes and advertisements. I have a passion for newspapers . . . read all the New

York dailies every day, and the Sunday editions of several foreign magazines too. The ones I don't buy I read standing at news stands. I average about five books a week . . . the normal length novel takes me about two hours. I enjoy thrillers and would like someday to write one. Though I prefer first-rate fiction, for the last few years my reading seems to have been concentrated on letters and journals and biographies. It doesn't bother me to read while I am writing . . . I mean, I don't suddenly find another writer's style seeping out of my pen. Though once, during a lengthy spell of James, my own sentences *did* get awfully long.

I: What writers have influenced you the most?

C: So far as I consciously know, I've never been aware of direct literary influence, though several critics have informed me that my early works owe a debt to Faulkner and Welty and McCullers. Possibly. I'm a great admirer of all three; and Katherine Anne Porter, too. Though I don't think, when really examined, that they have much in common with each other, or me, except that we were all born in the South. Between thirteen and sixteen are the ideal, if not the only ages for succumbing to Thomas Wolfe . . . he seemed to me a great genius then, and still does, though I can't read a line of it now. Just as other youthful flames have guttered: Poe, Dickens, Stevenson. I love them in memory, but find them unreadable. These are the enthusiasms that remain constant: Flaubert, Turgenev, Chekov, Jane Austen, James, E.M. Forster, De Maupassant, Rilke, Proust, Shaw, Willa Cather . . . oh the list is too long, so I'll end with James Agee, a beautiful writer whose death over two years ago was a real loss. Agee's work, by the way, was much influenced by the films. I think most of the younger writers have learned and borrowed from the visual, structural side of movie technique. I have.

I: You've written for the films, haven't you? What was that like?

C: A lark. At least the one picture I wrote, *Beat the Devil*, was tremendous fun. I worked on it with John Huston while the picture was actually being made on location in Italy. Sometimes scenes that were just about to be shot were written right on the set. The cast was completely bewildered . . . sometimes even Huston didn't seem to know what was going on. Naturally the scenes had to be written out of a sequence, and there were peculiar moments when I was carrying around in my head the only real outline of the so-called plot. You never saw it? Oh you should. It's a marvelous joke. Though I'm afraid the producer didn't laugh. The hell with them. Whenever there's a revival I go to see it and have a fine time.

Seriously though, I don't think a writer stands much chance of imposing himself on a film unless he works in the warmest rapport with the director or is himself the director. It's so much a director's medium that the movies have developed only one writer who, working exclusively as a scenarist, could be called a film-genius. I mean that shy delightful little peasant, Zavattini. What a visual sense! Eighty percent of the good Italian movies were made from Zavattini scripts . . . all of the Di Sica pictures, for instance. De Sica is a charming man, a gifted and deeply sophisticated person; nevertheless he's mostly a megaphone for Zavattini, his pictures are absolutely Zavattini's creations: every nuance, mood, every bit of business is clearly indicated in Zavattini's scripts.

I: What are some of your writing habits? Do you use a desk? Do you write on a machine?

C: I am a completely horizontal author . . . I can't think unless I'm lying down, either in bed or stretched on a couch and with a cigarette and coffee handy. I've got to be puffing and sipping. As the afternoon wears on, I shift from coffee to mint tea to sherry to martinis. No, I don't use a typewriter. Not in the beginning. I write my first version in long-hand (pencil). Then I do a complete revision, also long-hand. Essentially I think of myself as a stylist and stylists can become notoriously obsessed with the placing of a comma, the weight of a semi-colon. Obsessions of this sort, and the time I take over them, irritate me beyond endurance.

I: You seem to make a distinction between writers who are stylists and writers who aren't. Which writers would you call stylists and which not?

C: What is style? And "what" as the Zen Koan asks, "is the sound of one hand?" No one really *knows*; yet either you *know* or you don't. For myself, if you will excuse a rather cheap little image, I suppose style is the mirror of an artists's sensibility . . . more so than the *content* of his work. To some degree all writers have style . . . Ronald Firbank, bless his heart, had little else, and thank God he realized it. But the possession of style, a style, is often a hindrance, a negative force, not as it should be, and as it is . . . with, say E. M.

Forster and Colette and Flaubert and Mark Twain and Hemingway and Isak Dinesen, a reinforcement. Dreiser, for instance, has *a* style—but oh, Dio Buono! And Eugene O'Neill. And Faulkner, brilliant as he is. They all seem to me triumphs over strong but negative styles . . . styles that do not really add to the communication between writer and reader. Then there is the styleless stylist . . . which is very difficult, very admirable, and *always* very popular: Graham Greene, Maugham, Thornton Wilder, John Hersey, Willa Cather, Thurber, Sartre (remember, we're *not* discussing content), J. P. Marquand and so on. But yes, there *is* such an animal as a nonstylist. Only they're not writers. They're typists. Sweaty typists blacking up pounds of Bond with formless, eyeless, earless messages. Well, who are some of the younger writers who seem to know that style exists? P. H. Newby, Françoise Sagan, somewhat. Bill Styron. Flannery O'Connor . . . she has some fine moments, that girl. James Merrill. William Goyen . . . if he'd stop being hysterical. J. D. Salinger . . . especially in the colloquial tradition. Colin Wilson? Another typist.

I: You say that Ronald Firbank had little else but style. Do you think that style alone can make a writer a great one?

C: No, I don't think so . . . though, it could be argued: what happens to Proust if you separate him from his style? Style has never been a strong point with American writers. This though some of the best have been Americans. Hawthorne got us off to a fine start. For the past thirty years Hemingway, stylistically speaking, has influenced more writers on a world scale than anyone else. At the moment, I think our own Miss Porter knows as well as anyone what it's all about.

I: Can a writer learn style?

C: No, I don't think that style is consciously arrived at. Anymore than one arrives at the color of one's eyes. After all, Your style *is* you. At the end the personality of a writer has so much to do with the work. The personality has to be humanly there. Personality is a debased word, I know, but it's what I mean. The writer's individual humanity, his word or gesture toward the world, has to appear almost like a character that makes contact with the reader. If the personality is vague or confused or merely literary, *ça ne va pas.* Faulkner, McCullers—they project their personality at once.

I: It is interesting that your work has been so widely appreciated in France. Do you think style can be translated?

C: Why not? Provided the author and the translator are artistic twins.

I: Well, I'm afraid I interrupted you with your short story still in pencilled manuscript. What happens next?

C: Let's see, that was second draft. Then I type a third draft on yellow paper, a very special certain kind of yellow paper. No I don't get out of bed to do this . . . I balance the machine on my knees. Sure, it works fine . . . I can manage a hundred words a minute. Well, when the yellow draft is finished, I put the manuscript away for a while, a week, a month, sometimes longer. When I take it out again, I read it as coldly as possible, then read it aloud to a friend or two, and decide what changes I want to make and whether or not I want to publish it. I've thrown away rather a few short stories, an entire novel, and half of another. But if all goes well, I type the final version on white paper and that's that.

I: Is the book organized completely in your head before you begin it or does it unfold, surprising you as you go along?

C: Both. I invariably have the illusion that the whole play of a story, its start and middle and finish, occur in my mind simultaneously—that I'm seeing it in one flash. But in the working-out, the writing-out, infinite surprises happen. Thank God, because surprises, the twist, the phrase that comes at the right moment out of nowhere, is the unexpected dividend, that joyful little push that keeps a writer going.

At one time I used to keep notebooks with outlines for stories. But I found doing this somehow deadened the idea in my imagination. If the notion is good enough, if it truly belongs to *you*, then you can't forget it . . . it will haunt you till it's written.

I: How much of your work is autobiographical?

C: Very little, really. A little is *suggested* by real incidents or personages, although everything a writer writes is in some way autobiographical. *The Grass Harp* is the only true thing I ever wrote, and naturally everybody thought it all invented, and imagined *Other Voices, Other Rooms* to be autobiographical.

I: Do you have any definite ideas or projects for the future?

C: *(meditatively)* Well, yes, I believe so. I have always written what was easiest for me until now: I want to try something else, a kind of controlled extravagance. I want to use my mind more, use many more colors. Hemingway once said anybody can write a novel in the first person. I know now exactly what he means.

I: Were you ever tempted by any of the other arts?

C: I don't know if it's art, but I was stage-struck for years and more than anything I wanted to be a tap-dancer. I used to practice my buck-and-wing until everybody in the house was ready to kill me. Later on, I longed to play the guitar and sing in night-clubs. So I saved up for a guitar and took lessons for one whole winter, but in the end the only tune I could really play was a beginners thing called "I Wish I were Single Again." I got so tired of it that one day I just gave the guitar to a stranger in a bus station. I was also interested in painting, and studied for three years, but I'm afraid the fervor, *la vrai chose*, wasn't there.

I: Do you think criticism helps any?

C: Before publication, and if provided by persons whose judgment you trust, yes, of course criticism helps. But after something is published all I want to read or hear is praise. Anything less is a bore, and I'll give you fifty dollars if you produce a writer who can honestly say he was ever helped by the prissy carpings and condescensions of reviewers. I don't mean to say that none of the professional critics are worth paying attention to . . . but few of the good ones review on a regular basis. Most of all, I believe in hardening yourself against opinion. I've had, and continue to receive, my full share of abuse, some of it extremely personal, but it doesn't faze me anymore . . . I can read the most outrageous libel about myself and never skip a pulsebeat. And in this connection there is one piece of advice I strongly urge: never demean yourself by talking back to a critic, never. Write those letters to the editor in your head, but don't put them on paper.

I: What are some of your personal quirks?

C: I suppose my superstitiousness could be termed a quirk. I have to add up all numbers: there are some people I never telephone because their number adds up to an unlucky figure. Or I won't accept a hotel room for the same reason. I will not tolerate the presence of yellow roses . . . which is sad because they're my favorite flower. I can't allow three cigarette butts in the same ashtray. Won't travel on a plane with two nuns. Won't begin or end anything on a Friday. It's endless, the things I can't and won't. But I derive some curious comfort from obeying these primitive concepts.

I: You have been quoted as saying your preferred pastimes are "conversation, reading, travel, and writing, in that order." Do you mean that literally?

C: I think so. At least I'm pretty sure conversation will always come first with me. I like to listen, and I like to talk. Heavens, girl, can't you *see* I like to talk?

A Rainy Afternoon with Truman Capote
Eugene Walter/1957

From *Intro Bulletin: A Literary Newspaper of the Arts*, 2 (December 1957), 1-2.

Thunder behind Montmartre and puddly streets . . .

I carried a blankbook and two *points-Bic*, all prepared for my interview with Truman Capote, but not at all prepared to be the Anonymous Interviewer. I couldn't! Didn't Capote come, like me, from Alabama? Hadn't he become a local monument and a local myth? He did, he had. Wasn't I curious as all get-out about him? I was. I had happened to work in The Haunted Bookshop in Mobile in the year before Capote's first novel, *Other Voices, Other Rooms* appeared, and I had been amazed at the people drifting in from remote upcountry towns to ask for the book, long before the publisher even announced it. I had gawked at the three extraordinary young ladies who had appeared separately to order the book, each confiding dramatically that she was the original of "Henrietta" in the novel.

Capote was staying at the Hotel France et Choiseul, which is quite frankly red-plush and gilt. I went up in one of those original-patent-model elevators that make life in Europe so rich and full of incident, stumbled into a dim corridor, knocked at the first door I saw, and there—the door opening promptly— was Truman Capote. Quickly I refurbished my mental image: what I saw had nothing to do with the famous *chaise-longue* checked-vest photograph that amused half of America and made the other half nervous in 1948. Here was a small bulldog, a Dr. Johnson in the bud, with a splendidly shaped skull and a stocky body.

He ushered me in, but seemed scarcely to notice me, he was looking for something in the cluttered room . . .

Capote: Where are my flowers? I told that woman not to throw out any flowers until I told her to. Damn her meddling soul anyway.

(As if to reinforce my impression of Capote as bulldog, or at least to bolster comparison, just then a bulldog came into the room. He resembled Capote. Other dogs followed.)

Capote: Well, come in. Let's go in the other room; I've been sniffly and am staying in bed.

Interviewer: Thank you . . .

C: What would you like to drink? Martini?

I: Martini, thank you . . .

(We go into bedroom: brass bed. Two books on bedside table: *A Taste for Honey* by Gerald Heard; *Act of Passion* by Simenon. Capote bounds into bed, after locking animals in bathroom, and settles himself.)

C: Well, what are you going to ask me? (He is most amiable.)

I: Well for example, is it true that you were raised in the South: there are people who claim that you've never been further South than Philadelphia.

C: No, I was born in New Orleans and lived as a child near Mobile. I had to go into Mobile on Saturdays to the dentist—every Saturday—I had all kinds of things wrong, question of braces and that sort of mess, you know—and I joined the Sunshine Club that was organized by the Mobile Press-Register. There was a Children's Page with contests for writing and for coloring pictures and then every Saturday afternoon they had a kind of party with free Nehi and Coca-Cola. At that time I loathed school, loved Edgar Allan Poe and, well, loved all short stories; I loved to stay home from school, stay in bed and listen to soap operas on the radio. I was crazy about *Myrt and Marge*, and *Backstage Wife*.

I: It was then that you began to write?

C: Uh-huh. Ten-ish, eleven-ish. The Sunshine Page that I spoke of, well they had a story contest and for prize offered either a dog or a pony, can't remember which, but I wanted it badly. All this time I had been spying on some neighbors who were up to no good, no good at all. So I wrote a thing called "Old Mr. Busybody," a kind of *roman a clef* you know, and sent it in, and they decided to publish it, in two installments. So the first part came out, under my real name of Truman Streckfus Persons. But somebody, wish I knew who, realized it was local scandal dished up as literature, so it was never completed, and I didn't have a chance for the dog or pony or whatever.

I: But you went on writing?

C: No. Not really. But I went on reading. I discovered Flaubert's "Three Tales," for instance, which made a great impression on me. My favorite was "The Legend of St. Julien the Hospitaler." I've just written a story in the vein of "St. Julien" only with a cruel ending. It's a kind of psychological fairy story, about two brothers.

I: Where will it be published?

C: I don't know. I don't care a thing about publishing.

I: When did you begin to write in earnest?

C: At about the age of 15 I guess. By then I had moved to Connecticut, and had the great good fortune to have a very intelligent teacher who encouraged me. I wrote my story "My Side of the Matter" when I was seventeen. I published one or two stories in a little review in Chicago then I published "Miriam" in *Mademoiselle* and it was taken for the O. Henry Prize Collection—I've never stopped writing since.

I: What writers have been especially meaningful for you?

C: Well, Flaubert first of all, then James and Proust I suppose.

I: And Carson McCullers?

C: Yes, in another way, though, outside of my own writing. In her work there is a kind of sensibility I suddenly understood when I got really depressed.

I: How much of your work is autobiographical?

C: Very little, really. A little is *suggested* by real incidents or personages, although everything a writer writes is in some way autobiographical. *The Grass Harp* is the only true thing I ever wrote, and naturally everybody thought it all invented, and imagined *Other Voices, Other Rooms* to be autobiographical.

I: Do you have any definite ideas or projects for the future?

C: (thoughtfully) Oh, yes, to write and then to write some more. Until this moment I have written in the manner easiest for me. I want to try something quite different now, a larger scene, a wider range of colors.

I: As a constant traveller who has had the opportunity to compare, off and on, America and the rest of the world, what do you feel about the position of intellectuals in America. Do you think there is a kind of anti-intellectual climate in America?

C: Yes. (Shrugs, sips martini. Fishes onion out of glass and munches.) And it's probably better to write outside an anti-intellectual climate, than to hang together in bitterness—sherry-tippling bitterness, you understand. After all, most writers in America are ashamed to be intellectual!

I: Yes, amazing how intellectual is a kind of naughty word in America, while in Europe it designates a respected portion of the population.

C: Robert Frost once said, "I don't know what I am. I'm not a writer, I'm not a teacher, I guess I'm just a farmer." I told him, don't be absurd, you're no such thing. Faulkner is always singing the same song, very boring. I think they have some ancient frontier idea that writing is not an active life: I think writing is the most active. And then at the other end of the scale is something just as dreary: the aesthetic pose. Oh-so-sensitive, you know. Neither one is especially healthy. Something else that strikes me, too, is that in America young writers are not really kind to one another.

I: Don't you find, too, that there is a general feeling that writers should write constantly?

C: That's nonsense. I don't care about Maugham at all, but you must read "The Summing-Up." He has some good blunt things to say from a purely practical point of view.

I: And what about our "writing" courses? How do they strike you?

C: Shattering, with a very few exceptions. I think there are so few good teachers. I know an awful lot of academic people. Non-creative, self-devouring. Think of Kafka, Melville, James, Whitman—look what's been done to them! And the greedy devouring education thing: look at the courses, now, for instance, on young writers who've published one book. Well, I think, you see, that there is nothing so anti-intellectual as the intellectuals in America. Wonderful case are the employees of *Time*. A set of broken-down eggheads, slightly-soiled eggheads. *Time*, far more than any university, is one of the assembly lines dispensing anti-intellectuals. Finally, it means little to a writer who is writing: the *pros* and *cons* can't bother him, and no writing class can teach him to write. At the end, after all, the personality of a writer has so much to do with the work. The personality has to be humanly there. Personality is a debased word, I know, but it's what I mean. The writer's individual humanity, his word or gesture toward the world, has to appear almost like a character that makes contact with the reader. If the personality is vague or confused or merely literary, *ca ne va pas*. Faulkner, McCullers—they project their personality at once. So does Thurber. So does the late James Agee, one of the two or three best American writers of the decade. And I'll tell you a young writer who has what I mean: let's don't say personality, it is such a cheapened word. That's J. D. Salinger. He makes an immediate electrical contact. I like his stories very much. How's your martini?

(After another martini and some idle chatter, the Interviewer prepares to go. Capote rises from bed, admits dogs, and goes through red damask salon to door. He moves restlessly about, suddenly laughs.)

C: Here're my flowers after all! I thought she'd thrown them out.

(While the dogs are chasing about among the gilt tablelegs, Interviewer leaves amidst rumbling thunder and sound of hard shower.)

Truman Capote
Roy Newquist/1964

From *Counterpoint* (Chicago: Rand McNally & Company, 1964), 76-83. Copyright © 1964 by Rand McNally & Company. Reprinted by permission.

N: *Other Voices, Other Rooms* introduced one of the great literary talents of our time: Truman Capote. Without *Voices*, without *Tree of Night, The Grass Harp, The Muses are Heard,* and *Breakfast at Tiffany's*—to mention only some of his fiction and reportage—contemporary American letters would present a far slimmer file in the valuable pocket labeled "quality."

In talking to Mr. Capote I would first, naturally, like to begin by asking him for the essential autobiography—where he was born, reared, and educated, and when his interest in writing developed.

Capote: I was born in New Orleans in 1924. (By the way, my name isn't Capote at all—I'll explain that later.) My father's name is Persons, and he was a salesman. My mother was only sixteen years old when they were married, and she was very, very beautiful—a beauty contest-winner type of child who later on in life became an enormously sensitive and intelligent person. But she was only sixteen when she was married—a normal, beautiful girl, rather wild—and my father was twenty-four.

My mother wasn't able to cope with the situation. She had a baby and she traveled with my father all around the South, and when she was eighteen she decided that she wanted to go to college. So I went to college with her, all the way through, and by the time she was graduated she and my father were divorced so I went to live with relatives in a rather remote part of Alabama. This was a very strange household. It consisted of three elderly ladies and an elderly uncle. They were the people who had adopted my mother—her own parents had died when she was very young. I lived there until I was ten, and it was a very lonely life, and it was then that I became interested in writing. You see, I always could read. I have the illusion that I could read when I was four years old, and I actually could read before I ever went to school. In first grade, reading was the only thing I liked to do, because I had this lonely childhood and reading took me out of it. I began to write, and also to paint—another deep interest I had. (I was also interested in music, but for various reasons I was not allowed to take music lessons.) Anyway, I started to write when I was eight years old and wrote a book when I was nine.

I spent every summer in that town in Alabama until I was sixteen. In the meantime, my mother had gone to New York and had remarried, so I came to New York to school for three years. I went to different boarding schools around New York, and when I finally left school I was seventeen and went straight to work at *The New Yorker* in the art department.

Originally I was to work for *The New Yorker* in the "Talk of the Town" department. This was during the war, and I had been sending them stories and articles, and I went to see the people I had been corresponding with; they were going to give me a job. It was during the war and they had lost all their staff. Well, I arrived, and they took one look—I was seventeen and looked about ten years old—and realized they could never send this child labor case out to interview anybody, so in the end I worked in the art department and turned out ideas for "Talk of the Town" every week and suggested personalities for "Profiles." I worked there for two years, then began writing my first novel, *Other Voices, Other Rooms*. When I really got into the novel I went back to New Orleans to finish it, and I've never set foot in another office. I must say that I really hate offices.

N. You mentioned that your name really isn't Capote. How did you come to assume it?

Capote: My mother's second husband was a Cuban businessman named Capote, a name Spanish in origin. He adopted me, and my name was legally changed to Capote.

N. Now, *Other Voices, Other Rooms* created quite a stir for a first novel, and certainly established you in the front rank. What was your reaction to its success?

Capote: So many things happened that were extracurricular to the work on the book that I mostly remember being shocked. There were so many cruel things written about me at the time, and a great deal of comment about the photograph on the back of the book (which was perfectly innocent). Somehow, all the publicity I read about it in the newspapers . . . well, I wasn't used to reading about myself. I was so shocked and hurt that I never got any pleasure out of it at all. Everything was different than I had always thought or hoped it would be.

Of course, the book was a literary success, and it sold quite well, but it has only been in the last six years that I could bear to think about certain things surrounding that book. I know it's a very good book, and it's coming into perspective and focus, and finally I feel no pain about anything connected with it. I just feel gratitude because, in a sense, it freed me to go on and do my own work. If I hadn't had that success, no matter what it was based on—publicity, notoriety, whatever it may have been—I would never have had the freedom to go on developing and maturing as an artist. (Perhaps I would have; I don't really know.) But I don't think it hurt me to have a success at that very young age because it wasn't really a success in my own eyes. If I had had any sense of fulfillment, or any of the things that go with that degree of success, it might have had a bad effect on me. But since I didn't get that satisfaction from it—in fact, got the exact opposite—it just sobered me up a great deal and made me realize on what paths I truly must go.

N. There is a later book I would like to touch upon. What was your motivation in writing *The Muses Are Heard*?

Capote: This was the beginning of a long experiment. I've always had the theory that reportage is the great unexplored art form. I mean, most good writers, good literary craftsmen, seldom use this metier. For example, John Hersey is a very fine journalist and an excellent writer, but he's not an artist in the sense that I mean. Even Rebecca West at her best (and I think she's a remarkable reporter) doesn't do what I'm talking about. I've had this theory that a factual piece of work could explore whole new dimensions in writing that would have a double effect fiction does not have—the very fact of its being true, every word of it true, would add a double contribution of strength and impact. The "Porgy and Bess" piece, and one other piece I did for *The New Yorker*—a profile of Marlon Brando—were parts of this experiment. I originally did them just to see if I could do them. After I did the "Porgy and Bess" tour of Russia for *The New*

Yorker, I wanted to see what I could do within the scope of something truly banal, and I thought, "What is the most banal thing in journalism?" After a time I realized that it would be an interview with a film star, the sort of thing you would see in *Photoplay* magazine. I decided that it must not only be with a film star, but that it must follow the absolute path of these things, in that they're always done as interviews that take place at one time with a person more or less on the fly. So I put a number of names into a hat and pulled out, God knows why, Marlon Brando. He was in Japan at the same time, so I went to *The New Yorker* and asked them if they'd be interested in this, and they were. So I went to Japan and spent just the prescribed time with Brando—an evening. I had actually known Marlon Brando before, so in a way I was cheating, but I didn't know him very well. I had dinner with him and talked with him and then spent a year on the piece because it had to be perfection—because my part was to take this banal thing and turn it into a work of art.

Anyway, I'm pleased with that piece. Lots of people can't understand why I wrote it, especially Marlon Brando. But it definitely had a point for me—an artistic one—and I moved slowly on this path because all the time I knew I was going to write a book, based on heaven knows what. I didn't know what the theme was going to be, but I knew it would be reportage on an immense scale.

I worked on other things, now feeling in complete control of myself within this form, becoming technically adept, just like one becomes technically adept at drawing skeletons to become a doctor. What I wanted to do, of course, was a great deal more ambitious than sketching skeletons; I was then going to fill it in, flesh it out, as it were. But it wasn't until five years ago that I knew what the subject would be.

One day I picked up a paper, and in the business section of the *New York Times* I found this very small headline that read, "Eisenhower Appointee Murdered." The victim was a rancher in western Kansas, a wheat grower who had been an Eisenhower appointee to the Farm Credit Bureau. He, his wife, and two of their children had been murdered, and it was a complete mystery. They had no idea of who had done it or why, but the story struck me with tremendous force. I suddenly realized that perhaps a crime, after all, would be the ideal subject matter for the massive job of reportage I wanted to do. I would have a wide range of characters, and, most importantly, it would be timeless. I knew it would take me five years, perhaps eight or ten years, to do this, and I couldn't work on some ephemeral, momentary thing. It had to be an event related to permanent emotions in people.

Now, there are thousands of crimes I could have picked, but I felt that this was mysteriously ordained. Why should I go to a small Kansas town? Why should I be interested in the murder of a wheat grower? I don't know, but it hit me head-on. The next thing I knew I got on a train and went to this little town in western Kansas. I was there for seven months that first time, and I've been back there many, many times since. I've been working on the book for five years, and it's almost finished.

N. To turn briefly to a more general topic—since you, yourself, are southern-born, you might have some opinion as to why such a disproportionate number of our leading writers come from the South.

Capote: I don't think this is true any more. During the last ten years the large percentage of the more talented American writers are urban Jewish intellectuals.

N. But in decades prior to this—

Capote: Oh, yes, then a large number did come from the South and Southwest. I think one reason is that there is a definite code of values, of regional values, regional speech, regional attitudes toward religion, race, society. Rightly or wrongly, a whole code of behavior. I think all this is beginning to blur considerably, but in the South you knew where you stood and you knew where other people stood. If you lived in a southern town you could, from the time you were seven (provided you were reasonably bright), make a social chart of the whole town—morals, religion, social status. The rest of the country has rather lost this. It presented, for the artist, that "perfect prospect," as it were. In the sense that Jane Austen had a perfect prospect from which she could view life, southern artists, regionally oriented, have this—or did have it.

I, personally, have never thought of myself as a writer regionally oriented. My first book had a southern setting because I was writing about what I knew most deeply at the time. The raw material of my work usually depends on events lived ten years beforehand, (in fiction, not nonfiction). Now, of course, the South is so far behind me that it has ceased to furnish me with subject matter.

I don't think that *Other Voices, Other Rooms* can be called a southern novel. As a matter of fact it is sort of a poem, not a novel; it was a poem about an emotional situation. Everything in it has double meanings—it could as well have been set in Timbuctu or Brooklyn, except for certain physical descriptions. Actually, the only thing I've written that *depended* on its southern setting was a story called "A Christmas Memory" in *Breakfast at Tiffany's*. The moment I wrote that short story I knew I would never write another word about the South. I'm not going to be haunted by it any more, so I see no reason to deal with those people or those settings.

N. Another question in the realm of theory: What obligation, if any, do you feel the writer owes the subject matter he works with and the public for which he writes?

Capote: I think the only person a writer has an obligation to is himself. If what I write doesn't fulfill something in me, if I don't honestly feel it's the best I can do, then I'm miserable. In fact, I just don't publish it.

The only obligation any artist can have is to himself. His work means nothing, otherwise. It has no meaning. That's why it's so absolutely boring to write a film script. The great sense of self-obligation doesn't enter into it because too many people are involved. Thus the thing that propels me, that makes me proud of my work, is utterly absent. I've only written two film scripts and I must admit that in a peculiar way I enjoyed doing them, but the true gratification of writing was completely absent; the obligation was to producers and the actors, to what I was being paid to do, and not to myself.

The only really gratifying thing is to serve yourself. To give yourself free law, as it were.

N. If you were to give advice to a young person intent on a literary career, what would that advice be?

Capote: People are always asking me if I believe that writing can be taught. My answer is, "No—I don't think writing can be taught." But on the other hand, if I were a young writer and convinced of my talent, I could do a lot worse than to attend a really good college workshop—for one reason only. Any writer, and especially the talented writer, needs an audience. The more immediate that audience is, the better for him because it stimulates him in his work; he gets a better view of himself and a running criticism.

Young writers couldn't get this even if they were publishing stories all the time. You publish a story and there's no particular reaction. It's as though you shot an arrow into the dark. You may get letters from people who liked or didn't like it, or a lot of reviews that really don't mean anything, but if you are working in close quarters with others who are also interested in writing, and you've got an instructor with a good critical sense, there's a vast stimulation.

I've never had this happen to me, but I know it must be so. I've given various readings and lectures at universities, so I have had some first-hand observation of it, though I never attended such a workshop myself, but if I were a young writer I would. I think a college workshop would be enormously helpful and stimulating.

N. In looking at today's creative arts, literature in particular, what do you find that you most admire? Conversely, what do you most deplore?

Capote: I find that a very hard question to answer. I really don't deplore anything, because I like all creative actions just as actions themselves, whether I personally enjoy them or not. I can't deplore them just because I don't think they are right. Now, none of this "beat" writing interests me at all. I think it's fraudulent. I think it's all evasive. Where there is no discipline there is nothing. I don't even find that the beat writing has a surface liveliness—but that's neither here nor there because I'm sure that eventually something good will come out of it. Some extraordinary person will be encouraged by it who could never have accepted the rigid disciplines of what I consider good writing.

On the other hand, what do I most admire? Perhaps "admire" isn't the right word, but I think it's a fine thing that Katherine Anne Porter's *Ship of Fools* sold so well. Why? Because she's a remarkably good artist. And I think it's wonderful that her book was so popular and successful, whether people really read it or not.

I think it's fine that a young writer like John Updike can have a large success because he's an exceptionally gifted young man. The attention shown to young writers in this country is greater than anywhere else (except France) and this is encouraging. I suppose Russia gives their young writers more attention than any other country, but I don't happen to admire any of the young Russian writers. I like some of the Communist film makers, who do extraordinary work, but I don't care for the younger writers.

N. What do you think of American criticism and review as a whole?

Capote: I don't think the problem is as much a question of the level of American criticism as it is the outlets for it. I suppose the *New York Times*, commercially speaking, is the most influential of all book review outlets, and it's appalling. It's as middle-class and boring and as badly put together as it can possibly be. I thought it was interesting that the *Herald Tribune* started "Book Week." The way "Book Week" started out, it promised to be good, but it hasn't turned out that way. However, *The New York Review of Books* is excellent. This is really a step in the right direction.

As far as the little magazines are concerned, each seems to be in the hands of a separate fleet and is at war with all the other little fleets. You can't pay too much attention to them, if you're a writer. But then, I've developed a very thick skin about criticism. I've had to. I can read the most devastating things about myself, now, and it doesn't make my pulse skip a beat. You know, the writer is inclined to be a sensitive person, and he can read one hundred good reviews and one bad review and take that bad review to heart. I don't do it, not any more.

N. As far as your own career is concerned, could you state your own objectives? Perhaps this should be placed in the perspective you would like applied?

Capote: Well, I think I've had two careers. One was the career of precocity, the young person who published a series of books that were really quite remarkable. I can even read them now, and evaluate them favorably, as though they were the work of a stranger. In a way, they are. The person who wrote them doesn't exist any more. My metabolism, artistically and intellectually, has changed. I'm not saying it's for the better; it's just changed. The way one's hair changes color.

My second career began—I guess it really began with *Breakfast at Tiffany's*. It involves a different point of view, a different prose style to some degree. Actually, the prose style is an evolvement from one to the other—a pruning and thinning-out to a more subdued, clearer prose. I don't find it as evocative, in many respects, as the other, or even as original, but it is more difficult to do. But I'm nowhere near reaching what I want to do, where I want to go. Presumably this new book is as close as I'm going to get, at least stylistically. But I hope to expand from that point on in the multiplicity and range of characters I can deal with, because until recently I've been quite limited. Now I feel capable of handling all sorts of new and different characters which I couldn't approach before, and I think reportage has helped me. I think it freed many things inside of me—this opportunity to work with real people, then using real people under their own names. It has freed or unlocked something inside myself that now makes it possible for me to return to fiction with the ability to use a far greater range of characters.

The Story Behind a Nonfiction Novel
George Plimpton/1966

From *The New York Times Book Review,* 16 January 1966, 2-3, 38-43. Copyright © 1966 by The New York Times Company. Reprinted by permission.

In Cold Blood is remarkable for its objectivity—nowhere, despite his involvement, does the author intrude. In the following interview, done a few weeks ago, Truman Capote presents his own views on the case, its principals, and in particular he discusses the new literary art form which he calls the nonfiction novel.

Q. Why did you select the particular subject matter of murder; had you previously been interested in crime?

A. Not really, no. During the last years I've learned a good deal about crime, and the origins of the homicidal mentality. Still, it is a layman's knowledge and I don't pretend to anything deeper. The motivating factor in my choice of material—that is, choosing to write a true account of an actual murder case—was altogether literary. The decision was based on a theory I've harbored since I first began to write professionally, which is well over 20 years ago. It seemed to me that journalism, reportage, could be forced to yield a serious new art form: the "nonfiction novel," as I thought of it. Several admirable reporters—Rebecca West for one, and Joseph Mitchell and Lillian Ross—have shown the possibilities of narrative reportage; and Miss Ross, in her brilliant *Picture,* achieved at least a nonfiction novella. Still, on the whole, journalism is the most underestimated, the least explored of literary mediums.

Q. Why should that be so?

A. Because few first-class creative writers have ever bothered with journalism, except as a sideline, "hack-work," something to be done when the creative spirit is lacking, or as a means of making money quickly. Such writers say in effect: Why should we trouble with factual writing when we're able to invent our own stories, contrive our own characters and themes?—journalism is only literary photography, and unbecoming to the serious writer's artistic dignity.

Another deterrent—and not the smallest—is that the reporter, unlike the fantasist, has to deal with actual people who have real names. If they feel maligned, or just contrary, or greedy, they enrich lawyers (though rarely themselves) by instigating libel actions. This last is certainly a factor to consider, a most oppressive and repressive one. Because it's indeed difficult to portray, in any meaningful depth, another being, his appearance, speech, mentality, without to some degree, and often for quite trifling cause, offending him. The truth seems to be that no one likes to see himself described as he is, or cares to see exactly set down what he said and did. Well, even I can understand that—because I don't like it myself when I am the sitter and not the portraitist: the frailty of egos!—and the more accurate the strokes, the greater the resentment.

When I first formed my theories concerning the nonfiction novel, many people with whom I discussed the matter were unsympathetic. They felt that what I proposed, a narrative form that employed all the techniques of fictional art but was nevertheless immaculately factual, was little more than a literary solution for fatigued novelists suffering from "failure of imagination." Personally, I felt that this attitude represented a "failure of imagination" on their part.

Of course a properly done piece of narrative reporting requires imagination!—and a good deal of special technical equipment that is usually beyond the resources—and I don't doubt the interests—of most fictional writers: an ability to transcribe verbatim long conversations, and to do so without taking notes or using tape-recordings. Also, it is necessary to have a 20/20 eye for visual detail—in this sense, it is quite true that one must be a "literary photographer," though an exceedingly selective one. But, above all, the reporter must be able to empathize with personalities outside his usual imaginative range, mentalities unlike his own, kinds of people he would never have written about had he not been forced to by encountering them inside the journalistic situation. This last is what first attracted me to the notion of narrative reportage.

It seems to me that most contemporary novelists, especially the

Americans and the French, are too subjective, mesmerized by private demons; they're enraptured by their navels, and confined by a view that ends with their own toes. If I were naming names, I'd name myself among others. At any rate, I did at one time feel an artistic need to escape my self-created world. I wanted to exchange it, creatively speaking, for the everyday objective world we all inhabit. Not that I'd never written nonfiction before—I kept journals, and had published a small truthful book of travel impressions. *Local Color.* But I had never attempted an ambitious piece of reportage until 1956, when I wrote *The Muses Are Heard,* an account of the first theatrical cultural exchange between the U.S.A. and the U.S.S.R.—that is, the "Porgy and Bess" tour of Russia. It was published in *The New Yorker,* the only magazine I know of that encourages the serious practitioners of this art form. Later, I contributed a few other reportorial finger-exercises to the same magazine. Finally, I felt equipped and ready to undertake a full-scale narrative—in other words, a "nonfiction novel."

Q. How does John Hersey's *Hiroshima* or Oscar Lewis's *Children of Sanchez* compare with "the nonfiction novel"?

A. The Oscar Lewis book is a documentary, a job of editing from tapes, and however skillful and moving, it is not creative writing. *Hiroshima* is creative—in the sense that Hersey isn't taking something off a tape-recorder and editing it—but it still hasn't got anything to do with what I'm talking about. *Hiroshima* is a strict classical journalistic piece. What is closer is what Lillian Ross did with *Picture.* Or my own book, *The Muses are Heard*—which uses the techniques of the comic short novel.

It was natural that I should progress from that experiment, and get myself in much deeper water. I read in the paper the other day that I had been quoted as saying that reporting is now more interesting than fiction. Now that's *not* what I said, and it's important to me to get this straight. What I think is that reporting can be made *as* interesting as fiction, and done *as* artistically—underlining those two "as"es. I don't mean to say that one is a superior form to the other. I feel that creative reportage has been neglected and has great relevance to 20th-century writing. And while it can be an artistic outlet for the creative writer, it has never been particularly explored.

Q. What is your opinion of the so-called New Journalism—as it is practiced particularly at the *Herald Tribune*?

A. If you mean James Breslin and Tom Wolfe, and that crowd, they have nothing to do with creative journalism—in the sense that I use the term—because neither of them, nor any of that school of reporting have the proper fictional technical equipment. It's useless for a writer whose talent is essentially journalistic to attempt creative reportage, because it simply won't work. A writer like Rebecca West—always a good reporter—has never really used the form of creative reportage because the form, by necessity, demands that the writer be completely in control of fictional techniques—which means that, to be a good creative reporter, you have to be a very good fiction writer.

Q. Would it be fair to say, then, since many reporters use nonfiction techniques—Meyer Levin in *Compulsion,* Walter Lord in *A Night to Remember* and so forth—that the nonfiction novel can be defined by the degree of the fiction skills involved, and the extent of the author's absorption with his subject?

A. *Compulsion* is a fictional novel suggested by fact, but no way bound to it, I never read the other book. The nonfiction novel should not be confused with the documentary novel—a popular and interesting but impure genre, which allows all the latitude of the fiction writer, but usually contains neither the persuasiveness of fact nor the poetic altitude fiction is capable of reaching. The author lets his imagination run riot over the facts! If I sound querulous or arrogant about this, it's not only that I have to protect my child, but that I truly don't believe anything like it exists in the history of journalism.

Q. What is the first step in producing a "nonfiction novel?"

A. The difficulty was to choose a promising subject. If you intend to spend three or four or five years with a book, as I planned to do, then you want to be reasonably certain that the material will not soon "date." The content of much journalism so swiftly does, which is another of the medium's deterrents. A number of ideas occurred, but one after the other, and for one reason or another, each was eventually discarded, often after I'd done considerable preliminary work. Then one morning in November 1959, while flicking through the *New York Times,* I encountered, on a deep-inside page, this headline: Wealthy Farmer, 3 of Family Slain.

The story was brief, just several paragraphs stating the facts: A Mr. Herbert W. Clutter, who had served on the Farm Credit Board during the Eisenhower Administration, his wife and two teen-aged children, had been brutally, entirely mysteriously, murdered on a lonely wheat and cattle ranch in a remote part of Kansas. There was nothing really exceptional about it; one reads items concerning multiple murders many times in the course of a year.

Q. Then why did you decide it was the subject you had been looking for?

A. I didn't. Not immediately. But after reading the story it suddenly struck me that a crime, the study of one such, might provide the broad scope I needed to write the kind of book I wanted to write. Moreover, the human heart being what it is, murder was a theme not likely to darken and yellow with time.

I thought about it all that November day, and part of the next; and then I said to myself: Well, why not *this* crime? The Clutter case. Why not pack up and go to Kansas and see what happens? Of course it was a rather frightening thought!—to arrive alone in a small strange town, a town in the grip of an unsolved mass murder. Still, the circumstances of the place being altogether unfamiliar, geographically and atmospherically, made it that much more tempting. Everything would seem freshly minted—the people, their accents and attitudes, the landscape, its contours, the weather. All this, it seemed to me, could only sharpen my eye and quicken my ear.

In the end, I did not go alone. I went with a lifelong friend, Harper Lee. She is a gifted woman, courageous, and with a warmth that instantly kindles most people, however suspicious or dour. She had recently completed a first novel (*To Kill a Mockingbird*), and, feeling at loose ends, she said she would accompany me in the role of assistant researchist.

We traveled by train to St. Louis, changed trains and went to Manhattan, Kan., where we got off to consult Dr. James McClain, president of Mr. Clutter's alma mater, Kansas State University. Dr. McClain, a gracious man, seemed a little nonplussed by our interest in the case, but he gave us letters of introduction to several people in western Kansas. We rented a car and drove some 400 miles to Garden City. It was twilight when we arrived. I remember the car-radio was playing, and we heard: "Police authorities, continuing their investigation of the tragic Clutter slayings, have requested that anyone with pertinent information please contact the Sheriff's office. . . ."

If I had realized then what the future held, I never would have stopped in Garden City. I would have driven straight on. Like a bat out of hell.

Q. What was Harper Lee's contribution to your work?

A. She kept me company when I was based out there. I suppose she was with me about two months altogether. She went on a number of interviews; she typed her own notes, and I had these and could refer to them. She was extremely helpful in the beginning, when we weren't making much headway with the town's people, by making friends with the wives of the people I wanted to meet. She became friendly with all the churchgoers. A Kansas paper said the other day that everyone out there was so wonderfully cooperative because I was a famous writer. The fact of the matter is that not one single person in the town had ever heard of me.

Q. How long did it take for the town to thaw out enough so that you were accepted and you could get to your interviewing?

A. About a month. I think they finally just realized that we were there to stay—they'd have to make the best of it. Under the circumstances, they were suspicious. After all, there was an unsolved murder case, and the people in the town were tired of the thing, and frightened. But then after it all quieted down—after Perry and Dick were arrested—that was when we did most of the original interviews. Some of them went on for three years—though not on the same subject, of course. I suppose if I used just 20 per cent of all the material I put together over those years of interviewing, I'd still have a book two thousand pages long!

Q. How much research did you do other than through interviews with the principals in the case?

A. Oh, a great deal. I did months of comparative research on murder, murderers, the criminal mentality, and I interviewed quite a number of murderers—solely to give me perspective on these two boys. And then crime. I didn't know anything about crime or criminals when I began to do the book. I certainly do now! I'd say 80 per cent of the research I did I have never used. But it gave me such a grounding that I never had any hesitation in my consideration of the subject.

Q. What was the most singular interview you conducted?

A. I suppose the most startled interviewee was Mr. Bell, the meat-packing executive from Omaha. He was the man who picked up Perry and Dick when they were hitchhiking across Nebraska. They planned to murder him and then make off with his car. Quite unaware of all this, Bell was saved, as you'll remember, just as Perry was goiong to smash in his head from the seat behind, because he slowed down to pick up another hitchhiker, a Negro. The boys told me this story, and they had this man's business card. I decided to interview him. I wrote him a letter, but got no answer. Then I wrote a letter to the personnel manager of the meat-packing company in Omaha, asking if they had a Mr. Bell in their employ. I told them I wanted to talk to him about a pair of hitchhikers he'd picked up four months previously. The manager wrote back and said that they *did* have a Mr. Bell on their staff, but it was surely the *wrong* Mr. Bell since it was against company policy for employees to take hitchhikers in their cars. So I telephoned Mr. Bell and when he got on the phone he was very brusque: he said I didn't know what I was talking about.

The only thing to do was to go to Omaha personally. I went up there and walked in on Mr. Bell and put two photographs down on his desk. I asked him if he recognized the two men. He said, why? So I told him that the two were the hitchhikers he said he had never given a ride to, that they had planned to kill him and then bury him in the prairie—and how close they'd come to it. Well, he turned every conceivable kind of color. You can imagine. He recognized them all right. He was quite cooperative about telling me about the trip, but he asked me not to use his real name. There are only three people in the book whose names I've changed—his, the convict Perry admired so much (Willie-Jay he's called in the book), and also I changed Perry Smith's sister's name.

Q. How long after you went to Kansas did you sense the form of the book? Were there many false starts?

A. I worked for a year on the notes before I ever wrote one line. And when I wrote the first word, I had done the entire book in outline, down to the finest detail. Except for the last part, the final dispensation of the case—that was an evolving matter. It began of course, with interviews—with all the different characters of the book. Let me give you two examples of how I worked from these interviews. In the first part of the book—the part that's called "The Last to See Them Alive"—there's a long narration, word for word, given by the school teacher who went with the sheriff to the Clutter house and found the four bodies. Well, I simply set that into the book as a straight complete interview—though it was, in fact, done several times: each time there'd be some little thing which I'd add or change. But I hardly interfered at all. A slight editing job. The school teacher tells the whole story himself—exactly what happened from the moment they got to the house, and what they found there.

On the other hand, in that same first part, there's a scene between the postmistress and her mother when the mother reports that the ambulances have gone to the Clutter house. That's a straight dramatic scene—with quotes, dialogue, action, everything. But it evolved out of interviews just like the one with the school teacher. Except in this case I took what they had told me and transposed it into straight narrative terms. Of course, elsewhere in the book, very often it's direct observation, events I saw myself—the trial, the executions.

Q. You never used a tape-recorder?

A. Twelve years ago I began to train myself, for the purpose of this sort of book, to transcribe conversation without using a tape-recorder. I did it by having a friend read passages from a book, and then later I'd write them down to see how close I could come to the original. I had a natural facility for it, but after doing these exercises for a year and a half, for a couple of hours a day, I could get within 95 per cent of absolute accuracy, which is as close as you need. I felt it was essential. Even note-taking artificializes the atmosphere of an interview, or a scene-in-progress; it interferes with the communication between author and subject—the latter is usually self-conscious, or an untrusting wariness is induced. Certainly, a tape-recorder does so. Not long ago a French literary critic turned up with a tape-recorder. I don't like them, as I say, but I agreed to its use. In the middle of the interview it broke down. The French literary critic was desperately unhappy. He didn't know what to do. I said, "Well, let's just go on as if nothing had happened." He said, "It's not the same. I'm not accustomed to listen to what you're saying."

Q. You've kept yourself out of the book entirely. Why was that—considering your own involvement in the case?

A. My feeling is that for the nonfiction-novel form to be entirely successful, the author should not appear in the work. Ideally. Once the narrator does appear, he has to appear throughout, all the way down the line, and the I-I-I intrudes when it really shouldn't. I think the single most difficult thing in my book, technically, was to write it without ever appearing myself, and yet, at the same time, create total credibility.

Q. Being removed from the book, that is to say, keeping yourself out of it, do you find it difficult to present your own point of view? For example, your own view as to why Perry Smith committed the murders.

A. Of course it's by the selection of what you choose to tell. I believe Perry did what he did for the reasons he himself states—that his life was a constant accumulation of disillusionments and reverses and he suddenly found himself (in the Clutter house that night) in a psychological cul-de-sac. The Clutters were such a perfect set of symbols for every frustration in his life. As Perry himself said, "I didn't have anything against them, and they never did anything wrong to me—the way other people have all my life. Maybe they're just the ones who had to pay for it." Now in that particular section where Perry talks about the reason for the murders, I could have included other views. But Perry's happens to be the one I believe is the right one, and it's the one that Dr. Satten at the Menninger Clinic arrived at quite independently, never having done any interviews with Perry.

I could have added a lot of other opinions. But that would have confused the issue, and indeed the book. I had to make up my mind, and move towards that one view, always. You can say that the reportage is incomplete. But then it has to be. It's a question of selection, you wouldn't get anywhere if it wasn't for that. I've often thought of the book as being like something reduced to a seed. Instead of presenting the reader with a full plant, with all the foliage, a seed is planted in the soil of his mind. I've often thought of the book in that sense. I make my own comment by what I choose to tell and how I choose to tell it. It is true that an author is more in control of fictional characters because he can do anything he wants with them as long as they stay credible. But in the nonfiction novel one can also manipulate: if I put something in which I don't agree about I can always set it in a context of qualification without having to step into the story myself to set the reader straight.

Q. When did you first see the murderers—Perry and Dick?

A. The first time I ever saw them was the day they were returned to Garden City. I had been waiting in the crowd in the square for nearly five hours, frozen to death. That was the first time. I tried to interview them the next day—both completely unsuccessful interviews. I saw Perry first, but he was so cornered and suspicious—and quite rightly so—and paranoid that he couldn't have been less communicative. It was always easier with Dick. He was like someone you meet on a train, immensely garrulous, who starts up a conversation and is only too obliged to tell you *everything*. Perry became easier after the third or fourth month, but it wasn't until the last five years of his life that he was totally and absolutely honest with me, and came to trust me. I came to have great rapport with him right up through his last day. For the first year and a half, though, he would come just so close, and then no closer. He'd retreat into the forest and leave me standing outside. I'd hear him laugh in the dark. Then gradually he would come back. In the end, he could not have been more complete and candid.

Q. How did the two accept being used as subjects for a book?

A. They had no idea what I was going to do. Well, of course, at the end they did. Perry was always asking me: Why are you writing this book? What is it supposed to mean? I don't understand why you're doing it. Tell me in one sentence why you want to do it. So I would say that it didn't have anything to do with changing the readers' opinion about anything, nor did I have any moral reasons worthy of calling them such—it was just that I had a strictly aesthetic theory about creating a book which could result in a work of art.

"That's really the truth, Perry," I'd tell him, and Perry would say, "A work of art, a work of art," and then he'd laugh and say, "What an irony, what an irony." I'd ask what he meant, and he'd tell me that all he ever wanted to do in his life was to produce a work of art.

"That's all I ever wanted in my whole life," he said. "And now, what has happened? An incredible situation where I kill four people, and you're going to produce a work of art." Well, I'd have to agree with him. It was a pretty ironic situation.

Q. Did you ever show sections of the book to witnesses as you went along?

A. I have done it, but I don't believe in it. It's a mistake because it's almost impossible to write about anybody objectively and have that person really like it. People simply do not like to see themselves put down on paper. They're like somebody who goes to see his portrait in a gallery. He doesn't like it unless it's overwhelmingly flattering—I mean the ordinary person, not someone with genuine creative perception. Showing the thing in progress usually frightens the person and there's nothing to be gained by it. I showed various sections to five people in the book, and without exception each of them found something that he desperately wanted to change. Of the whole bunch, I changed my text for one of them because, although it was a silly thing, the person genuinely believed his entire life was going to be ruined if I *didn't* make the change.

Q. Did Dick and Perry see sections of the book?

A. They saw some sections of it. Perry wanted terribly much to see the book. I had to let him see it because it just would have been too unkind not to. Each only saw the manuscript in little pieces. Everything mailed to the prison went through the censor. I wasn't about to have my manuscript floating around between those censors—not with those Xerox machines going clickety-clack. So when I went to the prison to visit I would bring parts—some little thing for Perry to read. Perry's greatest objection was the title. He didn't like it because he said the crime wasn't committed in cold blood. I told him the title had a double meaning. What was the other meaning? he wanted to know. Well, that wasn't something I was going to tell him. Dick's reaction to the book was to start switching and changing his story, saying what I had written wasn't exactly true. He wasn't trying to flatter himself; he tried to change it to serve his purposes legally, to support the various appeals he was sending through the courts. He wanted the book to read as if it was a legal brief for presentation in his behalf before the Supreme Court. But you see I had a perfect control-agent—I could always tell when Dick or Perry wasn't telling the truth. During the first few months or so of interviewing them, they weren't allowed to speak to each other. They were in separate cells. So I would keep crossing their stories, and what correlated, what checked out identically, was the truth.

Q. How did the two compare in their recounting of the events?

A. Dick had an absolutely fantastic memory—one of the greatest memories I have ever come across. The reason I know it's great is that I lived the entire trip the boys went on from the time of the murders up to the moment of their arrest in Las Vegas—thousands of miles, what the boys called "the long ride." I went everywhere the boys had gone, all the hotel rooms, every single place in the book, Mexico, Acapulco, all of it. In the hotel in Miami Beach I stayed for three days until the manager realized why I was there and asked me to leave, which I was only too glad to do. Well, Dick could give me the names and addresses of any hotel or place along the route where they'd spent maybe just half a night. He told me when I got to Miami to take a taxi to such-and-such a place and get out on the boardwalk and it would be southwest of there, number 232, and opposite I'd find two umbrellas in the sand which advertised "Tan with Coppertone." That was how exact he was. He was the one who remembered the little card in the Mexico City hotel room—in the corner of the mirror—that reads "Your day ends at 2 P.M." He was extraordinary. Perry, on the other hand, was very bad at details of that sort, though he was good at remembering conversations and moods. He was concerned altogether in the overtones of things. He was much better at describing a general sort of mood or atmosphere than Dick who, though very sensitive, was impervious to that sort of thing.

Q. What turned them back to the Clutter house after they'd almost decided to give up on the job?

A. Oh, Dick was always quite frank about that. I mean after it was all over. When they set out for the house that night, Dick was determined, before he ever went, that if the girl, Nancy, was there he was going to rape her. It wouldn't have been an act of the moment—he had been thinking about it for weeks. He told me that was one of the main reasons he was so determined to go back after they thought, you know for a moment, they wouldn't go. Because he'd been thinking about raping this girl for weeks and weeks. He had no idea what she looked like—after all, Floyd Wells, the man in prison who told them about the Clutters, hadn't seen the girl in 10 years: it had to do with the fact that she was 15 or 16. He liked young girls, much younger than Nancy Clutter actually.

Q. What do you think would have happened if Perry had faltered and not begun the killings? Do you think Dick would have done it?

A. No. There is such a thing as the ability to kill. Perry's particular psychosis had produced this ability. Dick was merely ambitious—he could *plan* murder, but not commit it.

Q. What was the boys' reaction to the killing?

A. They both finally decided that they had thoroughly enjoyed it. Once they started going, it became an immense emotional release. And they thought it was funny. With the criminal mind—and both boys had criminal minds, believe me—what seems most extreme to us is very often, if it's the most expedient thing to do, the *easiest* thing for a criminal to do. Perry and Dick both used to say (a memorable phrase) that it was much easier to kill somebody than it was to cash a bad check. Passing a bad check requires a great deal of artistry and style, whereas just going in and killing somebody requires only that you pull a trigger.

There are some instances of this that aren't in the book. At one point, in Mexico, Perry and Dick, had a terrific falling-out, and Perry said he was going to kill Dick. He said that he'd already killed five people—he was lying, adding one more than he should have (that was the Negro he kept telling Dick he'd killed years before in Las Vegas) and that one more murder wouldn't matter. It was simple enough. Perry's cliché about it was that if you've killed one person you can kill anybody. He'd look at Dick, as they drove along together, and he'd say to himself, Well, I really ought to kill him, it's a question of expediency.

They had two other murders planned that aren't mentioned in the book. Neither of them came off. One "victim" was a man who ran a restaurant in Mexico City—a Swiss. They had become friendly with him eating in his restaurant and when they were out of money they evolved this whole plan about robbing and murdering him. They went to his apartment in Mexico City and waited for him all night long. He never showed up. The other "victim" was a man they never even knew—like the Clutters. He was a banker in a small Kansas town. Dick kept telling Perry that sure, they might have failed with the Clutter score, but this Kansas banker job was absolutely for certain. They were going to kidnap him and ask for ransom, though the plan was, as you might imagine, to murder him right away.

When they went back to Kansas completely broke, that was the main plot they had in mind. What saved the banker was the ride the two boys took with Mr. Bell, yet another "victim" who was spared, as you remember, when he slowed down the car to pick up the Negro hitchhiker. Mr. Bell offered Dick a job in his meat-packing company. Dick took him up on it and spent two days there on the pickle line—putting pickles in ham sandwiches, I think it was—before he and Perry went back on the road again.

Q. Do you think Perry and Dick were surprised by what they were doing when they began the killings?

A. Perry never meant to kill the Clutters at all. He had a brain explosion. I don't think Dick was surprised, although later on he pretended he was. He knew, even if Perry didn't, that Perry would do it, and he was right. It showed an awfully shrewd instinct on Dick's part. Perry was bothered by it to a certain extent because he'd actually done it. He was always trying to find out in his own mind why he did it. He was amazed he'd done it. Dick on the other hand, *wasn't* amazed, *didn't* want to talk about it, and simply wanted to forget the whole thing: he wanted to get on with life.

Q. Was there any sexual relationship, or such tendencies, between them?

A. No. None at all. Dick was aggressively heterosexual and had great success. Women liked him. As for Perry, his love for Willie-Jay in the State Prison was profound—and it was reciprocated, but never consummated physically, though there was the opportunity. The relationship between Perry and Dick was quite another matter. What is misleading, perhaps, is that in comparing himself with Dick, Perry used to say how totally "virile" Dick was. But he was referring, I think, to the practical and pragmatic sides of Dick—admiring them because as a dreamer he had none of that toughness himself at all.

Perry's sexual interests were practically nil. When Dick went to the whorehouses, Perry sat in the cafes, waiting. There was only one occasion—that was their first night in Mexico when the two of them went to a bordello run by an "old queen," according to Dick. Ten dollars was the price—which they weren't *about* to pay, and they said so. Well, the old queen looked at them and said perhaps he could arrange something for less; he disappeared and came out with this female midget about 3 feet 2 inches tall. Dick was disgusted, but Perry was madly excited. That was the only instance. Perry was such a little moralist after all.

Q. How long do you think the two would have stayed together had they not been picked up in Las Vegas? Was the odd bond that kept them together beginning to fray? One senses in the rashness of their acts and plans a subconscious urge to be captured.

A. Dick planned to ditch Perry in Las Vegas, and I think he would have done so. No, I certainly don't think this particular pair wanted to be caught—though this is a common criminal phenomenon.

Q. How do you yourself equate the sort of petty punk that Detective Alvin Dewey feels Dick is with the extraordinary violence in him—to "see hair all over the walls"?

A. Dick's was definitely a small-scale criminal mind. These violent phrases were simply a form of bragging meant to impress Perry, who *was* impressed, for he liked to think of Dick as being "tough." Perry was too sensitive to be "tough." Sensitive. But himself able to kill.

Q. Is it one of the artistic limitations of the nonfiction novel that the writer is placed at the whim of chance? Suppose, in the case of *In Cold Blood*, clemency had been granted? Or the two boys had been less interesting? Wouldn't the artistry of the book have suffered? Isn't luck involved?

A. It is true that I was in the peculiar situation of being involved in a slowly developing situation. I never knew until the events were well along whether a book was going to be possible. There was always the choice, after all, of whether to stop or go on. The book could have ended with the trial, with just a coda at the end explaining what had finally happened. If the principals had been uninteresting or completely uncooperative, I could have stopped and looked elsewhere, perhaps not very far. A nonfiction novel could have been written about any of the other prisoners in Death Row—York and Latham, or especially Lee Andrews. Andrews was the most *subtly* crazy person you can imagine—I mean there was just one thing wrong with him. He was the most rational, calm, bright young boy you'd ever want to meet. I mean *really* bright—which is what made him a truly awesome kind of person. Because his one flaw was, it didn't bother him *at all* to kill. Which is quite a trait. The people who crossed his path, well, to his way of thinking, the best thing to do with them was just to put them in their graves.

Q. What other than murder might be a subject suitable for the nonfiction novel?

A. The other day someone suggested that the break-up of a marriage would be an interesting topic for a nonfiction novel. I disagreed. First of all, you'd have to find two people who would be willing—who'd sign a release. Second, their respective views on the subject-matter would be incoherent. And third, any couple who'd subject themselves to the scrutiny demanded would quite likely be a pair of kooks. But it's amazing how many events *would* work with the theory of the nonfiction novel in mind—the Watts riots, for example. They would provide a subject that satisfied the first essential of the nonfiction novel—that there is a timeless quality about the cause and events. That's important. If its going to date, it can't be a work of art. The requisite would also be that you would have had to live through the riots, at least part of them, as a witness, so that a depth of perception could be acquired. That event, just three days. It would take years to do. You'd start with the family that instigated the riots without ever meaning to.

Q. With the nonfiction novel I suppose the temptation to fictionalize events, or a line of dialogue, for example, must at times be overwhelming. With *In Cold Blood* was there any invention of this sort to speak of—I was thinking specifically of the dog you described trotting along the road at the end of a section on Perry and Dick, and then later you introduce the next section on the two with Dick swerving to hit the dog. Was there actually a dog at that exact point in the narrative, or were you using this habit of Dick's as a fiction device to bridge the two sections?

A. No. There was a dog, and it was precisely as described. One doesn't spend almost six years on a book, the point of which is factual accuracy, and then give way to minor distortions. People are so suspicious. They ask, "How can you reconstruct the conversation of a dead girl, Nancy Clutter, without fictionalizing?" If they read the book carefully, they can see readily enough how it's done. It's a silly question. Each time Nancy appears in the narrative, there are witnesses to what she is saying and doing—phone calls, conversations, being overheard. When she walks the horse up from the river in the twilight, the hired man is a witness and talked to her then. The last time we see her, in her bedroom, Perry and Dick themselves were the witnesses, and told me what she had said. What is reported of her, even in the narrative form, is as accurate as many hours of questioning, over and over again, can make it. All of it is reconstructed from the evidence of witnesses—which is implicit in the title of the first section of the book—"The Last to See Them Alive."

Q. How conscious were you of film techniques in planning the book?

A. Consciously, not at all. Subconsciously, who knows?

Q. After their conviction, you spent years corresponding and visiting with the prisoners. What was the relationship between the two of them?

A. When they were taken to Death Row, they were right next door to each other. But they didn't talk much. Perry was intensely secretive and wouldn't ever talk because he didn't want the other prisoners—York, Latham, and particularly Andrews, whom he despised—to hear anything that he had to say. He would write Dick notes on "kites" as he called them. He would reach out his hand and zip the "kite" into Dick's cell. Dick didn't much enjoy receiving these communications because they were always one form or another of recrimination—nothing to do with the Clutter crime, but just general dissatisfaction with things there in prison and . . . the people, very often Dick himself. Perry'd send Dick a note: "If I hear you tell another of those filthy jokes again I'll kill you when we go to the shower!" He was quite a little moralist, Perry, as I've said.

It was over a moral question that he and I had a tremendous falling-out once. It lasted for about two months. I used to send them things to read—both books and magazines. Dick only wanted girlie magazines—either those or magazines that had to do with cars and motors. I sent them both whatever they wanted. Well, Perry said to me one time: "How could a person like you go on contributing to the degeneracy of Dick's mind by sending him all this 'degenerate filthy' literature?" Weren't they all sick enough without this further contribution towards their total moral decay? He'd got very grand talking in terms that way. I tried to explain to him that I was neither his judge nor Dick's—and if that was what Dick wanted to read, that was *his* business. Perry felt that was entirely wrong—that people had to fulfill an obligation towards moral leadership. Very grand. Well, I agree with him up to a point, but in the case of Dick's reading matter it was absurd, of course, and so we got into such a really serious argument about it that afterwards, for two months, he wouldn't speak or even write to me.

Q. How often did the two correspond with you?

A. Except for those occasional fallings-out, they'd write twice a week. I wrote them both twice a week all those years. One letter to the both of them didn't work. I had to write them both, and I had to be careful not to be repetitious, because they were very jealous of each other. Or rather, Perry was terribly jealous of Dick, and if Dick got one more letter than he did, that would create a great crisis. I wrote them about what I was doing, and where I was living, describing everything in the most careful detail. Perry was interested in my dog, and I would always write about him, and send along pictures. I often wrote them about their legal problems.

Q. Do you think if the social positions of the two boys had been different that their personalities would have been markedly different?

A. Of course there wasn't anything peculiar about Dick's social position. He was a very ordinary boy who simply couldn't sustain any kind of normal relationship with anybody. If he had been given $10,000, perhaps he might have settled into some small business. But I don't think so. He had a very natural criminal instinct towards everything. He was oriented towards stealing from the beginning. On the other hand, I think Perry could have been an entirely different person. I really do. His life had been so incredibly abysmal that I don't see what chance he had as a little child except to steal and run wild.

Of course, you could say that his brother, with exactly the same background, went ahead and became the head of his class. What does it matter that he later killed himself. No, it's there—it's the fact that the brother *did* kill himself, in spite of his success, that shows how really awry the background of the Smiths' lives were. Terrifying. Perry had extraordinary qualities, but they just weren't channeled properly—to put it mildly. He was really a talented boy in a limited way—he had a genuine sensitivity—and, as I've said, when he talked about himself as an artist, he wasn't really joking at all.

Q. You once said that emotionality made you lose writing control—that you had to exhaust emotion before you could get to work. Was there a problem with *In Cold Blood*, considering your involvement with the case and its principals?

A. Yes, it was a problem. Nevertheless, I felt in control throughout. However, I had great difficulty writing the last six or seven pages. This even took a physical form: hand paralysis. I finally used a typewriter—very awkward as I always write in longhand.

Q. Your feeling about capital punishment is implicit in the title of the book. How do you feel the lot of Perry and Dick should have been resolved?

A. I feel that capital crimes should all be handled by Federal Courts, and that those convicted should be imprisoned in a special Federal prison where, conceivably, a life-sentence could mean, as it does not in state courts, just that.

Q. Did you see the prisoners on their final day? Perry wrote you a 100-page letter that you received after the execution. Did he mention that he had written it?

A. Yes, I was with them the last hour before the execution. No, Perry did not mention the letter. He only kissed me on the cheek, and said, "Adios, amigo."

Q. What was the letter about?

A. It was a rambling letter, often intensely personal, often setting forth his various philosophies. He had been reading Santayana. Somewhere he had read *The Last Puritan,* and had been very impressed by it. What I really think impressed him about me was that I had once visited Santayana at the Convent of the Blue Nuns in Rome. He always wanted me to go into great detail about that visit, what Santayana had looked like, and the nuns, and all the physical details. Also, he had been reading Thoreau. Narratives didn't interest him at all. So in his letter he would write: "As Santayana says—" and then there'd be five pages of what Santayana *did* say. Or he'd write: "I agree with Thoreau about this. Do you?"—then he'd write that he didn't *care* what I thought, and he'd add five or ten pages of what he agreed with Thoreau about.

Q. The case must have left you with an extraordinary collection of memorabilia.

A. My files would almost fill a whole small room, right up to the ceiling. All my research. Hundreds of letters. Newspaper clippings. Court records—the court records almost fill two trunks. There were so many Federal hearings on the case. One Federal hearing was twice as long as the original court trial. A huge assemblage of stuff. I have some of the personal belongings—all of Perry's because he left me everything he owned; it was miserably little, his books, written in and annotated; the letters he received while in prison . . . not very many . . . his paintings and drawings. Rather a heart-breaking assemblage that arrived about a month after the execution. I simply couldn't bear to look at it for a long time. I finally sorted everything. Then, also, after the execution, that 100-page letter from Perry got to me. The last line of the letter—it's Thoreau, I think, a paraphrase, goes, "And suddenly I realize life is the father and death is the mother." The last line. Extraordinary.

Q. What will you do with this collection?

A. I think I may burn it all. You think I'm kidding? I'm not. The book is what is important. It exists in its own right. The rest of the material is extraneous, and it's personal, what's more. I don't really want people poking around in the material of six years of work and research. The book is the end result of all that, and it's exactly what I wanted to do from it.

Q. Detective Dewey told me that he felt the case and your stays in Garden City had changed you—even your style of dress . . . that you were more "conservative" now, and had given up detachable collars. . . .

A. Of course the case changed me! How could anyone live through such an experience without it profoundly affecting him? I've always been almost overly aware of the precipice we all walk along, the ridge and the abyss on either side; the last six years have increased this awareness to an almost all-pervading point. As for the rest—Mr. Dewey, a man for whom I have the utmost affection and respect, is perhaps confusing comparative youth (I was 35 when we first met) with the normal aging process. Six years ago I had four more teeth and considerably more hair than is now the case, and furthermore I lost 20 pounds. I dress to accommodate the physical situation. By the way, I have never worn a detachable collar.

Q. What are you going to work on now?

A. Well, having talked at such length about the nonfiction novel, I must admit I'm going to go on to write a *novel,* a straight novel, one I've had in mind for about 15 years. But I will attempt the nonfiction form again—when the time comes and the subject appears and I recognize the possibilities. I have one very good idea for another one, but I'm going to let it simmer on the back of my head for while. It's quite a step—to undertake the nonfiction novel. Because the amount of work is enormous. The relationship between the author and all the people he must deal with if he does the job properly—well, it's a full 24-hour-a-day job. Even when I wasn't working on the book, I was somehow involved with all the characters in it—with their personal lives, writing six or seven letters a day, taken up with their problems, a complete involvement. It's extraordinarily difficult and consuming, but for a writer who tries, doing it all the way down the line, the result can be a unique and exciting form of writing.

Q. What has been the response of readers of *In Cold Blood* to date?

A. I've been staggered by the letters I've received—their quality of sensibility, their articulateness, the compassion of their authors. The letters are not fan letters. They're from people deeply concerned about what it is I've written about. About 70 per cent of the letters think of the book as a reflection on American life—this collision between the desperate, ruthless, wandering, savage part of American life, and the other, which is insular and safe, more or less. It has struck them because there is something so awfully inevitable about what is going to happen: the people in the book are completely beyond their own control. For example, Perry wasn't an evil person. If he'd had any chance in life, things would have been different. But every illusion he'd ever had, well, they all evaporated, so that on that night he was so full of self-hatred and self-pity that I think he would have killed *somebody*—perhaps not that night, or the next, or the next. You can't get through life without ever getting anything you want, ever.

Q. At the very end of the book you give Alvin Dewey a scene in the country cemetery, a chance meeting with Sue Kidwell, which seems to synthesize the whole experience for him. Is there such a moment in your own case?

    A.   I'm still very much haunted by the whole thing. I have finished the book, but in a sense I *haven't* finished it: it keeps churning around in my head. It particularizes itself now and then, but not in the sense that it brings about a total conclusion. It's like the echo of E. M. Forster's Malabar Caves, the echo that's meaningless and yet it's there: one keeps hearing it all the time.

The Author
Haskell Frankel/1966

From *Saturday Review,* 49 (22 January 1966), 36-37. Copyright © 1966 by Saturday Review Magazine Company. Reprinted by permission.

"A dozen oysters," Mr. Capote told the waiter. "The little ones. Those big old ones get too fat."

His voice is high-pitched, but pleasant on the ear. It glides and swoops through the upper registers like some tissue-thin kite at the whim of a breeze. The voice is the only suggestion left of the slender man-child of twenty-three who posed recumbent on a couch, blond hair drooping on his forehead, for the dust jacket of his first novel, *Other Voices, Other Rooms.* At forty-one Truman Capote's short frame has thickened out as if to compensate for the hair, which has thinned and moved back. The blue eyes look our from behind brown horn rims. There is warmth in the eyes, compassion, understanding—and, if you look closely, somewhere far back there is steel.

"That picture," he said. "It was part of my complete naïveté." He pronounces it nah-vit-tay, an echo of his New Orleans childhood. "A friend took the picture. I had about nine or ten pictures. I didn't think anything about the picture, and when the publishers said, well, let's have a picture on the jacket of the book, I just sent all the pictures I had. I think it was general naïveté, period. There was nothing calculated about it at all. But when people read the book, and realized what the theme was, and coupled that with the picture, I mean the whole thing took on a kind of *outré* peculiar quality that it was never meant to have had. I mean, I could have had a completely simple straightforward picture, or not any at all. I've almost never had a picture on a book since then."

There is no author's photograph on the jacket of *In Cold Blood,* his ninth book (if one counts *Selected Writings,* made up from his other works). *In Cold Blood,* the meticulously detailed factual account of a small-town Kansas murder from the events preceding the crime through the execution of the murderers, was a guaranteed success, financially speaking, months prior to its publication. The *New Yorker* printed the novel in four consecutive issues and is rumored to have paid $70,000 for the privilege. Also rumored is the $700,000 paid by New American Library for the paperback rights; the motion picture rights have gone to Columbia Pictures in a near-million-dollar deal, and the work is the February selection of the Book-of-the-Month Club, another whopping source of author money. Whatever the hard facts and figures pertinent to *In Cold Blood* are, Truman Capote has worked hard and long—five years—for his reward.

"Well, for two years I had been looking for the subject to do this nonfiction novel about, and I had two or three that I had evolved one way or the other, and had done just a certain amount of work, when, one day, it suddenly occurred to me that a crime might be an excellent subject to make my big experiment with. *In Cold Blood*, you know, is what I call a nonfiction novel. It's a peculiar sort of hybrid form. I think it's a great unexplored art form.

"I wrote what I called a short comic nonfiction novel, *The Muses Are Heard*. About the people going to Russia. And then I got this idea of doing a really serious big work—it would be precisely like a novel, with a single difference: every word of it would be true from beginning to end. I called this, in my mind, a nonfiction novel.

"To get back, once I had decided on the possibility of a crime—and I am not interested in crime per se: I hate violence—I would half-consciously, when looking through the papers, always notice any item that had a reference to a crime. Well, one day in November 1959 I was thumbing through the *New York Times* and I saw this little headline, just a few paragraphs about this case. It was sort of as though one had been sitting for a long time watching for a certain kind of bird—if you were a bird-watcher—to come into view, and there it was. Almost instantaneously I thought, well, this is maybe exactly what I want to do, because I don't know anything about that part of the world. I've never been to Kansas, much less western Kansas. It all seems fresh to me. I'll go without any prejudices. And so I went.

"The book wasn't something reconstructed from some great

distance. I did it right along as it was happening. I lived the whole thing. The whole investigation of the case, the capture of the boys, the trial, all of the years on Death Row. All I really had to reconstruct, in an historical way, was the last days of the Clutter family's lives. It's not so awfully difficult to do—I was there three days after the murder, and I could talk to everybody who had seen the family.

"But there was a tremendous amount of research. All those endless interviews with all of those people, and I traveled all over the country and to all of the places that appear in the book, all those motels where the boys stayed, all those sordid motels and hotels in Acapulco and Miami. And I wrote 6,000 pages of notes before I ever sat down to write the book.

"I only write in longhand. Six thousand pages of interviews. Then I typed them, all by myself. Of course, Harper Lee helped me with the research the first two months. She went out to Kansas with me as my friend—we grew up together—and assistant. You know, I didn't exactly want to arrive out there all by myself, not knowing what I was walking into with the town in the grips of this immense murder case. A little town like that. So Harper Lee very kindly said she would go along for company, and then she did a lot of research and some special sort of interviews. At the time she had just finished her book, *To Kill a Mockingbird,* and it hadn't come out yet.

"Five years is a long time, you know, and I had to do so much more than research. I used to have to write sometimes up to ten letters a day to people just in connection with tiny little details. To give you an example, you know in the last part of the book where the notes appear that Hickock and Smith wrote to the psychiatrist at the time of the trial?

"Well, Hickock and Smith, who were very very good friends of mine (I mean became very close friends, very very close intimates in every conceivable way), would have gladly given me the things they wrote. They tried to reproduce them for me, but they couldn't, and it took me two years of constantly writing to Dr. Johnson before he finally gave me these things that they had actually written. That's just a small example. I used to have a chart up on the board of people I'd written to, things to be done, people who have answered, who haven't answered—the most minute little details—I would never do it again. I mean, if I had known what that book was going to cost in every conceivable way, emotionally, I never would have started it, and I really mean that.

"You know, you mustn't read the book all in one wave. The last half is so terribly complex and complicated, and by that time you're too tired, just too tired. When anybody asks me about it, I say, well, read parts one and two, put it away for a day and then read the last two parts.

"Yes, I have a very detached attitude about work *vis-à-vis* myself. I think it's a very valuable quality to have if you want to do the work that I do. I feel detached, but that doesn't mean I don't feel moved. I always have this theory, that if you want to move someone else as an artist, you yourself must necessarily be deeply moved by what it is that you are writing, but you must keep exploiting that emotion in yourself over and over and over until you can become completely cold about it or fairly cold, and then you write it, because from that area of detachment, you know exactly how to reproduce what it was that moved you about it originally."

The steel in his eyes now seemed closer to the surface. "If you've been training yourself since you were—let me see . . . I began to write so-called seriously certainly by the time I was fifteen and I'd already been writing four years. That sounds silly, but the fact of the matter is, it wasn't. I saw every thing in literary or writing terms. I was a highly trained and accomplished writer by the time I was eighteen. All I had to do then was something to myself. As far as technical ability, I could write as well when I was eighteen as I can today. I mean technically. But I had to do something to myself. You see, I had to recreate myself."

The oysters had long been removed, the coffee had grown cold, and the last cigarette was butted. Truman Capote rose to say goodbye. "About *In Cold Blood*: after I had worked on it for three years, I almost abandoned it. I'd become so emotionally involved that it was really a question of personal survival, and I'm not kidding.

"I just couldn't bear the morbidity all the time. There's just so much you can give to art. Nevertheless I didn't abandon it. I went through the whole damn thing. I did everything very thoroughly, and in the end I simply reduced it down. I built an oak and reduced it to a seed."

A Visit with Truman Capote
Gloria Steinem/1966

From *Glamour,* 55 (April 1966), 210-211, 239-241, 255. Copyright © 1966 by Gloria Steinem. Reprinted by permission.

It took all those balanced, carefully-worded critiques of *In Cold Blood* to get Truman Capote out of the gifted-but-marginal category and onto the list of first-rate American writers, but this article will not be so dispassionate. I like his writing, and I have always liked his writing. From the moment I picked up a book of short stories in a campus bookshop, silently mispronounced his name (it's Ca-*po*- te, not Ca-*pote*) and read straight through *A Christmas Memory,* unable to stop long enough to get the book home, totally hooked by this story of a seven-year-old boy and his spinster cousin that says more about love than most novels, I have been a Capote partisan.

That was 1958. Capote had already written two novels, *Other Voices, Other Rooms* (which made him quite famous at twenty-three) and *The Grass Harp;* a book of travel essays called *Local Color;* two collections of short stories, *Tree of Night* and *Breakfast at Tiffany's;* the funny, quixotic screenplay for *Beat the Devil; The Muses Are Heard,* a brilliant, novella-like account of the *Porgy and Bess* company in Russia; the book and some of the lyrics for a Broadway musical based on his short story, *House of Flowers;* and a number of other short pieces not then in book form, notably a profile of Marlon Brando for *The New Yorker.* All this had earned him, at the age of thirty-four, several literary awards, entry into New York's most desirable salons, enough money to maintain writing retreats in Switzerland and Long Island, and a sizable number of readers eager to buy anything he wrote.

Still, critics often dismissed his work as something between "derivative Southern-degenerate" and "stylistically interesting, but minor." Looking now at the reviews of *In Cold Blood*—on which Capote began his six years of work in 1959—those critics who praise it for what are clearly wrong or inadequate reasons (as a good adventure story of the "chase" school, for instance, or an excellent job of crime reporting) are often the same who failed to see the serious purpose inside the fancier, less perfect wrappings of his earlier stories. Alfred Chester, for instance, who reviewed *In Cold Blood* for the New York *Herald Tribune,* first expressed relief that Capote had switched from the "truly repulsive . . . molasses manner" of *A Christmas Memory* and "Children on Their Birthdays," and then praised the new, nonfiction novel as an allegory of "the state of the world (here disguised as two people badly needing to love each other)" or the death of six million Jews. Perhaps it's true that readers who reject the imperfect or difficult work of a given author are not really understanding the rest; that *Moby Dick* can't be fully perceived if *Pierre* was not, or *Crime and Punishment* without *Notes from the Underground,* or *Catcher in the Rye* by those who separate it completely from *Seymour,* or *In Cold Blood* by those who saw no glimmer of the same mind, twenty years younger, in, say, "Shut a Final Door." Because Capote's serious concerns were there, explored in fantasy rather than reporting: a preoccupation with the many versions of reality, with the impossibility of prescribing a "correct" one, and with the result when different versions collide.

Capote's public image, frozen at the age of twenty-three by a peculiarly riveting photograph on the jacket of *Other Voices, Other Rooms,* didn't encourage readers looking for depth. He appeared as a kind of teen-age, marzipan Peter Lorre in a tattersall vest, reclining on a Victorian sofa, and peering myopically into the camera from under corn-silk bangs. This image he attributes to his naïveté in sending the publisher every photograph he could find and letting the publicity department choose. ("When people read the book," he explained recently, "and realized what the theme was [an adolescent boy for whom growing up meant the acceptance of homosexual love], and coupled that with the picture, the whole thing took on a kind of *outré* peculiar quality that it was never meant to have had.") There is no author's photograph on the jacket of *In Cold Blood,* but those that appeared on many magazine covers when the book came out showed a forty-one-year-old man with thinning hair brushed straight back, steady blue eyes with or without hornrimmed glasses, and suits of which a banker would approve. ("I've gotten rid of the boy with the bangs," he explained to one interviewer. "It took an act of will because it was easy to be that person—he was exotic and strange and eccentric. I liked the idea of that person, but he had to go.")

Some of the old Capote partisans are taking an I-told-you-so kind of pleasure in his great success, and others seem a little dismayed at finding their youthful prodigy a best-selling author whom Bar Associations ask to speak on criminal law. But, as one friend and partisan said, "He's changed and grown; devoting nearly six years to one project was a very courageous thing to do, and it's paid off. But if you called up Central Casting and said, 'Send me a guy who can play a major American writer,' they'd never send anyone like Truman. People who think seriousness is Poetry Chairs and leather elbow patches are as thrown by him as ever."

Standing in his new five-room cooperative apartment, directing workmen as they put up bookshelves and shifted furniture, Capote looked cherubic, a little rumpled, much too healthy to be Peter Lorre anymore, and, by his own description, "about as tall as a shotgun and just as noisy." (He described Perry Smith—the more dangerous and sympathetic of the *In Cold Blood* killers—as "tall as a twelve-year-old child." Photographed with Perry, Capote at 5'3" appears to be smaller.) The most *outré* thing about him now is his voice. High-pitched, but in an unusual way—as if he were playing back at 45 rpm and tone recorded at 33—it is softened by a New Orleans accent and wrapped around a bizarre mixture of Southern and Jet Set constructions: "I'm here to tell you," "Yes, indeed," and "Bless your heart" turn up quite a bit, for instance, with *"la vrai chose,"* "ça va?" the Salingeresque "I mean . . ." and an occasional English "rather" thrown in for spice. The result is quite strange for the first half hour, and very pleasant afterwards.

Each room in the apartment has a south wall that is mostly glass, with a view over the East River, the United Nations complex, and a forest of skyscrapers. In the dining room-library, however, Capote poured champagne for three and discussed ideas that might give the view some competition. His elegant lady decorator—who had already provided deep red walls, a red-patterned carpet, curtains and upholstery of a bold shiny-surfaced floral print, and a heavy inlaid dining table—objected to the addition of a large wire plant rack.

"Don't you *see*," he said, arraying it with a number of plaster cats, some books, framed drawings, two vases, and an artificial plant, "that the idea is to put so many casual little things all up together, that you don't know *where* to look and suddenly it's one big *simple* thing?" She looked doubtful but agreed. They went through the same process with a small leopard-skin rug to be spread on top of the carpet, a frosted glass lamp with crystal pendants that she thought was too big for an antique marble-topped washstand, and the notion of banishing the washstand to the entrance hall. As workmen hammered noisily at the bookshelves and hung James Whitney Fosburgh's oil portrait of Capote over the sofa, we moved our champagne to a bed-sitting room.

This one, Capote's own room, had a large rug of blue-and-white needlepoint, a Bermuda bed, the view, and little else. He lit a cigarette and explained what furniture was going to be put where before Sunday when he was to leave for Switzerland. "New York is mostly for my two-months off—lots of parties and seeing friends. Then I go back to the beach studio or Switzerland and work four months straight; kind of like school. In the seven years I've been going to Switzerland, I haven't gone out once in the evening; literally not stepped outside my door." His discipline is legendary. Like Tennessee Williams, he seems almost compelled to write (he has been publishing regularly since he was sixteen), but in shirtsleeves, with broad polka dot tie loosened and an outsize champagne glass in hand, he looked smaller and more boyish than ever; slightly out of scale with the room. One could imagine the astonishment in a Kansas farming town when Capote, with a trunk full of French wine and Life cigarettes, arrived to write about a local murder. (Novelist Harper Lee, a childhood friend who went along to help him with research, said, "He was like someone coming off the moon—those people had never see anyone like Truman.") But one can also imagine they're growing to trust him, as they did, and tell him everything.

"*This* apartment," he was saying, "is kind of hurry-up, everything-at-once. But you must see my beach house. I furnished it myself, slowly, as I found things. The truth is I love to shop; to wander through old dusty places with the excuse of looking for something."

More workmen could be heard in the living room, moving

something and cautioning each other to be careful. "Oh, my lamp is here," said Capote, brightening.

"You must come see, it's fantastic."

In the library, the decorator was adjusting a huge and very beautiful Tiffany lamp on a table that seemed to grow out of the lamp's *art nouveau* base, and the workmen were walking gingerly as if near a baby. "Evie didn't want me to have it at all, did you Evie?" Capote said happily. "But look *look* how beautiful!" It went with nothing else, certainly not with the ornate floral sofa, but the room was beginning to take shape: a dusty-plush "best" parlor in the South seen through the eyes of Vuillard, and suspended twenty stories above Manhattan. "Tru, darling, you were right," the decorator said, gamely. "It actually looks quite . . . *perfect.*"

Back through the living room—a simpler, spacious kind of room, suitable for entertaining the Radziwills or Jackie Kennedy or any of Capote's many elegant friends—past round, draped tables displaying objects of crystal and Fabergé enamel and ivory and jade; down the hall papered in bright-striped cotton; and into the bedroom again where Capote, seated on a Bauhaus chair of leather and chrome, looked as if his feet shouldn't reach the ground. But they did, of course, and he was in command of everything.

"I've never understood why people compartmentalize their lives," he said, "and think that aesthetics should be limited. When I lived in my little apartment—just one big room, really—I still enjoyed making it beautiful." Did he mind that his taste for the elegant was sometimes thought frivolous? That more Bohemian writers were critical? "Not in the least," he said firmly. "I like people who are tasteful or accomplished or terribly beautiful or brilliant. It's the pursuit of excellence in all fields, I suppose, which is why I admire Jackie Kennedy. But I have all kinds of friends, not just rich ones. Among my close friends, I suppose only three or four could be called rich."

He reached out to steady his champagne glass, exposing an old-fashioned wristwatch with chaste Roman numerals. "Maybe that's why I don't know too many writers and stay out of the literary, little-magazine group. I don't enjoy all that competitive chatter about writing, you know, and besides," he added, making a little face, "there are all those depressing living rooms with sling chairs."

Had all the publicity and acclaim of *In Cold Blood*—not to mention the two million dollars earned from paperback and film sales—lost him friends? A blank look. And then, "Oh, *them.*" He smiled. "They all left me when my *first* book succeeded; *Other Voices, Other Rooms.* Suddenly, nobody called me, and friends got competitive and mean, and I felt I didn't have a person left in the world. It's quite true that success loses you more friends than failure, you know. But now I just don't have that kind of friend. Of course, there's still the problem of critics. One wrote a whole essay about some little remark I made to *Newsweek*—something like 'a boy's got to hustle his book'—and blamed me for all the publicity. Actually, I've turned down all the usual radio and television appearances that authors make, including one on "Meet the Press," though I was the only novelist they'd ever asked."

Having spent a few weeks waiting to see him myself, I was aware that he hadn't stayed in New York to collect laurels, but had retired to the luxury of his friend Gloria Guinness's residences—first in Palm Beach, then in Acapulco—instead. But what about the fate of the book itself? Had it been misinterpreted? What about Mr. X, one of the two or three critics who disliked it, or Mr. Y, who wrote disparagingly about the murdered family?

The blue eyes went a little steely behind their horn-rims and the voice became more precise. "The book is *exactly* what I wanted it to be. They can say anything they like. I've had such outrageous things written in the past that I've become nearly immune." Mr. X, he said, naming names, "can go right on foaming at the mouth. I suspect the clue to *his* character are the dozens and dozens of manuscripts he has produced that no one wants. As for Mr. Y, he is not only cruel but dead wrong. Have you see Rebecca West's review in *Harper's?* I felt that was the most accurate. She really said it all in the first few paragraphs.

"What does disturb me, though, is all this misunderstanding of the nonfiction novel as a term. I'm not claiming to have invented anything, but to have extended the range of this form; and it is a form, quite separate and distinct. Journalism, you see, always moves along on a horizontal plane, telling a story, while fiction—good fiction—moves vertically, taking you deeper and deeper into character and events. By treating a real event with fictional techniques (something that cannot be done by a journalist until he *learns* to write good fiction), it's possible to make this kind of synthesis: thus, the nonfiction novel. Of course, it remains one person's viewpoint proceeding both along the surface and beneath. I suppose the single most difficult thing technically was to write it without ever appearing myself, but had I used narration, I knew that constant I-I-I would come between the reader and the event. The writer makes his presence felt by selection, by the way he assembles the facts and actual quotes.

"And, of course, now that I've learned all this, I'm going right back and write a *novel*-novel, one that I've been working on for years." Titled *Answered Prayers,* it will have something to do with the world of those who have got what they wanted, though Capote if trying to quash rumors that it is a *roman à clef* peopled with all his rich and successful friends. *A Christmas Memory* is being made into an hour film which he will narrate, and next season will see *Breakfast at Tiffany's* as a Broadway musical, though not with a script by Capote. *The Grass Harp* also may be done as a musical in late summer. A nightclub fight between Irving Lazar, who was the agent in the sale of *In Cold Blood* film rights to Richard Brooks, and producer Otto Preminger, who wanted the rights, has already given headline publicity to that movie yet unmade. It's a bit like having children out there wandering around, getting into unknown trouble, but Capote has the good judgement to stay uninvolved with most of it and concentrate his energies on new work.

Workmen and decorator having left, we went back to the library where Capote asked if I liked Dionne Warwick and put on a record. "The Supremes read somewhere I liked their records, which I do, and sent me an invitation to their opening here. I'd go, but I'll be in Switzerland." We agreed to share a crosstown taxi and he left to put on a jacket for the evening's dinner party. He came back into the room doing a few shakes of a very creditable frug. "Why doesn't somebody revive tap dancing?" he said suddenly. "I'd like nothing better than to see a really good tap dancing show tonight." Was that part of his legend—that he had once tap danced on a Mississippi riverboat—really true? "Yes," he said, "but it was a riverboat my father worked on and I was only about five at the time. When I took trips with him, I used to perform—get all dressed up on my little suit and stand there, waiting for my big moment—I remember it well.

And I used to practice by buck and wing at home 'til I drove them all wild."

The discussion turned to another writer, much more visibly "serious," and I couldn't help thinking of the contrast they would make. As if reading my mind, Capote told the story of their one meeting at a dinner in Paris, together with a third American writer now dead. "They had invited me, you see," he said smiling, "and as I knew neither one of them, it was perfectly clear that they were just curious; I suppose because *Other Voices, Other Rooms* was then causing a bit of a stir. Anyway, I went, and I've never felt so much like a specimen under a microscope in my life. They kept asking me questions and peering at me for my reaction. So of course I told them lies, nothing but lies. I just thought of the most outrageous answer, something I didn't think at all, and then said it. They were fascinated; they probably think to this day that it's all true."

Out of a sympathy for the other writer—or envy of Capote's strength: I couldn't help thinking how *I* would have reacted, striving to make myself ever more likeable under their microscope—I launched into a rather boring explanation of their possible difficulty; seriousness that comes together with the unknown, and all that. "Then they don't know," he said firmly as I trailed off, "what seriousness is."

As we waited for a taxi, I thought of Perry Smith, murderer of four, who had wanted so much from life and got none of it: most of all to be taken seriously and to produce, as he told Capote, "a work of art." What would happen to the letters—sometimes two a week, the one just before his execution nearly a hundred pages long—that he had written to Capote during five years in prison? What would happen, for that matter, to all the trunks full of research, the 6,000 pages of notes Capote had taken, his dozens of interviews with other convicted murderers (the better to understand Smith and Hickock), and his study of criminal law and psychology?

Capote paused, and seemed tired. "When Perry's things arrived after his execution, I couldn't even look at them for a long time. It was a pretty pathetic collection . . . books with his notations in the margins, drawings he'd done in prison, the few letters he'd received. Our appeals system is inhuman, you know: all those years they spent living on Death Row. His letters were very strange. He had no interest in narrative, only in ideas; so he'd say, 'I agree with what Santayana says, do you?' and there would follow ten pages of what Santayana said.

"And then there's all the other research material, trunks full. I suppose I could do a book including some of these things that nonfiction novels cannot, a personal book. But not for awhile yet, not now. After three years of working on *In Cold Blood,* I almost abandoned it. I'd become so emotionally involved that it was almost a question of personal survival. I stuck with it, but toward the end, the emotional involvement even took a physical form: hand paralysis. I finally used a typewriter, very awkward as I always write in longhand. Now, I'm just kind of . . . weary of it all. Weary inside."

We got in a taxi and drove through the snow, talking of trivial things; this man who seemed so full of limits and was so nearly free of them. (Mrs. Al Dewey, wife of the local Kansas detective, said of Capote: "He's something more than any of us . . . when we went to New York after his book was done, we found out that Truman was no different there than he was here. All those famous people we met there—Jackie Kennedy, Barbara Paley, Bennett Cerf, Arlene Francis—they love Truman just as we did in Garden City. He enriched our lives.") In work and in life, his great strength is his gift for understanding many worlds and many realities; for writing about both the murderer and the murdered with a compassion that makes the reader trust him completely.

Capote patted my hand as he got out at a Park Avenue apartment building, and said cheerily, "Now you have my number, so just call me if you think of anything else." Halfway up the sidewalk, he turned and waved again, doing a little dance step against the wind.

Turman Capote Swings in the Sun
Alice Albright Hoge/1967

From *Chicago Daily News,* Panorama Section, 24 June 1967, 4. Copyright © 1986 by News Group Chicago, Inc. Reprinted by permission of the *Chicago Sun-Times.*

"Where did you get those sandals?" Truman walked from the Ambassador East to Goudy Square. "I can't find nice sandals anywhere."

Truman was wearing bare ankles. Also a biscuit-colored blazer, linen pants, pointed loafers, and gold-rimmed spectacles. He walked with an air, nose high and sniffing the lake breeze, nearly skipping because it was such fun to be away from work and out in the sunshine.

"I love Chicago, it's a marvelous place. I don't know a soul, except for a couple of people."

And not a soul on Astor St. turned around to look at Truman Capote, although the Fashion Foundation of America calls him one of the 10 best-dressed men in the country. Of course Truman Capote is awfully small, and, wedged in by myself and photographer John Tweedle, perhaps nobody saw him.

"People overestimate it," he told us, referring to his celebrity. "Sometimes I exist for days without being recognized.

"It seems to go in cycles. You can get on an airplane and not even the stewardess recognizes you. Or else people stroll up and down the aisles to have a stare . . . I don't mind being stared at in the least." A little shrug, a little giggle, amused by himself and by people.

The only people in Goudy Square were kids, and they all wanted their picture taken. Truman stood bareheaded under a shade tree, took off his spectacles, and looked like a kid himself, hair blonde and wisping, eyes so blue. He posed.

"I hate pop art to death," he was saying. "I have nine Warhols in my closet which Andy gave me. I've told this to his face."

As Truman posed, he switched expressions with the precision of a dancer moving his limbs. Intense. Then delighted. Then blissfully happy. One was conscious of his utter lack of self-consciousness. But of course he's been striking extraordinary poses for 20 years. Remember his book jacket picture for *Other Voices, Other Rooms,* the decadent in the hammock?

"But worse than pop in painting," he told us, "pop *writing.*" The subject of writing produced a businesslike expression. "Now William Burroughs. He's what I'd call a pop writer. He gets some very interesting effects on a page. But at the cost of total lack of communication with the reader. Which is a pretty serious cost, I think."

We moved to the little red slide, where Truman sat on the dusty steps and let kids clamber over him. He patted a couple of towheads as they slid past. We discussed the subject of the hour, his great, great friend Lee Radziwill, whose stage debut at the Ivanhoe Theater was only eight hours away.

"Look," he said, insisting that he be understood, "I don't waste my time on people I don't admire. She *really* is a disciplined serious person."

The nice thing now was that Truman was getting a kick out of posing for us. As he cocked his head and rested it on his hand, arch as a fiend, he talked photography.

"I'm thrilled with the way *Cold Blood* is being filmed. This is really one of the most original films technically." He explained about a new camera which has been built into a car for road scenes and about "an extraordinary kind of lens" which was used to film the whole scene of the murder.

"In total pitch dark," Truman said. His voice quavered and his hands waved. "The screen is black except for—SUDDEN RIPPLES—then breathing sounds, footsteps. Absolutely the end." He dropped the spooky voice and spoke flatly. "The quality of reality is almost unbearable."

One of his projects at the moment is a television documentary on capital punishment, which, he hopes, will have even more effect on public opinion than his book. He's also working on a major novel called *Answered Prayers*; filming for TV two short stories which eventually will be joined with *Christmas Memory* as a full-length movie; and another non-fiction novel, the subject of which is top secret. He just finished a novel and may or may not give it to a publisher.

"It was hard for me, because I'm a gregarious person, but I've trained myself to be alone when I work. I go off for months at a time without seeing a soul. I wrote much of *Cold Blood* on top of a Swiss Alp—in a little chalet, all by myself."

Often, it seems, Truman Capote is here among us, in Chicago, living in a hotel (he obviously won't tell which one) under an assumed name. He finds this is a marvelous place to work.

"When one is really writing, one must be in training and feel really good, physically good even, and be as fit for writing as a fighter is fit for fighting." Thus every morning Truman Capote turns on the radio and does exercises. He says he does the new dances, too, for the exercise. He likes folk-rock and is enthusiastic about a new number by the Jefferson Airplane called "Surrealistic Pillow."

The disciplined perfectionist. Posing like a professional model. Clothes perfect. His apartment in the United Nations Plaza building is perfect, his country house planned for effect to the last detail.

"When I was a kid," he said, "I made writing exercises a regular part of my day. For example, while I was working on qualities of narrative description, I went to the museum. I would try to describe each painting exactly, trying over and over again until I felt I had the *absolute quality*."

The same type of exercises could serve a photographer, Truman said. One could concentrate on photographing a particular subject—such as—shall we say—FREAKS. Yes, freaks. Do a whole photographic essay on freaks. Until one had distilled the absolute quality of freakishness.

And then, because it was such a pretty day, and because why not, we kicked one of the kids off a horsey swing so Truman Capote could have a ride. Click, click, GREAT POSE. A little faster and higher, we said. I'm getting seasick, he protested, head in the air, stirrups about the right length, reliving the childhood that probably wasn't that way at all. Click, click, click.

Truman's giggle floated on the wind. Look everybody, stick your heads out of your highrises and look at who's on the horsey swing in Goudy Square.

That night at Maxim's, after Lee's play, Truman Capote in black tie was making up for all the beautiful people who didn't materialize. The dignity of a famous man who isn't a bit defensive.

"Hello, lovey," he said when he saw me. "Didn't we have fun today?" No wonder the people liked him in Garden City, Kan.

"Go Right Ahead and Ask Me Anything." (And So She Did) An Interview with Truman Capote
Gloria Steinem/1967

From *McCall's* 95 (November 1967), 76-77, 148-152, 154.
Copyright © 1967 by Gloria Steinem. Reprinted by permission.

On this particular afternoon, Truman Capote had announced himself in New York and ready for talk, a clear sign that he was between bouts of writing.

Anyone who knows him gets used to an all-or-nothing schedule. For weeks and months at a time, he disappears into one of two writing retreats, a beach house on Long Island or a chalet in Switzerland. Then back again for a burst of socializing, brief but intense, with long, gossipy lunches every day, dinner parties given by the many hostesses who arrange their social calendars around his work breaks and frequent visits in the great houses of England or Acapulco or Algiers. "It's like school," Capote explains reasonably. "I concentrate really hard for three or four months. Then I *deserve* a vacation."

The size of the social burst varies directly with the amount of work done. (It was after the final revision on *In Cold Blood* that he gave the famous black-and-white masked ball for "five hundred people I like." The book had taken five years, and the party was chosen by the Museum of the City of New York—along with George Washington's Inaugural and a ball in honor of General Lafayette—to live on in its archives.) Today's escape came near the end of "The Thanksgiving Visitor," on page 75, a story that had been gestating for nearly a year but was not yet quite finished, and celebrations were to be correspondingly short: a film premiere in honor of the Duke and Duchess of Windsor; several lunches, to catch up on news of friends in New York; a trip to Chicago for the acting debut of another old friend, Lee Radziwill; and then straight back to Long Island.

"I'm so *slow*," mourned Capote, peering into a refrigerator stacked with very good champagne. "It should have been finished this week, but the end isn't right yet." He rejected the wine and poured a fizzing vitamin-C mixture over some ice cubes, instead. ("Very healthy, very refreshing, my dear," he explained, handing me a crystal tumbler, "and you can only buy it in Switzerland.") "Of course, the small boy in the story is me, and the lady is Miss Sook, the elderly cousin in *A Christmas Memory*, so it's more a reminiscence than a story." He gazed out the huge windows of this apartment tower, his official residence when not working, at the rainy afternoon and the East River below. On clearer days, its residents—Senator Robert F. Kennedy among them—have a princely view of Manhattan. "It all happened in this tiny Southern town where I grew up; the bully in the story and everything." A foghorn sounded somewhere in the mist. Did he know that, since the famous party, sight-seeing boats had identified this as *his* apartment building, ignoring Bobby Kennedy? "Yes," he said, delighted. "Isn't that a *ridiculous* thing to do?"

"The party did get a little out of hand. There were so many people wanting invitations that I finally just locked myself up in the beach house and turned off the phone." We wandered from library to living room, and he settled into a silk-covered sofa. I sat down, too; gratefully. At five feet three inches, Capote is much too confident to seem short. He just makes everyone else feel too tall. "Mostly they were people I didn't even *know* who felt their social position demanded an invitation. Can you imagine?

"And this is my other celebration," he added, giving the vitamin C an expert swirl. "As soon as I finished all those years on *In Cold Blood*, I developed a whole thing about being on a health cure. I've lost twenty pounds, become superhygienic and spent too much time at the tailor's. A long project like that absorbs all your vanity, all your energy, and then it all comes back in a rush.

"Ten years ago, I started another health regime, but I hope this one sticks. I want to wake up every morning feeling very—very *dancy*, and ready to work. There are four books—two nonfiction novels and two fiction ones—in some stage of progress or planned out in my head. Then there are some adaptations to do, and before any of those things, I want to finish a television documentary on capital punishment. You know, the executions are starting again—especially in Florida, California—and there are so many men waiting in Death Row right now."

He took off his horn-rimmed glasses and massaged the bridge of his nose; thoughtful for a moment, or tired. His eyes looked very serious, very vulnerable. Elegance, party giving and a high-pitched Southern drawl seem nearly as off-putting and contrary to serious-mindedness in a conservative forty-two-year-old as they did in the blond-banged, outrageously vested prodigy who looked out from the dust jacket of *Other Voices, Other Rooms*. But now, as then, his eyes give him away. Like a gift for writing compassionately about everyone from virginal old ladies to convicted murderers, they betray an Achilles heart.

"Of course, the truth of it is," said Capote, replacing his glasses and sitting up straight, "that the thing I like to do most in the whole world is *talk*." He reached out past a Fabergé box and carved *objets d'art* for an ashtray, opened a pack of cigarettes and settled back comfortably into the cushions, as if for life. "If I had to choose between writing and talking—well, I just don't know *what* I'd do!"

He smiled. As Perry once said of Dick in *In Cold Blood*, he had a smile that really worked. "Go ahead," he said cheerily. "Go right ahead and ask me anything."

Interviewer: If you were being described to someone who did not know you—as a person, as a writer—what would you like to have said? Without false modesty.

Capote: As a writer, that I'm a good artist, a serious craftsman; that my writing gives pleasure in itself, regardless of what I'm writing about. I spend a great deal of time with that object in mind. Because to me, the greatest pleasure of writing is not what it's about, but the inner music that words make.

Once, a critic called Stanley Edgar Hyman wrote an article about me in some magazine. I read it, and it was all right—neither flattering nor unflattering—but suddenly I came to a sentence that said, "Alas, Capote has a tin ear." *A tin ear!* I wondered what on earth ailed Mr. Hyman. Because the one thing I'm convinced of is that I have a good ear for prose writing.

Interviewer: And as a person?

Capote: If I were in another room and could overhear someone describing me? (*A long pause, then a smile.*) Well, they could say, "You may not like him, but you must admit he's very candid."

I: Is that what is actually said? Or close enough to what is said so that you're not unhappy about it?

C: No. I know all the criticisms. There are "friends" who make a great specialty of telling you what's being said, you know. The sort of thing that starts, "I had the biggest argument over you the other day. I told them it wasn't true, but they said—" Many of the unkind things told about me are true—up to a point. But on the whole, they seem unfair and prejudiced. Or based on jealousy.

Of course, if I were outside myself looking on, I'd probably be infuriated. I'm sure I'd put me down stronger than anybody else.

I: Does the literary establishment punish writers for personal fame?

C: There is a feeling that serious writers shouldn't be celebrities or even do work that receives popular attention. I found it quite interesting how *Ship of Fools,* by Katherine Anne Porter—which I liked very much—was criticized as unreadable by some people *after* it became a success. The same was true of Mary McCarthy's *The Group.* I know for a fact that one judge alone, Saul Maloff, talked the others out of giving me last year's National Book Award on the grounds that it should go to a less successful writer. If commercial failure is a criterion, they should say so in advance.

But I've never lived by other people's values. I wasn't able to, which I realized when I was very young; and I don't know where the hell I'd be now if I'd tried. I never felt the need of belonging to a clique. As a child, I was a loner; and I've just continued walking my own road.

I: Hemingway said that the trouble with American writers was they talked to each other.

C: Yes, all this ganging together is a kind of defense setup. I understand it, but associating with other writers never interested me particularly. I already *know* what they're about; it's like meeting some area of myself all over again. Other kinds of people seem mysterious and constantly intriguing. *All* other kinds. Someone is always saying to me, "But what do you see in that person? He's really very dumb and boring." Well, he isn't dumb or boring to me as long as I can *learn* something.

I: The striking thing about your guest list for the famous masked ball was its variety: you seem to know maharajas, police detectives and everybody in between. Is this mystery, this ability to be learned from, their common denominator?

C: Yes. And individuality. I guess none of my friends could be mistaken for any other.

It *was* a nice party, wasn't it? There was something warm and cozy about it; quite the opposite of all the publicity. I had been planning it for ages, and used to tell my friends how I was going to give this wonderful party, with people I liked from all over the world. The thing I resented most about some of the write-ups was the idea that the party was intended to promote me or my books. After all those years on one project, *In Cold Blood,* I was just tired and unable to work. So that summer, I began making my guest list: there were people I'd known when I was twelve and hadn't seen since. Even my old schoolteacher came.

I: What about the guests who got all the publicity: the Beautiful People? Do they have mystery? Is there something to be learned from them?

C: Of course. Most of my friends among the so-called Beautiful People have something more than that. It's a level of taste and—*freedom.* I think that's what always attracted me. The freedom to pursue an esthetic quality in life is an extra dimension, like being able to fly where others walk. It's marvelous to appreciate paintings, but why not *have* them? Why not create a whole esthetic ambience? Be your own living work of art? It has a good deal to do with money, but that's not all of it, by any means.

Not that freedom solves everything. *Answered Prayers,* a novel I've been working on for years, is about four people who got exactly what they set out to get in life. The title comes from something Saint Theresa is supposed to have said: "More tears are shed over answered prayers than unanswered ones."

I: Do you think of yourself as someone whose prayers have been answered?

C: No. In the first place, I've used only a small percentage of the abilities I honestly think I have. A great deal of time was spent developing a technique, a highly complicated apparatus that I tested on subjects that interested me but were limited as far as my overall range was concerned. Now I'm just beginning to feel confident enough to forget technique. It's like a good touch typist who doesn't have to think about the keys. That allows me to open areas of my mind that I've never used.

Besides, the ambitions of people in the novel are more or less material, but artistic ambitions are spiritual. Basically, all artistic problems are really religious problems, you know, and can't be completely satisfied. Perhaps a genuine Zen person, a monk or a nun who devotes a whole life to reaching an inner peace, a satisfaction and serenity—But how can a religious problem be solved? Only in moments—and one lives for those moments—when, rightly or wrongly, you feel in complete contact with this extraspatial thing and able to put it into some frozen form. I'm not a religious person, but when I see a painting or hear music or read something that seems beautiful and perfect, I think, How did they *do* that? They must have been in a state of grace. Flaubert's *A Simple Heart*, for instance. There isn't a thing in it that one would change.

Nothing in the world is as exhilarating as writing something you think *almost* has perfection. For some people, religion is the consolation for being human. For me, it's art. But that very personal feeling of contact with God happens rarely. Or accidentally. Something one thought was good turns out to be wrong, and something one did rather casually turns out to be good.

I: Is the book's message that prayers shouldn't be materialistic and answerable?

C: The book has no message.

I: Do you have a date by which you hope to finish?

C: No. Because I never think that way. I just go along, inch by inch.

I: When your books and stories are adapted for other forms—plays, television shows, movies—do you still feel they belong to you?

C: That depends. Did you see "A Christmas Memory" on television? I thought that was good and still mine. Almost nothing was changed. They're filming two other short stories, "Among the Paths to Eden" and "Miriam," so the three together will make a regular film, a triptych. But those were something I worked on, a true collaboration.

I haven't had a thing to do with the movie of *In Cold Blood*, but I watched the first reel—the movie will be released in December—and I think it's going to be extremely good. Of course, the musical of *Breakfast at Tiffany's* was a disaster. I had nothing to do with it, but I felt sorry for all those people who worked so hard. *House of Flowers*—a musical based on my story, for which I wrote the book and lyrics—was never produced properly. It's fragile, no more realistic than those pretty little scenes inside an Easter egg, but it was done overly large on Broadway. This year, it's being revived off-Broadway in a small theater, and it should be much better. I've written a new second act.

I: Is it true that during the filming of *Beat the Devil,* you threw Humphrey Bogart with a judo hold, sat on his chest and said, "Now, Bogey, if you're not nicer to me, I'll have to get rough"?

C: Wherever did you hear that? Well, it's true, but I didn't sit on his chest. Let's see, now, I'll tell you exactly.

We were in Ravello, Italy. All the actors were there, and John Huston was directing, but there was no script at all. I was writing it day by day, literally. I worked all night, and the parts would be handed out in the morning; the whole thing was quite mad.

Anyway, Bogart used to sit in the lounge and play this game of Indian hand wrestling, which he always won. One day I was watching him, and he said to me, "Caposy—" it was his little joke to always call me Caposy—"how about you? Would you like to take me on?" I said, "Well, I happen to be quite good at that," and he said, "Chuckle-chuckle-chuckle." So I told him we should bet. He said five dollars, but I said no, make it fifty dollars, and he looked at me, taking it seriously for the first time. We sat down at the table, locked arms and I pushed his hand down flat.

He said, "Would you mind doing that again?" "Sure," I said, "for another fifty dollars." So we sat down, and I pushed his arm down to the table again.

He stood up and looked at me as though he were having double vision or I had borrowed somebody else's arm, and he said, "I'd like to see you do that just one more time." I said, "You owe me a hundred dollars. This will make it a hundred and fifty. Okay?" He said okay, so we wrestled again, and I pushed his hand down again.

Well, he couldn't believe it, and he started sort of wrestling around the room, saying, "Gee, I didn't know Caposy was as strong as all that." I said, "It's not that I'm strong; it's just a trick. For instance, I could put you right on your bottom like *that.*" He said, "Oh, yeah?" And I did.

The only trouble was that he hurt his elbow and was out of the picture for three days. John Huston kept telling me, "You cost us twenty thousand dollars."

I: That's what people *really* say about you, Truman. That you're full of surprises. Did you learn how to fight like that as a child?

C: No, no. I was a sickly kid, with every conceivable sort of illness and operation. Of course, a lot of it was because I wanted to stay home and read. I was constantly inventing these illnesses. Also, I loved listening to soap operas on the radio. I'd have three days of this nice cold, get all involved with "Myrt and Marge" or "Backstage Wife," and it was just torture to go back to school and not know what was happening. What was "Our Gal Sunday" going to do?

I: Didn't she live in Black Swan Hall with Sir Henry Brinthrop? I always used to listen to that, and I'd send in box tops.

C: So did I!

I: Helen Trent's Bluebird of Happiness bracelet?

C: And Little Orphan Annie's Secret Code ring. I did *all* those things.

You know, I'll tell you something funny. Those people on the radio, in books or movies—even people I read about in the newspapers—seemed much more real than the people around me. The only real person I was *deeply* concerned with was Miss Sook, the old cousin of mine I wrote about in *A Christmas Memory,* and we lived a fantasy life together. "Sookie," I used to say to her, "someday you and I are going to Hollywood, and I'll be a tap dancer in the movies."

I: A whole generation of us wanted to be Shirley Temple. Or Sonja Henie.

C: Yes, Sonja Henie! I wanted to be a professional ice skater, too. I was obsessed by *anything* that would get me into the real world I read about.

I: Do you think this dreaming of dreams is part of the American experience?

C: Yes, I do. Sookie and I only identified with people outside the periphery of our little Southern town. I was extremely jealous of all children whose names or pictures were in the paper—Shirley Temple, Bobby Breen, Jackie Cooper, Jackie Coogan; everybody.

I: Were those dreams of getting out the reason you started to write so young?

C: No, I really *did* want to do it by being a tap dancer. I was quite serious about it, and used to drive the family wild with my practicing.

I: George Orwell used to say he wrote to show his third-grade teacher that she'd been wrong about him. Wasn't there any of this "I'll show you" motive in your wanting to write?

C: I suppose there was a little when I was seventeen and began to have things published, but that was a long time after the fact; I started writing when I was about eight. No, writing was always an obsession with me, quite simply something I *had* to do, and I don't understand exactly why this should have been true. It was as if I were an oyster and somebody forced a grain of sand into my shell—a grain of sand that I didn't know was there and didn't particularly welcome. Then a pearl started forming around the grain, and it irritated me, made me angry, tortured me sometimes. But the oyster can't help becoming obsessed with the pearl.

I: Do you suppose that is why you thought of yourself as a loner?

C: Yes, it's all part of the same thing, I suppose. The reason for it was a mystery to me and still is. I got on okay, mind you; but I was always a sort of two-headed calf and was aware of the fact even when I was very young.

I: Did you know anyone else with this sense of apartness?

C: Yes, there was Harper Lee, the girl who wrote *To Kill a Mockingbird*. She was an apart person, too, though in an entirely different way from me. She wanted to be a lawyer, like her father and her sister, and cared only about hanging around the courthouse and playing golf. She was extremely articulate on every kind of constitutional law known to man and in fact *did* go to law school, came within one week of graduating, and then decided she wanted to write, instead.

Anyway, when we were children, I had a typewriter and worked every day in a little room I used as an office. I convinced her she ought to write, too, so we would work there each day for two or three hours. She didn't really want to, but I held her to it. We kept up that routine for quite a long time.

I: Did you ever have the fantasy that you didn't really belong to your family? That someday your true relatives would come to claim you?

C: No. I know that fantasy, but I never had it. After my parents were separated, I was moved around among other relatives and was finally sent to boarding school. I didn't *have* to have a fantasy; I was living one!

The family wasn't unkind to me at all; it was just that we had different interests. In a way, it was harder on them. They definitely thought there was something very wrong with me.

When I first started school, I did well—I had learned to read at about four—so at least they had the consolation of thinking I was bright. But in the third grade, I started getting straight F's. And marks for bad behavior, too. They thought that something had happened to me between the second and third grade, or that I was retarded. Of course what had happened was I just got *bored* to death.

Anyway, this was during the Depression, and one of the WPA's projects was to send a team of researchers around the rural areas giving intelligence tests. They came to our little town in Alabama, gave the tests and were supposed to leave the next day. Only they *didn't* leave; they came around to our house and asked if I would take the test again. I did, and I got the highest score they'd ever seen. Well, the researchers were fascinated, and my teachers at school were laughing up their sleeves, saying, "These Yankees, you see what nonsense they're up to now!"

But the researchers convinced my mother that I really had this high IQ, so she let them bring me to New York. I spent a whole week at Columbia University, taking tests every day; psychological tests, aptitude tests, everything.

I went home again, *extremely* pleased with the whole thing. I think that was the first time in my life I was ever vain. It ws like thumbing my nose at them and saying, "Ha ha, you see?!"

That convinced my relatives I wasn't *stupid,* but they still thought I was very odd. They really hadn't wanted me to come home from New York a genius, just a nice normal boy. But the experience gave me confidence, and by the time I was ten, I was sitting up all night long to write. The excitement was so great that I couldn't relax at all until I discovered whisky. Then I would take a few swigs before going to bed. Eventually, my little hoard of bottles was discovered, and that put an end to that.

I: Was there anyone who encouraged you in your writing?

C: No, it was still a private obsession. Though later on, after my mother remarried and we were living in Greenwich, Connecticut, I had a high-school English teacher there who encouraged me in every way. Miss Catharine Wood.

There were authors who comforted me, too, and who opened my imagination a great deal. Beginning at twelve or thirteen, I had an *idée fixe* about Flaubert. People like Aubrey Beardsley and Oscar Wilde appealed to me: there's something about them that *demands* an imaginative response. Katherine Mansfield, Thomas Wolfe, Maupassant, Chekhov, Turgenev, Proust—I read them all. (Though I was never a fast reader, and I'm still not. I can't skim. I hear every word sounding in my head.) Proust may have had the greatest effect on me, more as a person than as an artist. I always felt he was a kind of secret friend.

The trouble was that I had no one to show my stories to, nobody to use as a sounding board. It was like playing tennis by myself. When I was about fifteen and started sending them off to little magazines, it was only to get some reaction. No one was more surprised than I was when they were accepted; I really was surprised. One day, when I was seventeen, I got my three first acceptances at once!

That same year, I met a fellow artist for the first time, and it was a turning point in my whole attitude.

We had moved East, you see, and I finished high school—well, more or less: I never really graduated. And I had a job at the *New Yorker*. It was during the war, and they were short-handed, but they couldn't send me out on interviews, because I looked about ten or eleven years old at the most. People would have thought it was child labor. So they used to give me little errands, or hand me packages to wrap or research jobs to do.

Quite often, I would go to the New York Society Library on Seventy-Ninth Street to do research, and three or four times I noticed this absolutely *marvelous*-looking woman. She had a wonderful, open, extraordinary face, and hair combed back in a bun. Her suits were soft, but rather severe—very distinguished-looking—and her *eyes*. Well, her eyes were the most amazing pale, pale blue. Like pieces of sky floating in her face.

One day about five-thirty, I came out of the library, and there she was, standing under the canopy. It was snowing hard, and she was looking this way and that, as if she couldn't decide whether to walk or wait for a taxi. I stood there, too, and she said she didn't think there *were* any taxis. I said no, I guessed there was no point trying to get back to the office, I guessed I'd just go home. Suddenly she said, "Would you like a hot chocolate? There's a Longchamps restaurant just around the corner, and we could walk there."

Well, we walked there, and she said she'd noticed me in the library several times. I told her I was from the South, was working on a magazine, and that I wanted to be a writer. She said, "Oh, really? What writers do you like?" We talked about Turgenev and Flaubert.

Then she asked what *American* writers I liked. I told her that my favorite was Willa Cather. Which of her works did I like best? Well, I said, *My Mortal Enemy* and *A Lost Lady* were both perfect works of art. "That's very interesting," she said. "Why?" So I told her why, and we talked for a while. "Well," she said finally, "I'm Willa Cather."

It was one of the great *frissons* of my life! I knew it was true the minute she said it. Of *course* she was Willa Cather!

We talked a little more, and when I finally got out in the street again, I was so bowled over that I walked right into a lamppost.

I: Did you see her after that?

C: Oh, yes, we became quite friendly. She was really one of my first intellectual friends. While I was growing up, I knew scarcely anyone who read books. Later on, at the *New Yorker*, I'd met writers who were talented, even very gifted. But somehow I never wanted to share my innermost self with them. My interest in writing, in art, was so intense and out-of-the-blue. It was almost like having a peculiar sex fetish—for doorknobs, say—that one else could conceivably understand. Willa Cather was the first person I'd ever met who was an artist as I defined the term; someone I respected and could talk to.

I: That sense of being different, of being an oyster with a pearl, has led a lot of artists toward mysticism.

C: Yes, I've often thought that reincarnation could explain the whole thing. But I have no answer.

I: Are you superstitious?

C: I used to be *fantastically* superstitious, I mean to the point of mania. I've tried to break myself of it, but I still do practically nothing on the thirteenth, a hat on the bed drives me into a frenzy, and I never put three cigarette butts in an ashtray.

I: Did you invent that one about the ashtray?

C: Yes. But the most serious superstitions are those you invent yourself. For instance, I used to walk along counting steps—one two three four five—and when I got to the thirteenth, I jumped. Now, isn't that ridiculous?

Even now, when I really really want something to come true, I do various hoodos around it. And I'm convinced that they work.

I: How do you do a hoodoo?

C: I can't explain exactly. They *vary*, you know. Usually, I just add up events and say to myself, "See? These happened in such-and-such a way, so I know *that* is going to happen." I also know when I *won't* get what I want.

I: Are you afflicted with pantheism, too? I mean, do you develop affection for objects because you believe they have a spirit?

C: I have a terrific thing about objects. That's why I accumulate so many. I have four houses—two on Long Island, one in Switzerland and this apartment—just crammed with nonsense.

I: Does superstition affect your work habits?

C: It used to. Now I just try to keep a sensible routine. I work four hours an afternoon, have dinner and go to bed. Then in the morning, when I'm very clear, I go over what I wrote and straighten out anything that seems wrong. That way, I don't wake up to the sad emptiness of a blank page.

Of course, when I'm working, I really think about it twenty-four hours a day anyway.

The one unbreakable hang-up I have is with cigarettes. They have a bad effect on me. They make me extremely nervous. But I started smoking at twelve, and I've never written a word without a cigarette in my hand.

I: What about astrology?

C: I like the idea, I'm always reading the newspaper charts, but I know that if I got serious about it, I'd never stop. I'd consult Carroll Righter before I got out of bed in the morning.

I: Have there been periods in your life when you couldn't write?

C: I've never had writer's block per se. There have been periods when I couldn't focus on work because of emotional problems, but they were unrelated to the act of writing.

You know, I've never been to a psychiatrist or analyst of any kind. Considering the many sorts of adjustments I've had to make, I've often wondered: Would analysis have made them easier? Would it have lessened the penalties I paid? Now, I think not. It's like a person on a diet. If you can do it without pills, then you adjust your metabolism to not eating, and you're less likely to gain when the diet stops.

I: Do you think that psychiatry might have analyzed away the magic, the talent, along with the obsession?

C: No, I think anything that makes your adjustment to *yourself* better, or easier, is just fine. Provided it *is* yourself, your own personal truth, and not just blending in.

Tennessee Williams was being analyzed for a while, about two years. One day I saw him and asked how it was going.

"I'm not happy about it," he said, "not happy at all."

"Why?" I said. "I thought it was doing you a lot of good."

"Maybe," he said, "but I'm going to stop. You know, Truman, that man is interfering with my *private life!*"

That's a pretty good analyst story, don't you think? "Interfering with my private life!"

I: Have you ever experimented with psychedelic drugs?

C: About eight years ago, before any of these things had been written about, I knew a doctor who asked a few of us to take LSD. It was his theory that the state LSD induces is a chemically exact replica of schizophrenia. Well, I took it twice, and was interested in the images and fantasies, but I quite disagreed with his theory. Because all the time you're under LSD, some part of your mind is saying, "My, isn't this interesting." You *know* that what you're seeing is not reality, which the true schizophrenic does not.

I: Did you find it useful at all in your writing?

C: No. It was an extraordinary visual thing, but I had no desire to repeat it. I've never had any real rapport with drugs. In fact, I forgot all about it and was quite surprised later when all the excitement started. I thought, Gee, can that be the same old stuff *I* took?

I used to be very much interested in dreams, though, as a form of literary exercise. For years, I kept a book to write them down in each morning, not out of any *great* interest in dreams themselves, but because describing them seems to tap gifts one has. It was like a pianist doing scales in the morning to limber up his fingers.

My most persistent dream—which I've discovered is a very common one—always took place backstage in a theater. I have a very important part to play. The only trouble is that I'm in a panic because I don't know my lines, I've never read the play, and I'm ashamed that people are going to find this out. Finally, the moment comes. I walk onstage. Everybody else is excellent, but I just stumble about, mortified. Have you ever had that dream?

I: Yes. A lot. And the remarkable thing about it is I know I'm dreaming, even while it's going on.

C: That's exactly what happened to me! Because the moment I began to keep that dream book, I was perfectly conscious that I was watching a dream. It was like being at the cinema; some part of my mind would be saying, "Now, don't forget *that* detail. That's really very good!"

I: Don't you know, even when you're drunk, that you could get up and walk quite soberly if you had to?

C: Yes, always. It must be a writer's trait: that strong detachment, or superego, or whatever.

I: Do you think there's something of the voyeur in every writer?

C: Well, there certainly is in me! I love listening to other people's conversations, no matter how dull they are. I can be mesmerized, as long as they have that quality of being overheard.

In fact, if I could have one wish granted, it would be to become the Invisible Man. I really have thoughts about that. I would drink a magic potion, walk around and watch everything that people are doing and saying; then drink this other little potion, and I'd be visible again.

I: Do you find that people confide in you easily? That they tell you their secrets?

C: Yes. Because I tell them mine. Reporters are always asking me about *In Cold Blood*, "But how did you get people to *tell* you all that?" They forget there were two sides to the conversation, even though, when it's written, I'm an invisible presence. The best policy is to be as candid with them as you want them to be with you. I interviewed many hostile, dangerous criminals. They asked me some pretty startling things, as if they were daring me to be offended. When I told the absolute truth, they were embarrassed at first, but then the floodgates would open. A very easy, intimate feeling took over.

I: Will you be interviewing prisoners again for the capital-punishment documentary you're doing for ABC television?

C: Prisoners in various states of appeal may have reservations about being interviewed, but yes, I hope quite a few can be filmed.

You know, even to those who believe in capital punishment—as I do not—the present system must seem indefensibly cruel. Right now, there are four hundred and forty men in this country on Death Row, not knowing whether they will be alive next week, or next month, or next year. The average time in those cells is three to five years, but many appeal procedures are even slower. In Louisiana, there are two men who have been locked in death cells for fourteen years.

Most states take them out once a week for a bath. Then they are put back. There is no real attempt at rehabilitation. It seems to me there would at least be psychiatric interest in them—what better way to study the mind's reasons for homicidal action?—but there is none. They just sit in a pointless coma.

Once in Hong Kong, I was walking through the market and saw all these little dogs in bamboo cages. The cages were stacked on top of each other, and the little dogs were stuffed inside; not yapping, nothing. It was very hot. I couldn't imagine what in the world they were there for, so I asked the Chinese girl who was with me. "Oh," she said, "they're for sale. They're waiting to be eaten. Soup is made out of those little dogs."

That was many years ago. But the first time I saw Death Row in one of our prisons, all I could think of was those little dogs.

I: Will there be any difficulty putting this show on television?

C: Well, ABC offered to put up the money, so we're going ahead. Actually, it will be quite neutral in feeling. I know some very kind, intelligent people—not cruel at all—who have a rather involved defense of capital punishment that seems to them correct. Obviously, an enormous number of law-enforcement people believe in it. I can even see why. But I doesn't *really* make sense if you know what's happening. During the five years I spent working on *In Cold Blood,* I was involved intimately, all the time, with people who were suffering through the whole excruciating business. It's simply indefensible.

Actually, the very first thing to be done is to see that it *isn't* a political hot potato any more. Now it gets all mixed up in local politics. Governors who don't believe in capital punishment at *all* end up killing men just because they're convinced they'll lose votes. If all murders were made a federal crime, then there would be some chance of keeping it out of the vote-getting area.

I: Is it possible to have reform until there's such a thing as a true life sentence?

C: No, it isn't. And that's just the point. Because with all convicted murderers in one maximum-security federal prison, there would be less chance of their escaping, or being wrongly paroled, to murder again.

Let me tell you the kind of thing that goes on now. A boy I interviewed in prison was under death sentence. About two weeks before his execution date, the governor commuted the sentence, which means he'll be out in seven to twelve years; nearer to seven. Within three days, the boy had walked out in the yard and killed another man. Of course, the authorities could do nothing about it, because when a murder happens in prison, you can never get anyone to testify. The boy stabbed this man to death in front of fifty people, but they could never get *one single witness*. No witness meant no trial. So, in a few years, a boy who has already committed two homicides will be walking out free.

It's this kind of case that turns gentle people into advocates of capital punishment.

But men who killed in a moment's passion, men who were sick and can be cured *are* executed. There is such a thing as the professional homicidal mind—a man who cannot be let loose, because he simply has no feeling for human life—but that is very rare. Most men on Death Row are emotional criminals, which is quite a different thing. They belong in a hospital more than a prison.

I: Isn't there any attempt to differentiate between the two now?

C: Not really. We're still thinking in terms of "good behavior," or the opinions of a governor and voters who've never laid eyes on the criminal.

My theory is that, with one or two federal prisons, the murderer could be committed to what's called an open sentence; with and without the possibility of parole. A really good staff specializing in only this problem, homicidal violence, would give therapy and psychiatric help. Prisoners wouldn't be shut up in little holes, but allowed to work, as in an ordinary prison. And it would be up to an expert staff to decide who should be paroled and *when*. Or decide, in the case of the inveterate homicidal mind, that they should simply be kept incarcerated for life.

I: Has this happened in any country?

C: No. It's never happened anywhere.

I: Do you think we ignore men on Death Row, like cancer victims, as a *memento mori*?

C: Maybe. Because people just don't want to *think* about it. Of course, there are many people who are deeply concerned, but for most, it's like something in a book. That man can live like that on Death Row, can then be really and truly hanged—it just seems too farfetched.

I: Do you feel strongly about other political issues?

C: I'm not a political person at all. Everything with me is extremely personal. Vietnam involves me emotionally, but not politically. The whole thing seems wrong, both Hanoi and Washington.

I: Nearly twenty years ago, in *Other Voices, Other Rooms*, you seemed concerned about injustice to the Negro.

C: I was and I am. Personally, as a child, almost *literally* all my friends were Negroes. Somehow, I always had more empathy with them than anyone else. The sole exceptions were my elderly cousin, Miss Sook, and Harper Lee. Most of the time, the relationships between white people and colored people in the South were kind. But then there would be that moment when you saw them stepping off the sidewalk for us to pass—I just couldn't accept that at all. Couldn't *believe* it, almost.

A little circus used to come to town. All the white children would ride on the merry-go-round, while the colored children just watched. I couldn't stand it. I never wanted to ride.

I: Did this consciousness set you apart from other white children?

C: I was apart from them anyway.

I: Is this apartness like a mark of Zorro that you can recognize now in others?

C: Sometimes. I get a lot of letters from young people. They've read somewhere that I never finished school, and they say, "I don't want to finish, either. I want to *write*."

If the letter is from parents, they'll send some manuscript of the child's. What they really want to know is not if he has talent, but "Can he make a living?" I read them if I can, and a few have been quite talented.

There's one fourteen-year-old boy I've been in correspondence with. He writes and draws with great imaginative qualities.

I tell them to go to college anyway, because they'll have an audience for their work, a sounding board. The audience may discourage them, but that's a good thing, too. The most pathetic thing in the world is a person who has been persuaded, through false friendship, that he has talent when he does not.

My whole education was a development of my own self-instructed tastes. I don't have an abstract mind at all. The literary art, painting and music: that's really all that concerns me.

In the end, I suppose *everybody* has to invent his own world, and that's truly what I did. I invented myself, and then I invented a world to fit me.

I: Do you still feel a loner, a two-headed calf?

C: There are numerous people I like very much; three or four I feel close to and love. Maybe they are two-headed calves themselves.

From the moment I felt secure in my talent, I didn't mind being a loner, anyway. As long as *that* wasn't a fantasy, I knew everything was going to be all right.

Truman Capote, Man About Town
Jerry Tallmer/1967

From *New York Post,* Weekend Magazine, 16 December 1967, 26. Copyright © 1967 by New York Post. Reprinted by permission.

Everybody snapped to Gallic attention, the proprietor, the waiters, the hatcheck girl, when the bantam gentleman in cap and pea jacket walked into the Lafayette restaurant.

"Bon jour," they said, *"bon jour, M'sieur Capote, comment allez vous?"*

"Fine, fine," said Truman Capote, doffing cap and pea jacket. The movie from his book, *In Cold Blood,* a recreation of the slaughter of the Clutter family of Holcomb, Kan., had opened that day at Cinema I, and the reviews the next morning were to call it superb.

They gave Capote a table near the door. He decided to start things off with a Bloody Mary frappe without Worcestershire sauce. To his luncheon companion, this reporter, he said, "There are only about four good restaurants left in New York and this is the one I like best" (the other three are the Colony, La Grenouille, 21).

The proprietor presented the menu.

"Oh well now," said Capote, "we know what Truman's going to have." He indicated a "fabulous omelet here" called the George Sand, all creamed chicken on the inside and smothered in a rich sauce. Then he switched signals and asked, "Do you have anything cold?" and opted for a luke-warm striped bass. So his interviewer took the omelet. It was fabulous. So was the tab.

What have you been doing, Truman, the past couple of years since the book came out?

"Well, I've written some short stories. I'm about halfway through a novel. I've done three or four things for TV. We might as well get the ads in. They're going to show my 'Among the Paths to Eden,' with Maureen Stapleton, Sunday from 8 to 9 p.m. on Ch. 7. And on

Tuesday from 8:30 to 9:30 [same channel] they're going to repeat my 'A Christmas Memory.' Have you seen that?"

No, as a matter of fact.

"Oh well, you should. Geraldine Page is just wonderful. And I've done a completely new version of *House of Flowers* [the Capote-Harold Arlen musical that flopped on Broadway in 1954] for a Jan. 24 opening at the Theater de Lys." Capote grinned. "And I can't wait to get my revenge." Wider grin. "Because I was right in the first place." Wider grin. "It's going to be marvelous." He signaled a waiter and asked for a vodka on the rocks with lemon peel. "So you see," said Capote, "I've been a little busy.'

He's also been busy as a consultant on the film *In Cold Blood* working closely with director Richard Brooks.

"Dick did the script because I was too close to it, too involved. But everything was done the way I wanted: a cast of unknowns, black and white, on location in Kansas. I feel I did the right thing. I could have had *any* director, from Antonioni to Jack Clayton. Well, that would have been another thing, you know—no doubt very beautiful, but . . .

"We wanted it to be really real: to make you know what happens inside the homicidal mind, and to get the whole thing of capital punishment. It's a shocking film, no doubt about it, but we meant it to be; to shock you into thinking. There's nothing in it the bit prurient, however, nothing that would appeal to the exhibitionistic, the masochistic, the sadistic."

A year ago Capote set the town agog with a famous party in the grand ballroom of the Hotel Plaza (". . . that little dance I gave last year"); since then he's been pretty well chained to the typewriter. He has a lush apartment at United Nations Plaza and a house in Switzerland, but for the most part he's been out at his place at Wainscott, near Bridgehampton, L. I., working hard on the novel, getting up at 5, writing until 11, then attending to his correspondence ("I answer the letters that are sort of serious, college kids and so forth"), then "lunch and a little nap, reading in the afternoon and a little exercise," working again from 5 to 7. "Then I have three drinks—two drinks—three drinks. Then I have my supper, go to bed, read, fall asleep around 9:30. So that's the glamorous life I lead."

What kind of house do you have out there, Truman?

"O well, what it is is it's two houses. One very cozy little cottage all covered with roses and grapevines, and then you walk down the road, a private road I built myself, to the studio where I work, right almost in the marsh before the ocean. Very lonely, nothing but seagulls. The studio is one huge room going up two floors, with a spiral staircase."

Somebody with a familiar face came into the Lafayette restaurant. "Hi, Truman," he said. "Hi, Mac," said Capote. Ah yes, McGeorge Bundy. "I hear your film's terrific," said Bundy. "You're looking very autumnal," said Capote.

Once last winter Capote was out on the Island, taking a stroll, wondering whether he should order a snowplow. Suddenly there was another person walking toward him. "My God, I thought, it looks like J.N.—and it was. A man I had interviewed for *In Cold Blood,* a former convict from California and a highly dangerous gentleman."

What did he want, money?

"M-mmm, hmmm. He stayed all day. A highly disturbing experience. Because you are so alone. A modified version of *The Desperate Hours.* I did have to give him money, but it turned out all right."

Capote broke into a laugh, and when Capote laughs the room lights up.

"So many creepy people," he said, "try to involve themselves in my life. My mail every day would send most people off to a mental ward. Talk about 'Marat/Sade'!"

He took a bottle of Pouilly-Fume, *accent aigu,* with his fish, and spoke of the Capote interview that's coming up in the February issue of *Playboy.* "You're really going to have a good time. It's really fun. I'm probably going to have to leave the country, but . . ."

What do you read, Truman?

"Oh, everything. Newspapers. Magazines. The last three months I've been re-reading Jane Austen for the umpteenth time. And the reason is I have this extraordinary grandmother, 92 years old. Mrs. M. K. Purcell, now living in Jacksonville, Fla.

"She was the first woman chemistry professor in this country. Her mind is just as clear as"—fleeting pause, to nail the exact smile—"Poland water. Well, she wrote me this letter that she had just finished reading three Jane Austen novels. She hadn't read any since she was 19. She had kept a diary at that time, and now whe re-read it. What a world of experience she's had in between, she wrote, and yet she still thought precisely what she'd thought at 19.

"My grandfather was a mathematician. My mother's family were all Southern country people, but my whole intellectual apparatus is so obviously counter . . . you know . . ."

Capote, as everybody also knows, was brought up mostly by aunts and grandmothers in Alabama, New York, New England, his mother having married at 15 and divorced early. Capote himself has been completely on his own since he was 17, when he landed a job sorting cartoons at *The New Yorker*. At 24 he skyrocketed out of nowhere with *Other Voices, Other Rooms*.

"I think it's a really fantastic book, I really do. It's being reissued by Random House in a 20th-anniversary edition. Put that in. With a whole new introduction."

How old are you, Truman?

"Oh, I never tell my age," He grinned. "I'm 43," he said.

The waiter came up to ask: "Coffee, M'sieur?"

"No, I'll have a little more of my wine," Capote said. He started to talk about writers and writing.

"The main thing with me," he said, "is I *can't* write. That's what nobody understands. When I write a letter I try to keep it down to about five words, all ending 'Love, Truman.'

"What I do is go through *such* an infinite process. It's just impossible for me to write a sentence. I have to think about it such a—long time. The thing that's most important is style; not what I'm saying but how I'm saying it; manner over matter. I realize it's the wrong point of view. I want to change it. I just can't, Unfortunately it got locked in me when I was about 15 years old."

Well, Truman, it may be hard for you to write, but you *do* write, and a lot. I mean, look at Flaubert—

Capote looked over in dead earnestness and said: "I think I put as much into *In Cold Blood* as he put into *Madame Bovary*."

He was asked for his opinions on Norman Mailer, whom he likes and is liked by, and William Styron.

"I'd like to have a marvelous house somewhere," he said, "and

Jerry Tallmer/1967

make Norman come there six months and *really* make him work. Because he's a fantastic talent . . . with an unfortunate lack of discipline. And yes, I liked the Styron book *The Confessions of Nat Turner.* Admired it more than liked it, but it's really an extraordinary achievement."

He laughed his laugh.

"I like to say," he said, "that since Flannery O'Connor and Carson McCullers died there are only three talented writers in this country, and that's Mr. Styron, Mr. Mailer, and Mr. Capote. Oh, there are others . . . Katherine Anne Porter, a marvelous artist . . . Eudora Welty, when she writes . . ."

A smoker since the age of 12, Capote has now kicked the habit, except for "a little bit" in the evening. "The hardest thing was: not while working. Once I got over that barrier . . ."

But that's the secret of your success, Truman, isn't it? You're a very disciplined guy.

"Well," he said, again in dead earnest, "that's the answer to everything. Discipline is everything. They say American writers have to burn themselves out, like Scott Fitzgerald. Well, it didn't happen to Henry James," he said somewhat primly. "A writer has to train like an athlete. Alas, writers live so much longer than athletes. Athletes can sink into a bowl of spaghetti at the age of 35. That's when writers start functioning, isn't that true?"

The management brought around a *creme de menthe.*

"It really amazes me," said Capote, "that Somerset Maugham and Raymond Chandler didn't start writing until they were 42, 43. On the other hand I started at 17, so I really had to stay in training.

"When I was 17 a man named Robert N. Linscott bought me, so to speak. He was an editor at Random House; he's dead now. He said to me: 'Now you're going to be a writer, an artist. We're going to support you, take you. You're like a race horse.'

"It didn't make any sense to me at the time. I thought it was crazy. But now," said Truman Capote, "I can see what the point of the whole thing was."

So can a lot of other people.

Playboy Interview: Truman Capote
Eric Norden/1968

From *Playboy*, 15 (March 1968), 51-53, 56, 58-62, 160-162, 164-170. Copyright © 1968 by Playboy. Reprinted by special permission of Playboy Magazine.

"WEALTHY FARMER, THREE OF FAMILY SLAIN: H.W. CLUTTER, WIFE AND TWO CHILDREN ARE FOUND SHOT IN KANSAS HOME." The UPI dispatch below this headline, buried in the back pages of the November 15, 1959, *New York Times,* was newsworthy outside Kansas only because H. W. Clutter was a former Eisenhower appointee to the Federal Farm Credit Board. But in New York City, the item had an electrifying effect on novelist Truman Capote. Within three days, he was in the small western Kansas farm town of Holcomb, interviewing friends and neighbors of the Clutter family and badgering local police for information about the crime, determined to probe deeply into the lives of both the Clutter family and their murderers.

At first the diminutive (5'3") Capote, with his exotic European clothes and high-pitched voice, was viewed askance by local residents, who often demanded to see his meager credentials—a letter of recommendation from the president of Kansas State University and a battered U.S. passport blackened with visas for over 30 nations. Nor was Capote, a darling of the jet set, initially at home on the plains of Kansas. "It was as strange to me," he said later, "as if I'd gone to Peking." But townspeople and police alike soon warmed to the effervescent elf; and for the next five and a half years, he relentlessly investigated the lives of the Clutter family and the two men convicted of (and eventually executed for) their murder—Richard Hickock and Perry Smith, who became his close friends.

Capote's research was exhaustive—and exhausting. "I wrote 6000 pages of notes before I ever sat down to write the book," he says. Everyone even remotely connected with the case was interviewed in depth, and no aspects of the lives of the Clutters or of their killers escaped Capote's scrutiny. The result was *In Cold Blood,* a 343-page "nonfiction novel"—Capote's own term—published by Random House in January 1966. An instantaneous critical and commercial success, the book soared within two weeks of publication to the top of the best-seller list, where it remained for over a year. In the process of selling 800,000 copies in hard cover and over 2,500,000 in paperback—in America alone—it became one of the biggest moneymakers in publishing history. Translated into 25 foreign languages (including Hebrew, Catalan, Afrikaans and Icelandic), it has already earned Capote over $3,000,000 including $500,000 for movies rights.

The author was even more pleased by the book's rave reviews than by its resounding commercial success. The icons of the literary establishment, who for years had merely tolerated Capote or, like Herbert Gold, dismissed him as "one of the chattering poets of decoration," now called him a towering figure in American letters. "Remarkable, tensely exciting, moving, superbly written," hailed *The New York Times.* "A masterpiece . . . a spellbinding work," echoed *Life.* "The best documentary account of an American crime ever written," declared *The New York Review of Books.* "One of the stupendous books of the decade," panegyrized London's *Sunday Express.* No book in recent years had been so widely and so lavishly praised.

Drowned out by the cheers were a few restive murmurs of dissent. Reviewing *In Cold Blood* for *New Republic,* critic Stanley Kauffmann wrote: "It is ridiculous in judgment and debasing of all of us to call this book literature. Are we so bankrupt, so avid for novelty that, merely because a famous writer produces an amplified magazine crime feature, the result is automatically elevated to serious literature?" Novelist Mary McCarthy derided the claim that Capote had invented the nonfiction novel and charged that his "greatest contribution to literary innovation was to publicize the author first, the book second."

Capote has always been a lightning rod for controversy. Born Truman Streckfus Persons (he later changed his surname legally to that of his mother's second husband) in New Orleans on September 30, 1924, Capote was four when his mother divorced a traveling salesman and packed her unwanted son off to live with three elderly aunts in Monroeville, Alabama. In the following years, he shuttled among various relatives throughout the rural South, seldom seeing his mother and completely out of touch with his father. Perhaps as an anodyne for parental rejection, he retreated into an inner world of fantasy and dreams. A precocious child, he began his writing career at the age of eight, and at twelve won first prize in a literary contest with a short story titled, "Old Mr. Busybody."

Capote dropped out of school at 17 and, after a brief stint as protégé of a fortuneteller, he traveled to New York and got a clerical job at *The New Yorker;* originally hired by the accounting department, he confessed after one day that he could not add and was transferred to the art department. But his literary talents were soon recognized and he graduated from cataloging cartoons to writing items for "The Talk of the Town" department. He also found time to moonlight as a movie-script reader and to grind out free-lance anecdotes for a popular digest magazine. That same year, he wrote his first piece of published fiction, and at 19 won the O. Henry Prize for a short story called "Miriam," a schizophrenia-tinged tale about a mysterious child who enters the life of a middle-aged woman and slowly destroys her. All of Capote's early work dealt, as critic John K. Hutchens puts it, with a "macabre, isolated world of shadowy characters in flight from sundry terrors."

By 1948, a series of such stories had won him *succès d'estime* within the world of letters, but he was still unknown to the general public. Then his first novel, *Other Voices, Other Rooms,* was published and Capote became an overnight celebrity. The *New York Herald Tribune* called the book "the most exciting first novel by a young American in many years," and critics began to compare its author with Norman Mailer, Irwin Shaw and Gore Vidal—the brightest literary lights of the early post-War period. Overshadowing the paeans, however, and perhaps as responsible for the book's success as its luminous prose, was the photograph of Capote on the dust jacket. Gazing limpidly out of a thousand bookshop windows at a public alternately beguiled, outraged and amused was a portrait of Capote reclining on a couch, fastidiously attired in a tattersall vest and black bow tie, blond bangs dangling over his forehead, full lips moist and pouting. Critic George Davis quickly dubbed him "the perverted

Huck Finn of American Letters." Thus was Capote stamped indelibly with the image of a decadent, orchidaceous aesthete.

As the years passed, his florid personal legend grew apace with his reputation as a writer. *Other Voices, Other Rooms* was followed with a string of equally successful, if less controversial, books. *A Tree of Night,* an anthology of eight hauntingly evocative short stories, appeared in 1949 and was followed in 1950 by *Local Color,* a collection of perceptive and civilized travel pieces that marked Capote's first literary departure from the shadowy borderland between dream and reality. *The Grass Harp,* his second published novel (1951), once more reflected Capote's preoccupation with the world of childhood but evidenced a new feeling of human warmth and a life-affirming faith. In 1956, Capote unveiled yet another dimension of his evolving talents with the publication of *The Muses Are Heard,* a bitingly witty documentary account of his trip through Russia with the touring company of "Porgy and Bess"—and the precursor of his preoccupation with journalism. In 1958 came *Breakfast at Tiffany's,* his celebrated *novella* about Holly Golightly, the wistfully whimsical demimondaine subsequently immortalized on film by Audrey Hepburn. Capote adapted "House of Flowers," another story from this period, for the stage; it was a flop—but a revised version opened on Broadway early this year. In 1963, Capote's *Selected Writings* appeared—again, to mixed reviews. But the critics' objections didn't trouble Capote; he was then almost halfway through his most monumental work, *In Cold Blood.*

In the years since then, Capote's stature as a world-acclaimed author has won him entree to the *salons* of international society, and he reciprocated on November 29, 1966, by throwing a gala—and widely reported—masked ball for his friends. Among the several hundred intimates who packed the Grand Ballroom of the Plaza Hotel were Rose Kennedy, Princess Lee Radziwill, Mrs. Stavros Niarchos, Lynda Bird Johnson, Mr. and Mrs. Henry Ford II, Princess d'Arenberg, Countess Gianni Agnelli, Alfred Gwynne Vanderbilt, Margaret Truman Daniels, Countess Rudi Crespi and Undersecretary of State Nicholas Katzenbach.

Capote, who has never been accused of modesty, forthwith accepted Elsa Maxwell's guttering torch with grace: "I'm an absolute social smash," he announced. Though he has been called a snob, members of his self-styled court are not selected on the basis of their standing in "Burke's Peerage" or with Dun and Bradstreet; beauty, wit and elegance are his criteria. Nor are Capote's courtiers, who range from royalty to Long Island potato farmers, drawn to him because of his reputation as a best-selling author. As Suzy Knickerbocker, guru of the gossip columnists, puts it: "All his friends like and love him—not because he's a big literary lion, not because it's the thing to do, but because Truman is Truman...."

To discover what makes Truman Truman and to fathom the complexities and contradictions of the man and the artist, PLAYBOY interviewed Capote at his New York residence, a five-room co-op on the 22nd floor of the luxurious new United Nations Plaza apartment building, a millionaire's mecca (Capote's next-door neighbors: Senator Robert F. Kennedy and Johnny Carson). Capote does the bulk of his writing at a two-house estate in Bridgehampton, Long Island; he also maintains a home in Palm Springs, California, and a mountainside villa in Verbier, Switzerland, but does most of his entertaining—and grants most of his infrequent interviews—in his New York apartment, surrounded by a collection of turn-of-the-century Tiffany lamps, animal *bibelots*, antique paperweights and yellowing photographs. Now 43, Capote is no longer the fey youth on the dust jacket of *Other Voices, Other Rooms*: His blond hair is thinning, his jowls are fuller and the years have traced fine lines about his eyes. But at our first interview session, as he uncorked a bottle of French champagne—his refrigerator holds little else—and settled himself, scruffily accoutered in T-shirt, windbreaker and sunglasses, on a window seat overlooking a view of the East River, the impish *enfant terrible* of 20 years ago seemed not so far away. "Have at me," Capote commanded in his lilting, near-contralto voice. PLAYBOY interviewer Eric Norden began by asking him about that other self.

Playboy: Do you think the public's initial image of you as a kind of literary Aubrey Beardsley helped or hindered your career?

Capote: It certainly didn't do me any good in official academic circles, but then, I never cared about all those gray people with their drab quarterly reviews. On the other hand, a number of people who were concerned about my welfare and my emerging career did feel that this image harmed me, since many in the literary establishment were bound to resent my eccentricities and mannerisms and to feel that I received far too much publicity for a serious writer. But it's not true, as so many people seem to think, that I did a great deal to encourage this image in an effort to build an "atmosphere" around myself. From the beginning, I've never done anything but try to be myself and go my own way. I think there are certain people who have a natural charisma that generates public awareness and interest. You have it or you don't; and if you don't have it, there's nothing you can do to create it. For better or worse, I've had this charisma from the start; and I can't say whether it's helped or hurt me. It all depends on whether you think fame is an asset or a hindrance in an artistic career. I feel rather indifferent about the whole thing, but then, I've been in public life over 20 years now, and you become neutral about publicity. I never pay attention to what people write about me anymore. It takes a lot to make my pulse skip a beat.

Playboy: The image that grew up around Ernest Hemingway—big-game hunter, bullfight *aficionado*, belting whiskey and swearing like a stevedore—was just the opposite of your image, as you once described it in Paris to Art Buchwald: "fragile and aesthetic . . . although I'm not that at all." Do you think that in both cases the image may have tended to obscure the real man and his work?

Capote: Yes, in both instances the myth is erroneous and almost comically misleading. I am secretly several of the things the hairy one pretended to be. But don't expect me to elaborate on that doubtless curious-sounding statement, for the operative word is *secretly*.

Playboy: Despite—or perhaps because of—your famous dust-jacket photo on *Other Voices, Other Rooms*, you became an instantaneous literary celebrity. How did all that publicity affect your personal life and your writing?

Capote: Mostly, it gave me confidence. Also, it improved my love life; a wide variety of attractive people became highly available.

Playboy: Would you care to elaborate on *that*?

Capote: No.

Playboy: All right. You have said of *Other Voices, Other Rooms*, "I feel a stranger to the book. . . . I'm terribly parnoid about the whole thing." Why?

Capote: That was true once, but it isn't true now. The reason I felt alienated from it for so many years was that I didn't want to face the fact that the book was all about *me* and my problems. I hadn't reread it for many years—I'm always a little afraid of rereading my own work, for fear I'll discover that my harsher critics are correct—but a new edition is coming out this year, so I recently read it through in one sitting. And I realized that the book is a prose poem in which I have taken my own emotional problems and transformed them into psychological symbols. Every one of the characters represented some aspect of myself. Do you remember the young boy who goes to a crumbling mansion in search of his father and finds an old man who is crippled and can't speak and can communicate only by bouncing red tennis balls down the stairs? Well, I suddenly understood that, of course, this represented my search for my own father, whom I seldom saw, and the fact that the old man is crippled and mute was my way of transferring my own inability to communicate with my father; I was not only the boy in the story but also the old man. So the central theme of the book was my search for my father—a father who, in the deepest sense, was nonexistent. This seems so clear and obvious today that it's hard to understand why I never grasped the fact at the time; it was a classic case of self-deception. I now realize that what I was attempting in *Other Voices, Other Rooms* was to exorcise my own devils, the subterranean anxieties that dominated my feelings and imagination: and my ignorance of this was probably a protective shield between me and the subconscious well-spring of my material. And, of course, this explains why so much of my earlier work is written in a fantastic vein; I was attempting to escape from the realities of my own troubled life, which wasn't easy. My underlying motivation was a quest for some sense of serenity, some particular kind of affection that I needed and wanted and have finally found. As I reread the book, I realized that I've lost touch with that anguished youth of 20 years ago; only a dimming shadow of him remains inside me: I felt I was reading the work of a stranger. He impressed me—but he is no longer me.

Playboy: Why did your childhood experiences have such a strong impact on your early writings?

Capote: Well, I had a difficult childhood. I was born in New Orleans and my parents were divorced when I was four years old, with a great deal of bitterness on both sides. After that, I spent most of my time wandering between the households of relatives in

Louisiana, Alabama and Mississippi. My story *A Christmas Memory*, about a boy with elderly female relatives, is altogether drawn from life. As I grew older, I was packed off to different boarding schools all across the country, and I was lonely and very insecure. Who wouldn't be? I was an only child, very sensitive and intelligent, with no sense of being particularly wanted by *anybody*. I rarely saw my father; he remarried three or four times. My mother wasn't unkind to me; she simply had other interests. She remarried, too, and that's how I got the name Capoté; it's not the name I was born with, but that of my mother's second husband, a Cuban gentleman. I wasn't neglected financially; there was always enough money to send me to good schools, and all that. It was just a total *emotional* neglect. I never felt I belonged anywhere. All my family thought there was something wrong with me. When I grew bored at school after the third grade and started getting straight Fs and bad-conduct marks, they began to think I was retarded. Then a WPA project—this was back in the Thirties—sent a team of researchers to our town one day to give intelligence tests to the school children, and I received the highest score they'd ever encountered. They were intrigued and paid my expenses to New York, where Columbia University gave me a whole battery of I.Q. and aptitude tests: and I returned home knowing I was extremely intelligent. That was the first time I ever felt proud of myself and I flaunted the test results to my relatives. They now knew I wasn't retarded, but they still considered me very peculiar. I always thought of myself as a kind of two-headed calf. Well, that's all I want to say about it. I've never been psychoanalyzed; I've never even consulted a psychiatrist. I now consider myself a mentally healthy person. I work out all my problems in my work.

Playboy: How old were you when you first began to write?

Capote: I was eight. I was a sickly kid. Or I *pretended* to be; I was always inventing a new illness so that I could stay home and read. I loved Poe and Dickens and Twain and I just couldn't get enough of them. The desire to write became an obsession, something I had no control over. I made myself a little office in one room with an old typewriter and each day I worked there for a certain number of hours; and before I reached my teens, I had developed a definite style. I began staying up all night, writing in a state of feverish excitement. And I read more and more: Oscar Wilde, De

Maupassant, Henry James, Hawthorne, Flaubert, Jane Austen, Proust, Chekhov, Turgenev, Emily Brontë, Sarah Orne Jewett, E. M. Forster. They all contributed to my literary intelligence, each in a different way. Thus reading was of far more value to me than anything I ever learned in a classroom. My official education was a total waste of time and I dropped out of school at 17 and traveled to New York, where I got my first job, at *The New Yorker.* That job wasn't very glamorous, just clipping newspapers and filing cartoons, but I was delighted to have it, because I was determined never to set foot inside a college classroom. If I was a writer, fine; if I wasn't, no professor on earth was going to make me one. So ever since childhood, there has never been a moment when I wasn't concerned with writing.

Playboy: What prompted you to make the creative leap from your dreamlike and poetic earlier work to the harsh realm of documentary writing such as *In Cold Blood*?

Capote: I don't believe I was making any "leap" at all. I'd *always* been experimenting with journalism, my first attempt was a long *New Yorker* profile of Marlon Brando and I followed that with a book, *The Muses Are Heard,* which describes my tour of Russia as an observer of the *Porgy and Bess* company. In both cases, I was moving slowly toward *In Cold Blood.* But the truth of the matter is that there's no difference at all between the prose style of a story like *A Christmas Memory* and, say, the opening chapter of *In Cold Blood.* If you examine *In Cold Blood* carefully, you'll realize that it's every bit as lyrical as my earlier work.

Playboy: Critic Granville Hicks believes there is a greater gulf between your earlier work and your current documentary writing than you've just indicated. He claims that there are "two Capotes: the author of delicate, often exquisite, sometimes sentimental stories about children and the shrewd, alert, sophisticated reporter of events in the 'real' world." Are there "two Capotes"? And, if so, will they continue to coexist?

Capote: Dear old Granny Hicks. As far as the "two Capotes" goes, I occasionally read articles in these little literary quarterlies about the coexistence of two or three personalities and styles in the one writer—the "dark" Capote and the "bright" Capote, the "shadowy" one and the "sunny" one; I think it's all a lot of *merde.*

Like any artist, such as a singer or a pianist, I change my tone and color range to suit my subject; and as a result, it *seems* as though there is some extraordinary difference of approach and style, when there is none whatever. Of course, the color tone of *Breakfast at Tiffany's* is totally unsuited to books like *The Muses Are Heard* or *In Cold Blood*; but if anybody at all *soigné* in his knowledge of writing technique reads all three, he will see that the style doesn't change at all; there is merely a melodic adjustment of language to suit the shifting material. And why *shouldn't* a writer extend his subject matter? So the two Capotes Hicks refers to won't continue to coexist, because they *don't* exist.

Playboy: Yet you have said of the time prior to your decision to write *In Cold Blood* that "I had to do something to myself, I had to re-create myself." What did you mean by that?

Capote: Most American writers, as Scott Fitzgerald said, never have a second chance. I realized that if I were ever going to have that chance, it was necessary for me to make a radical change; I had to get outside of my own imagination and learn to exist in the imagination and lives of other people. I knew that it would help me enormously to expand my own range of interest and material and understanding, because I had become too obsessed with my particular internal images. That was the main reason I turned to journalism; and I must say, the shift of emphasis caused me to gain in creative range and gave me the confidence to deal with a wide spectrum of people I otherwise would never have written about. Take most of the characters in *The Muses Are Heard* or *In Cold Blood*; as an *imaginative* writer, I wouldn't have written one word about them, because they didn't come within my scope of interests. But by working journalistically, I was forced by the medium's own criteria to empathize with them and understand their motives and objectively describe their language and action and emotions; and as a result, I now have a vastly wider literary range. So I haven't shattered the mold; I've merely expanded it.

Playboy: The publisher's blurb for *In Cold Blood* claims that the book "represents the culmination of Capote's long-standing desire to make a contribution toward the establishment of a serious new literary form: the nonfiction novel." Isn't the "nonfiction novel" a contradiction in terms—literarily as well as literally?

Capote: Perhaps it's an awkward phrase, but I couldn't think of any better words to describe what I was attempting, which was to write a journalistic narrative that employed all the creative devices and techniques of fiction to tell a true story in a manner that would read precisely like a novel. So even though the phrase "nonfiction novel" is technically a *non sequitur*, it's the only description I could devise.

Playboy: Some critics saw in the phraseology of that cover blurb an implied claim that you were the *inventor* of the nonfiction novel—and have pointed to many earlier experiments in the genre to prove that you weren't. Did you intend any such claim?

Capote: Let me stress that the blurb you quoted reads: "make a contribution toward the *establishment* of a serious new literary form." Many people, of course, have experimented in this field before, and what I meant by saying I wished to contribute to the *establishment* of the nonfiction novel was that I wanted to present the technique in its most fully developed form. I have never claimed to have *invented* narrative journalism; I do claim to have undertaken the most comprehensive and far-reaching experiment to date in the medium of reportage. The dust-jacket copy on my book was thoughtfully written, but it was still misinterpreted. The real demarcation between my book and anything that has gone before is that it contains a technical innovation that gives it both the reality and the atmosphere of a novel; and that device is that *I* never once appear in the book. Never. Always before in this genre, the author has been faced with a technical problem of credibility: The reader wants to know *how* does the writer know this person said this to someone else, *how* does he know this background material? Now, previously the problem has always been solved by the narrator intruding himself into the scene: *I* discovered this, *I* saw that, *I* overheard this. The first-person pronoun permeates the whole composition and it thus becomes a piece of straight surface journalism. It only moves *horizontally* throughout. But what I wanted to do was bring to journalism the technique of fiction, which moves both horizontally and vertically at the same time: horizontally on the narrative side and vertically by entering *inside* its characters. And that, of course, is what gives fiction its peculiar depth and impact. Now, in my effort to give journalism this vertical interior movement—and that was the whole purpose of my experiment—I had to remove the narrator entirely. I had to make the book flow uninterruptedly from beginning to end, just like a novel, and thus the narrator never enters the picture and there is no interpretation of people and events. I wanted the story to exist completely in its own right; except for the selection of detail, I am totally absent from the development of the book, and the people are re-created as they are in life. That's why I feel it's not comparable with anything else in the history of journalism.

Playboy: You have said, "In 1955 I began to develop a theory that I could become a human tape recorder. I practiced over a period of two years and I ended with a high proportion of accuracy." *In Cold Blood* certainly demonstrates your talent as an interviewer and researcher; but in the process of becoming a recorder rather than an interpreter of events, isn't there a danger of sacrificing one dimension of your creativity and becoming a journalist rather than a novelist?

Capote: The two disciplines, at their highest level, are not mutually exclusive; if I hadn't thought it possible that journalism and novelistic technique could be artistically wedded, I never would have set out on my experiment in the first place. As for my being a "human tape recorder," I've always had what amounts to the auditory version of a photographic memory, and all I did was perfect this gift. This is of great importance in the kind of reportage I do, because it is absolutely fatal to ever take a note or use a tape recorder when you interview somebody. Most people are quite unsophisticated about being interviewed, and if you erect any kind of mechanical barrier, it destroys the mood and inhibits people from talking freely. In the case of *In Cold Blood*, as I said a moment ago, it was vital for me to live *inside* the situation, to become part of the scene I was recording and not cut myself off from them in any way. And so I trained myself in this so-called human-tape-recorder technique. Anybody could learn to do it, but it's useful only to a specialist like me.

Playboy: How do you react to those critics who deride the form of documentary crime writing employed in *In Cold Blood* as inferior to the novel?

Capote: What can I say, except that I think they're ignorant? If they can't comprehend that journalism is really the most avant-garde form of writing existent today, then their heads are in the sand. These critics seem unable to realize, or accept, that creative fiction writing has gone as far as it can experimentally. It reached its peak in the Twenties and hasn't budged since. Of course, we have writers like William Burroughs, whose brand of verbal surface trivia is amusing and occasionally fascinating, but there's no base for moving *forward* in that area—whereas journalism is actually the last great unexplored literary frontier. There is so *much* that can be done with journalism. It's the only really serious and creative field of literary experimentation we have today, and I feel rather sorry for those critics who are so ossified and so fearful of relinquishing their prejudices that they fail to recognize the fact. As Napoleon said of the Bourbons, they've learned nothing and forgotten nothing. In a way, I guess it's unfortunate that I selected a crime for my first big experiment in the genre, because that made it easier for them to mistakenly lump together the material and the technique and think of it as a true crime story. But a nonfiction novel can be about *anything*—from crime to butterfly collecting.

Playboy: Of all the crimes, catastrophes, wars, political conspiracies and international crises you could have chosen as the theme for such an exhaustively researched work of nonfiction, why did you select the murder of an obscure Kansas farmer and his family?

Capote: I *didn't* select this Kansas farmer and his family; in a very real sense, they selected *me*. I'd been experimenting for a long time with the theory of writing a nonfiction novel, and I'd had several dry runs that didn't work out. I was searching for a suitable subject and, like a bacteriologist, I kept putting slides under the microscope, scrutinizing them and finally rejecting them as unsuitable. It was like trying to solve a quadratic equation with the X—in this case, the subject matter—missing. And then one day I was reading *The New York Times* and buried in the back pages I found a little item about the murder of a family in Kansas and suddenly I thought: Why not a crime? Maybe if I applied my theory and the technical apparatus I'd devised to a crime, it would give me the necessary range of material to make the experiment succeed. I had no natural attraction to the subject matter; it was just suddenly meshed into the equation. Anyway, I traveled to this small town in Kansas and started to investigate the crime and immediately faced innumerable difficulties.

Remember, all the material was not just waiting out there for me, as some people seem to think; when I began, I was dealing with an unsolved murder and initially I got very little cooperation either from the Clutters' relatives and neighbors or from the local police. I didn't know from minute to minute what was going to happen with the case, so I simply drudged on, gathering material. In fact, I didn't definitely decide that I was going to write the book until I had been working on it for more than a year. There were so many things that could have frustrated me; even after the two boys were arrested for the murder, what would have happened if, as was highly probable, they weren't interested in what I was doing and refused to cooperate with me? Of course, I did win their confidence and we became very close, but I had no assurance of that at the outset. And then, as the years dragged on and the legal delays and complications multiplied, I still didn't really know if I was going to be able to finish the book or even if there was any book there. After three years of work, I almost abandoned the whole project; I had become too emotionally involved and I couldn't stand the constant morbidity of the situation. It was becoming for me a question of personal survival. But I forced myself to keep going and pushed through the whole damned thing. It's a book that was written on the edge of my nerves. If I had ever known what I was going to have to endure over those six years—no matter what has happened since—I never would have started the book. It was too painful. Nothing is worth it.

Playboy: Are you the same man you were when you began work on the book in the fall of 1959?

Capote: Obviously I'm not. It wasn't the problem of writing it; I had to *live* it, day in and day out, for six years. I had to become a part of all those people's lives, some of whom weren't naturally sympathetic to me and with whom I had little in common. I had to surrender my entire life to this experience. Try to think what it means to totally immerse yourself in the lives of two men waiting to be hanged, to feel the passage of hours with them, to share every emotion. Short of actually living in a death cell myself, I couldn't have come closer to the experience. I lived a life totally alien to anything I had ever undergone before and I came to understand that death is the central factor of life. And the simple comprehension of this fact alters your entire perspective. Curiously enough, as a result of this constant awareness of imminent death, you develop a peculiar kind of humor—gallows humor, literally. My conversations with Smith and Hickock would have shocked and perhaps revolted anyone of the least sensitivity, because they were so stark, so brutal. But one *is* brutalized in that kind of situation, and overly sensitized at the same time. The experience served to heighten my feeling of the tragic view of life, which I've always held and which accounts for the side of me that appears extremely frivolous; that part of me is always standing in a darkened hallway, mocking tragedy and death. That's why I love champagne and stay at the Ritz.

Playboy: Despite the efforts you made on behalf of Hickock and Smith, all their appeals for commutation were rejected and on the night of April 14, 1965, you witnessed their death on the gallows. How did you feel that evening?

Capote: It was the worst experience of my life. Period.

Playboy: Did it affect your views on capital punishment?

Capote: They had already been formed. I'm against it—but not for any of the usual reasons. I feel that capital punishment could very well be a deterrent if it were evenly enforced and used more generally. But today, because of all the legal machinery and the interminable slowness of appeal procedure, there is this incredible stupidity and cruelty of keeping men in death rows for years on end. At this very moment, 440 men are in death rows across the country, not knowing whether they will be executed tomorrow or next year, or spared by the whim of some governor. The average time a convicted murderer spends on death row is five years; but in Louisiana, two men wasted in death cells for almost 14 years waiting for new trials. There isn't a pretense of rehabilitation or even an attempt to find out what makes them tick; they're left to vegetate. Now, I'm no bleeding heart about murderers; most of them have no conscience at all and their sole regret is that they were caught. I know them and I'm realistic about them. But as capital punishment functions today, it is so erratic in its application and *so creakingly* accomplished that it really does constitute "cruel and unusual" punishment as proscribed by the Constitution. If the system was clear-cut and a person was sentenced and executed within a six-month period on an even, regularized basis, then it might become a singularly effective deterrent; I think professional murderers would really think twice. By professional murderer, of course, I mean not the killer for hire or the Syndicate assassin but the man who commits a crime with the intention of killing the man he is robbing, often in the belief that he will thus not be identified to the police by his victim. He considers murder a necessary *by-product* of his crime. Of course, this type of criminal is generally motivated by pathological drives, but he is rational; and if he knew that death would be his unavoidable punishment, I believe it would give him pause. Today, however, when some are executed and some spared almost by happenstance, as if the legal system were drawing straws, capital punishment has no value as punishment and really constitutes a kind of institutionalized sadism.

Playboy: Why isn't the prospect of life imprisonment as effective a deterrent as death?

Capote: It might be if a life sentence really *meant* life imprisonment. But in the ordinary American prison, a man sentenced to life on a first-degree homicide charge is paroled and out on the street again within seven years. And almost no one is ever held longer than 12 years. That's why I'm against the way the parole system operates in homicide cases. There is an enormous number of recidivists among these parolees, and I believe that society has a right to protect itself against, say, a sexual psychopath who has no control over his compulsions. It might appear that there is no middle-ground choice between killing people and letting them out of prison prematurely; that's why so many people say, "Let's just extinguish this man so he won't go out and kill again." But there *is* a solution: I believe that all homicide cases, of whatever nature, from the psychopathic murderer to the obviously unpremeditated act of an enraged husband who kills his wife after catching her *flagrante delicto,* should be made a Federal crime, not a state crime, and every killer should be sent to a special maximum-security Federal prison. An immediate advantage here would be that all murder cases would go to trial outside the jurisdiction where the crime was committed; a man who commits murder in New York, for example, might be tried in California. And this would solve one of our major problems—that of pretrial publicity prejudicing the jurors. The key to this system would be that whenever a man is convicted of first-degree homicide, he would receive no precise sentence but an indeterminate sentence of from one day to life, and the actual length of his sentence would be determined not by a parole board but by an expert psychiatric staff attached to the Federal prison. The prison itself would be as much a hospital as a jail and, unlike most of our prisons, whose so-called psychiatric staffs are merely a joke, a true effort would be made to cure the inmates. Under this system, the board might determine that the man who killed his wife in a spasm of passion would be incarcerated for only three months, since his was not a repeatable crime, while a man like Perry Smith would probably have to stay there the rest of his life.

Playboy: But is psychiatry sufficiently precise to make a valid judgment about whether or not a man is cured? Isn't it still possible under your plan that a cunning psychopath could con a board of psychiatrists into releasing him and then kill again?

Capote: Oh, I don't pretend that my idea is foolproof. But it would certainly be a damn sight better than the situation you have today, with the inmates being handled by a lot of underpaid ex-Army sergeants and the parole board staffed by a combination of political hacks and naïve do-gooders. I think it's a feasible idea and it would remove as much of the element of unfairness from the system as possible. The biggest stumbling block is that shifting homicide from state to Federal jurisdiction would require amending the Constitution. But sooner or later, it will have to happen.

Playboy: You said that under your penal plan, Perry Smith would probably have been incarcerated for life because of his uncontrollable homicidal compulsions. Do you feel that rehabilitation would have been out of the question in his case?

Capote: Not necessarily. He wanted very deeply to paint and write and he also had genuine talent as a musician. He had a natural ear and could play five or six instruments; the guitar, in particular, he played extremely well. But one of the things he used to tell me over and over again was what a tragedy it was that never in his life had anyone, neither his father nor the staffs of the various reform schools or correctional institutions, encouraged him in any single creative thing he wanted to do. He said he often tried to get someone interested in him in the hope that he could receive lessons in music or writing, but *nobody* ever paid the slightest bit of attention to him. As a result, Smith came to live in a kind of schizophrenic dream fantasy where he was a great musician or the creator of a brilliant piece of art. Obviously, if at any time in his life another human being had shown him some sustained affection or even interest, Smith could have revealed something of himself and his aspirations and thus been able to lessen his bitter feeling of being so utterly deprived and alone and jealous and ousted from the world. If this had ever happened, I believe that the drive precipitating his psychotic outbursts of violence might have been aborted. Of course, in the five years I knew him after the murders, Smith showed great improvement. He had nothing to do but sit in his cell on death row and wait and sweat; so when I sent him four or five books a week, he read them avidly and sent me opinions on them, very intelligent and perceptive opinions, and I put him on a systematic reading program. He grew particularly enamored of Thoreau and Santayana in his last years and really became, unlikely as it sounds, something of a Santayana expert.

Playboy: Surely you don't intend to imply that the fact that Smith had artistic talent and an appreciation of Santayana would justify his release from prison.

Capote: Not in itself, of course. But there is such a thing as *partial* rehabilitation. Emotionally and intellectually, Perry had improved considerably during his stay on death row, but his homicidal compulsions ran very deep and I'm not sure he could ever have fully overcome them in the outside world. But the whole point of the psychiatric board attached to the hospital under my plan is to ensure that Perry would undergo extensive examination during his years in prison. It would then be up to the board to decide whether or not he was cured. If Perry had genuinely overcome his homicidal drives, I see no reason why he could not have been freed and allowed to play a productive role in society. It's really rather extraordinary that so many of the people I've interviewed on death rows across the country do change dramatically, primarily because for the first time in their lives they have the *time*, with no distractions whatever, to really think about their lives and probe inward to discover all kinds of things about themselves. So there's no doubt that people do have a capacity to rehabilitate themselves. For example, I visited a boy in Colorado State Prison named Michael John Bell, who has been on death row for almost five years now and has really evolved into an extraordinarily sensitive and perceptive guy. He's had six stays of execution and may be dead by the time this is in print, and it's a real shame. But this argument can be exaggerated; you mustn't forget that the people who are rehabilitated or who rehabilitate themselves are the exceptions and decidedly not the majority. And not all the rejuvenations take, either. Look at Paul Crump, who's one of the most celebrated examples of this sort of thing. He wrote a novel in prison, eventually had his sentence commuted; but he has gone downhill ever since his commutation and is now a problem character.

Playboy: What about Caryl Chessman? Do you share the view of those who feel that it was a tragic waste to execute a man who had changed so dramatically since his conviction?

Capote: I'm afraid there has been a lot of bleeding-heart nonsense printed about Chessman. He was a very, very dangerous psychotic who was anything but rehabilitated. He had a sympathetic personality that attracted people to his cause, a certain flair for writing that fooled a lot of people into thinking he was a saint and, God knows, he was articulate; but if Chessman had been let out of San Quentin, he would have returned to his old habits. The man had a *hopelessly* criminal mind. Of course, I'm not saying he should have been executed. Nobody should be executed for rape, even though the victims sometimes suffer aftereffects that are worse than being killed; one of Chessman's victims remember, is still in a mental institution. I wouldn't have objected to commuting Chessman's sentence to life imprisonment, but I think we should dispense with all this romanticizing about him.

Playboy: You have characterized Perry Smith as "psychotic." But was either Smith or Hickock clinically insane?

Capote: No, at least not by the current legal definition of insanity. But you've got to make a distinction between Hickock and Smith. Perry Smith was a serious psychopath and to some degree paranoid, with the kind of mind that is able to kill without passion and without remorse, just as you or I would swat a fly. I've known several Perry types, and human life means nothing to them; it's as if they have a talent for destruction, the kind of death-dealing ability hired killers have. These men have what I call the professional homicidal mind; they think nothing about murdering a man in the course of a robbery or a sexual assault. They can cut a man's throat from ear to ear and walk away and go to a movie and never think about what they've just done, because they place no value whatever on human life. It's almost as if somewhere along the line a surgeon had operated on them and removed some vital part of their brain, leaving them with this ability to kill. There is another type of killer whom I would describe as the *emotional* homicide. This is a man rather like Charles Whitman, the Texas tower murderer, or Robert Benjamin Smith, who walked into an Arizona beauty parlor, forced all the patrons to lie down on the floor and then shot them. This is murder on stage; they're doing it with a *desire* to be caught, because their own anonymity and inadequacy make them desperately require recognition. This type of killer is motivated by a desire to become *somebody*, because he thinks he's nothing; the act of murder becomes the sole release for his frustrations. One of the most interesting things about *Bonnie and Clyde*, which I consider an excellent film, is that it recognizes that the simple desire for notoriety is one of the strongest incitements to crime. Very few people have the vaguest idea of how strong a criminal motivation this is.

But Perry Smith's accomplice, Richard Hickock, doesn't fit either of these categories. Hickock wasn't capable of solo murder at all; he had the sly, quick mind of the petty thief, a kind of check-bouncing mentality. But you might say that in a sense he was a murderer, too, because he recognized the homicidal drive in Perry and he attached himself to it and encouraged it. Hickock was responsible for arranging the crime and the murdering was left to Perry. But Perry, once he was inside the Clutters' house, didn't really *want* to kill; he was reluctant about it, though the outcome was inevitable from the moment he saw Mr. Clutter. Do you remember what he said? "I didn't want to harm the man. I thought he was a very nice gentleman. Soft-spoken. I thought so right up to the moment I cut his throat." Insanity? Perhaps; but no court would recognize it as such.

Playboy: You say that Smith and Hickock could not be judged insane by the current legal definition of insanity, which in most states is the M'Naghten Rule. Do you think the M'Naghten Rule should be scrapped or amended?

Capote: It should certainly be amended. The M'Naghten Rule stipulates that the only proof of insanity is a man's inability to distinguish between right and wrong at the time of the crime. It's completely black and white; you have to be literally foaming at the mouth to be classified insane under this rule; anything short of that and the courts have no choice but to adjudge you sane. It's absurdly simplistic, because a man can succumb to a terrible inner compulsion to kill, know it's wrong and yet be powerless to resist it. But under the M'Naghten Rule, he will be judged sane and hanged; while by any remotely civilized legal standard, he should be incarcerated in a mental institution. Our laws in this area are about as modern and enlightened as the rack and the bastinado.

Playboy: You have said that Smith and Hickock would have gone on killing if they hadn't been apprehended. How can you be so sure?

Capote: A pattern of homicide had become so ingrained in them that it was inevitable they would have killed again if they had remained free. Let me give you an example that for space reasons I had to omit from the book. After Smith and Hickock murdered the Clutters, they fled to Mexico and in Mexico City they became chummy with a Swiss man who owned a restaurant. He was a homosexual and Hickock arranged to be picked up by him and go to his apartment. Incidentally, there was no homosexual relationship between Hickock and Smith; Perry once had an affair with a man and had definite homosexual fixations, but he had nothing to do with Hickock; they were completely frank about such matters and would have told me like a shot. Anyway, once Hickock arrived at the apartment, Perry planned to show up and together they were going to murder and rob this man. This assignation fell through at the last moment, but they had every intention of murdering him. You'll find another instance in my book where the two of them are hitchhiking and they agree to murder anybody who picks them up. So this pattern of homicide had already set in; and if they had gotten away with the Clutter murder, they would have set forth on one of those cross-country murder sprees that have become so common. I must stress again that Smith and Hickock had absolutely no qualms about killing. The only thing that bothered them or, rather, disturbed Perry, was a recurrent superstitious dread that something terrible was going to happen, that they wouldn't get away with it. But conscience didn't enter into it at all; Perry Smith, as a matter of fact, told me he was somewhat upset that he *didn't* have any conscience. So the murder of the Clutter family would have been only the first of many.

Playboy: The gulf between someone of your background and two such brutal criminals would seem impossible to bridge. But you've said, "Hickock and Smith became very, very good friends of mine—perhaps the closest friends I've ever had in my life." How did you establish rapport with them?

Capote: I treated them as *men*, not as murderers. To most people, a man loses his humanity the minute they learn he's a murderer; they could be talking with him one moment and then the next someone would whisper, "Do you know he killed five people?" and from that moment on, the man would become unreal to them, an uncomfortable abstraction. But I find it relatively easy to establish rapport with murderers; in the past few years, I've interviewed more than 30 of them in all parts of the country. Before I began *In Cold Blood*, I knew nothing about crime and wasn't interested in it; but once the book was under way, I began interviewing murderers—or homicidal minds, as I call them—in order to have a basis of comparison for Smith and Hickock; and I met many more recently while doing a television documentary on capital punishment. The second we begin talking, I find that they are ordinary men with extraordinary problems, set apart only by their ability to kill; in some it's a total lack of conscience, in others a passionate destruction drive. But I have found a certain pattern. One common denominator, for example, is their fetish for tattoos. I have seldom met a murderer who wasn't tattooed. Of course, the reason is rather clear; most murderers are extremely weak men who are sexually undecided and quite frequently impotent. Thus the tattoo, with all its obvious masculine symbolism. Another common denominator is that murderers almost always laugh when they're discussing their crimes. I've met few killers who didn't start laughing when I finally managed to force them to discuss the murder—which isn't easy. When Perry Smith started to tell me about the murder of the Clutter family, for example, he said, "I know this isn't funny, but I can't help laughing about it." Just a while ago, I interviewed a 21-year-old boy named Bassett in the San Quentin death house who is extremely intelligent. He's a slight, thin boy, with a delicate face and figure, a college student, and he writes poetry and short stories. He murdered his mother and father when he was 18; he'd been planning to do it since he was 10 years old. And when he started telling me about how he killed his parents, he began laughing and cracking little jokes, just as though he was telling me the most humorous story. They're mostly like that; they'll tell you how they cut someone's throat and it's as if they were watching a clown slip on a banana peel.

Playboy: *In Cold Blood* scrupulously refrains from speculating about the motives of the two murderers. You thus avoid answering the crucial question, Why? Is there no answer—or did you just fail to find one?

Capote: There *is* an answer and it's implicit in the book. In the last section of Part Four, called "The Corner," I describe at some length a study by several psychiatrists at the Menninger Clinic entitled "Murder Without Apparent Motive," which deals with cases in which a man commits an act of exceptional violence, one out of all proportion to the situation, as Perry Smith did. These doctors analyzed many such cases and found that the backgrounds of all the murderers interviewed were remarkably similar: All of them had experienced a childhood marked by parental brutality, rejection, insecurity. One of the Menninger psychiatrists, Dr. Joseph Satten, concentrated extensively on Perry Smith, and his conclusion was that the person Perry was murdering that night in a Kansas farmhouse was not Mr. Clutter but his own father. I agree. It also became quite clear from many of the things Perry told me over the years that this was his *own* evaluation of what had happened. The only murder of psychological importance in this case is the first one, because once it was committed, the others were imperative, but not in themselves psychologically motivated; they were automatic and almost incidental. So the why is quite clear: Perry identified Mr. Clutter, an authority figure, with the father he loved-hated and he unleashed all his inner resentment in an act of violence. This was a pattern in Perry's life; each time he tried to kill someone, that person was an obvious authority figure, a father surrogate. For example, he told me many times about his attempt to murder a military policeman in Japan; he picked him up and then threw him off a bridge. In each instance, what triggered Perry's violence was his own love-hate relationship with his father. That was the motivation for the crime. In this respect, Smith was very much like Richard Speck, who murdered the eight nurses in Chicago. I haven't interviewed Speck, but I've studied his case and, once again, you have a man full of random, violent hatred that is psychologically triggered by subliminal compulsions. I believe

Speck when he says that he didn't intend to kill the eight nurses; what happened was that he identified the last of the girls he tied up, the girl he raped, with his own wife, whom he detested. In Perry's case, it was a father surrogate whom he killed: in Speck's, a wife surrogate. And for Speck, as for Smith, it was only the *first* murder that counted; once he killed the girl he identified with his wife, the other murders were inevitable. I'm always surprised to read reviews of *In Cold Blood* that lament, "But Mr. Capote didn't tell us *why.*" Well, short of getting a baseball bat and clubbing you over the head with it, I don't see how I could have made the point any more clearly.

Playboy: Throughout *In Cold Blood*, you starkly and systematically emphasize the contrast between the wholesome, prototypically rural-American Clutter family and the brutal, disinvolved and desensitized drifters, Hickock and Smith. Some critics have wondered which you intended to imply more truly represents the *real* America of the Sixties—the Clutter family or their murderers.

Capote: This contrast does exist, and even though I didn't start out on the book with any preconceived theme—at first I didn't know anything about the Clutter family, much less their killers—this gulf between victim and murderer became so intriguing that it was one of the major factors behind my decision to invest years of time and effort in the book. The contrast was so exaggerated that it became symbolic in a kind of textbook fashion. Here you have the Clutter family on one hand—such a perfect prototype of the good, solid, landed American gentry, as you point out—and on the other hand you have Hickock and Smith, particularly Smith, representing the dangerous psychotic element, empty of compassion or conscience. And these two extremes mated in the act of murder. The Clutter family and Hickock and Smith do represent the opposite poles in American society; if you ask me who best represents the *real* America, I have to say a very modified and much more soiled and complicated version of the Clutter family. But Perry Smith—and I single him out because he had a deeply psychotic criminal mind, whereas Hickock was just a smart-aleck, small-time crook—does represent a very real side of American life; he is typical of the conscienceless yet perversely sensitive violence that runs through such phenomena as the motorcycle gangs and the drifting herds of brutalized children wandering across the country. Of course, in Perry's case—and in the case of the thousands like him—the arbitrary act of violence springs from the poverty of his life, its deep insecurity and emptiness. That doesn't excuse what he did, of course, but it does help explain it. In a way, all this had to happen; there was a quality of inevitability about it. Given what Perry was, and what the Clutters represented, the only possible outcome of their convergence was death.

Playboy: In addition to the type of depersonalized violence represented by Smith and Hickock, other forms of *anomie* permeate American society. In Forest Hills, New York, on March 26, 1964, Kitty Genovese was murdered while 38 witnesses stood by and did nothing to help for the half hour it took her assailant to kill her. Instances of this sort in our major cities have become as common as cases in which spectators gleefully shout "Jump!" to potential suicides on window ledges. What do you think accounts for this widespread apathy to the sufferings of others?

Capote: The two instances you cite are basically quite different. The Kitty Genovese case is a completely *urban* phenomenon; I don't think anything like it could ever happen anywhere in rural America. But in our big cities, people are afraid to become involved, because the city *itself* is frightening. The city dweller lives in his isolated unit, his apartment or furnished room, with bolts on the door; and his reaction to another person in trouble is, "I can't do anything, because I really don't know what's out there. I can't get involved." It's not surprising that they have no sense of community responsibility; they don't even know who their *neighbors* are. So why risk their own lives for a stranger? While nothing can excuse the people who watched Kitty Genovese murdered and didn't even call the police, it *is* understandable, in the context of the current urban brutality, why people are afraid to intervene in acts of violence. It's lamentable, but in some ways you can hardly blame them. If you understand the psychology involved, you can see why this kind of thing could never happen in a small town, where people have roots, where they are not afraid of their environment, where they know their neighbors and feel part of a recognized society. But the cities are anonymous, as Kitty Genovese discovered. The second point, about the spectators who shout "Jump!" to some poor suicide crouched on a window ledge, is just the opposite of the passivity and fear of involvement displayed in the Genovese case: This is the classic lynch-mob mentality. There is a sadistic component of the human mind that is seldom manifested in the individual but that is somehow liberated in the collective; you can have a crowd watching anything from a fire to a fist fight and it's amazing how quickly it can be sparked into a mob. When I was a child in Alabama, lynchings occasionally happened; and I've known hundreds of people perfectly capable of attending a lynching. It's amazing how easily an individual can become depersonalized and swept up into the lynch-mob mentality; people will tell you how they hate violence and how they could never imagine themselves involved in a lynching and then you'll see news photographs of a lynch mob and there they are, their faces glazed with joy and sadism. If the Kitty Genovese case is an urban phenomenon, the lynch-mob mentality is, I fear, a human phenomenon.

Playboy: Ten thousand murders are committed in the U.S. each year—in New York City alone, about four times as many as in the whole of Great Britain. Our crime rate is one of the highest in the world and increases yearly. Four U.S. Presidents have been assassinated while in office and four others have survived assassination attempts. Mass murders are becoming commonplace; extremist paramilitary groups arm to fight off their enemies; and race riots wrack more and more cities. Social critic Max Lerner contends that we are living in a "climate of violence—a climate of frustration, of emotional deprivation, of hate." He feels there is something peculiarly American about this high incidence of violence, perhaps rooted in our frontier psychology, which dictated that disputes be settled by guns. Do you agree?

Capote: I'm constantly reading in the popular psychological press about this residue of frontier mentality accounting for the violence in our society, but I just don't agree. After all, for centuries, assassination has been almost a way of life, or death, in the Orient and the Arab world; and Russia has a pretty neat record of assassination, too. I just don't subscribe to the whole idea that America is more violent than other countries. What makes it *appear* that way statistically is that when you take America and put her next to France or Sweden or Liechtenstein, we have more of everything, from assassination to psoriasis. But the United States is an enormous part of a whole continent and comparisons like this are meaningless unless you first lump all the nations of Europe into one country and for good measure throw in a couple of Arab states; then you'd have a fair basis for statistical comparison, and I'm sure you would find the incidences of violence are quite similar.

Playboy: Even if America is no worse than other countries in this respect, you have frequently expressed alarm over the rising tide of violent crime in our society. In November 1966, you appeared before a Senate Judiciary subcommittee and attacked recent Supreme Court rulings strengthening the rights of suspects in criminal cases, charging that if those rulings had been in effect at the time of Hickock and Smith's arrest, both men would have gone free to kill again. Why are you so opposed to these rulings?

Capote: I'm not opposed to all the Court's rulings on the civil liberties of suspects in criminal cases. The Court has delivered two major decisions, *Miranda* and *Escobedo*. The *Escobedo* ruling states that if a suspect requests a lawyer, he must be supplied one, whatever his financial status. I have no objection at all to that decision. But the *Miranda* decision, which stipulates that a suspect must be advised that he has the right to remain silent and the right to the presence of an attorney before any questioning, is absurd and extremely detrimental to effective law enforcement. Just the other day, *reductio ad absurdum*, a nine-year-old boy was picked up for shoplifting in Missouri and he told the arresting officers that he wouldn't go to the police station and wouldn't answer any questions: "I know my rights! You get a lawyer here this minute!" That's a true story, believe it or not; and aside from its humorous aspects, it holds a sinister message: From now on, no prisoner is going to confess to any crime with a lawyer in the room, because no lawyer worth his salt will *allow* a prisoner to confess, even if he wants to. As a result, the number of convictions law-enforcement agencies will obtain is going to be considerably reduced; you don't have eyewitnesses at every crime, and frequently a confession is the only way a criminal's guilt will stand up in court. But as a result of the *Miranda* ruling, the police are hamstrung. I don't think this is fair either to the police or to the public at large.

Playboy: Even if the *Miranda* decision does restrict police power to some extent, isn't it true that for years, suspects in criminal cases have been coerced into signing confessions by police strong-arm techniques? And isn't it more important to protect the civil liberties of the defendant than to ensure a 100-percent conviction rate?

Capote: I'm well acquainted with this argument, but I think it applies to only an infinitesimal percentage of criminal cases. Of course, there are occasionally bad situations where the police use third-degree tactics, but I think that is being corrected by the police forces themselves, which are growing more enlightened every day. But I would still prefer the occasional situation where police exceed their authority to the situation we have today as a result of the *Miranda* ruling. The Supreme Court has handcuffed the police and thus bears a share of responsibility for the vast increase of crime in our society.

Playboy: You don't agree, then, with the adage that it's better for a dozen guilty men to go free than for one innocent man to be unjustly convicted?

Capote: It's a charming sentiment, but more apropos in the halcyon days of yore, when our cities had not yet been turned into jungles and a citizen could still stroll the streets in safety. I'm afraid that today, for the very self-protection of our society, it's better that one innocent man be *punished* than that a dozen guilty men go free. It's unfortunate, but that's the harsh reality we face.

Playboy: You have consistently defended the police against their critics, but you've never addressed yourself to the problem of police brutality—and corruption—across the country. Why?

Capote: I know it's become fashionable to depict the police as sadistic Cossacks riding down innocent citizens, but I've become well enough acquainted with law-enforcement agencies across the country to know that's just not the case. Of course, a certain small percentage of policemen are irresponsible, just as a certain percentage of lawyers and doctors and insurance salesmen are irresponsible, but that doesn't justify the current unjust barrage of propaganda against a tribe of men who are hard-working, underpaid and daily risking their lives to protect *us*. I'm sure there are isolated instances of police brutality, but the rising crime rate and urban violence constitute a far, far more pressing problem.

Playboy: Are you opposed to civilian review boards to supervise the police?

Capote: Not on principle, but I do think that any such board is unworkable in practice and really little more than a piece of propaganda.

Playboy: Crimes of sexual violence have been rising in recent years. Do you feel, as some proponents of censorship contend, that there is a discernible relationship between the reading of pornographic material and the commission of sex offenses?

Capote: Pornography doesn't drive a man out into the streets to rape; if anything, it has the opposite effect. After all, the major purpose of pornography is to activate masturbation; thus, it serves to release sexual tensions, not to exacerbate them. The people who commit rape or other sexual assaults are suffering from a pathological condition, a kind of claustrophobic compulsion to burst out of their sexual frustrations by the commission of a violent act. They have been stimulated by interior drives that can find an outlet only in violence, and a salacious book would have as much effect on their behavior as a copy of *The Christian Science Monitor.* Pornography literally has no meaning for them; if it did, they would buy it and stay in their rooms, peacefully masturbating. But for those people who are less disturbed but still have sexual problems, pornography can be a quite healthy form of release and serve as a tranquilizer for the libido.

Playboy: Do you believe it is possible to establish any objective legal guidelines for censorship?

Capote: Of course not, for the very simple reason that nobody can even define what pornography is. It's all in the eye of the beholder, and what seems pornographic to one person may appear as benign as December snow to somebody else. I'm sure that there are people who consider the *Song of Songs* in the Bible pornographic. So if it's impossible to even establish a valid definition of something how can you legislate against it? But even if you could define it, I'd be against censorship; I've never been able to understand the whole obsession with the "evils" of pornography. What possible harm can pornography do? I know some people argue that it falls into the hands of young people and corrupts them, but that's nonsense; any child who reaches the age of 14 is already knowledgeable sexually, even if the only thing he's ever read is *Rebecca of Sunnybrook Farm.*

Playboy: Though the Supreme Court has considerably liberalized censorship laws in recent years, the Court departed from its tolerant stance in 1966 and upheld the obscenity conviction of publisher Ralph Ginzburg on the grounds that his advertising material—not the contents of his publications—was "titilating." What do you think of the *Ginzburg* ruling?

Capote: The only obscene thing about it was the Court's own decision. But then, nothing this particular Supreme Court does surprises me. Not that I want anybody impeached—except, perhaps, Justice Douglas.

Playboy: Why Douglas?

Capote: I decline to answer, on the grounds that I prefer to be enigmatic.

Playboy: Censorship, of course, is not the only area in which our sexual mores have evolved. In recent years, wife-swapping clubs and correspondence societies catering to offbeat erotic tastes have burgeoned across the country, and some consider this an unhealthy social phenomenon. Do you?

Capote: It's always been going on beneath the surface, and now, with the loosening of censorship regulations, it just appears more obvious. What's new about orgies? The only original development is that people have now begun to select their sexual partners in the most convenient way—by putting an ad in the paper.

Playboy: Those who place such ads sometimes get an unexpected response—from the U.S. Post Office. In recent years, the postal authorities have adopted a policy of opening first-class mail in search of pornography and turning over the offenders for prosecution. How do you feel about this policy?

Capote: It's disgraceful. The Post Office's sole function, after all, is to ensure the delivery of mail—not to interfere with its contents. But they have arrogated this right to themselves and, as a result, have caused intense personal suffering for countless people. To give a case in point, a very good friend of mine was the late Professor Newton Arvin of Smith College, who was one of the foremost distinguished American literary critics of the century and has been cited as such by Edmund Wilson, Lionel Trilling and many others. One of Professor Arvin's hobbies was the collecting of pornography, which he frequently ordered through the mail—a perfectly harmless pursuit, as far as I'm concerned. But the defenders of public morality who run the Northampton, Massachusetts, Post Office began opening his first-class mail—in violation of the law—and then resealing it and sending it on to him. Finally, after a few months of this surveillance, they went to his home with a search warrant, turned the premises upside down, impounded Professor Arvin's collection of pornography, and arrested him. Though he could have been sent to jail for several years for the "crime" of possessing pornography, he pleaded guilty and was allowed to go free on probation. But the episode ruined his life and his career; Smith College tried to be decent, but they had to release him because of the publicity surrounding his arrest, and no other university would give him a position. So this charming, brilliant, civilized individual, one of America's four or five finest critics, died in shadow. And I'm afraid this kind of thing is going on every day. Only two things can correct it: the passage of legislation allowing a person to possess pornography if he so desires and the institution of measures preventing the Post Office from snooping into the mail of private citizens.

Playboy: As you know, the Post Office isn't alone in invading the citizen's privacy. Vance Packard and other social critics, joined recently by Senator Edward Long, have warned that similar privacy invasions—by electronic eavesdropping, Internal Revenue Service investigations, Government "security" checks, intensive psychometric testing for job placement, etc.—are subtly ushering us into the age of Big Brother. Do you agree?

Capote: I couldn't agree more. I think this systematic invasion of privacy is one of the most dangerous developments of the past 15 years, and I wish the public would become more exercised about it. There's no reason why we should meekly submit to this kind of creeping totalitarianism. But as it stands right now, Big Brother is having a field day.

Playboy: The Post Office's attempt to sanitize the mail, as well as the Ginzburg decision, appear to constitute the rearguard stand of traditionalism in its campaign against the so-called new morality, midwifed by the pill and the re-examination of sexual mores that began with the Kinsey Report. Do you consider this new morality a positive development?

Capote: I certainly do. Anything that frees people of fear and makes them less inhibited is a damn good thing. Of course, I've read recently about various researchers who have polled college students across the country and discovered that today's girls aren't really any more lenient than girls 30 years ago, but I just don't believe it. There is a new morality; it was bound to happen, and I'm delighted it did.

Playboy: One of the early fictional precursors of this trend was your own Holly Golightly, the heroine of *Breakfast at Tiffany's*. Would you elaborate on your comment that Holly was the prototype of today's liberated female and representative of "a whole breed of girls who live off men but are not prostitutes. They're our version of the geisha girl."?

Capote: Holly Golightly was not precisely a callgirl. She had no job, but accompanied expense-account men to the best restaurants and night clubs, with the understanding that her escort was obligated to give her some sort of gift, perhaps jewelry or a check. Holly was always running to the girl's room and asking her date, "May I have a little powder-room change?" And the man would give her $50. Usually, her escort was a married man from out of town who was lonely, and she would flatter him and make a good impression on his associates, but there was no emotional involvement on either side; the girl expected nothing but a present and the man nothing but some good company and ego bolstering—although if she felt like it, she might take her escort home for the night. So these girls are the authentic American geishas, and they're much more prevalent now than in 1943 or 1944, which was Holly's era. Every year, New York is flooded with these girls; and two or three, usually models, always become prominent and get their names in the gossip columns and are seen in all the prominent places with all the Beautiful People. And then they fade away and marry some accountant or dentist, and a new crop of girls arrives from Michigan or South Carolina and the process starts all over again. The main reason I wrote about Holly, outside of the fact that I liked her so much, was that she was such a symbol of all these girls who come to New York and spin in the sun for a moment like May flies and then disappear. I wanted to rescue one girl from that anonymity and preserve her for posterity.

Playboy: Shortly after publication of *Breakfast at Tiffany's*, a writer named Bonnie Golightly sued you for $800,000, on the grounds that she was the real-life inspiration for your fictional heroine. At least four other New York girls about town countered with the claim that *they* were the prototype of Holly. Was the characterization of Holly based on a real person?

Capote: Yes, but not on any of the people you refer to. The real Holly Golightly was a girl exactly like the girl in *Breakfast at Tiffany's*, with the single exception that in the book she comes from Texas, whereas the real Holly was a German refugee who arrived in New York at the beginning of the War, when she was 17 years old. Very few people were aware of this, however, because she spoke English without any trace of an accent. She had an apartment in the brownstone where I lived and we became great friends. Everything I wrote about her is literally true—not about her friendship with a gangster called Sally Tomato and all that, but everything about her personality and her approach to life, even the most apparently preposterous parts of the book. For instance, do you remember, in the beginning, where a man comes into a bar with photographs of an African wood carving of a girl's head he had found in the jungle and the girl could only be Holly? Well, my real-life Holly did disappear into Portuguese Africa and was never heard from again. But after the War, a man named John La Touche, a well-known song lyricist and writer, traveled to the Belgian Congo to make a documentary film: and in a jungle village he discovered this wooden head carving of Holly. It's all the evidence of her existence that remains.

Playboy: Holly Golightly alludes to her onetime Lesbian roommate and obliquely expresses a sexual interest in other women. Was Holly a Lesbian?

Capote: Let's leave Holly out of it. It's a well-known fact that *most* prostitutes are Lesbians—at least 80 percent of them, in any case. And so are a great many of the models and showgirls in New York; just off the top of my head, I can think of three top professional models who are Lesbians. Of course, there's a Lesbian component in every woman, but what intrigues me is the heterosexual male's fascination with Lesbians. I find it extraordinary that so many men I know consider Lesbian women exciting and attractive; among their most treasured erotic dreams is the idea of going to bed with two Lesbians. These men seem to find the role of voyeur in that kind of *ménage à trois* irresistible. It's a curious phenomenon. I don't know precisely what accounts for it, but it's certainly one of the most widespread male erotic fantasies I've encountered.

Playboy: Isn't the livelihood of Manhattan's Holly Golightlys being threatened by the increasing influx of "amateur" bachelor girls who come to New York in search of fun and games as well as careers and husbands?

Capote: Oh, yes. All these bars along Second and Third avenues, with names like The Little Jolly Brown Jug, are packed with airline stewardesses and miniskirted secretaries waiting to be picked up by some guy. And when *they* ask for change for the powder room, they only expect a quarter.

Playboy: Do you think prostitution should be legalized?

Capote: Why not? It goes on all the time anyway, and the laws we have on the books certainly do nothing to restrict it. There are more prostitutes in New York today than there have ever been; you can hardly walk down Broadway without being propositioned. If it were legalized, there would be hygienic centers where the girls could be inspected to check the spread of venereal disease, and perhaps prostitutes could be localized in certain designated areas of the city where they could be supervised by the authorities. What's more, the Government would have an additional source of tax revenue. But as it stands today, it's like Prohibition; people will go on drinking bad whiskey, so why not remove the restrictions and let them drink *good* whiskey? It's all so hypocritical. The last stand of puritanism is in our lawbooks; a considerable percentage of the population has freed itself of the old taboos, but laws always lag behind reality. So let's change the laws.

Playboy: Your position on such questions as capital punishment, censorship and prostitution would seem to fall under the traditional liberal classification; but on other issues, such as the Supreme Court rulings on the rights of suspects in criminal cases, you adopt an essentially conservative stance. Where would you place yourself on the political spectrum—right, left or center?

Capote: Nowhere. I have never considered myself right, left or center. On some issues, such as law enforcement, I do sound like a Birchite; and on others, more like Fidel Castro after two quarts of Appleton's rum. I never label myself; I decide how I feel about a specific political issue on its own merits, without evaluating everything from a rigid ideological position. As a result, my opinions don't always add up to a harmonious whole, but I've never known anybody altogether consistent who wasn't either a psychopath or a cretin—or both. To take a case in point, I have never been able to understand a group like the John Birch Society. I know three or four admitted Birchites and have discussed politics with them, and I find their position totally unrealistic; anybody who is so rigidly consistent about such a complex question as communism, say, is just a fanatic. I don't believe there can be any genuinely intelligent approach to a given issue unless one has a great mental flexibility, and the trouble with all these far-right and far-left mentalities is that they can encompass only one side of an argument and are congenitally incapable of holding two opinions in their heads at the same time. Of course, the middle-of-the-roader isn't always correct, either, because sometimes an extreme left- or right-wing opinion happens to be correct; you have to pick and choose. Anybody who is consistently middle-of-the-road is just another type of extremist; you can't always straddle the fence.

Playboy: Do you believe that a writer should be *l'homme engagé*, as Sartre put it, deeply committed to the social and political issues of his time? Or should he write only about what he subjectively perceives and not become involved in political controversy?

Capote: I prefer not to become involved in politics. But there are certain writer-intellectuals—words that don't necessarily cohabit—whose sole distinction is their treatment of political and sociological subjects. Usually, these are men who can brilliantly perceive abstractions—and usually they are *not* artists. The essay is their natural medium, not poetry or narrative prose. Camus did manage to combine artistry with the *homme engagé* concept, with some success; also Malraux. But not Sartre. He's an interesting philosophical theoretician, but he is definitely *not* an artist. His novels are on a par with those of Simone de Beauvoir; together they constitute the dullest of intellectual vaudeville teams.

Playboy: One of your few ventures into politics occurred in 1961, when you became a sponsor of the Fair Play for Cuba Committee and signed a full-page advertisement in *The New York Times* exhorting Washington to adopt a more conciliatory attitude toward the Castro regime. Do you regret your association with the Fair Play for Cuba Committee?

Capote: Yes, I do. I'm sorry I signed that advertisement. But at the time, I honestly thought Castro was an admirable young insurgent who was being unjustly abused in the American press. So when I was asked to sign this Fair Play for Cuba advertisement, I agreed, although only on the condition that the committee assure me they were paying for the space themselves, without any assistance from the Castro government. They swore they were just a legitimate organization with no ties to Havana, so I lent them my name. But some time afterward, I discovered that the advertisement *had* been paid for by the Cuban government; the money was passed in cash to the Fair Play organizers by Raulito Roa, the son of Cuba's foreign minister. Naturally, I felt that the officers of the committee had been deceitful and unscrupulous, and I regret ever getting involved with them.

Playboy: Apart from the duplicity of the advertisement's sponsors, do you now also disagree with the opinions expressed in the ad? Or do you still feel that the hostile American attitude toward Castro forced him into the arms of Russia?

Capote: I suppose that may be true to some extent, but I now believe that Castro was a Communist from the very beginning and was lying when he styled himself a democratic agrarian reformer. I'm just sorry I believed him; I even believed Che Guevara's disavowals. There's little doubt that sooner or later, whatever Washington's attitude, Castro would have declared his government Communist and at that point would have no alternative but to turn to Russia and the Communist bloc for support. But it is possible that if both sides had shown more forbearance, we might never have gotten trapped into such a bitterly hostile relationship. After all, there are nationalistic variants of communism, and it's much better to coexist with a country like Yugoslavia than live in a state of antagonism, as we do today with Cuba.

Playboy: Senator Fulbright contends that the Cold War has frozen us into an unrealistically rigid attitude toward world communism and has conditioned the public to view every Communist state as our mortal enemy, thus inhibiting the flexibility of our foreign policy and increasing the likelihood of war. Do you feel that's true?

Capote: Yes, but I think that in recent years the United States Government has improved relations with Russia considerably and now *does* have a much more flexible attitude toward the Communist states. We are now peacefully coexisting with Russia to a degree that would have seemed impossible to most people ten years ago. And I think the central reason is China; both Washington and Moscow understand the threat posed by China, Russia even more than the United States. If we have mended our fences, it's primarily because both countries fear China more than each other. That's the main thing that keeps the thaw going.

Playboy: Critics of American involvement in the war in Vietnam fear it will escalate into a confrontation with China that could precipitate World War Three. For this and other reasons, they urge an immediate cessation of hostilities and withdrawal of U.S. troops, unilaterally, if necessary. Do you agree?

Capote: I can't give you a pat dove-hawk answer, because my preoccupations with the war are primarily emotional, not political. I think both sides, Hanoi and Washington, are terribly, tragically wrong. And the mistakes of statesmen are always written in young men's blood.

Playboy: Many artists and writers, including Robert Lowell and Arthur Miller, have boycotted White House cultural events to express their abhorrence of the war. Do you believe an artist should demonstrate his opposition to Government policy in such a matter?

Capote: No. The isuance of an invitation is a private matter and its acceptance or rejection should also be private. Robert Lowell is a friend of mine and I have the greatest respect for him as a man and as an artist, but I think he was mistaken to publicly announce what by any standard of good manners should have been a privately conveyed regret. This has nothing to do with dissent, mind you, just good manners. But let me add that if Lowell really felt deeply that this was the best way to dramatize his opposition to the war, then that is his right, his freedom, his manhood—and to hell with etiquette. I just would have handled it differently.

Playboy: Opponents of the Vietnam conflict, from Bertrand Russell to Senator Eugene McCarthy, are united in their condemnation of Lyndon Johnson and his conduct of the war. Do you share their estimation of the President?

Capote: I think the attitude of the press and the intelligentsia toward him is unfair. He's the most maligned man since Lincoln. The

President is confronting and dealing with situations on the basis of information to which the rest of us have no access; it's always easy to condemn a course of action when you're unaware of the hard facts on which it's based. Of course, it can be argued that our very lack of inside information is in itself an indictment of this man's Administration, but that is to totally ignore the tactics of our political opponents. President Johnson is a pragmatist who handles our interests without subtlety—but with a realism that requires a certain emotional control that I respect.

Playboy: President Johnson's critics contend that he has deliberately misled the public, particularly in regard to the war in Vietnam, and has thus created a serious credibility gap. Do you agree?

Capote: It's true that the Administration has made promises about Vietnam that haven't been fulfilled, but that doesn't mean there's any conscious deceit involved. For example, McNamara predicted that U.S. troops would be out of Vietnam by the end of 1965; but did it ever occur to you that at the time he made the statement he really thought those troops *would* be leaving? Just because things don't happen doesn't necessarily mean they weren't said in good faith the first time around; you can promise something and have every reason to believe it's true when you say it and place all your faith in it and then find that new developments change the whole situation and dictate a new course of action. President Johnson may be mistaken in some of his policies, but I don't believe he has been deliberately lying.

Playboy: To cite a specific instance, *Newsweek's* White House correspondent Charles Roberts and former Assistant Secretary of State for Far Eastern Affairs Roger Hillsman have both reported that Johnson made the decision to escalate the war and bomb North Vietnam as early as December 1963 but withheld this information from the public until after the election so that he could counter Goldwater's hawkish campaign appeals with a promise to limit the war "and not go north." Isn't this an example of the so-called credibility gap?

Capote: If it's true, yes.

Playboy: Recent Presidential preference polls have shown both New York Governor Nelson Rockefeller and California Governor

Ronald Reagan running close to President Johnson. What do you think of the two men as possible candidates?

Capote: Well, Rockefeller is definitely back in contention for the 1968 Republican Presidential nomination. And I hope he gets it, too. He certainly deserves it. Without a doubt, he's the ablest man the Republicans could offer. As for Ronald Reagan, I met him recently for the first time and he's really a disarming fellow, not just the California aberration all the *cognoscenti* seem to think. He's a modest man with a genuine sense of self-deprecating humor and he talks easily, with a certain relaxed alertness, on quite a wide range of subjects. While he may not be my own choice politically, I can certainly understand why he appeals to the California voter. Don't underestimate him.

Playboy: President Johnson's main rival within the Democratic Party is Senator Robert F. Kennedy, a personal friend of yours. How would you answer the charges of such political commentators as Victor Lasky and Ralph de Toledano that Senator Kennedy is ruthless and power hungry?

Capote: Have you ever met a politician who wasn't? Actually, I think this particular Senator is quite considerate of other people's feelings and, on certain occasions, is even more loyal to those feelings than to the pursuit of his own ambition.

Playboy: Do you believe Kennedy intends to run for the Presidency in either 1968 or 1972?

Capote: 1972. But who really knows?

Playboy: Do you think he'd make a good President?

Capote: If Bob Kennedy were elected President, it would be rather like a career diplomat who starts out in the Foreign Service as a clerk and is finally appointed an ambassador; it's a post he's been trained for all his life, just as Bob Kennedy has been trained for the Presidency. Of course, that doesn't necessarily mean he'll ever get it, but he is certainly fully equipped for the job.

Playboy: R.F.K.'s critics warn that his past actions—including his work for Joe McCarthy and his hounding of Jimmy Hoffa—would make him a dangerously authoritarian President likely to run roughshod over the civil liberties of his opponents. Do you feel that this is a valid apprehension?

Capote: No, because Bob Kennedy would certainly be no worse in this respect than any of the other likely contenders for the

Presidency. If he were to become President, I think his sense of responsibility would rise to the altitude of his position. That's what happens to most people who are elected to high office; they become acutely aware of their own power and the responsibilities it entails and they learn how to gauge and apply it. I don't think Bob Kennedy is a ruthless or malicious person at all. He is human and, when he gets riled, he wants to go after his enemies; who doesn't?

Playboy: One former associate of Kennedy's who is unlikely to agree with your evaluation of him is William Manchester. What did you think of his book *The Death of a President?*

Capote: This has nothing to do with my friendship for the Kennedys, but the book is a literary and historic disaster.

Playboy: Apart from the literary merits of Manchester's book, do you feel that Robert Kennedy behaved properly throughout the affair?

Capote: I certainly do. What else could he have done? The Kennedy family commissioned the book; they requested certain conditions and Manchester signed a statement promising to respect those conditions—and then turned around and broke the agreement. Manchester could never have done the book without the assistance of the Kennedys and he was honor bound to abide by his word and respect their feelings. Of course, I don't think Bob Kennedy would ever have gotten involved in the whole mess except for Mrs. Kennedy; he was, in effect, coming to her defense. But I think that he behaved as a good brother-in-law and as a man standing up for his own rights. I have never been able to understand the attitude of the press toward the controversy. Manchester made an agreement and then didn't live up to it. It's as simple as that.

Playboy: Even if Manchester did fail to honor his agreement, do you think the Kennedys had any right to exact such conditions? Weren't they, in effect, demanding censorship of history?

Capote: No, they weren't. Bob Kennedy had every right to insist on certain conditions, since the Kennedy family was supplying the relevant material to Manchester, speaking freely to him and ensuring that others spoke freely to him. The Kennedys *gave* the book to him, in return for his word that he would grant them a measure of editorial control. Manchester had the right to accept or reject those conditions at the outset; but he had *no* right, ethically or legally, to accept them when it was convenient and then reject them after he had gotten all he needed from the Kennedys. This all boils down to a simple question of contract. If a publisher negotiates a contract with me, he has every right to say, "Now, Truman, I want 60 percent of this material in the book and 40 percent of that." If I sign such a contract, I have to fulfill my obligations. If I don't fulfill them and my publisher insists that I stick to the terms of our contract, I certainly would have no right to holler that my muse was being violated.

Playboy: But this book was an examination of the circumstances surrounding the assassination of the President of the United States—and the facts of that tragedy belong to the public. Some feel that Manchester had a higher obligation to the truth than to his agreement with the Kennedy family. Do you disagree?

Capote: Manchester had a higher obligation, all right—to the Book-of-the-Month Club, *Look* magazine and his accountants. But the most important point here is that the Kennedys were never thinking in such terms about Manchester's book; they didn't envision him doing a definitive, deathless study of the Kennedy assassination that would be pored over by scholars 300 years from now. They just didn't consider it a historical project; that task they left to Arthur Schlesinger, a highly competent historian who is compiling a comprehensive examination of the assassination for the Kennedy Library, to be released some years from now. The Kennedys asked Manchester to do a popular book on the subject because a slew of third-rate journalists had expressed their intentions to do the literary equivalent of those ghoulish J.F.K. memorabilia gimcracks that blossomed on the market after the assassination. To head off an onslaught of such commercial trash, the Kennedys contacted Manchester and provided him with information that was denied all other journalists. Bob Kennedy and Jacqueline Kennedy hoped that by cooperating with Manchester, they would prevent a lot of people from making money out of their brother and husband's death. Instead, they lost their privacy and made him rich.

Playboy: Manchester generally confirmed the conclusions of the Warren Report, but its findings have been under heavy fire recently from best-selling author Mark Lane and New Orleans District Attorney Jim Garrison, among others. What's your opinion of the Warren Report and the current controversy raging over it?

Capote: The Warren Report is correct. Oswald, acting alone, killed the President. And that's it.

Playboy: Nevertheless, a whole body of literature has sprung up challenging the Warren Commission's conclusions on the assassination. In addition to Lane, such authors as Edward Epstein, Sylvia Meagher, Leo Sauvage, Josiah Thompson and Harold Weisberg have examined in depth the Commission's own evidence and discovered many contradictions and discrepancies. Don't you think these critics have scored some valid points against the Warren Commission?

Capote: Of course they've scored some points. Obviously, there are many mistakes in the Warren Report, generally minor technical errors and omissions. The Report isn't Holy Writ, after all. But I've read three or four of the most prominent books critical of the Commission, and I've also read the Warren Report, and by every rule of logic and sanity I believe the Report is correct in all its essentials. I'm unable to understand why any intelligent and objective person cannot clearly see the basic correctness of the Warren Reports. But I *do* understand very well all this nit-picking and speculation that's going on, because most of it is monetary; a bunch of vultures has discovered that pecking at the carrion of a dead President is an easy way to make a living.

Playboy: If the authors of books critical of the Warren Commission are just "nit-picking," what about Garrison's claim to have discovered a well-organized assassination plot? Do you exclude the possibility that he's on to something?

Capote: Mr. Garrison is on to something, all right—a good press agent. As far as I'm concerned, Garrison is a man on the make politically who's seized hold of this alleged conspiracy as a method of advancing his career. But I think he bit off more than he can chew and is now forced to ride the thing to the dirty end. I'll bet Garrison is sorry he ever started his so-called investigation.

Playboy: Garrison answers the charge that he is politically motivated by arguing that an ambitious man would never crawl out on such a limb unless he had the facts to back him up. If Garrison doesn't have a case, why would he have started something that could only discredit him and scuttle his career?

Capote: Well, if he really does have some cards up his sleeve, why doesn't he show them to us? I'm convinced his whole "case" is a lot of hot air. If Garrison really does have anything at all to back up his charges, it will be a great surprise to me. I think he's a faker.

Playboy: Garrison contends that it's not his job to show his cards in public but to prove his case in a court of law. By not allowing his charges to stand or fall in court, aren't you prejudging the case?

Capote: Of course I'm prejudging the case, for the simple reason that I don't believe he *has* any case. The man has behaved with outrageous irresponsibility, caused great emotional damage to a number of innocent people and, in general, conducted himself in a manner that makes Huey Long look like Orphan Annie. I'm not going to suspend my critical faculties just because the jury hasn't rendered a verdict. And if the jury *did* find Shaw guilty, I would still refuse to believe Garrison has a case. I was born in New Orleans and I know how the courts operate down there. I have about as much faith in New Orleans jurisprudence as I would in a moral-uplift campaign conducted by the local Mafia.

Playboy: Has Robert Kennedy or any other member of the Kennedy family ever expressed to you their feelings about the assassination and the controversy over the Warren Report?

Capote: They never discuss anything to do with the assassination. The feeling of Senator Kennedy and Jacqueline Kennedy is that their brother and husband was murdered and nothing is ever going to change that. The one central fact that matters is that he's gone. Why it happened, how it happened and who did it doesn't concern them.

Playboy: Then Robert Kennedy really knows no more about the assassination and the controversy surrounding it than the average man on the street?

Capote: He doesn't pretend to.

Playboy: The only figure on the right with political sex appeal comparable with that of Bobby Kennedy is William Buckley, who is reported to be considering a crack at the Republican nomination for the New York Senate seat currently held by Jacob Javits. How would you evaluate the "new conservatism" articulated by Buckley and his *National Review*?

Capote: I prefer Buckley to his politics. I see *National Review* only occasionally, but I would say that the four best-edited commercial magazines extant are (1) *The New Yorker*, (2) *Time*, (3) *Vogue* and (4) *National Review*, in that order.

Playboy: Thank you.

Capote: This has nothing to do with the content; it's simply that each has an identifiable editorial approach that is like a signature. Buckley has the hardest row to hoe, but he is one smooth article—clever, logical, witty, almost excessively articulate, with a vocabulary as baroque as an 18th Century Austrian palace. If Buckley were a political candidate, he wouldn't get my vote, but he's certainly one of the live ones—and Forest Lawn has a real franchise on 90 percent of the rest.

Playboy: Although both Buckley and Kennedy number many young political activists among their most ardent admirers, a growing percentage of the so-called under-25 generation that will soon dominate the country's population is refusing to buy its traditional values. Do you share their disenchantment?

Capote: No, but I like today's younger generation. I think they have great verve and creativity and I particularly like their music, as exemplified by such groups as The Doors and the Jefferson Airplane. It's extraordinary and far better than most of the so-called serious music being produced either here or in Europe. Just the other day, I was passing one of those little stores where you buy pop posters and I saw this poster of me together with all the Beatles and a lot of other youngsters. I was delighted; I've never been more flattered.

Playboy: What do you think of Timothy Leary and the psychedelic subculture that has sprung up across the country?

Capote: I think Dr. Leary is a thoroughly delightful, harmless do-gooder—a true innocent. His heart is in the right place. But I don't think his theory of understanding oneself and expanding consciousness through psychedelic drugs is at all valid. Out of my boundless curiosity, I've experimented with LSD myself once or twice, but I haven't derived much benefit from it. My own imagination is psychedelic enough.

Playboy: Do you agree with Dr. Leary's contention that the American middle class is hag-ridden by ethical and spiritual hang-ups stemming from the pursuit of mediocrity?

Capote: Well, of course, they're hag-ridden, but not by the *pursuit* of mediocrity; they *are* mediocre. You don't pursue the essence of your being.

Playboy: Would you share the views of those social critics who argue that the mediocrity and materialism of the middle class account for the rising tide of drug-taking juvenile delinquency and hippie dropouts?

Capote: What society *isn't* totally concerned with materialism? It's not a question of economic systems, either, because Russia is the most materialistic country in the world; everybody, from the Politburo member on down to the street cleaner, is obsessed with consumer commodities and acquisitions. And what else is materialism? Does all this account for the younger generation's rejection of its parents' values? Well, it's a truism that youth revolts against the older generation in one form or another, but a youngster doesn't become a juvenile delinquent just because his parents are bourgeois. The reasons are more intimate. And many things account for the growing use of drugs. In my youth, drugs were just in the offing, a harbinger of the future, and now they're beginning to come into their own. It's inevitable that drugs will play a significant role in life. Alcohol is very *démodé*. Regarding middle-class responsibility for hippie dropouts, my one real criticism of the hippies is that they themselves are so middle-class in their values and so invincibly conformist; they conform about different things, but their insistence on adherence to their own rigid behavioral code, in everything from dress to language, is a form of middle-classism in itself. Of course, almost all of these kids do come from middle-to-upper class homes, and there would probably never be a hippie if there weren't an Oak Road in Cleveland with a nice white frame house and a neatly pruned garden. Eighty percent of these kids will eventually settle down and there will be a rebellious wave of another kind. Each generation spawns its rebels, but eventually they wander back into the fold and are absorbed. Alas!

Playboy: Some political activists of the New Left are critical of the hippies' turn on, tune in, drop out philosophy, on the grounds that it benefits the power structure by diverting potentially rebellious youths into a harmless Soma world. As Rap Brown put it recently, "When the Federal troops march on Harlem, the hippies will be standing on the corner of 125th Street, handing them daffodils." Do you feel that in a sense the hippie subculture is subtly serving the interests of the establishment?

Capote: I can well understand the argument of some radicals that they're contributing nothing whatsoever to a legitimate political rebellion, but that's not what they're all about. They're after something quite different. Theirs is a so-called aesthetic movement, isn't it? Politicians belong in their own union hall, not with the Jefferson Airplane! As far as Rap Brown goes, I'm sure he would rather have people hurling hand grenades than passing out daffodils; he is so incredibly irresponsible in his tactics and utterances as to subvert one's confidence in his capacity for responsible action and thus render him worthless as a leader. It's a pity, too, because both he and Stokely Carmichael are very intelligent. But how can anybody, black or white, rationally back such extremists?

Playboy: Are there any Negro leaders whom you respect?

Capote: There is no leader on the Negro left of any real ability; in fact, there is no leader at all, just a handful of neurotic notoriety seekers who've appointed themselves spokesmen for a few shattered splinter groups and follow the television cameras across the country. There has been only one man of our generation who could have led a united and constructive radical Negro movement: Malcolm X. I always admired Malcolm and I think his assassination was a tragedy. He was an extremely intelligent man and, in the long run, I believe he was quite sensible in his outlook. He could have been a real leader and of great value.

Playboy: Does your dislike of Brown and Carmichael extend to the philosophy of black power they articulate?

Capote: There are only three kinds of real power in our society: economic power, political power and military power. When the phrase "black power" was originally coined, I understood it to mean that Negroes would press for the kind of economic power that would automatically generate political power and I considered that a constructive goal. Unfortunately, the very people who first launched the term have perverted it to mean *military* power—the power to kill and burn to achieve one's aims. So if black power means black armies racing through the streets, creating havoc, that certainly does nothing to advance the legitimate political and economic aspirations of the black community. Just the opposite, in fact.

Playboy: Negro militants answer that objection by saying that racism is so endemic in our social structure and so institutionalized in our economy that they have been driven to violence as the only means of dramatizing their demands. Do you think there's any truth in this?

Capote: Well, if they think a few Molotov cocktails are going to bring down the whole system and build something new, I'm afraid they're just indulging in wishful thinking. In any case, I have to deny their basic premise: I don't believe America *is* a hopelessly racist society, despite the awful abuses of the past. Racism is not a problem you find only in America. Look at India, where the caste system determines every person's role in society. The Brahmans at the top are pale-skinned; the untouchables at the bottom are black and it's gradation of color that determines the destiny of the intermediate castes. Take England, which now has an explosive racial situation stemming from the huge colored immigration from the Commonwealth; England has ghettos as bad as Harlem, and Negroes are discriminated against socially and economically. Even Africa has its own intertribal racism. And in those countries where race isn't a pressing problem, you have rigid class divisions, as in Russia. Of course, none of this in any way justifies our own situation, but I think it does demonstrate that racism and exploitation are not a peculiarly American phenomenon but a universal human phenomenon.

Playboy: Do you think that you, yourself, are entirely free of racism?

Capote: Well, I think I am, but who really knows? Emotionally, I *feel* I am, because I have always had the closest personal relationship with Negroes. When I was a child, all the people I cared about, with two exceptions, were Negroes; and I felt an intense pain whenever they were slighted or abused. Of course, most of the white-Negro relationships I witnessed were relatively humane, but then I would walk down the street and see Negroes stepping into the gutter to let white people pass by and I just couldn't comprehend it. Throughout my life I have never had any feeling other than complete identification with colored people who were on any kind of wave length at all with me. It's something that I've stopped thinking about, really. I fully realize, of course, that this is not true of most white people, but I think the argument that *no* whites are free of racism is quite erroneous. But then, on another level, does it really matter if anybody is free of *any* negative feeling about *anything*? No matter how much you love somebody, you know, there's some part of him you don't like.

Playboy: Are you impressed with the work of any of the new Negro writers?

Capote: No. LeRoi Jones, who is a sort of avatar of this trend, is a total fraud, both artistically and politically. I was particularly amused to note that he was recently awarded a Guggenheim fellowship; well, a Guggenheim is something an artist applies for—*begs* for, actually—and if LeRoi Jones so violently hates the white race and all its works, why is he down on his knees pleading for several thousand of Guggenheim's filthy white capitalist dollars? You can't raise riots at the front door and then run around to the back door with an alms cup. He's just another hypocrite.

Playboy: What about James Baldwin?

Capote: He's another story entirely. When I first met him in Paris, he was a literary critic and essayist, and a first-rate one, although it was his fiction that saved him from starvation. But I think it is as an essayist that he will survive. You know, you've got to remember one thing whenever you discuss writers, white or black: Most people assume that because a man is a writer, he must, a priori, be intelligent. Not at all. It's possible to be greatly gifted and grievously stupid. For example, two of America's four leading playwrights are exceedingly dumb. But Jimmy Baldwin is one writer who is also a deeply intelligent man.

Playboy: Who are the two "exceedingly dumb" playwrights you refer to?

Capote: No comment. I want to have a few friends left after this interview!

Playboy: Irrespective of their I.Q. ratings, whom do you consider the most able contemporary American playwrights?

Capote: Tennessee Williams and Edward Albee.

Playboy: Are there any authors on the current literary scene whom you consider truly great?

Capote: Yes. Truman Capote. There are a number of others who, while not quite in this exalted orbit, are still commendable: Norman

Mailer and Bill Styron and Katherine Anne Porter and my friends Glenway Wescott and Jack Dunphy and Donald Windham and Harper Lee, and writers like Jimmy Baldwin and Jane Bowles and the late Flannery O'Connor and Carson McCullers. I also think John Updike is a gifted fellow. Norman Mailer says he can't write, but in fact he can, and beautifully, although he doesn't write *about* anything; reading Updike is like trying to grab a piece of smoke.

Playboy: For many years, American letters seemed dominated by Southern writers, but, as you have said, "during the last ten years the large percentage of the more talented American writers are urban Jewish intellectuals." How do you feel about this shift in ethinc, geographic and literary emphasis?

Capote: Well, it has brought about the rise of what I call the Jewish Mafia in American letters. This is a clique of New York—oriented writers and critics who control much of the literary scene through the influence of the quarterlies and intellectual magazines. All these publications are Jewish-dominated and this particular coterie employs them to make or break writers by advancing or withholding attention. I don't think there's any conscious, sinister conspiracy on their part—just a determination to see that members of their particular clique rise to the top. Bernard Malamud and Saul Bellow and Philip Roth and Isaac Bashevis Singer and Norman Mailer are all fine writers, but they're not the *only* writers in the country, as the Jewish literary Mafia would have us believe. I could give you a list of excellent writers, such as John Knowles and Vance Bourjaily and James Purdy and Donald Windham and Reynolds Price and James Leo Herlihy and Calder Willingham and John Hawkes and William Goyen; the odds are you haven't heard of most of them, for the simple reason that the Jewish Mafia has systematically frozen them out of the literary scene. Now, mind you, I'm not against any particular group adhering to its own literary values and advancing its own favored authors; such cliques have always existed in American letters. I only object when any one particular group—and it could just as well be Southern, or Roman Catholic, or Marxist, or vegetarian—gets a strangle hold on American criticism and squeezes out anybody who doesn't conform to its own standards. It's fine to write about specifically Jewish problems, and it often makes valid and exciting literature—but the people who have other messages to convey, other styles and other backgrounds should also be given a chance. Today, because of the predominance of the Jewish Mafia, they're not being given that opportunity. This is something everyone in the literary world knows but never writes about.

Playboy: Aren't you opening yourself up to a charge of anti-Semitism?

Capote: No, because anti-Semitism has nothing to do with it. As I've already indicated, I would be just as opposed to a clique of white Anglo-Saxon Protestant authors and critics exercising exclusive control over American letters and excluding talented Jewish writers. I'm against ghettoization from *any* source. And let me point out that this Jewish Mafia is based more on a state of mind than on race; gentile writers such as Dwight MacDonald who toe the line are made honorary members, while gifted Jewish writers are read out of the club for nonconformity. Irwin Shaw, for example, an excellent writer of Jewish origin, has been damaged by the Jewish Mafia, which has studiously ignored him, despite the fact that his early short stories are superior to any of the contemporary idols. Almost as many Jewish writers as gentiles have suffered at their hands. The ax falls, ecumenically, on the head of anybody, Jew or gentile, who doesn't share this group's parochial preoccupations. The regrettable aspect of all this is that there is so much room for diversity, plenty of space for everybody, if the Jewish Mafia could only accept that other people exist.

Playboy: Mary McCarthy has said that American letters, Jewish and gentile alike, represent "the mirror on the whorehouse ceiling." Do you think that the current literary preoccupation with violence, sexual perversion, mental illness and death is a sign of decadence?

Capote: Can you tell me of any age that hasn't been preoccupied with violence, sex and death? Was Shakespeare decadent? Society today is greatly more relaxed, especially sexually, and at least in that one area shows encouraging progress. Progress, of course, *is* often misinterpreted as decadence.

Playboy: This process of relaxation has been particularly pronounced in Hollywood, which in the past few years has dealt candidly with such hitherto taboo subjects as incest, homosexuality and nymphomania. But the old Production Code still prevailed in 1961, when your novelette *Breakfast at Tiffany's* was adapted for the screen, and its heroine was transmogrified from a pseudo prostitute to a flighty but inwardly untrammeled ingénue. Were you disturbed by this cinematic bowdlerizing?

Capote: Of course. The book was really rather bitter, and Holly Golightly was *real*—a tough character, not an Audrey Hepburn type at all. The film became a mawkish valentine to New York City and Holly and, as a result, was thin and pretty, whereas it should have been rich and ugly. It bore as much resemblance to my work as the Rockettes do to Ulanova.

Playboy: Is the film version of *In Cold Blood* more faithful to the original?

Capote: Yes, it's as accurate a rendering of the book as I could have hoped, with the single exception that if it were done the way I would *really* have liked, it would have had to be at least nine hours long. As it stands, it runs about two hours; but those two hours are verbatim from the book and brilliantly done. I cooperated fully with Richard Brooks, who directed the film and did the screenplay, and we never had the slightest disagreement. The actors who play Perry Smith and Dick Hickock, by the way, turn in remarkable performances. Even the physical resemblance is uncanny; when I first saw the boy selected to play Smith, it was as if Perry had come back from the grave.

Playboy: In addition to novel and short-story writing, you have also sidelined as a television playwright and adapted two of your works, *House of Flowers* and *The Grass Harp,* for the Broadway stage. Do your writing habits vary with each project or remain essentially uniform?

Capote: They vary, but according to my personal habits rather than the medium in which I'm working. I used to write from midnight until five or six in the morning, but now I write only during the day. For the past ten years, my schedule has been to work eight months out of the year, separated into four-month periods, with a two-month interlude between each stretch. I still work during these "vacations," of course, but not with the same intensity. During my work bouts, I run a very tight ship; an artist, in my opinion, has to be as healthy and disciplined as a champion athlete. I go to bed at ten in the evening, get up at five, start work at six, stop at ten or eleven and attend to my correspondence—a heavy burden, yet I feel guilty not answering a letter, even though I can manage only one out of ten—have lunch at one, take a nap, then read or take a stroll, work again from five to seven, have several drinks, dinner, go to bed and start the cycle all over again.

Playboy: How do you outline and organize your books?

Capote: I've always had the illusion that a story or a novel springs into my mind *in toto*—plot, characters, scenes, dialog, everything—all in one long rush. Whether this is really true or not I don't know, but it certainly *seems* as if this is what happens. I suppose all good writing involves a tapping of the subconscious, and perhaps in my case, the process is a bit more instantaneous. But once I start to write a story or a novel, I have it very thoroughly outlined in my mind and often down on paper in considerable detail, too. I occasionally deviate from these outlines when I see a means of improving on them, but I generally follow them quite closely. Frequently, before I even write the opening words of a book, I will have written bits and pieces that fall one third of the way through, or halfway through, or at the very end; and as I write, I fit all these segments together into a kind of mosaic. The most important question in my mind is always: How does it end? I try to have the concluding two or three pages written before I start the book, because that's what I'm driving toward from the very beginning and I always want to keep the book's central point clear. But the writing of a novel is such a complex and intimate process that you can't really recite it like a formula.

Playboy: You're reported to be working on a new novel called *Answered Prayers*, with a theme revolving around a statement by Saint Theresa that "more tears are shed over answered prayers than unanswered ones." Does this indicate a return from the nonfiction novel to more traditional literary forms?

Capote: Well, this book is rather a *roman à clef*, drawn from life yet suffused with fictional elements and partaking of both my reportorial abilities and imaginative gifts. However, this doesn't mean that I've abandoned the nonfiction novel in its purest form. In fact, I have one in the works right now. The subject matter is very ordinary and the color tone is gray-pastel; but if I can bring it off, I think I will have proved once and for all the point that journalism, regardless of its subject matter, is capable of reaching an artistic level equal to the most superior fiction. Not *better*, but equal.

Playboy: When you're not working, you enjoy a highly publicized social life that crescendoed with that masked ball you held late in 1966 at New York's Plaza Hotel. But there were those who frowned on the opulence of the affair. Drew Pearson, for example, criticized the ball for being in poor taste when Americans were dying in Vietnam and racial violence was wracking the nation's ghettos. Pearson wrote, "If a fraction of the money spent on the fantastic New York party were spent on curing juvenile delinquency, there would have been no Perry Smith or Dick Hickock to commit one of the most cold-blooded murders in Midwest history." How would you reply to Pearson?

Capote: The gentleman guilty of "poor taste" is Mr. Pearson. To supply the background, my party was given in honor of Mrs. Katherine Graham, a close friend of mine who publishes the *Washington Post*. I asked Mrs. Graham whom she wanted invited from Washington, and she supplied a list of 20 or so people, including Mr. Drew Pearson. So here you have a person attending a private dance because he is acquainted with the guest of honor and who then hurries to his typewriter and produces a column acutely critical of both his host and his fellow guests. If that's not dubious taste, I don't know what is. As to the substance of his criticism—what there is of it—is someone automatically blind to social injustice just because he chooses to have a private party for his friends? If so, we might as well declare a moratorium on all social events until the millennium. And remember, although this particular party was accorded an inordinate amount of attention, there are parties given every day of the week that are many times more extravagant, and nobody bothers to comment on them. As far as I'm concerned, this was a private occasion and nobody's business but mine.

Playboy: In the aftermath of your masked ball, one critic commented that your busy social life actually derives from your own essential loneliness. Many of the characters in your earlier fiction, which you have indicated was subconsciously autobiographical, have a great tenderness and capacity to love and an almost commensurate inability to express that love. Do you feel you may have the same problem?

Capote: Oh, no! I've always been able to communicate my feelings to anybody I care about. I'm really a very warm person, although you might have trouble believing it from some of my answers to your questions. But for those who have my affection, I sing a different tune altogether. If I really like somebody, they *know* it.

Playboy: Has your personal happiness matched your professional success?

Capote: Well, I'll only say I'm not an *unhappy* person. I don't know *anybody* whom I could honestly say I considered happy. Anybody who is totally happy would have to be incredibly stupid. Only imbeciles and sweet idiots wandering around in the sunshine of a spring day are happy.

Playboy: If you had the power to live your life over again, would you still select writing as your profession?

Capote: Quite frankly, I think I could have done well at anything I set my mind to. I would have made a first-rate lawyer and I certainly could have done extremely well in business; if my concern had been to make money, I'd be one of the richest men in the world. The reason is that I have the ability to concentrate completely on one thing at a time and I also have discipline and a unique memory. It just so happened that from my childhood on, the thing that was always riding the top of my mind and dominating my inner self was art and creativity and writing. So I became an artist. But I believe that I could have accomplished anything I wanted to.

Playboy: Somerset Maugham once called you "the hope of modern literature." Looking back on the past 20 years of your career, do you think you've realized your full creative potential?

Capote: Of course not. I've always been too preoccupied with technique and the acquisition of a virtuoso apparatus; that's the principal reason the fields I've worked in have been so varied. And the result is that I've exposed far too few layers of my actual knowledge and perception. I'm 43, so perhaps, if luck allows and discipline holds, I will have time to arrive at higher altitudes, where the air is thin but the view exhilarating.

Truman Capote Talks, Talks, Talks
C. Robert Jennings/1968

From *New York*, 1 (13 May 1968), 53-55.

Palm Springs, where they roil the pools with vapid doxies and stuff golf balls with Seconol, is not burdened with style. It wears Ike like a comfortable old slipper; but it hasn't the foggiest what to make of Truman Capote during his recent vacation there, and small wonder: he is style quintessenced; he is not exactly zonked by celebrity golf tournaments or zircon charity balls; he cordially loathes the Racquet Club; he does not pay court to the rather dazed resident Establishment; he is there to work while others play, or rot; he has never heard of Smoke Tree Ranch; and about the only time he is visible is on sun-slanted afternoons when he "messes about in all those marvelous whirlpools and things" at The Spa or rides a bay horse across the yucca flats or makes like Sonja Henie, an early idol of his, at the Palm Springs Ice Skating Center: "I *like* ice skating. I'm usually the only person there. I'm very good, and they don't know who I am—they think I'm very mysterious with my beautiful imported skates and a sort of outer-space Courrèges number, with lots of zippers—ha-ha-ha-ha-ha. I can do all these marvelous spins by myself in the blue *gloom* of the Ice Palace." While Ike and Those Others golf in golden El Dorado.

We find Truman in an impeccable, tan-awninged, antique-burdened house on Paseo El Mirador, where between wrestling bouts with his new electric typewriter ("I haven't quite learned how to work it yet—it sort of runs away"), he lolls about a geranium-bordered pool like Nancy Mitford's Sun King, tawny as Kansas wheat-stubble in a blue stretch swimsuit, sybaritically supine and inert. By his own admission, he is a horizontal writer.

Capote sought the sere desert spaces simply because, he says, "I wanted to try the desert. I never have. I wrote one book on the island of Paros, another on a mountaintop in Sicily, another in Morocco, and now that I own a house in Verbier, Switzerland, I usually go there. I looked around Scottsdale, Arizona but didn't find a house, so I came here and this one I really liked—the Lazars found it for me. You might as well be in the Greek Islands: I haven't heard the first sound; there are flowers and orange trees and blue sky and bright sun and those barren hills. Of course, when you step out the door it's all rather Sodom and Gomorrah." Big sassy laugh again. Tinkle of ice cubes now through limpid Polish vodka, glinting like icicles in the winter sun. Quincy Jones' *In Cold Blood* score careens out of the stereo set, and Truman Capote makes the supreme effort of pushing his small cinnamon form up from the beach towel—"Let's play something *merry*"—changes LPs and bugaloos back to cool crashing sounds from The Doors.

The manuscript of *Answered Prayers* awaits. "It's a sort of *roman à clef*, drawn from some people I've known and places I've been. It is very strangely constructed, moving in time both past, present and future all at the same time, but it is a completely realistic novel—nothing experimental about it other than technique. I've been working on it for a year and a half and will finish by January of '69. Santa Teresa said more tears are shed over answered prayers than unanswered ones—and four or five people in the book get precisely what they wanted and the result? I'm not tellin', baby."

Lee Radziwill calls Capote her very own "answered prayer" and said as much on a recent gift. Lined schoolboys' notebooks and a lot of yellow paper and a little white bond litter a corner of the simple guest bedroom, recently vacated by the princess, where *Answered Prayers* is being written—first in longhand in the notebooks (in a chicken-scrawl), then on yellow—"yellow gives everything a sense of impermanence"—and finally on white via the electric machine. If Hemingway is the Paganini of the paragraph and Henry James, as Capote puts it, "is the maestro of the semi-colon", Truman is the Toscanini of the colon. To paraphrase Oscar Wilde, he may spend the morning just putting one in, the afternoon taking it out.

There is a large parcel from Colonel Thomas Andrew Parker—"Elvis nude, no doubt," says Capote, spilling El's latest LPs onto a tangerine beach towel with tassels. "We're going to star in a *blue* movie together, ha-ha-ha." Actually, Truman has never seen or heard the Solid Gold Cornpone in his life, so he puts one of the recordings on the stereo. "I think," he says matter-of-factly, "that something is wrong with the machine." El is swiftly displaced by The Jefferson Airplane.

He rubs his eyes—serious, searching—over an illustration in *Los Angeles Magazine* of himself swinging a tennis racket ("I don't play tennis") amid members of "Palm Springs party society." "I don't know *any* of those people and don't intend to." He files his nails—one finger is encircled with a stunning gold and sapphire ring from Tiffany's—and smokes True cigarettes and languidly moves from one white chaise to another to take the phone. Each buzzing makes him wince. It is Lee Radziwill calling from New York just prior to flying to London: "Where'd you have lunch? That's an *awful* place. How were you looking—good? . . . Oh, dear, oh golly, what time are you leaving? . . . That's right, lovey. Listen, darling, it was wonderful having you here. Hugs and kisses. Bye, bye."

Capote's talk is disarmingly candid, frequently funny, always intelligent, sometimes hair-curling. A random sampling:

On Edward Albee: "Exceedingly bright—and a shrewd little cookie-cutter."

On Ernest Hemingway: "He was the greatest old closet queen ever to come down the pike, truly one of the dis*honest* people. I've said I am *secretly* some of the things the hairy one pretended to be, without further comment. Well, he pre*tended* to be a hearty, courageous person, but I don't think he could have *possibly* survived the five years that I did in Kansas. And I don't think women liked him at all—he was just a big blowhard, the Closet Quean Compleat. But they are absolutely crazy about *me*, and that's a *fact*, baby. Why? Because I like them, and I don't think most men do and are incapable of being friends with them."

On Bobby Kennedy: Unprintable, but not negatively unprintable, just juicily unprintable.

On Oscars: "It's all outrageous, really. It simply *proves* that the Academy awards have nothing to do with merit. The only three good American films last year were *Bonnie and Clyde, The Graduate* and *In Cold Blood. In the Heat of Night* was a good bad picture. *Guess Who's Coming to Dinner* is a bad movie that got there for sentimental reasons and all that political *merde*." He added that if the Oscar gurus had any imagination they would have lumped Scott Wilson's and Robert Blake's performances in *ICB* into a single achievement, which at the very least would have provoked attention, like a sideshow of Siamese twins who can also act up a storm.

On Jackie Kennedy: "All absolute complete lies the reports that *I* started the marriage rumors. Your *Times* gossip picked it up from *Women's Wear Daily*—they just use your name any way they want because they know you won't sue. They have to blame it on *some*one so they say, oh, well, blame it on Capote. They said one of Jackie's guests at the Whitney plantation called me about it—they're referring to Mrs. [William] Paley, whom I hadn't spoken to in over a month."

On Gore Vidal: "I really enjoy him, but neither of us would *dare* say anything nice about the other's works. But have you looked at *Myra Breckenridge*? I never thought the day would come I'd ever say anything good about Gore's contributions, but some of the scenes in it are terrifically funny. Of course the dildo scene is *really* repulsive, but up to that time it was really amusing."

On current practitioners of journalism-*cum*-art: "I can only think of *one*, baby."

On graffiti: "Some of the most vivid writing in America is on the walls of restrooms. The men's room in the Albany, N.Y. railroad station, for instance, should be preserved as a national shrine: there is more wit there than in *any* Broadway hit!"

On marijuana: "Pot makes the most stupid people sound amusing—that's the best thing about it. They never turn mean, they laugh at everything, and they turn charming even if they are dull."

On Mary McCarthy: (apropos her remark that American letters represent "the mirror on the whorehouse ceiling."): "If there's anyone in American literature who knows what a whore would see when she looks at the ceiling, it's Mary McCarthy."

On the urban intellectual Jewish writers: "Very talented, very powerful, and very parochial. I call them the Jewish Mafia. They exclude too many good writers. They're afraid of me. I can manipulate beyond their reaches. I never would play the game. Styron is accepted because if ever there was a goy Yid, it's Bill Styron."

On The Beautiful People: "There are mutations and gradations and I don't bother with the ones that don't interest me—some are unbelievably dumb, aren't they? [Yes.] The main thing with me is *intelligence*. I've got to feel that you don't have to finish sentences with a person, you can sort of talk in hieroglyphics and communicate still. I do like marvelous-looking people, if they have discipline and great style. I can't stand people who are sloppy. I have *sympathy* for them, but people should be in control of their physical appearance, their mind, and their emotions."

On psychiatry: "I'm for anything that helps people accept themselves, but I never felt the need for analysis—I had to face such real problems and solve them myself at such an early age. I exorcised my own demons in my writing and through certain acts of will. I have no particular inhibitions now. If I get anxiety it's because I've taken on more than I can chew, trying to do more than I can. I've gotten rid of whatever it is that caused such terrible difficulty in my life. I just arrange everything around my work, where I can always work out my problems."

On sex: "To me sex is like sneezing; if you sneeze about six times in a row it's as good as an orgasm. It's the quarry that counts. Incidentally, my doctor tells me you get the most fantastic orgasm if you are terribly hung over. Unfortunately, I never have hangovers."

And no wonder. At this particular juncture, Truman Capote piles into his wagon (in Manhattan it's a green XK-E Jaguar, "Green Girl"), scurries off to the doctor's for his daily B-12 shot, then to The Spa for his daily sauna, whirlpool bath, and the zingiest massage in town.

Five-thirty p.m. The sun has plummeted well behind snow-sprinkled San Jacinto, and Truman Capote is back at his schoolboy notebooks, zapped by exotic masseur-oils and mineral waters from unknown depths. At seven-thirty he puts down his pencil, cracks open the J&B Scotch, and dresses for the evening: jaunty Cardin cap, brown Bill Blass sweater over white turtleneck shirt, square-toed Cardin shoes and a vast handbag from Mark Cross, a veritable attic of money and meaningless treasures. "I do tend to collect things," says Truman, who has more paperweights than most artists have hives. And people: "I'd like to have little replicas made of all the people I like and send them around to all my other friends."

We have drinks off antique tables in the bar-den and tell tall tales and laugh a lot. Capote is startingly intuitive, sweetly-cynical, and generous in spirit.

He is amused at Charles Portis' new novel, *True Grit*. But the truly surprising thing—and Capote is loaded with surprises—is that he is also reading *Return of the Native* and *Vanity Fair*. "And I am about to start The Proust Plunge, which I do about every five years. You take a big breath and go under for about six weeks with him. I used to do that with Jane Austen, but I've memorized all of Jane now so I don't go back to her anymore."

Truman introduced Babe Paley to Marcel Proust, who suggested that Society is the most sensitive indicator of fluctuating power-values in the regnant hierarchies. Truman and Babe are subtle arrangers of hierarchies or, as his friend Bill Buckley has it, he practices the science of regulation and control, "the regulation being that of ordering the attitudes, value judgments and reflexes of society."

He confesses that he and the late Harry Kurnitz once wickedly compiled a list of "The Thirty Most Boring People in the World" which, if ever published, would rock quite a few of The Right People off their power-perches including, incidentally, some choice members of The Hollywood Establishment. "To play the game fair," he explains, "it has to be *somebody* that other people think is interesting, so they are all famous people."

Nine o'clock. Truman Capote sashays into Ethel's Hideaway swinging his Mark Cross purse, Cardin cap rakishly agley on his taffy head, and all the people in their Perry Como sweaters glom onto him. They are witnessing a bit of *art nouveau* with its very own *Wanderschaft*, a walking *objet d'art* out of The Yellow Nineties. Over rare filets and rivers of Chambertin he is reminded of a startling piece of personal exfoliation in an interview, when he said that it was his own essentially tragic view of life that accounted for the fribble side of him. "That is the truest thing I've ever said in my life—I didn't mean to let it slip out. (Huge—defensive?—laughter.) I don't care what you write about me, as long as it's all lies. It's just the truth one can't bear. The stories about me still repeat the things I said about myself on the dust jacket of *Other Voices*. But I had nothing to say on the jacket. I had never *done* anything but write, so I made up all that *hooey* about being the protegé of a fortune-teller, a river-boat dancer, and reader of motion picture scripts—it's all a lot of *merde*. Such a send-up! But it's still printed in *Who's Who*: 'author and painter on glass.' I never painted anything in my whole life, much less on *glass*."

It is two o'clock in the morning at a tawdry discotheque called IJ's in soporific Palm Springs, and the hard-rock sounds mercifully halt. Truman Capote removes his gold-rimmed glasses revealing an oddly-handsome face suffused with something like *Weltschmertz*, reaches for his handkerchief, and without embarrassment, rubs tears from haunted eyes.

Six a.m., the following day. Truman Capote has slept sounder than General Westmoreland during the Tet lunar holiday. He reads two chapters of *Vanity Fair* before doing battle with the electric typewriter, which still gallops away from him. At ten he breaks to check on his guest, voice deliberately pitched higher than usual: "This is Nancy Reagan. We're having a *gas*sing up at San Quentin and wondered if you could come." Big sassy laugh. "Hung *over*? Black-outs? I am sorry . . . Oh, Heavens no, I'm clear as a bell. Get your suit on, honey, have a swim and a little vodka something . . ."

We Talk to . . . Truman Capote
Barbara Packer, Laurie Deutsch, Barbara Bussmann, Ann Beattie, and Judi Silverman/1968

From *Mademoiselle*, 67 (August 1968), 366-367. Copyright © 1968 by The Condé Nast Publications Inc. Reprinted by permission.

Sitting beneath glittering stained glass in his antique-and-curio-cluttered apartment overlooking the New York skyline, Truman Capote relaxed with Barbara Packer, Laurie Deutsch, Barbara Bussmann, Ann Beattie, and Judi Silverman.

Q. Do you think the U.S. is a violent country?

A. I think the "frontier theory" is an excuse. I don't think America is any more violent than any other country, although recent events don't seem to bear that out. Compared statistically to other nations of its size, I don't think ours is noticeably a criminal culture. Speaking of statistics, did you know that 80 per cent of all hitchhikers have served some time in prison?

Q. What are your views of capital punishment?

A. I'm sure the Supreme Court will rule capital punishment cruel and unusual treatment because of the rarity with which it is enforced. If it were strictly enforced it might deter the professionally homicidal mind, the person who kills as an accessory to his crime. If he really thought death would be the outcome of his action, he would think twice.

Q. What do you think of student protests?

A. I think the whole student rebellion is not really a rebellion at all, but prone for a kind of grim "fun." It's not for anything. They want a certain kind of identity; they're jockeying with each other for political power in their own culture. The basis for this behavior is a desire for notoriety. That they want to have an identity and not be anonymous, I can understand, but I can't see seeking notoriety as a group, as a mass movement. The hippie communities, too, have to conform. You might as well be living in Shaker Heights.

Q. You've said your material chooses you.

A. That's the difference between the serious artist and the craftsman—the craftsman can take material and because of his abilities do a professional job of it. The serious artist, like Proust, is like an object caught by a wave and swept to shore. He's obsessed by his material; it's like a venom working in his blood and the art is the antidote.

Q. You once said your education was a waste of time.

A. But I went to rotten schools. Alabama in the Depression wasn't aflame with brilliant teachers. I educated myself. I think everyone has to create themselves. But some people start from a strange point of view and have no one to pattern themselves after. Take the Brontes; they lived in such a remote part of England that they made themselves into completely original people.

Q. Do you consider your public image a creation, too?

A. Not exactly. There's a certain point where a celebrity image starts to be self-perpetuating. It's like a stone you sink in the sea where the shells and barnacles attach to it until you don't know the truth yourself. Last night I turned on the radio—sometimes the drone of the talk shows helps me fall asleep—and I suddenly realized they were talking about me. It was boring. There is a certain kind of serenity that comes with that feeling.

Q. You said you have a tragic view of life.

A. I just assume everything is going to turn out for the worst and if it doesn't that's just so much gravy.

When Does a Writer Become a Star? Truman Capote
David Frost/1970

From *The Americans* (New York: Stein and Day, 1970), 17-23. Copyright (c) 1970 by David Frost. Reprinted by permission of Stein and Day Publishers.

Frost: About a year ago I was talking to Noel Coward, and I asked him at what age he knew that he was a star, and he said, "Two!" You're a star. At what age did you realize that you were a star-writer personality?

Capote: You've got to separate those two things. A personality or a writer?

F: Well, you're a mixture of the two, aren't you?

C: Well, I realized that I could get away with murder when I was about six.

F: Really?

C: In school.

F: What sort of things could you get away with?

C: Well, all the teachers thought that I was much brighter than I was. And so I could get away with anything—if that's what you mean, having a sort of certainty of your own ability to do a thing.

F: What was your first great coup? The first thing you really got away with?

C: I guess maybe I didn't really mean it in that sense, but the first thing that happened to me in my career that gave me a sense of confidence—because, you see, I didn't finish high school. I didn't want to because I had begun to publish stories when I was fourteen, fifteen, and I wanted to come to live in New York, and I was living in New Orleans. And I came to work with the *New Yorker* magazine. But they didn't know how old I was. I mean, I'd been sending them material and stories and things and I actually was about seventeen years old, and I came up to New York. They had written me a letter and said they would be very pleased to give me an interview to work there as a reporter. And so I arrived, and I was taken to see the managing editor, who is now the editor of the *New Yorker*, and when I was seventeen I looked about ten years old. And this man nearly fainted. And so I said, "But I've come all the way from New Orleans." He said, "But we can't do this—it's child labor. We can't send you out to interview anybody." But in the end they let me stay, and I had a job there; and I worked there for two years, until I published a book.

F: Between the age of six, when you realized you could get away with anything, and the age of seventeen, you had lots of other ambitions, didn't you? You wanted to be a tap dancer?

(*Laughter*)

C: Oh, that's just something I put in *Who's Who*.

F: It's not true?

C: No. You know, they send you these forms to fill out, what you wanted to do or be in *Who's Who in America*, and I just sent them back a sort of a joke thing. I said that I painted on glass and wrote political speeches and wanted to be a tap dancer, but it was none of it true.

F: Well, how do we know that the other story you just told us is true?

C: Maybe it isn't. (*Laughter, applause*)

F: But what about the rumor that you also had said that you were desperate to learn to play the guitar and learn a song called "I Wish I Were Single Again"? Did you do that, or did you make that up?

C: No, I did do that, but that's the only song I ever did learn. I got so tired of that guitar I left it in the bus station in Mobile, Alabama.

F: Were you a lovable child?

C: Those who knew me well thought so. Those who didn't, no.

F: Why? Because you were daunting first time out?

C: I had a sharp tongue.

F: You haven't lost it. You said on one occasion, in fact, that you'd developed the muscles of a veritable barracuda in dealing with your enemies. What bit of dealing with your enemies are you proudest of?

C: Doing in Kenneth Tynan. Remember when I had my feud with Kenneth Tynan?

F: Over *In Cold Blood*? What was it that really convinced you you'd succeeded in doing him in?

C: Because my reply was much better than his attack.

F: Have you always been superstitious?

C: Yes, but not any more. I was until about ten years ago. I was very interested in horoscopes and things like that, and just one day I took all of them and tore them up, and I'm not going to let myself be victimized by this junk any longer.

F: But you had some marvelous superstitions. Half of them you invented yourself, didn't you?

C: Oh, yes. I only have one with which I still drive people crazy. I won't have three cigarettes in the same ashtray. I keep taking them out and putting them in my pockets and all over my suit, just so I never have more than two cigarette butts in other people's. I won't let other people have it either. And they keep saying, "What are you doing?"

F: Have you any spare cigarette butts with you now?

C: No, no, no. I just changed my suit.

F: At one stage you always said that you didn't like to travel on an airplane with two nuns?

C: I still wouldn't do that. (*Laughter*) I wouldn't go anywhere with two nuns.

F: Were you afraid of being hijacked to the Vatican or what? (*Laughter*)

C: Maybe there's just something gloomy about it.

F: What about *three* nuns?

C: Oh, I wouldn't do that either.

F: How would you feel about one nun?

C: That's all right. (*Laughter*)

F: You also had a thing about phone numbers at one time.

C: Recently I had a very bad automobile accident, and I hit a tree at forty hours an hour. I went through the windshield. And I was lying on the ground there waiting for the ambulance, and it took about thirty-five minutes before it got there. And during that whole time I was completely conscious. But all that was going through my mind was old telephone numbers. I kept thinking of a telephone and thinking, "Who does that telephone number belong to?" It was a very curious thing, but I entertained and occupied myself, and felt no pain the whole time.

F: Really? But before that you found certain combinations of numbers unlucky, didn't you?

C: Yes, well, I won't dial them. I had a great fight once with Tennessee Williams. We went to Capri together. This was a long time ago, fifteen years ago. And we went to this hotel, and when they brought the keys with the numbers on them, I looked at my number and I didn't like it. I said to Tennessee, "Would you mind if I had your room and you gave me your key?" And he said, "All right." I went upstairs, and then I came down. We were having a drink, and he walked into the bar with a terrible look on his face, and said—because he's even more superstitious than I am—he said, "I just figured out why you wanted me to have that number instead of you: because it adds up to thirteen."

F: What did he do?

C: He was furious with me. He said I had no right to put this jinx on him.

F: What about the stars and astrology? You believed in those at one stage?

C: Not any more.

F: Why not? You just decided to chuck them out of the window? What about the belief in God? You said on one occasion that for you art really took the place of religion. Do you believe in a god?

C: Not in that specific sense. What I meant when I said I believed in art as a religion is that art can be a comfort and a guide in the passage through life. Art is a recompense for the difficulties of simply living.

F: What do you believe in the strongest?

C: Art.

F: Anything else?

C: Friendship.

F: Which is more powerful, do you think—friendship or love?

C: Friendship. Actually, I think friendship and love are exactly the same thing.

F: How do you mean?

C: Obviously sex is not love. It's a temporary situation, isn't it? Sex can lead to love, but friendship, real friendship, inevitably leads to love. There can't be any friendship unless it's a real friendship, but then, one doesn't have that many friends in a lifetime.

F: Have you ever been in love?

C: Oh, yes.

F: Often?

C: No. Twice.

F: And was it just like heightened friendship then?

C: Yes. *(Laughter)*

F: Heightened in what way?

C: Well, I didn't have to finish sentences.

F: That's a great definition. But if friendship leads to love, does it normally lead to sex too?

C: No.

F: You don't seem to have a very high opinion of sex.

C: Well, that's not true either. I just don't see in what connection this really falls, because you see I don't think sex has anything to do with friendship. It's very difficult to have a sort of sexual relationship with somebody who actually is a friend. Because there's a kind of tension and antagonism that goes on in a sexual relationship that's the antithesis of friendship, because friendship is the perfect sort of trust and belief and not lying to one another. People who are having a love-sex relationship are continuously lying to each other because the very nature of the relationship demands that they do, because you have to make a love object of this person, which means that you editorialize about them. You know? You cut out what you don't want to see, you add this if it isn't there. And so therefore you're building a lie. But in a friendship you don't do that. You do exactly the reverse. You try more and more to be as completely pure and straight as you can be.

F: Have you found you've had more sex relationships than love relationships, or less?

C: No, I've had more love relationships than sex relationships.

F: But you've only had two love relationships.

C: Yes. No, wait— *(Laughter, applause)* Pretty good, pretty good, but you didn't quite get away with it. Let's see now. Let's really figure this out. I tell you what. I've never been to a psychoanalyst, but after this I'll go and consult one, and then I'll have him call you up, and then maybe he can tell you the whole situation.

F: More, then, not less.

C: I'm going to leave it to the analyst.

F: You once said, "Sex is like sneezing."

C: Yes. I meant that literally. I was making a metaphor for orgasm. What is the nearest thing in physical sensation to an orgasm? And I came up with the idea that it was sneezing. (*Laughter*)

F: You also said once, when you were analyzing whether you would have gone to a psychiatrist, that it might "have lessened the penalties I pay." I can't imagine you ever paying penalties. Have you?

C: Sure, everybody pays penalties.

F: What sort of people pay?

C: In the process of maturing, if you mature at all, one has to pay a certain price.

F: What do you mean?

C: I don't think it's possible to go through life, unless you're a complete idiot, without being continuously hurt one way or another. The only thing that doesn't hurt me is to pick up a newspaper and read some libelous thing about me or some bad review of something. That doesn't bother me at all. But if I feel somebody has betrayed me in some way or been disloyal about something, I get terribly upset about it.

F: You said once the only thing you hate reading about yourself in the papers is the truth.

C: That's it.

F: The lies are fine?

C: I don't care what anybody says about me as long as it isn't true. (*Laughter and applause*)

Truman Capote on Christmas, Places, Memories
Mary Cantwell/1971

From *Mademoiselle*, 74 (December 1971), 122-123, 176. Copyright © 1971 by The Condé Nast Publications Inc. Reprinted by permission.

Truman Capote is a writer of extraordinary diversity and extraordinary accomplishment, not the least of which is a memoir published in *Mademoiselle* in 1956, "A Christmas Memory," which ranks among the few truly moving pieces on a subject which has evoked centuries of bathos and bad writing. He has recorded "A Christmas Memory"; it was made into a distinguished television play; it will probably be anthologized until Armageddon yet no amount of exposure can weather its freshness and immediacy, or numb the feeling of loss which pervades it. To catch up on Mr. Capote and Christmas . . . and a few other things, a *Mlle* editor sat recently in his super-Victorian apartment (in a super-modern building) and taped the following.

ON CHRISTMAS

Q: If I say Christmas, what is the first word you think of?

A: Crayons.

Q: Why?

A: Well, when I was a child living in Alabama, we were too poor to buy Christmas presents and we always used to make our own Christmas presents and there were two or three I used to make—like my story, "Christmas Memory." I used to make kites—I was quite an expert kite maker—and I used to decorate them with crayon drawings and another thing I used to do is, I used to get, you know that scratch paper—sandpaper and I'd get this sort of thick kind of sandpaper and I would cut all kinds of animals out of it and then put them on boards and I would decorate the boards with all sorts of wax drawings and put them up by the fireplace and they would be used to light matches with. We used to get all these different sorts of dyes and by what we now call tie-dying—at that time I don't remember seeing anybody really doing it except in the South—we used to make all these kinds of bandannas for presents by tie-dying them. And the other thing was we'd get all kinds of different colored cellophane and save it all through the year and you take this cellophane and wrap it in a special sort of way and weave it into belts that really lasted for a long time and were really pretty—red and green and yellow and orange cellophane.

Q: Who did you give all these presents to?

A: My cousins and my friends at school. And of course living in a small town like that, everybody made a big thing about Christmas and nobody had any money anyway. It was during the Depression, in the deepest, most rural part of the South, so everybody was in the same boat. But Christmas was a big thing that way. There was certainly nothing commercial about it.

Q: Was Christmas a good time for you?

A: I loved Christmas up until the time I was about 12 years old and then I went away to boarding school and quite often for one reason or another I had to stay over in the school over the Christmas holiday and it became the most unhappy period—but it was a very happy period most of my childhood.

Q: Were you excited all the time? Feeling very giving or did you feel that you were getting?

A: I was looking forward to what I was going to get, but I liked to make things too.

Q: Were there religious connotations to your Christmas?

A: No. A great deal of singing and I liked all the party part of it. In fact, it's the only time I liked going to church. But I never liked going to church. I was never a very religious person—I was sort of anti the whole thing. Which was odd in that particular atmosphere and that town which was extremely either Baptist or Methodist and almost everyone's social life centered around the church. Especially Sunday—if you didn't go to church there wasn't anything to do at all. No one was allowed to play cards or go to the movies—there weren't any movies. You weren't allowed to turn on a radio.

Q: So you're not a repository of Baptist hymns?

A: No. I'm not. But I used to go to church. I had to. I was forced to. I liked to go to Negro churches curiously. I always enjoyed that and I would go quite willingly to any Negro church because the music was so good and the singing was so good. I rather liked the preachers because they were so emotional—spoke sort of a strange marvelous rhetoric I enjoyed and there was something kind of real and emotional about it. And I used to go to colored churches all on my own—really for the theatricality of it more than anything else. In fact, entirely for the theatricality.

ON CHRISTMAS PLACES

Q: When was Christmas ever good again?

A: I have a little chalet in Switzerland. High up in the Alps. And I spend most every Christmas there. From my house you can look over valleys for 50, 60, 70 miles. Everything is in deep snow. And there's this marvelous silvery jingly thing about it. A kind of deep quiet. Big wood-burning fires. A coziness about it that I like, a great sort of purity. It seems to be in the spirit of everything.

One Christmas I can remember with great distinctness was about 1953. I was in Italy and a friend and I decided to spend Christmas in Venice. When we arrived, it was terribly cold and all the gondolas were covered with thick black velvet and were trimmed with little silver bells so that they could hear each other as they were going through the canals. Everything was so dark. Venice was almost totally deserted, just one or two lights flickering in a window. And it was snowing—the snow sort of drifting. In this dark wintry Venetian night. Sitting with this little kerosene stove burning in the gondola. We arrived at the Grand Hotel which had just one floor open, and we ate all our meals at Harry's Bar. They had a stove in Harry's Bar. And all of these people who hadn't been out of their old palaces since 1903 came creeping over there and had a big Christmas dinner with martinis and cheese sandwiches. Harry's Bar was marvelous.

There was another Christmas—when I was first in New York. I had met Carson McCullers and her sister Margarita Smith and they were living in a house about 40 miles up on the Hudson. I was working for *The New Yorker* and didn't get very much of a salary, but I saved up some money and bought them and a few other people Christmas presents. On Christmas Eve, I went out and when I came back my apartment had been robbed and everything in it had been taken. I went up anyway and we played old Marlene Dietrich records and drank wine. It was a very southern Christmas—my last southern Christmas up north—and we had all kinds of fried chicken and pies and cakes. And everybody was very kind about my not giving them a present although they all gave me one.

Q: Tell me about your most horrible Christmas.

A: The very worst Christmas I ever spent, in fact one of the worst experiences of my life in any way, was in Russia. In Leningrad. It was unbelievably cold; you could have walked down the street, sat down, and had an appendectomy and never felt a thing. Permanently Novocainized. And one night it was Christmas Eve. A man who is a professor at the University of Leningrad phoned and said that he'd like to take me out for dinner. We walked from the hotel to the restaurant—it turned out to be about three miles—and when we got there I could scarcely move. So he ordered this special vodka with red pepper in it. It's warm and you just have to dash it down in one big gulp and it makes you start breathing again. There was a terrible little orchestra among some desiccated palm trees—a piano, a fiddle and something playing "Good Night Ladies" is the last thing I remember. Because suddenly this vodka hit me, just like somebody clapped an ether mask over my face. Although I remained conscious, I don't remember a thing from that point on. Apparently we had dinner, and then he took me to a nightclub on the waterfront where they were having some crazy, wild Russian Christmas dance. I'd come to every now and then and see some terrible big dirty filthy thing with a beard dancing around. And I was drinking Russian brandy then which there is nothing like in the world. This poor professor got me back to my hotel and when I got to my room I somehow got the windows open. The next day I didn't come to at all. And no maids ever come to your room; you have to get out and yell "Fire" before one comes anywhere near you. A day and a night passed. The second day I woke up and didn't know where I was: the entire room was filled with snow. The bed, the floors, the chairs—the snow kept blowing into the room. I got out of bed and tried to find the door, but the next thing it was total darkness. When I came to again, it was the middle of the night and there I was crashing around in this snow and slush. Finally I was about 2½ days in this room, only coming to now and then until finally I got out. There's a matron at the end of each corridor in every Russian hotel and I walked into it like a cave man—covered with snow, snow pouring out of the bedroom. I was in the hospital four days with pneumonia and they said if I hadn't been so chock full of Russian brandy I'd have died. (To the interviewer's comment that that was the loveliest Christmas story she'd ever heard, Capote replied "Even better than 'Christmas Memory.' ")

ON HOME
  Q: Where is home?
  A: Home is where your hat hangs. Where you hang your hat. I've always wandered. I lived in Europe for 16 years and had some terribly nice houses. But I've always moved to get moving. . . . I always knew who I was because I always knew what I wanted to do. And I guess somehow the two things are synonymous—at least they are with me. I was always in the middle of a project as it were. And in that sense the project became my sort of chauffeur or mobile home.

ON VULNERABILITY
  Q: How did you get so tough?
  A: I'm not tough. In fact my greatest problem is that I am infinitely more aware of what is going on in other people than I am in what is happening to me. I was always much more aware of their sensibilities and sensitivities and needs than I was of my own—and my own seemed unimportant in comparison. As a result, I haven't been sufficiently selfish or tough, haven't gotten or enjoyed as many things in life as I should have. . . . I once said to someone that nothing I could read in a newspaper or hear about myself could cause me any distress. I also thought that even in private life it would be extremely difficult for someone to hurt me because they would have to disappoint me to some extraordinary degree that I didn't think they could. I was right in the sense that nothing anybody could write or say about me could hurt me—but I found out later that I can be hurt, and that I am capable of crying. Because I cried quite a lot then.
  Q: If I say family. What do you think?
  A: Well. I have many relatives. But I would not say that I have any

family. As the word is generally understood. Mostly since I was 12 years old, my family has been what I consider just my friends. You know my story "Christmas Memory"—which you published in your magazine—that is the story of my childhood—that is the story up to that point: I did have a family with this elderly cousin, the house I lived in. But after that point, when she died and I started going to different schools, I never did.

But you had enough from those 12 years to sustain you for the rest.

ON CHANCE

Q: So many people lean on religion, or astrology, or the I Ching—anything so long as it suggests a pattern or a plan. But you don't, do you?

A: Everything is up to chance. I don't think there's any point in making any particular plan. You can make out of your life what you want it to be if you really want to. Either you believe there's a pattern in life or you don't. I just don't. Obviously it takes a great effort and will to write a book: I mean it isn't just to take up my time. But I don't have the need to do things that other people have. I don't care whether I work or don't work. If work weren't my project, a kind of nothingness would be my project. Kind of drifting. I just make the things up as I go along. I look for love and that's about it.

Q: Is love everything? Is it enough?

A: Yes. Except that one has to keep finding it over and over.

Self-Portrait
Truman Capote/1972

From *The Dogs Bark: Public People and Private Places* (New York: Random House, 1974), 405-419. Copyright © 1974 by Random House, Inc. Reprinted by permission.

Q: If you had to live in just one place—without ever leaving—where would it be?

A: Oh, dear. What a devastating notion. To be grounded in just one place. After all, for thirty years I've lived everywhere and had houses all over the world. But curiously, no matter where I lived, Spain or Italy or Switzerland, Hong Kong or California, Kansas or London, I *always* kept an apartment in New York. That must signify something. So, if really forced to choose, I'd say New York.

Q: But *why*? It's dirty. Dangerous. In every way difficult.

A: Hmmm. Yes. But though I can live for long stretches in mountainous or seaside solitude, primarily I am a city fellow. I like *pavement*. The sound of my shoes on pavement; stuffed windows; all-night restaurants; sirens in the night—sinister but alive; book and record shops that, on impulse, you can visit at midnight.

And in that sense, New York is the world's only city *city*. Rome is noisy and provincial. Paris is sullen, insular, and, odd to say, extraordinarily puritanical. London? All my American friends who have gone to live there bore one so by saying, "But it's so civilized." I don't know. To be totally dead, utterly dull—is that civilized? And to top it all, London is also highly provincial. The same people see the same people. Everybody knows your business. At most, it is only possible to lead *two* separate lives there.

And that is the great advantage of New York, why it is *the* city. One can be a multiple person there: ten different people with ten different sets of friends none overlapping.

Q: Do you prefer animals to people?

A: I like them about equally. Still, I've usually found there is something secretively cruel about people who really feel more warmly toward dogs and cats and horses than people.

Q: Are you cruel?

A: Occasionally. In conversation. Let's put it this way: I'd rather be a friend of mine than an enemy.

Q: Do you have many friends?

A: About seven or so whom I can entirely rely upon. And about twenty more I more or less trust.

Q: What qualities do you look for in friends?

A: Firstly, they mustn't be stupid. I've once or twice been in love with persons who were stupid, indeed very much so; but that is another matter—one can be in love with someone without feeling the least in communication with that person. God, that's how most people get married and why most marriages are unhappy.

Usually, I can tell quite early on whether it is possible for someone and myself to be friends. Because one doesn't have to finish sentences. I mean, you start to say something, then realize, midway, that he or she has already understood. It is a form of mental-emotional conversational shorthand.

Intelligence apart, attention is important: I pay attention to my friends, am concerned about them, and expect the same in return.

Q: Are you often disappointed by a friend?

A: Not really. I've sometimes formed dubious attachments (don't we all?); I've always done it with my eyes open. The only hurt that hurts is one that takes you by surprise. I am seldom surprised. Though I have a few times been outraged.

Q: Are you a truthful person?

A: As a writer—yes, I think so. Privately—well, that is a matter of opinion; some of my friends think that when relating an event or piece of news, I am inclined to alter and overelaborate. Myself, I just call it making something "come alive." In other words, a form of art. Art and truth are not necessarily compatible bedfellows.

Q: How do you like best to occupy your spare time?

A: Not sexually, though I have had my enthusiastic periods. But, as more than a casual pastime, it is too heart-scalding and costly, however you interpret the latter adjective.

Really, I like to read. Always have. There are not many

contemporary writers I like too well. Though I have admired, among our own Americans, the late Flannery O'Connor, and Norman Mailer, William Styron, Eudora Welty, Katherine Anne Porter, the early Salinger. And oh, really, a number of others. I've never liked Gore Vidal's fiction, but I think his nonfiction is first-class. James Baldwin, ditto. But for the last decade or so I prefer to read writers I've already read. Proven wine. Proust. Flaubert. Jane Austen. Raymond Chandler (one of the *great* American artists). Dickens (I had read all of Dickens before I was sixteen, and have just now completed the full cycle again).

I am partial to films, too—though I leave in the middle quite a lot. But I only like to go to films alone, and only in the daytime when the theatre is mostly empty. That way I can concentrate on what I'm seeing, and depart when I feel like it without having to discuss the merits of the project with someone else: with me, such discussions always lead to argument and irritation.

I prefer to work in the mornings, usually for about four or five hours, and then, if I'm alone in a city, any city, I meet a friend for lunch at some favorite restaurant (in New York: Lafayette, La Côte Basque, Orsini's, the Oak Room at The Plaza, and, until its unhappy demise, the Colony). Many people say they hate to lunch; it fattens them, fatigues them, altogether spoils their day. It makes mine. There are some men I enjoy lunching with, but by and large I prefer beautiful, or at least extremely attractive, alert, and *au courant* women. I count in this category several very young ladies (Lally Weymouth, Amanda Burden, Penelope Tree, Louise Melhado—the latter, alas, married to a very square stockbroker). But I don't consider that any woman deserves full marks until she attains and maintains qualities of style and appearance and amusing good sense beyond the point of easy youthful beguilement: this, a partial list, and a prejudicial one, would have to include Barbara Paley, Gloria Guinness, Lee Radziwill, Oona Chaplin, Gloria Cooper, Slim Keith, Phyllis Cerf, Kay Meehan, Viola Loewy, D. D. Ryan, Evelyn Avedon, Pamela Harriman, Kay Graham—well, one could go on for quite a while, though certainly the names would not top fifty. Notice, the persons I mention are private citizens, not public; after all, for certain public characters—Garbo (an ultimately selfish and tiresome woman) or Elizabeth Taylor (a sensitive, self-educated lady with a tough but essentially innocent attitude—if you sleep with a guy, gosh, that means you have to marry him!)—*allure* is their trade.

Though I know I'm supposed to be very sociable, and though some of the above statements would seem to testify to that, I like to be alone. I like fast, finely made cars, I like lonely motels with their ice machines and eerie anonymity; so sometimes I get behind the wheel and, without warning, without particular destination, drive all alone as far as a thousand miles. I've only once consulted a psychiatrist; instead, I should have gone for a drive with the top down and a wind blowing and a sun shining.

Q: Of what are you most afraid?

A: Not death. Well, I don't want to *suffer*. But if one night I went to sleep and failed to wake, that thought doesn't trouble me much. At least it would be something different. In 1966 I was nearly killed in an auto accident—was flung through the windshield head-on, and though seriously wounded and certain that what Henry James called The Distinguished Thing (death) was nearby, lay fully conscious in pools of blood reciting to myself the telephone numbers of various friends. Since then, I've had a cancer operation, and the only altogether upsetting part was that I had to loiter around an aimless week between the day of diagnosis and the morning of the knives.

Anyway, it strikes me as absurd and rather obscene, this whole cosmetic and medical industry based on lust for youth, age-fear, death-terror. Who the hell wants to live forever? Most of us, apparently; but it's idiotic. After all, there *is* such a thing as life-saturation: the point when everything is pure effort and total repetition.

Poverty? Fanny Brice said, "I've been rich and I've been poor. Believe me, rich is better." Well, I disagree; at least I don't think money makes any ultimate difference to anyone's personal adjustment or (moronic word) "happiness." I know very well a considerable number of very rich people (I don't count anyone rich who can't quite quickly summon up fifty million dollars in hard currency); and there are some who say, when feeling in a bitchy mood, that I don't know anybody else (to which one can best reply, at least they sometimes pick up the check, and never ask for a loan). But the point is: I can't think of a single rich person who, in terms of contentment, or a lessening of the general human anxiety, has it easier than the rest of us. As for me, I can accept it either way: a furnished room on some side street in Detroit or Cole Porter's old apartment in the Waldorf Towers, which the decorator Billy Baldwin transformed into such an island of sublime and subtle luxury. What I couldn't survive is the middle ground: the sound of lawn mowers and water sprinklers outside a two-car-garage ranch split-level in Scarsdale or Shaker Heights. Well, I never said I wasn't a snob. I only said I wasn't afraid of being poor.

Failure? Failure is the condiment that gives success its flavor. No, I've drunk that special hemlock, bit that bullet (especially working in the theatre) enough to now scorn it. Honestly, I don't give a damn what anybody says about me, either privately or in print. Of course, that was not true when I was young and first began to publish. And it is not true now on one count—a betrayal of affection can still traumatically disturb me. Otherwise, defeat and criticism are matters of indifference, remote as the mountains of the moon.

Q: Then what does frighten you?

A: The thought that I might lose my sense of humor. Become a mind without a soul, start down the path to madness, and thereby, as the Zen riddle runs, spend the rest of a ruined life listening to the sound of one hand clapping.

Q: What shocks you? If anything?

A: Deliberate cruelty. Cruelty for its own sake, verbal or physical. Murder. Capital punishment. Child-beaters. Animal-baiters.

Once, long ago, I discovered that my best friend, aged eighteen, was having a fully realized love affair with his stepmother. At the time I was shocked; needless to add, I'm not now, and thinking back, can see that it was probably a positive benefit to them both. Since then, I've never been surprised, not to say shocked, by any sexual-moral arrangement. If so, I'd have to lead the parade of our nation's million-upon-million hypocrites.

Q: It is now six years since you published *In Cold Blood*. What have you been working on since then?

A: Published as a book a long short story, "The Thanksgiving Visitor." Collaborated on a film, *Trilogy*, based on three of my short stories ("A Christmas Memory," "Miriam," "Among the Paths to Eden"); made a documentary film about capital punishment, *Death*

Row U.S.A., which was commissioned by ABC but never shown in this country (others, yes; Canada, for one) for reasons still mysterious and unexplained. Have also recently completed a screenplay of Fitzgerald's *The Great Gatsby*—a nearly perfect short novel (or, really, long short story), but hell to dramatize because it consists almost entirely of long-ago exposition and, as it were, offstage scenes. Personally, I like my adaptation, but the producers, Paramount Pictures, are of a different opinion; my pity to whoever attempts a rewrite.

It took five years to write *In Cold Blood*, and a year to recover—*if* recovery is the word; not a day passes that some aspect of that experience doesn't shadow my mind.

However, prior to beginning *In Cold Blood*, in fact soon after finishing *Breakfast at Tiffany's* in 1957, I began to prepare the notes and structure for an ambitious novel then entitled, and entitled now, *Answered Prayers*, which derives from a remark of St. Theresa's: "More tears are shed over answered prayers than unanswered ones." I think that's true: no matter what desires are requited, they are always replaced by another. It's like those racing greyhounds and the mechanical rabbit—one can never catch it. It makes for the worst and best in life. I remember a friend at Robert Kennedy's funeral, someone very close to him, and she said: "It was such a hot day. Sweltering. And there was the grave waiting in the grass under this great cool green tree. And suddenly I envied him. Envied him all that green peacefulness. I thought, Bless you, Bobby, you don't have to fight any more. You're safe."

Answered Prayers is complicated technically and much the longest work I've done—indeed, triple the length of all my other books combined. During the past year or so I've been under great pressure to finish it; but literature has its own life, and insists on dancing to its own measure. *Answered Prayers* is like a wheel with a dozen spokes; the fuel that spins the wheel is an extraordinary young woman who has had fifty affairs, could have married virtually anyone, but for twelve years has loved an "older" man who can't marry because he is married, and *won't* divorce because he expects, with reasonable cause, to be the next President of the United States.

Q: If you hadn't decided on writing, a creative life, what would you have done?

A: Become a lawyer. I often considered it, and many lawyers, including one attorney general and a Supreme Court justice, have told me I would have made a first-class trial lawyer, though my voice, often described as "high and childish" (*among* other things), might have been a detriment.

Also, I wouldn't have minded being kept, but no one has ever wanted to keep me—not more than a week or so.

Q: Do you take any form of exercise?

A: Yes. Massage.

Q: Can you cook?

A: Not for company. For myself, I always dish up the same cuisine. Crackers and cream of tomato soup. Or a baked potato stuffed with fresh caviar.

Q: If *Reader's Digest* ever commissioned from you an "Unforgettable Character" article, whom would you write about?

A: God forbid that such a degrading assignment should ever come my way. But if it did—ahem, let's see. Robert Frost, America's Poet Laureate, was fairly memorable. An old bastard, if ever there was one. I met him when I was eighteen; apparently he didn't consider me a sufficiently humble worshiper at the altar of his ego. Anyway, by writing a scurrilous letter to Harold Ross, the late editor of *The New Yorker*, where I was then employed, he got me fired from my first and last time-clock job. Perhaps he did me a favor; because then I sat down and wrote my first book, *Other Voices, Other Rooms*.

As a child, I lived until I was ten or so with an elderly spinster relative in a rural, remote part of Alabama. Miss Sook Faulk. She herself was not more than twelve years old mentally, which is what accounted for her purity, timidity, her strange, unexpected wisdom. I have written two stories about her, "A Christmas Memory" and "The Thanksgiving Visitor"—both of which were filmed for television with Geraldine Page portraying Miss Faulk with an uncanny beauty and accuracy.

Miss Page is rather unforgettable, come to consider: a Jekyll and Hyde; Dr. Jekyll on stage, Mr. Hyde off. It is purely a matter of appearance; she has better legs than Dietrich and as an actress can project an illusion of infinite allure—but in private she insists, Lord knows why, in disguising herself under witchlike wigs and costumes of consummate eccentricity.

Of course, I don't care much for actresses *or* actors. A friend, I can't remember just now who, said, "All actresses are more than women, and all actors are less than men." A half-true observation; still, true enough to be, in my opinion, the root cause of the prevailing theatrical neurosis. But the trouble with most actors (*and* actresses) is that they are dumb. And, in many instances, the dumbest are the most gifted. Sir John Gielgud, the kindest man alive, an incomparable technician, brilliant voice; but, alas, all his brains are in his voice. Marlon Brando. No actor of my generation possesses greater natural gifts; but none other has transported intellectual falsity to higher levels of hilarious pretension. Except, perhaps, Bob Dylan: a sophisticated musical (?) con man pretending to be a simple-hearted (?) revolutionary but sentimental hillbilly.

But enough of this question. It was stupid to start with.

Q: What is the most hopeful word in any language?
A: Love.
Q: And the most dangerous?
A: Love.
Q: Have you ever wanted to kill anybody?
A: Haven't you? No? Cross your heart? Well, I still don't believe you. Everybody at one time or another has wanted to kill someone. The true reason why many people commit suicide is because they are cowards who prefer to murder themselves rather than murder their tormentor. As for me, if desire had ever been transferred into action, I'd be right up there with Jack the Ripper. Anyway, it's amusing to think about: the plotting, the planning, the surprise and regret imprinting the face of the villain-turned-victim. Very relaxing. Better than counting sheep.

Not long ago my doctor suggested that I adopt some healthier hobby other than wine-tasting and fornication. He asked if I could think of anything. I said, "Yes, murder." He laughed, we both did, except I wasn't laughing. Poor man, little did he know what a painful and perfect demise I'd planned for him when, after eight days abed with something closely resembling black cholera, he still refused to pay me a house call.

Q: What are your political interests?
A: I've known a few politicians whom I liked, and a more surrealist montage could not be imagined. Adlai Stevenson was a friend, and

always a generous one; we were staying as guests in the same house when he died, and I remember watching a manservant pack his belongings, and then, when the suitcases were so pathetically filled, but still unclosed, I walked in and helped myself to one of his ties—a sort of sentimental theft, because the night before I'd complimented him on the tie and he'd promised to give it to me. On the other hand, I like Ronald Reagan, too. Many of my friends think I'm teasing them when I say that. I'm not. Though Governor Stevenson and Governor Reagan are quite different spirits, the latter shares with the former a modesty, an "I'm looking you in the eye and I mean what I say" directness that is rare enough among us folk, not to mention politicians. I suppose New York's Senator Jacob Javits and Governor Reagan, for purely reflex reasons, feel antipathetical toward each other. Actually, I think they would get along fine, and would make an interesting political combination. (Of course, the real reason I always speak well of Governor Reagan and Senator Javits is that I like both their wives, though they are even less alike than their husbands, Mrs. Javits being a lacquered but still untamed city urchin, a smoochy-voiced and sexy-eyed child-woman with a vocabulary as fresh and salty and Brooklyn-bred as the waves that spank the beaches at Coney Island. As for Mrs. Reagan—I don't know, there is about her something so small-town American and nostalgia-making: the homecoming queen riding past on a throne of roses.)

The two politicians I've known best were President Kennedy and his brother, Robert. They, too, were quite unalike, and not as close as generally believed; at any rate, the younger brother was very much afraid of the elder—

Q: Do we really have to hear *any* more about *any* Kennedy? Moreover, you're sidestepping the question, which wasn't about politicians but your own interest in politics.

A: I have none. I've never voted. Though, if invited, I suppose I might join almost anyone's protest parade: Anti-war, Free Angela, Gay Liberation, Ladies' Lib, etc.

Q: If you could be anything, what would you most like to be?

A: Invisible. To be visible or invisible at will. I mean, think of the possibilities: the power, the riches, the constant erotic amusement.

Q: What are your chief vices? And virtues?

A: I have no vices. The concept doesn't exist in my vocabulary. My chief virtue is gratitude. So far as I know, I've never betrayed anyone who was kind to me. But as art is life's compensation for the flawed delights of living, I reserve my greatest gratitude for those poets, painters, composers who have compensated me most. A work of art is the one mystery, the one extreme magic; everything else is either arithmetic or biology. I think I understand a considerable lot about writing; nevertheless, when I read something good, in fact, a work of art, my senses sail away into a universe of wonder: How did he do it? How is it possible?

Q: Looking back, it would seem as though some of your answers are rather inconsistent. Deliberate cruelty, you say, is the one unforgivable sin. Then you confess to occasional verbal cruelty, and later on admit that you have contemplated prepared murder.

A: Anyone consistently consistent has a head made of biscuit. My head, the interior, may be made of something odd, but it isn't biscuit.

Q: Suppose you were drowning. What images, in the classic tradition, do you envision rolling across your mind?

A: A hot Alabama day in, oh, 1932, so I must be eight, and I am in a vegetable garden humming with bees and heat waves, and I am picking and putting into a basket turnips and slushy scarlet tomatoes. Then I am running through a pine and honeysuckle woods toward a deep cool creek, where I bathe and wash the turnips, the tomatoes. Birds, bird-music, leaf-light, the stringent taste of raw turnip on my tongue: pleasures everlasting, hallelujah. Not far away a snake, a cotton-mouth moccasin, writhes, ripples across the water; I'm not afraid of it.

Ten years later. New York. A wartime jazz joint on West 52nd Street: The Famous Door. Featuring my most beloved American singer—then, now, forever: Miss Billie Holiday. *Lady Day.* Billie, an orchid in her hair, her drug-dimmed eyes shifting in the cheap lavender light, her mouth twisting out the words: *Good mornin', Heartache—You're here again to stay—*

June, 1947. Paris. Having a *fine l'eau* at a sidewalk café with Albert Camus, who tells me I must learn to be less sensitive to criticism. (Ah! If he could have lived to see me now.)

Standing at the window of *a pension* on a Mediterranean island watching the afternoon passenger boat arrive from the mainland. Suddenly, there on the wharf carrying a suitcase is someone I know.

Very well. Someone who had said goodby to me, in what I took to be final tones, not many days prior. Someone who had apparently had a change of mind. So: is it the real turtle soup?—or only the mock? Or is it at long last love? (It was.)

A young man with black cowlicked hair. He is wearing a leather harness that keeps his arms strapped to his sides. He is trembling; but he is speaking to me, smiling. All I can hear is the roar of blood in my ears. Twenty minutes later he is dead, hanging from the end of a rope.

Two years later. Driving down from the April snows of the Alps into the valleys of an Italian spring.

Visiting, at Père-Lachaise in Paris, the grave of Oscar Wilde— overshadowed by Epstein's rather awkward rendition of an angel; I don't think Oscar would have cared for it much.

Paris. January, 1966. The Ritz. An unusual friend comes to call, bringing as gifts masses of white lilac and a baby owl in a cage. The owl, it seems, must be fed live mice. A waiter at the Ritz very kindly sent it to live with his farm-family in Provence.

Oh, but now the mental slides are moving very fast. The waves are closing over. Picking apples on an autumn afternoon. Nursing to life a bulldog puppy ill-to-death with distemper. And she lives. A garden in the California desert. The surf-sound of wind in the palm trees. A face, close by. Is it the Taj Mahal I see? Or merely Asbury Park? Or is it at long last love? (It wasn't—God no, was it ever not.)

Suddenly, everything is again spinning backward; my friend Miss Faulk is making a scrap-quilt, the design is of roses and grapes, and now she is drawing the quilt up to my chin. There is a kerosene lamp by the bed; she wishes me happy birthday, and blows out the light.

And at midnight when the church-bell chimes I'm eight.

Once more, the creek. The taste of raw turnip on my tongue, the flow of summer water embracing my nakedness. And there, *just* there, swiveling, tangoing on the sun-dappled surface, the exquisitely limber and lethal cottonmouth moccasin. But I'm not afraid; am I?

Checking in with Truman Capote
Gerald Clarke/1972

From *Esquire*, 78 (November 1972), 136-137, 187-188, 190.
Copyright © 1972 by Esquire. Reprinted by permission.

"I always see myself described as delicate," complained Truman Capote. "There's nothing delicate about me. Do I look delicate?" he asked, pushing away his martini glass and rising from his chair to show two chubby, totally indelicate legs under his blue summer shorts and beneath his blue-and-white-striped shirt a large, middle-age bulge that would look at home on a steelworker. His annoyance subsided and he sat down. "In actual fact, I have a strong, sturdy, peasant frame and an oversized head. I have *always* worn the biggest hat." If Truman Capote were in the terminal stage of the black plague, he would somehow find the disease to his credit and expect envious, "Where-can-I-buy-it?" glances at La Grenouille. The funny thing is—he would probably get them.

At forty-eight, Capote is no longer the slim, exotic-looking faun who was pictured on the dust jacket of his first novel, *Other Voices, Other Rooms*. "At that time," he says, in the quarrelsome tone of a pioneer who finds his territory suddenly crowding up, "I was considered way beyond the pale. I made a whole life-style twenty years before its time. I was the only public character who didn't care what anybody said or thought." The wispy, childlike voice—"It is not a lisp," he says firmly—and the peculiar, yes, delicate, mannerisms that seemed so shocking in 1948 are now amusing eccentricities, always good for sales, and Capote himself has been canonized by Suzy and Johnny Carson as a Public Character, St. Truman of The Tonight Show.

After spending half a lifetime with his nose pressed against the glass—"He wants awfully to be on the inside staring out," Holly Golightly said of Capote the narrator in *Breakfast at Tiffany's*—Truman finds that most of the world is staring at him. His party at The

Plaza was one of the social events of the Sixties, and he is still busy hopping from yacht to yacht, Palm Beach to Acapulco. He lunches with New York's grandes dames at New York's grand restaurants, and he cried when the Colony, one of the four or five he considers worth the trouble of lifting fork to face, closed in 1971, depriving him evermore of his special back table under the TV set. ("Well, I didn't actually go boohoo," he told me, "but tears did come to my eyes. It was such a shock. I have been going there forever.")

He owns houses in Palm Springs, California; in Wainscott, Long Island, midway between the glittering poles of Southampton and East Hampton; and in Verbier, Switzerland, not to mention a luxurious five-room apartment on the twenty-second floor of the United Nations Plaza, overlooking the East River and the United Nations. An animal fancier, he lives there surrounded by, nearly smothered by, a hundred or more small animal representations: a seal, a rabbit, an owl, a Japanese deer, a Portuguese giraffe with a head that moves up and down, a rooster, a parrot, a frog, a bull, an ivory mouse, a duck, various butterflies, a turkey, several dogs, innumerable cats in innumerable colors, a lion holding up a table, and a snake in the form of a stick. He also has a real cat, Diotima, named for a woman philosopher, a teacher of Socrates, and Maggie, an English bulldog that enjoys dining on the clothes and flowers of his friends. "She is," says Truman, "very munchy."

Still, even in the years of fame and riches that followed his ball, Truman has had more than a few of the common ordinary problems. He was in a near-fatal automobile accident. He spent three days in a California jail for contempt of court after he failed to give evidence about a defendant he had interviewed. He was hospitalized for exhaustion, and, in 1971, was operated on for cancer of the groin. "People say that if you have cancer, you can't feel it. I'm here to tell you you can. I couldn't sleep for more than two hours a night, and I was dripping with sweat. Finally, I went to a doctor. When I got up from the examining table, the nurse wouldn't look at me and neither would he. It was like a jury about to hang me." We both meditate on that awful moment before he continues. "I saw Tennessee Williams some time ago and he said that Gore Vidal had told him that 'Truman is broke and dyin' of cancer.' " Capote's voice drops several octaves to approximate Williams' drawl, itself an imitation, doubtless, of Vidal's cheery report. "I said: 'Well, if wishes could come true, I would be.' Actually, Tennessee has been telling everybody for the past twenty-five years that he was dying of cancer, and, Jesus, Gore has been concerned about heart attacks for years to my certain knowledge. But *I'm* the *only* one who did have cancer."

When I talked with Capote, mostly in his New York apartment and on Long Island, his problems seemed well behind him, however, and he was all sunny geniality, with only an occasional cloud interrupting his beaming beneficence. In New York, in fact, he was so relaxed that he talked to me lying down, peering at me over his feet. "I'm never unkind to anyone," he sighed, as if confessing a shameful, neurotic weakness. "I mean, except intentionally. My great fault is that I understand everything. When somebody does something duplicitous to me, I always understand their motivations."

His comments on most of his fellow novelists are, in this generous spirit, almost olympian in their detachment, and he seems genuinely sorry that he has only so many good words and that they have already been taken by such favorites—all, fortunately, quite dead—as Jane Austen, Flaubert, Proust, Dickens, Henry James, Willa Cather, F. Scott Fitzgerald, Raymond Chandler ("one of the *great* American artists"), and Sarah Orne Jewett. "Sarah who?" I ask. "Sarah Orne Jewett. She wrote a marvelous book called *The Country of the Pointed Firs*. It had a purity I admired greatly, and it had a great effect on me. I like—and I don't like—Herman Melville," he adds crossly, uncertain just where he should place on the list that troublesome giant. "I'm having my problems with him. It took me three times till I finished *Moby Dick*. I was," he chortles, "thrice thrashed." Melville, clearly, has abused his patience and tested the boundaries of his goodwill.

In such an exalted gathering there is no room, even if Melville is invited, for a Faulkner or a Hemingway, much less a Mailer or an Updike. "I find Faulkner's prose so cumbersome and tanglesome, the exact opposite of what I admire and try to do myself. There is so much undergrowth and so much machete work that has to be done. Hemingway had the misfortune of being imitated so much that he came to seem like a parody of himself. Besides that, he was a bully. When I was twenty-one or twenty-two, Nelson Algren published *The Man with the Golden Arm* and Hemingway was quoted on the dust jacket: 'All you Capote fans, get your hats and coats and leave the room. Here comes a *real* writer.' I said to myself: 'Jesus Christ, here's this great guy Hemingway, and he knocks a kid in the head that hard.' I would call that pretty bullying."

For his living colleagues, none of whom would dare bully a writer named Capote, he measures his praise as stingily as if it were a rare, irreplaceable brandy. None of them is likely to find it intoxicating. "Norman Mailer is a good essayist. I don't think he can write fiction. Gore Vidal? I don't think Gore can create anything. The same thing is true of Mailer, but he is a *much* better writer than Gore ever thought of being. John Updike writes so well. But isn't it Norman who said that Updike's vice was writing? All the effects are on the surface, with nothing underneath. I can't remember what one of his stories is about when I've finished it. There's something wrong when you're aware all the time of the writing, don't you think? It's like trying to grasp smoke. *Rabbit, Run* has one marvelous scene, where she drowns the baby. The rest is hooey." Nabokov? "I liked *Lolita* and *Laughter in the Dark*. Other than that I've never particularly enjoyed him. I do think he writes well, though." Kurt Vonnegut? The worst possible fate. "I haven't read him." Saul Bellow? "I like him, yah, but I get bogged down in all of his urban intellectual Jewish jokes. I get so sick and tired of the whole Jewish mafia that I'm really no judge. They all seem as if they were squeezing out of the same toothpaste tube." Philip Roth? "This new book of his [*Our Gang*] is unreadable." To show that he is not entirely negative on the others who ply his trade, Capote concludes with friendly if somewhat opaque words for William Styron. "I think Bill Styron is very good, but then everybody says that. Just as everyone has a token Jew or a token homosexual, Styron is everybody's favorite good writer." While I sit quietly, silenced by the unexpected accolade for Styron, whom he apparently places on a level with the admirable Miss Jewett, Capote bounces up to refill my glass, "What we in the South," he winks, "call sweeten it up." A moment later he returns for his own glass. "You're not the only one entitled to ice around here," he jokingly pouts.

One reason for Capote's ostensible cheer may be that his newest novel, *Answered Prayers*—"more tears are shed over answered prayers than unanswered ones," wrote Saint Theresa—is now two-thirds finished and progressing well. Projected at eight hundred pages, the work will be almost as long as all of Capote's other books put together. "For me," he admits, "that is a fantastic length. I never wrote anything remotely that complicated. I began it in 1958 with notes, a full outline, and an ending. In 1959 I got involved in *In Cold Blood*, never dreaming I would spend five years on it. It was 1966 before I went back to the novel. I worked on my notes and construction from the end of 1966 to the end of 1969. In 1969 I began writing. I always planned this book as being my principal work, the thing I always have been working toward." One of the editors at Random House is the only other person, according to Truman, who has seen what he has written. The editor calls what he has read "brilliant, malicious, very funny, acerbic, bitchy, and unputdownable."

"There once was a great young philosopher," the book unputdownably begins, "named Agnes Otley, age eight, who said: 'If I could do anything I wanted to do, I'd like to go to the interior of the planet earth and there discover unspoiled monsters.'" Capote, who has removed his glasses and rubbed his eyes while he quoted the first sentence, taken from a selection of children's sayings, chuckles wickedly. "My book is about spoiled monsters, and I didn't have to go to the interior of the earth to find them." At the center of his *magnum opus* is an "extraordinary young woman who has had fifty affairs," but who loves an older, married man, a politician who is probably destined to be the next President of the U.S. "I'm going to call it a novel, but in actual fact it's a *roman à clef*. Almost everything in it is true, and it has in it every sort of person I've ever had any dealings with. I have a cast of thousands." It should be quite a cast. Besides lunching with the Paleys and weekending with the Guinnesses, Truman periodically explores New York's seamy netherworld—all, of course, in the interests of research. George Plimpton was taken along on one such foray to a dive on West Forty-fifth Street inhabited by "midnight cowboys," as Plimpton decorously calls them. Truman was eager to introduce him to "the Spook," a black pimp who has a stable of twenty-five girls, who sports an ankle-length white ermine coat, and who displays a diamond ring on every finger. The Spook, who will be one of the characters in the book, was busy on his rounds that night, however, and, to Truman's quite visible disgust, two sports fans latched on to Plimpton and spent the night talking football.

Whether Truman, who admires tightness and precision in writing, can conquer the difficulties of a large novel remains a serious question and there have been rumors in publishing circles that he is suffering from a bad case of writer's block. *In Cold Blood*, after all, came out seven years ago, and, except for some television and movie scripts, there has not been much from Capote's pen since. Truman hotly denies that there is, or has been, a problem. "I'm not being held up by any kind of block," he asserts, "just by my own standards. I have a terrific critical tension. When you get to know so much, you become critical because *you* know the difference. I *am* too self-critical. I could get a hell of a lot more work done if I could free myself of this neurosis." That he has the material for eight hundred pages, or, for that matter, eighteen hundred pages, is not, however, open to dispute. No other American novelist knows so many levels of life so intimately, and no other has observed so closely as has Truman the spoiled monsters that inhabit the rarefied reaches of the very rich. To hear him tell it, in fact, his passion for associating with the rich and famous has been, like the trip to the bar on Forty-fifth Street, little more than a giant research project. "I was gathering my grapes from which I would trample my wine," he assures me. "I've always been basically a reporter. Now that I've got what I want out of it [the partying] I'm no longer interested. I have no social life. I never go out."

That statement is not literally—or even approximately—true, and Capote has a reputation for rearranging facts to suit his fancy or his need. "He improves on the poverty of God's own imagination," is Wyatt Cooper's artful way of phrasing it. "His view of reality and mine are very different," is novelist Donald Windham's. Truman, apparently, is used to the charge and writes his own defense in a recent issue of *Cosmopolitan*: "I just call it making something 'come alive.' In other words, a form of art. Art and truth are not necessarily compatible bedfellows."

They are about the only ones who are not in the Capote world, and Truman, the supreme, ultimate gossip, knows, or pretends to know, the sexual habits of nearly everyone. He told me, for instance, all about the homosexual underlife of a male movie star, famous as a sex symbol ("Don't you know, anything?" he hooted at me. "But, Truman, I can't print that anyway," I protested. "It's libelous." "Oh, I *know* that, but I thought *you* would like to know"), and all about a famous politician's affair with another, female star ("He only went to bed with her twice, but apparently she thought it was love"). He was crestfallen when I expressed no great surprise at that familiar story. "I suppose everybody's heard that," he murmured, looking disappointed and a little embarrassed, as if I had rejected a present he had picked out just for me. "Truman is like a child at a birthday party," observes Plimpton, "and he loves to present you with delights. He makes his gossip into a story, setting it into a really quite lovely form."

Plimpton's image of Truman as the artful jeweler, the Fabergé of small tales, is not subscribed to by everyone, and Vidal, perhaps predictably, translates Capote's penchant for gossip into a major character flaw. "He has no conversation except telling scandalous stories about famous people. I used to watch him in action when we were very young. He was so strange looking that everybody took against him on first sight. His way of winning over famous and/or rich people—who were his only interest—was to tell them scandalous stories, usually about their ex-husbands or wives. This would immediately catch their interest, needless to say, and then he would be included in their circle."

Still, Vidal is wrong in claiming that gossip is the only way Capote holds his friends, and Truman does have a steadfast and intensely loyal band of admirers. "He wears very, very well, he's not a man to let a friend down," is the word from Lauren Bacall. "He has a sort of genius for friendship," adds novelist John Knowles, "and he takes this extraordinary interest in his friends. He feels that almost everybody he knows doesn't know how to live or run his life, and he wants to manage the life of everybody he likes." His interest in Knowles, for instance, consisted of advice on the promotion of Knowles's first novel, *A Separate Peace*. "He told me how to make literary politics—literary self-promotion—work and explained the whole game of capturing the public."

It was a secret I felt should not be so tightly held, and I ask Truman to play Machiavelli once again and to pretend that I, too, have a book to sell. "You've managed to promote yourself very well since you were twenty," I begin.

"Since I was sixteen," he corrects.

"Well, how do you do it?"

"My theory about publishing a book is that everything—the reviews, the interviews, and everything else—has to happen within two weeks of publication. If it's scattered, it's not going to work. But if it all comes together simultaneously, you'll spin right up the list."

"Yes, but how do you do it?" I persist.

"You use your God-given brain." He looks straight at me, and his chill, light-blue eyes suggest that I am a very slow, if not altogether stupid pupil. Still, he relents. "It takes about six months of organization. You just sort of time it right. I can't explain it. There's a pattern—thought out by me. When *In Cold Blood* came out, I was on the covers of three magazines simultaneously—*Newsweek*, *Life*, and *Saturday Review*—and I had a lead review in every Sunday book supplement across the country. That's a parlay that has never been beaten and never will be." He waits for a challenge I am not about to make. Who, after all, could question Truman Capote's talent for self-promotion? "I would have been great as either a super-lawyer or an advertising executive. What I could do with an ad account hasn't even been dreamed of!"

What he can do with a bank account has been, and Capote is equally, admirably frank about money, the end result of all that organization. "I have a very strong sense of my own value," he tells me. "I know exactly what my name means, in terms of audiences and everything else, and I want to be paid accordingly. I never ask more than the traffic will bear, however, and if a publisher thinks it's too much, that's all right. They can get someone else and there are no hard feelings." (They usually do accept his price, however. For the three-and-a-half-page "Portrait of Myself" in *Cosmopolitan*, for example, on which he claims he worked only two hours, he received $5,000, several times what the magazine ordinarily pays.) He pauses midway through his discourse to complain about high taxes and fourteen audits by the Internal Revenue Service in fourteen years before going on in a more philosophical vein. "I spent a lot of money, but I don't really need money to function or be content. I'm perfectly content to live simply in a one-room apartment." I can't erase an involuntary smirk at the picture of Truman cooking for Barbara Paley on a grease-spattered hot plate, then pulling—Voila!—from his tiny refrigerator a bottle of, God help us, Cold Duck.

"But, Truman, you can't be serious," I interject, trying with a helpless, inarticulate wave of the hand to conjure up the world of yachts, Gucci bags, and little doodads from Cartier, the world that in my ignorance I had assumed he had been hungering for since he was a child in Monroeville, Alabama. "You have so many things," I conclude lamely.

"That's because I'm a collector. I'm like a magpie, but I don't *love* things once I've got them. I have no sense of possession. If I have learned anything, it is that you can't own anything, especially people." The subject, I discover, has changed. "Are you a jealous person?" he asks. "It's the one uncontrollable thing with me—this intense jealousy. My whole life has been dominated by it. I've never been psychoanalyzed—well, I did once go to a therapist—but it finally penetrated that jealousy is only selfishness. I found out too late, however, only after it had caused a lot of damage, mostly to myself."

Capote implies, though he never actually puts it into words, that he was brought up half a step above the poverty line. In *A Christmas Memory*, a sad, sentimental little story he recommended to me as a description of his early childhood, he writes of scrounging dimes to buy Christmas presents. The story may be accurate certainly, but his mother's family, with which he spent most of his early childhood in Monroeville, seems to have been comfortable, even well established. His parents separated when he was two, however, and his sense of impoverishment was probably real enough. His father worked on Mississippi riverboats, and his mother, who died in 1953, was a very pretty, but, according to him, an alcoholic Southern belle. His aunts and his grandmother took care of him instead, and he was misunderstood and bitterly unhappy. "I've had my trauma. When I was five years old, living in Alabama. I might as well have been a deaf mute living there. I understood everything. I could see everything. I was a very, very super-intelligent child, beyond anything you've ever seen. I had the highest intelligence of any child in the United States, an I.Q. of 215." Truman's childhood friend, Harper Lee, in her novel *To Kill a Mockingbird*, gives what he thinks is a good account of him in those days. "We came to know [him] as a pocket Merlin," she writes, "whose head teemed with eccentric plans, strange longings, and quaint fancies."

Eventually Truman was sent north to military schools, which he hated, and, after his mother remarried, to schools in Manhattan and Greenwich, Connecticut. His stepfather, a wealthy Cuban businessman, adopted him, and his given, Waspish surname, Persons, was changed to the Latin Capote. A job with *The New Yorker* followed high school—he had given up by this time his early ambition to be a tap dancer—but he was soon fired for unintentionally but injudiciously offending Robert Frost. It seems that Truman had gone to Vermont on vacation, staying at an inn where Frost was giving a reading. Ill with the flu, Truman kept to his room, venturing down to the reading only on the pleadings of the manager, who had heard that he was from *The New Yorker*. Capote was sicker than he thought, however, and soon left. A copy of Frost's poems, thrown by the outraged poet himself, sailed after him. "Who the hell is this Truman Capote, anyway?" asked *New Yorker* editor Harold Ross the next day. Truman went back to Alabama to write *Other Voices, Other Rooms*. He still remembers Frost as "the meanest man who ever drew breath, an old fake dragging around with a shaggy head of hair and followed by pathetic old ladies from the Middle West."

Novel and author were soon famous, and, still in his early twenties, Truman took off for Europe, where he spent much of the late Forties and early Fifties. About that time he met Vidal. "He was usually being turned out of hotels because of a strange appearance," remembers Vidal. "He would arrive, with this long scarf trailing the floor, and check into a small room in a very grand hotel, like Claridge's. They always managed to hold something like the International Pheasant Harvest the next day, and Truman would have to make room. 'The hotels here can't hold me,' he would say."

Capote's friendship with Vidal, in fact, was quite short and ended in Tennessee Williams' Manhattan apartment in the Summer of 1949. "They began to criticize each other's work," recalls Williams, the unhappy referee. "Gore told Truman he got all his plots out of Carson McCullers and Eudora Welty. Truman said: 'Well, maybe you get all of yours from the *Daily News*.' And so the fight was on. They never got over it." Though Williams recalls the event with seeming distaste, he did not disagree with Vidal's explanation of Capote's literary family tree. "I've always found Truman's fiction a bit derivative and sometimes a bit saccharine, if you want my candid opinion," he told me. "I thought that *In Cold Blood* was an excellent piece of reporting, however, and I think he's found his métier in reportage."

About that time, too, Capote met Jack Dunphy, another novelist, ten years older than he was, who has been his companion on and off ever since. A picture that now hangs on the dark rose wall of Capote's New York dining room shows them during that period: taken in some peaceful garden, the two of them are lying on the grass, with Truman's head, in perfect repose, resting on Jack's chest. Like even most of Truman's friends, I was to get no closer to Dunphy, the man who is, undoubtedly, the most important person in his life.

"I'd like to talk with Jack," I told Truman.

"Oh, Jack won't talk with you." He laughed. "Jack won't talk to *anybody* about *anything*." During the three months they stayed in Switzerland last winter, Jack, however, apparently talked to everybody. "Jack speaks French better than anybody you've ever seen," Truman said proudly. (Despite his visits to France, his own French, by all accounts, is mostly confined to eloquent hand gestures.) "He can even fake dialects. He talks to people on the ski lift and makes them guess where he's from. Most people up there think he's some sort of spy from behind the Iron Curtain."

There are certain of Truman's friends that Dunphy will see and certain others, by far the greater number, that he will not see at all. Tennessee Williams, one of the happy few, remembers him as being "very, very shy" and walking away at the approach of strangers. Someone else who knows him is reminded of Van Gogh: "Jack has a freckled, red, mad look." A third suggests that the very fact that he is so withdrawn and that he has so little interest in Truman's madcap world gives him stability and integrity in Truman's eyes. Dunphy, I finally decided, piecing together various descriptions, is, and has been almost from the day the twenty-one-year-old Capote met him, Truman's stable alter ego.

A few weeks after my first interview with him, I happened to meet Capote one Friday at a private, prerelease screening of the film from Knowles's *A Separate Peace*. After the screening I joined Capote, Knowles, and Jason Epstein, a vice-president of Random House, for a drink. Like everyone else, I am charmed by Capote, who, like an infallible compass, always points toward the most interesting topic of conversation. "Why did Philip Roth leave Random House?" he asked Epstein. He was fascinated when Epstein told him that Roth had left for more money. Epstein excused himself from our group after an hour, and Truman invited me to join him and Knowles for dinner at Trader Vic's, whose appetizers he adores. I bowed out, saying that I had to attend a birthday party—my own.

"Well, we must give you a present," said Truman, who thereupon examined himself from head to toe and, finding nothing but an ordinary seersucker jacket, nondescript trousers, and sockless sneakers, pulled off his Cartier watch and handed it to me. "Here, take off that hideous thing you're wearing and put this on," he commanded.

"Oh, thank you, Truman, but I couldn't . . ." I began, flattered, embarrassed and altogether nonplussed.

"No, no, you must."

"I'm really very touched," I said taking off the hideous thing I was wearing and replacing it with his handsome Yves St. Laurent-designed timepiece. On Monday I sent it back with what I hoped was an appropriate note of gratitude and regret. Truman had gone off to follow the tour of The Rolling Stones for a possible article, and there was no reply. Two weeks later I called him, and after describing The Stones in some detail ("unisexual zombies" was the gist of it), he attended to me.

"Why in the *world* did you send me back that watch? That was a *stupid* thing to do."

"I felt that it was your watch, Truman, and that it belonged with you."

"I've got lots of watches. Jack Knowles told me you would return it. He said you have an uptight, puritan character."

"Jack is very perceptive."

"He said that you should put the whole episode in your piece because it tells so much about both of us." The suggestion, relayed in what was now a sweet, genial voice obviously met with Truman's approval. Jack later told me that the watch had cost $1,600—and that Truman had seven more just like it. "He loves to make princely gestures and pretend he's a rajah," Knowles explained.

A week later still I met Capote in East Hampton for a drive through his Long Island territory. He seemed mollified. "Don't you love to just wander?" he asked as he opened the door of what he calls his "touring car" and what I would call a new Buick Riviera. He nearly disappeared behind the wheel and, like Mr. Magoo, squinted uncertainly through the windshield (his new, stronger eyeglass prescription had given him trouble, and he had gone back to the old, weaker pair) and steered as if maneuvering an unwieldy tug through a crowded harbor. "Sometimes I just get in the car and drive all day." He turned on the car's stereo. "I like to write with records going. I think music has influenced my writing more than other writing has." Our wanderings that day took us to the cemetery where Jacqueline Onassis' father is buried and where both she and her sister Lee have plots, to a beach where Truman walks Maggie, and, finally, to the bar of the American Hotel in Sag Harbor, an old whaling town on the north shore, where we stopped for a drink.

"Have you ever talked publicly about your sexual orientation?" I ask him as we are riding.

"No," he replies, totally unperturbed. "But only because I don't want to give the critics an extra stick to beat me with. Everybody *knows* what I do anyway. I don't have many secrets. Once on a television program Groucho Marx asked me if I'd ever been married. I said, 'No, why?' 'Well, I'd marry you anytime,' he answered. I looked him straight in the eye. 'Is that an honest offer or a proposition?' That shut him up."

The last time I talked with Capote he had just returned to New York from California, and he was spending his nights and mornings with The Rolling Stones, who were appearing at Madison Square Garden and partying everywhere.

"I saw you on television the other night," I said, meaning the Johnny Carson show.

"That's not an unusual thing to do, is it?" he suggested in a voice both tired and bored.

"You looked very elegant in your big hat," I added, as if I hadn't heard him.

"My black and white hat," he corrected. "My black and white sweater. My black and white tennis shoes. My black and white teeth."

"You're also mentioned in The *Times* article on The Stones this morning." That captured his drowsy interest, and I was pleased to be the first to read to him the not particularly flattering account of The New York Times reporter: "The pudgy figure of Truman Capote, in a Stetson hat and sunglasses, could be seen jumping up and down behind the stage speakers."

"I was merely doing my Charlotte Selver exercises," he replied, as if he were not sure whether to be miffed or amused. He finally settled on the latter. I had never seen him angry, but I had seen and felt his snappy or, more exactly, his peevish temper, and was happy in his choice. "Pudgy, they said. Ummm. . . ."

I took advantage of his good humor to test on him a couple of my theories about him. For several days I had been trying, without much success, to get a fix on his character—Truman tells everything about himself, but in some ways he tells nothing, as if all the spicy little tidbits of personal confession were only so much bait to lead away those who would pry too deeply. Very candid people are often candid with a purpose. Wyatt Cooper, one of his closest friends, had suggested to me that Capote, because of his lonely, unhappy childhood, had been forced to create "a world of his own, a world in which he was God—his own creator. He is a natural aristocrat, one of those people who live by their own lights." The sentence struck me and explained what I thought I had perceived in Capote. Along with the gaiety and humor, there is also the sometimes bitter loneliness of the perpetual rebel. It is not easy being God, I suspect, and it is certainly not easy being Truman Capote.

I had been struck also by a passage Capote recently wrote in which he described a pilgrimage to the grave of Oscar Wilde, another elegant rebel, at Père Lachaise in Paris. I decided to try on him a line from Wilde. Ostensibly about playing the piano, it was, in fact, about Wilde himself. I felt it could do for Capote as well. "I don't play accurately—anyone can play accurately—but I play with wonderful expression." He thought that the line was a good capsule summary of his own character—"I think that's very fitting"—but he was quick to knock down any other resemblance to Wilde. Wilde, after all, was delicate. Capote, as I should have known by that time, is not. "I'm rather a tough little nut," he reminded me. "I'm really a peasant. I don't think there is anybody like me." To which, finally and begrudgingly, I agreed.

Truman Capote
Denis Brian/1972

From *Murderers and Other Friendly People: The Public and Private Worlds of Interviewers* (New York: McGraw-Hill Book Company, 1972), 103-133. Reprinted by permission.

Truman Capote's early writings were poetic and fictionalized accounts of the terrors and loneliness of his childhood in Alabama. His parents were divorced in 1928, when he was four, and Capote was brought up by elderly aunts and cousins.

Of the few friends he made, one, Martha Beck, grew up to be a murderess and was electrocuted in Sing Sing for her part in the Lonely Hearts killings; another, Harper Lee, became a novelist who portrayed Capote as a child in her *To Kill a Mockingbird*.

From the beginning Capote the fiction writer showed sympathy for eccentrics and misfits and an interest in the world of outsiders. And when he chose to move from fiction to fact, he turned to the real-life nightmare world of murderers. The result was *In Cold Blood*. After that triumph he took a TV camera into prisons throughout America, to interview murderers in death row.

Until *In Cold Blood*, Capote's most spectacular interview had been with friend Marlon Brando. The published account, which Brando resented, revealed an oversensitive, troubled, slightly paranoid man. Brando didn't challenge its truthfulness, but Capote's right to reveal the truth.

To produce *In Cold Blood* Capote lived three years in Kansas, a place as foreign to him, he said, as the moon: where he exhaustively interviewed two murderers, friends and neighbors of the four victims and the lawmen on the case.

The book (first published in *The New Yorker* in 1965) was built out of hundreds of these interviews. To persuade people to recall for him in detail not only their actions but their thoughts, Capote made them his friends. Motivated by curiosity, empathy for outcasts, and a passion for the right word, Capote produced a vivid portrait of one of the killers, Perry Smith. The brutal little man whose unfulfilled dream was to create one work of art at first resisted Capote's efforts to draw him out. But after a year, Smith began to confide in Capote and the result of their alliance was a work of art Smith wouldn't live to see.

Capote, a lonely, frightened, awkward little mouse of a boy, grew up to be a social lion. When he invited 500 people to a dance at the Plaza Hotel in New York, most of them world-famous, very few declined his invitation, and *The New York Times* devoted a page to an account of the party and reprinted the entire guest list. The outsider had become an insider. But even then he spent most of the time just watching others enjoying themselves. "What interests me—what I dwell on and dream of—are not the little nuances of my own life but the lives of people around me," Capote once told Jane Howard of *Life*.

Capote told me that he always knows when an interviewer is going to treat him sympathetically or not. The unsympathetic, he said, very early in the piece mention his unusual voice. But I agree with Donald Cullivan that through the fascination of Capote's talk you soon forget the voice—and just listen to the man.

My attempt to test Capote's reputed powers of total recall failed. He wasn't in the mood. But to test his reputed accuracy I interviewed Donald Cullivan and Duane West. Donald Cullivan was an army acquaintance of Perry Smith; Duane West was prosecuting attorney at Perry's trial. Capote wrote of both men in his *In Cold Blood*. How accurately? I asked them.

During my interview with Capote he called poet Robert Frost the meanest man he's ever met and explained why he thought so. I interviewed Robert Frost's daughter, Lesley, to see if there was another side to the story.

Capote spoke to me from his Long Island home, in an all blue room which goes up two floors, mirrors filling one wall and reflecting the blue. It has a winding staircase up to a balcony. And the wall opposite the mirrors has a white fireplace reaching to the ceiling, and floor-to-ceiling bookcases on either side, with a sliding red ladder to reach the topmost books. Capote describes it as the inside of an Easter egg. Glancing out of the window he could see the moors and the ocean. Within stroking distance were his two cats and bulldog.

Brian: It's strange that you should become so involved with murderers. Perry Smith became a close friend. You've made a documentary film about murderers. And even as a small child you ran away with a girl who grew up to become a murderer. (Martha Beck of "The Lonely Hearts Murders.") Did you stay away long?

Capote: No, just overnight. She had an uncle in Evergreen, Alabama, who ran a small hotel.

B: Did you lose contact with her after that?

C: Oh yes. After that her family took her away. I didn't even realize it was the same person until years later all my relatives in that town said: "Oh that's the girl who was here that summer. She's the one you ran away with."

B: Her motive for murder was greed, according to psychiatrist Fredric Wertham.

C: Yes, sexual greed on her part and financial greed on the man's part. But I hadn't any particular interest in crime. I wrote *In Cold Blood* by accident. I don't have a particular interest in crime now, except that I know a great deal about it.

B: To produce *In Cold Blood* you trained your memory so you could recall accurately almost 95 percent of what you heard. Would you at the end of this interview be able to repeat something I'd said earlier on?

C: I don't think I can today because I'm not in a very good mood. I'm not feeling so well. So don't let's try anything tricky . . . [Chuckles.]

B: All right. Back to *In Cold Blood*. Did Perry Smith and Richard Hickock lie to you, or try to mislead you, in the early stages of your contact with them?

C: I suppose so, inasmuch as Perry Smith had always told me that Dick killed the other two. I mean, that's what he told me earlier on. Then later, he told me the truth.

B: What d'you think was his reason for cooperating with you?

C: Loneliness. There they were, the first year I knew them, and I knew them almost six years, in this little town in Kansas. Nobody talked to them. Nobody would do anything for them. Nobody had heard of them. Nobody had even heard of their case. You know, there was nothing. I was this person who was there doing this thing and I was very attentive to them. I was drawing them out: out of boredom and out of loneliness, if nothing else. Who else was paying any attention to them? They were very grateful to me, although they were both very suspicious about what I was doing.

B: Weren't psychiatrists showing any interest?

C: There was only one psychiatrist and I don't think he was interested in them until he found out that I was. And he only saw them once. [Sigh.]

B: You say they were suspicious of why you were doing it. Did you ever tell them why?

C: Certainly. I told them the truth from the very beginning. But they couldn't understand. I mean, they didn't understand what I was doing. Well, why should they? None of my friends did, either. Nobody could understand what it was that I was doing. They couldn't understand what the end result of it was going to be.

B: Did your interviewing technique change over the years you were gathering material for *In Cold Blood*?

C: After a bit I wouldn't say it was interviewing in any real sense of the word: it was just talking. I was very, very friendly with them. In fact I was the only friend they had in the world.

B: How did you persuade the townspeople to talk about such a tragic and depressing subject?

C: It wasn't a matter of my just going in there bang, bang, bang, like some ordinary reporter. I went to that town and I moved into the town. And I began to cultivate people, you know. And on a very friendly basis, they'd introduce me to another person, who introduced me to another person. When I first lived there the case had only just happened. It was a couple of months before it was solved. Nobody had ever heard of Perry and Dick. I didn't know whether I'd have a book or not. And so I just cultivated people and by the time the case broke, I was on such friendly terms with the detective in charge of the case (Alvin Dewey), that I was the first person he told.

B: You had done this very deliberately?

C: Of course. I don't ordinarily go to Sunday school, I can tell you that. The first time I ever went to Sunday school classes.

B: Did you enjoy it?

C: Not much. [Laughs.] I came to respect all of those people, though.

B: You gave $50 apiece to Perry Smith and Hickock to get them to talk with you initially. Could you tell me the gist of your talk then, when you tried to get them to agree to be interviewed—after they'd accepted the money?

C: It was very brief, because they had their lawyers in the room and were terribly uptight. They'd only just been caught. This was maybe the day after they were returned to Garden City. They wanted $50. They wouldn't speak to any other reporter and I think that the only reason that the lawyers were able to arrange it was the money. If it hadn't been for that I would never have been able to have spoken, so the whole thing would never have started. I just wanted to establish a contact with them on which I could build. From that point on I supplied them with magazines and writing paper and all the little things that nobody else would think of doing, and they became very dependent on me, you see.

B: Did the payments for releases to the others you interviewed amount to a lot of money?

C: Oh golly, I've forgotten now. Mostly I tried to get the releases as I went along. But some of them I let go too long . . . and it was all my own money.

B: Could you ever feel warmly toward Hickock, knowing that he delighted in killing dogs by hitting them with his car?

C: It isn't a question of feeling warmly, but when you get to know somebody as well as I got to know those two boys—I knew them better than they knew themselves—feelings don't enter, of like or dislike. It's some kind of extraordinary condition of knowledge takes place. I found that, of course, appalling and repulsive, you know. (The killing of dogs). But there it is, it was part of his insensitivity and indifference to life in general.

B: Were you serious when you said of the *In Cold Blood* interview that you could tell if people weren't being accurate, by their eyes shifting from right to left?

C: I don't know if I said that, but I've often noticed it. When you get right down to hard ground with them, their eyes will start shifting. Shifty eyes [chuckles] is an old phrase.

B: Any other clues that indicated to you that people weren't telling the truth?

C: You know, all of that's so instinctual. After you get the feel of a person, can't you always tell more or less when somebody's really not leveling with you?

B: I think so, yes. The accuracy of *In Cold Blood* was challenged by Phillip K. Tompkins in *Esquire* of June 1966. According to him Mrs. Meier denied that she said she had seen worse men than Perry, denied that she ever heard him cry, denied that he ever held her hand and said: "I'm embraced by shame." And although you say that Perry Smith killed all the victims, Duane West (prosecuting attorney) and Alvin Dewey (chief detective) still believe that Dick Hickock killed the two women. Is this just a difference of opinion: you say it's true and they say it isn't?

C: What I wrote in the book was true. It is absolutely accurate. Mrs. Meier, wife of the under sheriff at the jail, turned against me. And Duane West is one of my bitterest enemies. And they were sort of working tooth and tong. As for Alvin Dewey, I don't know why he believed that. He always has and I don't know why he does because it's absolutely untrue. And Mrs. Meier is just not telling the truth.

B: Malcolm Cowley said to me that although *In Cold Blood* was meant to be a plea against capital punishment, he felt that it supported it, in that the execution of the two men was the only thing that gave their lives any stature, esthetically.

C: Meaning what? Or does he mean in respect to the book? If the boys hadn't been then . . . that was one of Tynan's great things . . . if the boys hadn't been executed then I wouldn't have had an effective ending for the book.

B: Tynan's was a snide thing, wasn't it? He was implying that you would have wanted them to die. But Cowley doesn't imply that you wanted that. He says that men like them, who do gruesome things and lead "worthless" lives, can only achieve stature, either as characters in a book or as human beings, by being executed.

C: I don't see his point about it in terms of life. The fact of a person being executed—what has estheticism got to do with that? Estheticism is purely something in terms of art.

B: Of course executions make heroes and martyrs as well. You're not struck by his comment?

C: I've heard variations of it before.

B: What surprised me about *In Cold Blood* was that there was no obscene language from either of the men.

C: That's what *The New York Times* pointed out. They said: "If these things are absolutely accurate, why is the language so," you know . . . As a matter of fact Perry Smith was extraordinarily prissy in conversation. I make a great point of it.

B: Did you use any euphemisms for Hickock's language?

C: No, I really didn't. The only word that Dick used to say all the time was "shit." But Perry would never say that.

B: Was there anything remarkable or moving in the hundred-page farewell letter Perry wrote to you just before he was executed?

C: I don't know if I ever said it or not. It was about . . . it was about . . . Oh my God, I really shouldn't go into all this. It just upsets me so much anyway. [Sighs.] All the time they had been in prison, all those years, they were only allowed to have a certain amount of money. And I always gave them each whatever it was they were allowed to have. Anyway, the thing was that in the letter there was a check for the money. Perry had never spent a penny of it and he was, you know, giving it back to me. I don't know why, but that one thing upset me more than any other thing. It just tore me up. Because I mean . . . oh God . . . it was touching, as though that all along . . . I can't go into it . . .

B: For which of the other murderers you've interviewed have you felt the most empathy?

C: A girl called Jeannace Freeman on Death Row at Oregon State Penitentiary. A fantastic story. She's a fascinating girl. She's now had her sentence commuted. But she's been on Death Row at Oregon about five or six years. I just find her a fascinating girl. Strange, curious, a monster. Terribly good-looking. She's not in the film. I went there for that purpose but in the end I edited it out.

B: Why, if you felt such empathy for her?

C: I liked her personally but my interview with her wasn't any good.

B: Did the Edgar Smith case interest you? (He was convicted of the murder of a fifteen-year-old girl in Mahwah, New Jersey, and William F. Buckley, Jr., befriended him.)

C: I read his book *Brief Against Death* (Alfred Knopf 1968). I thought it would have been a much more interesting book if he'd have admitted that he killed the girl. But since he doesn't, I find something about the whole book untrue, and unimpressive, because I'm convinced that he did kill the girl.

B: I told Buckley that the only thing that worried me was Smith's lack of memory for the crucial time. Particularly as he was supposed to be a man in control of his emotions. And Buckley said the same thing worried him. But don't you agree that the evidence against the other suspect seemed very strong?

C: You can make anything seem very strong. No, I think he did do it. I mean, I'm convinced that he did.

B: Whitney in *TV Guide* said that for your TV film about murderers, Prettyman took over much of the interviewing of the murderers because "Capote's high baby voice, seductive in jet set salons, proved somewhat less effective in the yard of San Quentin." Was that true?

C: No it wasn't. [Chuckles.] Because, in actual fact, I prepared all of the interviews for the different prisoners. And then, because of the terrible technical difficulties that we had in the prisons sometimes, the lighting was so bad and the lighting currents alternated so much that we worked in such awful conditions that, actually, there were three of us doing the interviews. I mean we would be together and then, as the subject was talking, whichever one of us wanted to, could interrupt and ask something. One was Mary Bailey Gimbel and one was Barry Freeman and one was me. Barry Freeman was really a lawyer, front man for the operation.

B: You were almost like friendly detectives.

C: Uh-huh.

B: You interviewed an ex-convict for *In Cold Blood*. And then he suddenly appeared at your home, stayed all day and got away with some money . . .

C: How did you know about that?

B: You told Jerry Tallmer of *The New York Post*.

C: Well, it happened anyway. I didn't remember that I'd ever told anybody. I mean I told certain friends about it. But I didn't realize I'd ever told the press. It was quite frightening. A bit like *The Desperate Hours*.

B: How can you avoid that sort of thing happening again?

C: I guess you can't. Something very similar happened last summer. It was similar in the sense that it wasn't somebody that I'd interviewed and met: but it was a psychopath who was out of a mental institution fairly recently, a rather good-looking young man, but so sinister. He just walked in through the lane and through the fields and up to this house and the next thing I knew he was knocking at the door. And I went there and there he was. And he was an instantly recognizable psychopath. He began talking to me, in what seemed a normal way and he was in the house before I knew what I could do and it took me forever to get him out of here. And then I had to drive him to the railroad station. And all the way he kept hammering his hand against his fist. He had found out where I was. He had taken a great deal of time and research and located this house out here in the country. I mean, how he found me here is just amazing because I come and go so, you know. It was really frightening. Extraordinary. And afterwards he appeared several times in a building where I live in New York, but I was never there. And finally the doorman there called the police about it. But there's nothing you can do about that. Everybody has . . . I mean, my mail [chuckles] lots of days it would make most people climb the walls.

B: But curiosity makes you read it?

C: Actually I can tell a lot of times, just by the quality of the handwriting, and I don't bother to read it.

B: I imagine all celebrities get that sort of mail?

C: But I have the extra burden of receiving an enormous amount of mail from the prison population of the world. They all want to tell me their stories. "If only you could write my story, I know that the world would listen." Or, you know, making me a deal. And if they aren't doing it, their lawyers are. I get tons of letters from lawyers asking me don't I want to write the story of their clients, to have the exclusive rights? Now, for instance, this boy who really committed all those Manson murders, the one that just got extradited, Watson. His lawyer from a little town wrote me this long letter right after they were all caught and in prison and asked me would I be willing to buy the story of this boy's life, exclusive rights to write about him for $50,000. [Laughs.] Can you imagine?

B: You've often written about death. Do you believe in life after death?

C: Do I believe? No, of course I don't.

B: Ever had any extrasensory experiences?

C: Just the ones that everybody's had. Thinking about somebody you haven't thought about in months and the phone rings and there they are.

B: If Jesus Christ returned to earth and invited you to question him, would there be a question you'd want to ask him?

C: No, because I don't believe he ever existed.

B: Have you ever heard John Allegro's theory that Christ was a mushroom?

C: [Laughing.] No. Whose theory is this?

B: Allegro. He's an expert on philology and one of the translators of the Dead Sea Scrolls. And in his book he says that early Christianity was a cult of drug-taking, the mushroom drug, and Jesus Christ was the mushroom.

C: [Laughing.] I think that's quite good. I like it.

B: When the cultists wrote or talked about the mushroom, they used the word Jesus as a code for mushroom.

C: [Laughing.] I think that's pretty good.

B: Is there any biggest disappointment in your life?

C: Well, I believe people that I shouldn't have believed, that's about what it comes to. I'm very gullible. I'm not gullible at all as a writer, or as an interviewer. But I'm very gullible personally, just in a purely social way. I really and truly believe what people tell me. If I were going to put them in a book or story or an article, I examine what they tell me. But if you say something to me, I just take it automatically and believe it. And then, when it's something important, I get a real sinking feeling. That's happened several times in my life.

B: Could you be specific?

C: No.

B: D'you think of yourself as frank and open?

C: Yes.

B: Have you ever met anyone you'd call a saint?

C: Did you ever read that story of mine called "A Christmas Memory"? In many ways, I suppose, Sook Faulk was a saint. Most people would think of her as a saint. I just think she was a good person.

B: Met anyone absolutely evil?

C: Absolutely evil? Let me think. I think Kenneth Tynan is absolutely evil, I really do. He's evil because he's the ultimate in hypocrisy and duplicity.

B: You never settled the argument where he accused you of not making any effort to prevent Smith and Hickock from being executed?

C: Oh, we settled it. I wrote a piece about it in the *Observer* that went on and on for a month. To me it has everything to do with duplicity and what not because he was pretending to be such a friend of mine, and living in my house, and I was so generous to him in every way. And all the time, months before the book came out, he was plotting this attack on me, for no reason, except what he was going to get out of it. It was reprinted everywhere in the world and he made a lot of money out of it. To me, that's really evil.

B: And you think his motive was greed?

C: Greed and jealousy.

B: What makes you cry?

C: Oh lord, anything to do with cruelty to animals. Or cruelty in any event. Deliberate cruelty is the only thing I can't forgive.

B: What scares you?

C: I don't think I used to be scared of anything that I automatically saw, but after doing all the research for *In Cold Blood* and all the murderers that I interviewed, hundreds of them, the very sight of a hitchhiker gives me a shiver. I've driven back and forth across the country several times and the idea of running out of gas in one of those lonely Midwestern places creates a tremendous sense of anxiety in me. And I have a real, true dread of being on some isolated road, depending on the kindness of strangers [chuckles], as Blanche Dubois would say.

B: What delights you?

C: Oh, I don't know. Unexpected pleasant sexual experience, I suppose.

B: Would you be very surprised if Kenneth Tynan apologized to you?

C: If I ever see him I'm going to kill him. He'd better stay out of my path. [Laughs.]

B: I'll have to record that you laughed when you said that.

C: But I usually laugh when I mean it the most. [Chuckles].

B: Did you read the statement by a maid of Mrs. Kennedy Onassis that Jackie was a very selfish and self-centered woman? And a newspaper's comment, that her father having been an alcoholic would explain why Mrs. Kennedy would be more self-centered than for example, Ethel Kennedy, whom they called outgoing and unselfish?

C: They're totally different people. I know them both. Jackie Kennedy and her sister are both extremely intelligent, sensitive people. Her sister even more so than she is. They had a difficult childhood. Their father was an alcoholic. That wasn't the problem. They adored their father. His alcoholism was not part of their unhappiness. It was just that their mother and father were separated. Jackie was always a very shy, sensitive, withdrawn person. And through various circumstances and accidents of fate, she feels she's been turned into a permanent freak of some kind. I don't think she's self-centered. That little horror that made the statement! Talk about self-centered people!

B: It's always a bit suspect when they're making money out of their revelations, isn't it? There's always got to be a knife in somewhere, or it doesn't sell. I know you don't believe in an afterlife. But do you believe there's a purpose to this life?

C: I'm beginning to wonder, let's put it that way.

B: You once said: "I developed the muscles of a veritable barracuda, especially in the art of dealing with one's enemies." Are there more, other than Kenneth Tynan?

C: Oh, one has many enemies in this world. I'm sure you do, too.

B: What is your technique with them?

C: I get even with them finally.

B: Did you have any frightening or wonderful experiences as a child, that you often recall?

C: When I was about four years old, I was in the St. Louis Zoo with some colored woman; I guess she must have been working for my mother. And two lions got loose from a cage. That was frightening. And then I was bitten by a snake when I was twelve years old. Bitten by a water moccasin and nearly died. Spent the whole summer in bed. I quite often recall those experiences in one form or another. Comes back to me as some form of anxiety.

B: Do you have a theory of interviewing? Some people think genuine curiosity is essential.

C: So do I. And I think you need to know a great deal about the person before you interview them. But the kind of thing I do, they're usually quite anonymous people that I have to get to know: like the book I did about the theatrical company traveling through Russia, *The Muses Are Heard*. The way I work . . . it's rather a tricky thing to do, but nevertheless it always works. If you're having a difficult time with a subject, then you, in effect, change roles. And you, the interviewer, begin by making little confidences of your own that are rather similar to things that you think you will draw out of them. And suddenly they'll be saying: "Ah yes, my mother ran away with five repairmen, too." See what I mean? Or: "Ah, yes, my father robbed a bank and was sent to prison for ten years, too. Isn't it extraordinary we should have those same things happen in our lives?" etc. And then you find you're off to the races.

B: You've been the subject of hundreds of interviews. Do you find that you reveal yourself more fully to a peer? Would Norman Mailer, for example, be the ideal man to interview you?

C: No. To me it doesn't make any difference. I can tell fairly early on in an interview whether it's going to have any quality or not. It's a question of the person's intelligence. It doesn't matter to me who they are. A man has just written a book about me, Professor William Nance from Texas. I think it's quite an interesting book (*The Worlds of Truman Capote*) and rather well written—but you would think from the first pages of the book and the remarks he makes that he had interviewed me many, many times. In actual fact I met him once in my life and talked for just a couple of hours. He was trying to give an impression that he knew me intimately, when in fact he did not know me intimately.

B: In fact he implies that he interviewed you twice, not once. He puts the dates as November 9 and November 10, 1966.

C: It's not true, though. I was in Austin, Texas, where the University is, and I gave a lecture there and I saw him just before the lecture and then afterwards he came to the hotel and I was very tired and I got into bed and had myself a drink (Evelyn Waugh was interviewed in bed by a *Paris Review* interviewer) and he sat down in a chair and I talked to him, maybe for an hour and a half, two hours.

B: Was it about midnight?

C: Yes, it was late.

B: Technically he's right, I suppose. He's got the two dates in as before and after midnight.

C: Oh, I see. [Chuckles.] Clever. [Laughs.]

B: Professor Benjamin DeMott's objection to almost all printed interviews is that the reporter eliminates his own reactions and his own personality from an interview, and so it becomes artificial.

C: I know the argument, but I don't agree with it because there's a whole other school where interviewers are constantly putting themselves into the interview and I think that's a thousand times worse, and easier. Rex Reed and all of these young reporters today are continually writing about themselves and the problems they had in getting the interview in the first place, and then their own personal reactions to the person. Anybody can do that. It's wrong. Because the ideal portrait is something in which the interviewer is totally removed and you set the whole thing up so that if it's good, the person that it's about comes across with no distortions on the part of the interviewer—well, of course if he's any good he's an artist, and any artist distorts whatever he touches. But it's not artificial: it's just a form of art. Well, then, all art is artificial. My point is that life is life and art is art. You can't take actual life to make it into art. It's impossible. Given the most careful documentary kind of writing, or filming, it's impossible. Because, by the very nature of what you're doing, framing something, it turns it into an art.

B: Do you agree that the First Amendment should be interpreted to mean that there should be no libel law and that one should be able to write or say anything about anyone else without fear of prosecution?

C: Yes, I agree with that. I personally don't care what anyone writes or says about me, so I'd just as soon [chuckles] that whole right was given to me.

B: As the subject of interviews, is there one that was most refreshing to you in that the questions were bright and unexpected and that you personally found it really interesting?

C: Yes, yours is very bright and fresh.

B: That's great. But are there any famous ones, for example?

C: There was this strange girl called Barbara something who writes for *The Village Voice*, who did a piece about me for *Esquire*. I didn't like the piece but I must say I thought she had a lot of talent. Strange girl. That was a couple of years ago.

B: Why didn't you like it, although you liked her?

C: I liked her quality. Now there's an interview in which the interviewer's in it completely. It's really much more about her than it is about me. But I think she's an interesting person. There's something fascinating about her: grotesque and weird. Really bright. She could have gone a long way, but I thought there was something quite peculiar about her.

B: What do you think of Studs Terkel?

C: I just read his book *Hard Times*. I thought that was quite good.

B: David Frost?

C: I've done his program. I like him. He's a little mechanical. Everything is totally prepared by his staff. And he's simply coming on there, hoping he can keep all those cards ahead, as he's shuffling through. He's thoroughly professional and he doesn't leave you in the lurch, like so many of them do.

B: Rex Reed?

C: His interviews are clever and amusing. A little too emotional, though.

B: William Buckley, Jr.?

C: He gives as much as you're supposed to give. It's like a discourse, a debate.

B: Mike Wallace?

C: He used to beg me to be on his show. And at that time I had never been on any television show. And finally, after months and months, I said I would do it. And then, at the last minute, I called him up and said I was sorry, I'd changed my mind because I'd finally gotten around to seeing his show [laughs] and I just wasn't about to subject myself to any of that nonsense. [Laughs.] He was very upset.

B: Which show had you seen?

C: I think it was poor Tennessee Williams.

B: Have you ever refused to answer certain questions?

C: Only if it involved somebody else. I've refused to give interviews quite a lot of times because I've been too busy. I've refused to be on television because the people were boring or I didn't want to be on their program. I never would be on Merv Griffin's program.

B: You think he's a bore?

C: Well, yes. I like Dick Cavett. I think he's nice. You see, I hardly ever watch, for one thing. I don't have a television in New York.

B: After a *Playboy* interviewer interviewed you, you said to Jerry Tallmer: "It's really fun. I'm probably going to have to leave the country." What had you said to the *Playboy* interviewer in 1968 that would cause you to leave the country?

C: Undoubtedly it was a reference to things that were taken out of the interview. They took an awful lot of things out, on grounds of libel.

B: For example?

C: Some of the things I said about Kenneth Tynan were absolutely hair-raising and they took those out because Kenneth Tynan was a great buddy of the *Playboy* people, which I didn't know at that time, in fact, practically an editor [chuckles]. And Hemingway, I said a lot of things about. Oh, Bobby Kennedy, yes. I had quite a lot to say about Bobby. I rather liked Bobby. I think they took the whole thing out.

B: Do you imagine you'd give fuller and franker answers to a close friend than to me, for example?

C: Well, no. I'm trying to be as frank as I can be.

B: I think you are. But I wondered if with a friend you might pull out the stops more. Maybe the reverse would be true.

C: I don't know. I'm answering the questions as I feel. So I'm being as honest as I can be.

B: I feel you are too. Do you regard the 500 people you had to your famous Plaza Hotel party as friends?

C: No, about forty-five of them were friends. But I knew everybody and I more or less liked them for one reason or another, or I wouldn't have invited them.

B: If you wanted to interview the entire 500 at that party, in depth, about how many do you think would give you good interviews, be expansive and frank? An educated guess . . . ?

C: Anybody can be interviewed if you go about it the right way. If you study the problem, there isn't a single person in the world, from violent prison hermits to chatterbox starlets, that if you really map out the problem you can't get to talk about themselves. If you're talking about interviewing public characters, well that's one problem. What I think is the most interesting and difficult form of interview is with people who don't expect to be interviewed, and in fact don't know that they are being interviewed.

B: I think that's Studs Terkel's technique.

C: He uses a tape recorder and I feel that's a great mistake, because the moment you introduce a mechanical device into the interview technique, you are creating an atmosphere in which the person isn't going to feel really relaxed, because they're watching themselves.

B: You said to George Plimpton: "No one likes to see himself as he is or cares to see exactly set down what he said or did. I don't like to myself when I am the sitter and not the portraitist. And the more accurate the strokes, the greater the resentment." Was there one particular interview you resented that was very accurate?

C: Oh, I don't know. I can always tell in the opening paragraph whether the interview is essentially going to be sympathetic or unsympathetic by the way they describe my voice. They'll go on about my height or something and then they'll have some kind of thing about this funny voice that he has, you know, several different allusions to this strange, funny little voice that Capote has. And I can always tell by where that is placed in the thing and the way the arrangements of adjectives are, whether the interview is going to be sympathetic or unsympathetic.

B: What did you think of Gay Talese's book about *The New York Times, The Kingdom and the Power*?

C: I thought it was very good.

B: Talese apparently tries to discover the thoughts of people. Do you think it comes off?

C: Ah, but he stole that from me. That was all my theory and he'll admit it.

B: He acknowledges it, does he?

C: I don't know that he acknowledges it, but he read the manuscript of *In Cold Blood* long before it came out in *The New Yorker*, and he was fascinated by the whole technique. That was the first time that anybody used that thing of people thinking. They're thinking in there but thinking what they told me they were thinking.

B: In *TV Guide* Dwight Whitney describes you as "looks like a small well-bred English bull." How do you react?

C: I just felt it wasn't true. Didn't he say bulldog?

B: Bulldog, was it? (No, it was bull.) Were you amused by it?

C: I just didn't feel he was very accurate. I happen to have a bulldog [chuckles]. I know I don't look like her. He does that voice description thing too, doesn't he?

B: What description by others of yourself most amused you?

C: In Harold Nicolson's memoirs there's rather an amusing description of when I was very young. Somebody took me to lunch with him. That was quite good. And then in David Lilienthal's memoirs there's—oh, a very long, quite amusing description of me.

B: What description most offended you?

C: Well there's a guy that was really . . . I mean it was a hatchet job. It was meant to be a hatchet job. It was meant to be as mean as it could possibly be. At the time I had that big dance at the Plaza, he wrote an outrageous column. You know, he wasn't invited or anything. He was just hanging around outside the hotel and he wrote a really outrageous piece about me. What's his name? (Dick Schaap in *The New York Post.*)

B: Didn't he intersperse the dance scene with scenes from the war in Vietnam?

C: That's it. It was so corny you couldn't believe it. Terribly corny. William Buckley wrote a very funny piece about it. (Buckley was at the dance and he supported Capote's right to throw a party.)

B: You're considered an outstanding interviewer, not only because of the years of interviews you did for *In Cold Blood* but for your *New Yorker* piece on Marlon Brando of November 9, 1957.

C: And that was a hatchet job. [Chuckles, mixture of benign and diabolic.]

B: There were reports that Brando didn't realize he was being interviewed by you.

C: That's not true. Of course he knew it. When I said it was a hatchet job I didn't mean that at all. I was just making a joke. I basically felt the piece was very sympathetic to him. He didn't think so and wrote me the most fantastic letter, which I wish I had kept, just as a souvenir. Originally I was going to do a larger piece about the making of the *Sayonara* film for *The New Yorker*. And in the end I thought it was all a big bore, you know, the whole thing. So I just decided to do this one part of it. But he knew perfectly well he was being interviewed.

B: The report that came out was that he told you moving things about his life and you had told him moving things about yours.

C: Yes, but I *know* Marlon Brando. And I told you one of the things that I do when I find the subject a little difficult—not that I found him that way—is to become very confidential.

B: Do you feel that when he saw what he'd said in print he wanted to take it back, or was upset about it?

C: I think they think you're going to edit the whole thing somehow, for them. And then they're shocked when you, according to their lights, didn't have the good taste to leave this out or that out.

B: Did you ever meet Hemingway?

C: No, but I hated him.

B: What did you think of the Lillian Ross piece about him in *The New Yorker*?

C: He was such a total hypocrite: he went on pretending to be a friend of hers afterwards. I thought it was rather a good piece, but I didn't like him, so it doesn't matter.

B: Do you think from reading his writings and other people's interviews with him, that he was a hypocrite?

C: A total hypocrite. And he was mean. I did know Robert Frost and he was about the meanest single man that ever drew breath. But I disliked Hemingway intensely. He was always writing little things about me, when I was very, very young. I was about eighteen or nineteen when I thought: "My God, here's this man fifty years old, this famous man. What the hell does he always want to be knocking me in the teeth about?"—you know. And then, when Nelson Algren's book *The Man with the Golden Arm* came out, Hemingway gave him a quote which the publisher used and the quote said: "All you Truman Capote fans get your hats and coats and leave the room. Here comes a real writer." Well, I thought that, really, I mean, it's really too much. When my *Breakfast at Tiffany's* came out he wrote me a little note telling me how good it was, or how much he liked it. And I thought: "There's more of your hypocrisy for you."

B: Mary Hemingway, interviewed by Oriana Fallaci, said: "Unlike a prima donna or an actress, a writer has a right to privacy, if he wants it. People should be prohibited from writing about others' intimate lives." Do you agree?

C: Mrs. Hemingway said that?

B: Yes. She had wanted to hide the fact that Hemingway killed himself.

C: No, I don't agree with what she said.

B: According to Hotchner, Mrs. Hemingway wanted to stop him writing a biography of Hemingway because she was cooperating with Carlos Baker.

C: And that was a bad book, too. [Chuckles.]

B: Because it had no point of view or because it was just facts?

C: The Baker book was bad all the way through. It was dull, it was uninteresting, it was badly put together, it had no selectivity, it was an atrocious piece of writing. And then on top of the whole thing [chuckles], considering how much the Hemingway estate backed him up and cooperated with him, it was a piece of duplicity, too. He was shoving the knife in there all the time. I mean, I never read a book in which I came away more with the feeling that the author hated the man he was writing about.

B: You said Robert Frost was the meanest man you ever met. Could you give me an example of how he was mean to you?

C: When I was about eighteen years old there was a thing called the Bread Loaf Writers Conference. I was invited up there and the great mogul of the thing was Robert Frost. You know, a glob of all these old Midwestern ladies and librarians and what not, oohing and ahhing and carrying on—he was such a ham. Anyway, one rainy day I stepped into this sort of barn—he was in this barn escaping from the rain—and the two of us had a little conversation. And I think he thought that I wasn't particularly awed by Mr. Frost, or something. Anyway, the chemistry was not particularly good. But the next day he had a poetry reading and I had the flu and I said I wasn't going to come. The director of the conference said to me that Mr. Frost was furious and thought I was insulting him. And so I said: "Well, I'll come but I've really got this fever." So I went, and about half way through the thing I felt so badly I thought I was going to faint, because it was terribly hot. So I got up and tried to ease along this aisle to go out this door. And Frost picked up this book and he threw it at me as hard as he could. And [chuckles] shouted, I don't know, something. And he refused to go on with the reading. And I went back to my room and the director of the conference came and asked me would I leave immediately because Mr. Frost was so upset about it. And with the flu and a fever of 103 I had to leave there. And then Robert Frost wrote a letter to *The New Yorker* Magazine and got lots of other people at the conference to write, saying how insulting I had been, as though I were representing *The New Yorker*. *The New Yorker* had nothing to do with it, you know, except that I worked there.

B: Did he hit you with the book?

C: Yep.

B: Did you read the recent biography of Robert Frost by Lawrance Thompson?

C: No. But I don't have to read. I know he comes out as such a monster. But I know he's a monster [laughs]. I don't have to read it.

B: A woman wrote in *The New York Times* book review section, saying he was even more of a monster than the book portrayed.

C: [Laughing.] Well, I guess I'll have to add my two bits.

B: Do you think it was innate unpleasantness with him? Or do you think it was a result of what he had gone through in life?

C: I think he was just a mean man, I really do. There are lots of mean people in the world, you know.

B: If you were ever in a position when you thought you were just about to die, could you tell me how you felt?

C: Three times. Once was the snake bite when I was twelve years old. I told you about that. Once when I had acute appendicitis and was in absolute agony and nobody could help me. And when I lost control of my car and it hit a tree and I went through the windshield. The tree was coming up and I was going through the windshield and I said: "Well, this is it, buster." [Chuckles.]

B: Were you scared or calm?

C: When I came to I was incredibly calm. I guess I was in a state of shock.

B: As you were flying through the air and saying, "This is it, buster," were you reasonably calm?

C: Yep.

B: If you could communicate with the world, say on international TV, is there any subject you'd specially want to talk about?

C: My mind doesn't work that way. If I said I wanted to talk of the need for peace I'd be a hypocrite, because I don't care about it. I suppose that shocks you. There's no subject I could imagine talking about to an international audience, to try to convince them, that I wouldn't feel hypocritical about.

B: I was trying to get at what most concerns you about life, or any aspect of living. If you could appear before people who could change the order of things, what would you ask them to change? For example, pollution might particularly concern you.

C: But it doesn't, you see. I really, truly don't *care* enough about any of these subjects to get up and talk about them.

B: Do you feel that might be because you haven't any children? Do you think if you had a son of eight and a daughter of six?

C: Probably. But I'm not that disconnected. When I think about myself being killed in the automobile accident, I think of certain people and I want to be sure they're provided for, a little bit here and there and what not. I don't feel *totally* disconnected. But I *suppose* if you have children it really does enter into it.

B: Do you think your answers to my questions give a fairly good picture of quite a few aspects of you?

C: I guess so. I think it's very good what you're doing. But to be perfectly frank with you some of my answers to these questions would be quite different under other circumstances. I've just been in a deep depression for about two months, you know, one of those things that one slides into? So my answers, if I were in a different mood, might be much brighter, more alert, not so "I don't know." So it's really a question of the particular sort of mood that I'm in. But nevertheless I've tried to answer as best I could.

B: I was going to ask you why you were depressed the first time I spoke with you. I had that down as question number one this time but I thought I'd leave it because it might make you more depressed. But it's just general depression, is it?

C: Yes. I do, every few years or so, slide into one of these things and it's not at all pleasant.

B: I remember you mentioned once that you suffered from severe headaches.

C: That's it. It starts that way.

B: I know you're very fond of Lee Radziwill, because you told me that although you like Jackie Onassis, or Jackie O as I believe she's called now [Capote chuckles], you think that Princess Radziwill is an even finer person.

C: Much. I think there are very few people in the world who are as extraordinary as that girl. She gets no credit for it, of course. She might as well be completely in oblivion. But she's really a brilliant girl and she's got tremendous style and kindness and heart and brains and energy and courage and she's really somebody.

B: To the public, of course, she's just a jet setter.

C: Well, she's just Jackie Kennedy's sister. I don't even know what a jet setter is. She's a very good mother. She runs a very good house. I suppose, yes, she does travel in those worlds.

B: Wouldn't Jackie Kennedy be upset if she knew you thought her sister was much finer?

C: She knows it. I've told her. [Chuckles.] I told her in just so many words. She agrees with me about it 100 percent, always has.

B: When she wrote to you after reading one of your books and then you had lunch together, do you recall which book it was?

C: It was the little book about going to Russia, the Porgy and Bess book, *The Muses Are Heard*.

B: Kennedy was a senator then, was he?

C: Yes. And she was very attractive and bright and charming and we became very good friends.

B: What's your instant reaction to these names: Robert Kennedy?

C: He was a friend of mine, you know. I liked Bobby very much. I don't know whether he was . . . Anyway, go on to the next.

B: Did you think he was ruthless?

C: Yes. He could be quite ruthless. He was most ruthless to the people who were closest to him in a sense. What was that marvelous word he used . . . ? "Hunkers." He used to call various people, who are still weeping and crying over him, you know, those who ran for his clean shirts, to tie up his shoelaces, and who ran after him with a lot of things, he used to refer to them as hunkers. And I said to him: "What is a hunker?" And he said: "A hunker is somebody who rushes ahead of you and sees that the revolving door is spinning by the time you get there." [Laughs.]

B: That's an overactive gofor. Norman Mailer?

C: Ah, Norman. Well, I've always had the very best possible relations with Norman. He's always been very careful with me, very polite. I used to see quite a lot of him. He used to come and see me quite often and . . . I mean, I've never had any bad experiences with him, like everybody else. And I like him and I respect him as a writer, too.

B: Malcolm X.

C: Ah, well, he's the only one of the Negro intellectuals, or whatever you want to call them, for whom I have any respect at all. He was quite an extraordinary man and I think that book of his, *Malcolm X*, is the only one of any of those books, and I mean any of them, that's good. I think Eldridge Cleaver's book was one of mind-blowing boredom and talentlessness.

B: Vice President Agnew?

C: I think there's something rather beguiling about him. But I wouldn't want to spend any time with him.

B: Tennessee Williams?

C: We've always been great friends. I feel sorry for him. He's just let something inside get completely out of control. The only thing that really matters to Tennessee is writing and he was always a compulsive writer. He's a compulsive writer like some people are compulsive readers or drinkers or whatever it is. And of course he'll just go on writing and writing and writing and writing, when what he ought to do is not write, and for a long time. And then come back to it with a whole new vision or something.

B: John Fitzgerald Kennedy?

C: I liked him very much. He was straightforward. He had a nice offbeat smile and an offbeat sense of humor. He was unshockable. You could tell him absolutely anything.

B: You heard people trying it, did you?

C: I used to do it. I used to tell him all kinds of things about other people or myself.

B: He liked gossip, did he?

C: Oh yes, loved it.

B: Can you give me an example?

C: [Chuckling.] I can tell you something I told him in front of about fifteen people at a State dinner. It's a true story. The previous week I had gone to a party that was also attended by a famous designer. He was with a famous actress and they were sitting on a couch, in front of me. And I was having a drink and idly listening to this conversation they were having, or over-listening to it. And the designer was saying: "You know, my dear, the older I become, I find the most extraordinary thing, the most depressing thing is happening: my private parts are shrinking." There was a long pause and then the actress said: "Uh, if ONLY I could say the same!" . . . So anyway, at this State dinner, there were all these people being very quiet, upstairs in the Kennedys' living room. And I just suddenly began telling him this anecdote and after a minute he roared with laughter. But the whole room was completely still until he laughed. They were really shocked that I would have the gall to tell something like that, in front of all those people.

B: You had the gall because you knew Kennedy would enjoy it?

C: Oh yes. It's a funny story. [Laughs.]

B: What was your reaction to the Buckley–Vidal controversy?

C: Well, I thought Buckley—you're talking about the *Esquire* pieces?—I thought Buckley was very foolish to have written that article. I mean, why, when he had already had this thing on TV, why drag it all up again? Very questionable, the whole thing. I certainly think he was in the wrong. On the other hand I think Gore was stupid to have answered him. He should have just kept quiet. He shouldn't have bothered to answer it. Neither of their pieces were any good. They were just embarrassing.

B: Did you ever know why Gore Vidal was so anti-Robert Kennedy?

C: Yes, sure.

B: Could you say why?

C: Sure, don't you know? Jacqueline Kennedy was wearing an obi. A Japanese dress with an obi. And I think it was the only time they'd ever invited Gore there and he had spent the whole time whispering in her ear. And as he was walking out of the room, he put his hand on her bottom, of this Japanese obi dress. And so Bobby Kennedy walked over to him and grabbed hold of his hand and said: "Cut that out, Gore. That stuff doesn't go around here." The exact quote. And Gore turned on him and told him to take his damned hands off him and said to him: "You Kennedys really think you have it all made, don't you?" And began this crazy sort of tirade . . . (next sentence omitted to avoid libel suit). And after that Gore sat down and wrote that piece for *Esquire* "The Holy Kennedys."

B: You got that from an unimpeachable source, did you?

C: I sure did.

B: You couldn't tell me who?
C: If you're not going to print it. [He then tells me.]
B: How do you respond to the name Gore Vidal?
C: Ah, Gore, poor Gore. [Chuckles.]
B: He won't like to hear that, "poor Gore."
C: [Laughs.] That's all I have to say. Well, I tell you: you ask him what he thinks of me and that's exactly what I think of him. [Laughing.] You can quote it.

Sunday with Mister C.:
An Audiodocumentary by Andy Warhol Starring Truman Capote
Andy Warhol/1973

From *Rolling Stone,* 12 April 1973, 28-30, 32, 34, 36-37, 39-40, 42-44, 46, 48. Reprinted by permission.

(Andy arrives at Truman's New York apartment.)
    Andy (to elevator man): Truman Capote's?
(Riding up in elevator.)
    Andy: What kind of dogs does Truman have? Does he have little dogs?
    Elevator man: He has one.
    Andy: I was going to bring mine. Is it a big dog?
    Elevator man: I think they call it a Chinese pug.
    Andy: Oh, it's a small one? Then I could have brought mine!
    Elevator man (laughs): Wait a minute. Maybe I gave it the wrong name, because this one's kind of huge. Maybe it's—a bulldog, and it's like a brownish color. . . .
    Andy: I always thought he had more than one. He just has one?
    Elevator man: Well, Charlie died. There's just Maggie now. . . . That's it. To your right.
    Truman: Come on in, Andy.
    Andy: I was going to bring my—Archie—he's a dachsund—but then I was afraid, and I'm so sorry now that I didn't. They would have had fun.
    He's so cute . . . so great.
    Truman: Oh, she's got your camera.
    Andy: She can have it. . . .
    Truman: What a nice tie you've got on. . . .
    Andy: It's so beautiful here. . . . Oh, isn't sun wonderful? I think sun is the most exciting thing to have in an apartment. I live in a dark—dump.

Truman: There's sun all through this place. . . .
Truman: Did you see my TV series—the prison documentary?
Andy: Yes. It was great.
Truman: Well, it's in two parts and the second one's coming up, and it's better than part one. . . . I just want to show you some photos that are sort of extraordinary. . . . Here's Bobby Beausoleil.
Andy: Look how beautiful he looks. How could a person like that kill.
Truman: Yes, isn't this an incredible photograph?
Andy: That's the most handsome-looking boy I've ever seen. . . . Look at that . . . Does he have Life?
Truman: Oh, yes. He was on Death Row. He was the reason for all the Manson murders.
Andy: Can you pick out a murderer now? Can you tell if you see one on the subway?
Truman: No, no one can do that. But I can tell pretty well . . . Here's all the different pictures of a boy who was murdered while I was there. . . .
Andy: How did you get these pictures?
Truman: The prison photographer took them, and Peter Beard rephotographed them from his prints.
Andy: And they gave them to you?
Truman: Yes.
Andy: Why are his lips so blue?
Truman: They aren't his lips. It's part of a tube.
Andy: Well, who put it in his mouth?
Truman: A doctor. He was bleeding through his mouth.
Andy: Oh. To stop the blood. . . . But this is another boy. Is he dead, too?
Truman: Yes, these are all different victims. They bump 'em off there right and left. . . . Come on Maggie! Cut it out!
Andy: It's all right, Maggie. You can use my leg. . . .
(Phone rings; it's Truman's house keeper Myrtle in Palm Springs.)
Truman: Hello? . . . Oh, hello, honey. . . . Well, I was planning to come out the first of February. . . . Well, then maybe I'll come along sooner. . . . Well, other than a little cold, I'm perfectly all right. Been getting a little work done, had the phone turned off for a couple of days, but how're you? That's more important. Everything fine? . . .

(Door buzzer: Bob MacBride, who works with Truman on their television production, comes in.)

Truman: Hello, Robert. How are you?

Bob: Here are your photos.

Truman: Oh, good. Show Andy the poster we had taken in New Orleans. They're really fun. . . .

Andy: That's great. . . .

Truman: Bayou Boys, Inc. . . .

Andy: Do they have a murder a day at this place?

Truman: Practically.

Andy: Well, this is another beauty right here. What do they fight over?

Truman: Their lovers, number one. Number two, bad debts. . . . They make what they call shivs. They make them out of anything, mostly out of screwdrivers from the shop. . . . This is a man who committed suicide and with his own blood wrote all that on the wall. . . .

Come here Maggie! Stop pickin' on everybody. Come here! I'm going to give you a cookie!

Andy: Did you bring the Stones to see any of the prisoners when you were there? Because it was done after the tour. Did you ever talk to them about the Stones?

Truman: They aren't interested in things like that.

Andy: Not in music? Do they have radios?

Truman: Well . . . they like country and western. Their idea of something great is Johnny Cash. . . . Here is the boy who murdered Ramon Navarro. He's in the second production. Here is a boy called Nathan Eli. He was on Death Row for seven years and he turned into a extraordinary intellectual. He's in the second program. He was a salesman of vacuum cleaners and he was demonstrating a vacuum cleaner to a woman when he decided to rape her, and in the course of it he strangled her with the cord.

Andy: Do you think all these people have chemical levels in their bodies that make them different?

Truman (laughs): No.

Bob: Chromosomes?

Andy: Well, both chromosomes and chemical balances.

Truman: Well, there are chromosome homocidal types like

Richard Speck. That's been proven, but it has nothing to do with these. . . .

Andy: Well, then why do these people do it?

Truman: Because something happens to them—a certain set of circumstances happens and it just—ends up as a homicidal mind. . . .

(Rod Stewart's "Never a Dull Moment" album plays in the background.)

Andy: But I never understand why people kill, when instead they could just not be thinking about it. That's why I think chemical levels control your perspective. And some people have the right chemical balances and some people are missing some chemicals.

Truman: Well, sometimes they kill out of what they—now, listen, Maggie! You're really too much. . . . She'll quiet down in a minute. She's excited because company's come. . . . There was something I wanted to tell Bob. . . . Oh yes . . . I've written 65 pages . . . On *Dead Loss,* an original screenplay Bob and I are working on. . . . Can I offer you anything?

Andy: No, thanks.

Truman: Where would you like to go to lunch? It's Sunday. Do you like Trader Vic's?

Andy: Oh yes.

Truman: It must be open for lunch on Sunday. . . . Do you like . . . *objets?*

Andy: Yes . . .

Truman: Well these are two Chinese Boxes . . . 18th Century boxes. But—open them up yourself. They're ivory. . . .
(Truman goes into another room)

Andy: Why are they so thin?

Bob: What did they contain . . . spices?

Andy: Drugs. [laughs] Haven't little boxes always been for drugs? Haven't they always made little bottles for snuff, or pills, or—something? And they're always really beautiful and small? When did you get them?

Truman: Someone gave them to me as a Christmas present.

Andy: What's the banana?

Truman: Now there is the original Pop Art. That's pre-Andy Warhol. By about 400 years.

Andy: That's Chinese?

Truman: Yes. That's about 500 years old.

Bob: But that's Indian corn over there. The Chinese certainly didn't have Indian corn.

Truman: No, but it is Chinese and it is 18th Century.

Bob: Maybe the ships coming back to China from America brought back pictures they had drawn . . . because these are so exact they're almost—scientific.

Truman: Yes, and I've often wondered if that's not what they were meant to be. Maggie! What is this great crush you have on Andy? . . . I saw one of these as a pineapple on auction at Sotheby's in London. But it was more than I could pay. . . .

Andy: I watched *The American Family* the other night. Did you see it?

Truman: No, I haven't yet.

Andy: Well, they picked a good family because they seemed to want to—entertain. I guess it was the mother who really wanted to be—somebody. So she was probably the one who wanted it. Because, I mean, if Lance knew about art when he was 12 and 13, then she must have really got him interested and stuff . . .

Truman: You mentioned the other night that he's been writing you since he was 13. . . . Were they fan letters?

Andy: They were—cute little letters. Well, the thing was, he would mail them from his father's business place, so they were always special delivery . . . And it was more the idea that they were special delivery than that they were letters.

Bob: Truman thinks I should do the story on Lance—on what happens to Lance.

Truman: It's like seeing what's happening now to Marjoe or Tiny Tim.

Bob: But what possibilities does Lance have, really?

Truman: Can he do anything?

Bob: He thinks vaguely about being an underground movie star, but he's not an actor. He's not a writer or anything else.

Truman (laughs): You don't have to be an actor to be in underground or above-ground movies . . .

Andy: I think he'll do something, I mean, look—I used to write to Truman every day for—years—until his mother told me to stop it. Remember?

Truman: I don't remember my mother doing that, no.

Andy: She did. She called me up and said it. She was really sweet.

Truman: She was drunk. But you think Lance will go on and do something?

Andy: I think so, yes. He's really imaginative. He cut his hair off and dyed it red. . . . In the beginning, what David Bowie did was, he saw our play group in London, hired them all for his entourage, dyed his hair, wore dresses, and became the biggest star.

Truman: David Bowie has talent, though.

Andy: Did the Louds get money for all of that? Because somebody told me that they have gotten a lot of money for it.

Truman: I don't think so. I understand they're very bitter.

Andy: They shouldn't be. I think it makes them glamorous. It really does. I mean, I just picked up a *Vogue* and there was an article on her in it.

Bob: They're all very bitter about it. Lance's father said it's an Eastern left-wing liberal plot to make Middle America look bad.

Andy: I don't think they looked bad. I don't.

Truman: I haven't seen the film at all, but that' not what I understood.

Andy: The mother is wonderful. The mother is understanding and really cares about the kids. She's young. That makes it American. And they're rich, and she's trying to find out things and she, you know, smokes a lot . . . and she's pretty, and Lance is somebody really imagivative. . . .

Truman: You know, we could have all flown out to the Rolling Stones concert in L.A. last night.

Andy: You mean the night before. Really?

Truman: Yes, the concert for Nicaragua. There was this private plane going out and I started to call you up. . . . We were all invited. Just for the evening and the concert, and then we would fly back. I don't know . . . I mean, I was a little bit more than stoned after all those Rolling Stones concerts. . . . You were sort of in love with the idea of being a Rolling Stone yourself. . . . It was something foreign to my nature, but all the people when we were on that tour—every single one of them in their imagination was a performer on the stage doing one or another of those acts. Do you know what I mean?

It was fascinating to watch a person like Marshall Chess with the recording thing—those earphones—he has them on all the time, and he's just pumping his hips away nymphomaniacally. You know, edging nearer and nearer to the spotlight until he's practically all tangled up in Mick Jagger's legs and Keith Richard's armpits and God knows what. Because all of the technicians became psychological Rolling Stones. It was, I thought, a terribly unattractive and unappealing part of the atmosphere.

Andy: But you were onstage and you saw all of that. Out in the audience it was really exciting, you know, just as a performance.

Truman: Oh, sure, I think they put on a terrific performance. Bob saw it both ways—backstage and frontstage, and he said that it was an incomparable difference. I never really saw it any place but backstage.

Bob: The audience was a great factor. The audience turned itself on to a degree, especially with this—communal grass—floating around. . . .

Truman: Self-hypnosis. . . . But as a matter of fact, I always found the show itself basically boring until they got to "Midnight Rambler" and I thought, why is it that it's at exactly this point that I become interested in the program? Suddenly I realized that it's at that moment that the audience gets turned on. It's like they were waiting for something and they all kind of rose up . . . and the whole thing sort of took on some terrific drive and beat. . . .

But it's amazing, the whole rock & roll thing of the seeming spontaneity, when in actual fact there's no spontaneity at all. I saw dozens of those Rolling Stones concerts, and they didn't vary an iota. It's the most choreographed note-by-note thing that I've ever known in my life. There wasn't an ounce of spontaneity. Including the crowds. It's a highly professionalized worked-out program. Chip Monck's lighting effects had a lot to do with it.

Sometimes I used to say to myself, "This not only is the same audience; it really *is* the same audience. They pack them on buses and rush them to the next town." They always did exactly the same thing at exactly the same moment. The very moment "Midnight Rambler" began they rrrrrose up. And then they were with it all the way through.

Andy: But every performer I've ever known sort of does that. You know, they know when the audience is going to laugh, and when it's going to get really interested. I like things that are different every time. But I don't know how you can make a performer do that. Because after a while, they know they can make a person laugh by saying some one specific thing, so they say it every time.

Truman: You mean they get to know what works and what doesn't work.

Andy: Yes, and they stick to exactly what works. That's why I like the stuff that the kids do down on Second Avenue because—you just never know. If two people see the same show on different nights and start talking about it to each other it turns out that nothing was the same in the two shows. Somtimes it's *so bad*. But at least it's different from the next night. They change it all the time. Every performance. Only the name of the play stays the same. Even the plot changes.

Truman: Did you see the Cockettes? [laughs]

Andy: I saw their show and I thought they were wonderful. I didn't see it on opening night. I went on a good night. When the theater was empty. . . . But then drag queens have a way of making things not work for themselves. That's what happens to drag queens. For the first few shows they had the best people down there to see them and they just ruined it. But by the time I saw the performance it was just great, only no one was coming down to see them any more.

Truman: I saw them in San Francisco and I thought they were wonderful.

Andy: I know, and they just ruined it for themselves. It's just what those kids do. They get too nervous. People shouldn't have been so hard on them, because they could have been so exciting . . .

Truman: Well they went back to San Francisco very embittered.

Andy: Yes, well it was because of their opening night that it all worked out badly for them. If it had all pulled together opening night they would have still been around.

Truman: Do you want to go to lunch? Trader Vic's? . . . I guess you'd better put on a tie, though. . . . One of the saddest things— when Trader Vic's was in a different place from where it is now . . . I can't remember. . . .

Andy: Yes . . . 60th Street. . . .

Truman: One night Monty Clift was—you know—not altogether dealing with a full deck by that time, but he came by and he was . . .

sober: He used to take these pills every day because he had this terrific pain from a car accident. And anyway, he didn't have on a tie so he walked in and first the manager said, "I'm very sorry but you can't come in without a tie." And so later the check came and Monty insisted on paying the check, so he just wrote his name on it and the man said he was very sorry but he didn't have a charge account and he'd have to see some identification, and Monty looked up absolutely stupefied and said the saddest line I've ever heard in my life. He said, "My face is my identification."

Bob: Can I borrow a tie?

Andy: I'm following you.

(Goes into bedroom to get tie.)

Truman: Here I am! A little pickaninny eating watermelon. This is me and that's my cousin. . . . Here's a picture with Cecil!

Andy: Oh that's my favorite picture of you. That's when *The Grass Harp* was on Broadway.

Truman: Yes, I guess it was. It was in *Vogue*, I remember. I like it because it's with Cecil.

Truman: Do you want your overcoat?

Andy: Yes, it's cold out . . . Bye, Maggie.

(They leave Truman's apartment and ride in the elevator.)

Andy: Do you like the building here?

Truman: Yes, very much. It's a very well-run building.

Andy: I could have had an apartment here, but it was on the other side. It didn't have a view.

Truman: There's no point living in this building if you don't have a view. At night it's really spectacular. You see all of Wall Street, that honeycomb of light . . . and all the bridges strung out with those green lights.

(Lady gets on the elevator with her dog, Hogan.)

Lady: Hogan! Come here!

Truman (laughing): Sit! All we do with dogs today is tell them "Sit down! Shut up!"

Lady: It doesn't do any good, as you see.

Truman (to doorman): Can we get a taxi?

Doorman: Sure.

Andy: Does Maggie sleep with you?

Truman: On and off. . . .

(In the cab.)
Driver: What hotel?
Bob: The Plaza.
Andy: We met one of your best friends last week—Marella Agnelli. [Mme. Agnelli is the wife of the owner of Fiat.]
Truman: We have really been around the world together. We're the only two people in the world who've done the Anatola coast of Turkey together, not once, but twice. And that's punishment way beyond the call of duty. But it's beautiful. You really must do it sometime.
Andy: Marella's so great. She wants to do a lot.
Truman: She has a zest. She's always complaining about this, that and the other thing, and I said, "For goodness sake. If we can't get an ice-cold Coca Cola here in Maxim's, what's the use of being rich?" [laughs]

Ah, it's closed. I thought Trader Vic's was open on Sundays.
Andy: When does it open? It opens later?
Truman: In the evening, I guess. . . . Well there's lots of places. We can go to the Oak Room . . . Green Tulip Room . . . Pretty corny . . . You know that quiet back booth with the black leather?
(In the Oak Room.)
Andy: This is really nice.
Truman: I just like this little area right here. Would you like something to drink? A glass of sherry or something?
Andy: Oh yes. Sherry. Dry.
Truman: Robert?
Bob: I'll have dry sherry.
Truman: Uh, I will have—Listen to exactly what I want, because it's a little complicated—I want a daiquiri. On the rocks. A daiquiri on the rocks. And with it, on the side, I want a jigger of white rum. I want them to make the daiquiri just like a straight daiquiri on the rocks, and on the side I want a jigger of white rum.
Waiter: Very good.
Andy: Sounds great.
Truman: As I drink I put drops of rum in . . .
Andy: At one time this must have been one of the great rooms. . . .
Truman: It's still beautiful.

Andy: But the menu looks different from what it used to be. It's time for a "Bring Back the Oak Room" campaign. I'm really fascinated as to how *The Great Gatsby's* going to turn out. We read the script and it didn't look like anything.

Truman: Did you read my script?

Andy: No.

Truman: I did the original.

Andy: This one's not too good.

Truman: Well, I didn't think my script was too wonderful. The only straight forward comment I ever got from any of them was, "But, Truman, this script is exactly like the book." I said, "Well, I was under the impression that you wanted to make a film called *The Great Gatsby*. You know? And that that was what the film was supposed to be about." Other than that I never got a straight comment.

Waiter? Can we have someone around here to order something? I mean, the service here is getting grim. . . .

Bob: Did you tell Andy how much you liked *Heat*?

Truman: Oh, no! We went to see *Heat* and we like it a lot. I thought it was very good.

Bob: Really funny . . . The girl who played the daughter. . . .

Truman: That's the girl who committed suicide.

Andy: Yes.

Truman: She was awfully good.

Andy: She was really well then, when Paul was filming it, and it wasn't until about a year later when she got depressed again.

Truman: Was she a manic-depressive?

Andy: She was out on the streets, you know, at 14; just running around. But she did her death as drama, too. Wrote a hundred letters and wroter her mother saying, "I'm going for the Big Time. Heaven."

Truman: That's really good. Unless she was kidding.

Andy: She seemed so strong, and if I'd thought she was really going to do something like that I would have really tried to help. I just thought that since she had gone through so much already and come out of it, that this was just another phase. Because she really was strong. She was a wonderful comedienne, and we used her in about three or four movies and finally just when she could have had such a great career. . . .

Truman: But was there any specific thing that prompted it?

Andy: No, it was just timing. We found out later that she had had fights with everyone at the same time, so no one was talking to her, but nobody knew that everybody else wasn't. . . . She was losing a lot of weight . . . But she was really brave. . . . I guess her chemicals were unbalanced. . . . That's why I was asking you about criminals.

Truman: Well I'll tell you a story. I had a conversation with a boy who killed both his mother and his father. He's not in either of the documentaries that I've done—he's one of the 200 or so murderers that I've interviewed over the years in great detail. His story is, in a way, typical.

When I interviewed this boy he had been on Death Row for two years, and this was in 1957. At the time he was 22 years old. He was extremely bright, but in a way he's a typical murderer of a kind. He was in college at the time of the murders.

He said, "When I was 14 years old I decided I was going to kill my mother and father. It came into my head one day that I would have to kill my mother and father, because otherwise I could never be a free person. The only way I can be free is when they're dead. One of us had to go."

His main thing was a hatred of his mother, not so much his father, but they both had to go at the same time. He said, "When I was 15 and 16 I told them that I was going to kill them, but because I seemed to be normal in every other way they thought this was just some kind of nervous joke that I was making. Like the reverse joke of 'I'm going to kill myself because you're so mean to me and then you'll be sorry.' But I was saying 'I'm going to kill you.' It was like a joke in reverse. They didn't believe me, and I was perfectly sane enough to know that I was going to do it, because I was under compulsion to do it. I went to two or three doctors and told them, 'I am going to kill my mother and father because I have to do it.' They paid no attention.

"So then finally time went by and time went by, and then the day came. I never knew what day it would be, but I knew the day was going to come, and it wasn't going to be about any particular thing. I was well-prepared for it. I knew it was going to happen. The day came, and my mother walked in the door and I shot her dead and I left her in the living room. And I waited until my father came home and as he walked into the living room I killed him.

"The day came," he said, "and that was it."

Now obviously the boy's a psychopath to an extreme degree. On the other hand, two different juries ruled that he was perfectly sane—that, in fact, the murder was "*over*-premeditated, but by a complete psychopath.

Now this is an extreme example of what we're talking about. You say, "Why do people kill?" Now this was something that the person planned, literally, for six years. The key sentence to it is, and then the day came. Now, in the lives of most murderers, whether it spontaneously happens, you know, between five minutes and the next five minutes, what really is happening is, "And then the day came . . ." You see what I mean? Because always, whether they were really planning it or not, there was this element, this spark, this thing . . . And I've never met a murderer in my life—at least I've never met a multiple murderer—let's put it that way, because there is a big difference—I've never met a multiple murderer in my life who has any regrets whatsoever. They couldn't care less. It's a kind of . . . You should eat your rice, there, Bob, or it'll get cold. . . .

Andy: But I think there's some missing chemicals in them that lets them feel as if they're watching a movie when they're doing it.

Truman: That's exactly what they say. Not all of them, but so many times when I go into talking about a specific crime, they will use that exact image. They'll say, "Well, it was just like I wan't there. It's like I was outside of myself. It's like I was outside of my own control and was watching myself on film."

Andy: New York is like a Wild West town now. You can pick up a newspaper and see people being held hostage in the sporting goods store in Brooklyn. They're still in there. Four robbers, ten hostages and a doctor. They've been in there for days, and the police don't know how to get them out. It's been on the news for days.

Truman: In the series of documentaries that Bob and I are doing for ABC, we're working on the research of something that should be, if it's done exactly right, altogether extraordinary, and very serious and moving and human and funny at the same time. Here's the proposition:

On the program we'll have about ten people, but just for now we'll tell you about seven of the people we're going to have. The thing for you to tell us at the end of it is, "What do these people have in common?" We won't go through the whole ten but I'll do seven . . . The title of the program is *Second Chance*.

(Tape ends and in between sides Truman describes seven men and women, all of different ages, from different parts of the country, of different professions, etc., and then Truman asks):

Now, Andy, you tell me what you think these people have in common.

Andy: They committed suicide once?

Truman: Now use your mind.

Truman: They're sex changes—transsexuals. Midway in life, they decided to change their lives and submerge themselves in an entirely different life. To get sexual "reassignment."

Andy: And a lot of them were married?

Truman: Well, it's usually their lovers who pay for the operation . . . I'm just going to have my salad now . . . Waiter? . . . They would like some dessert . . . Bob, tell about the letter. Do you remember the thing where the boy went in to rob the bank so that his boyfriend could have the operation?

Andy: Oh, yes. In Brooklyn. The two guys went in and robbed a bank and the police came and they couldn't get out of the bank and all the people were still inside. And while they were holding everybody inside it comes out that one of the robbers is robbing the bank to get money for his boyfriend's sex change, and it was on all the New York front pages. And then Arthur Bell, who writes for the *Village Voice,* heard the news broadcasts and knew the robber, so he called the bank while they were still inside holding hostages, and the robber picks up the phone and says, "Is that you, Arthur?" And then there were other crazy things, like they let some people go out to the pizza stand to get food. . . . Did you know the one who wanted the operation?

Bob: Truman got a very short, succinct letter from the girl in the case—the boyfriend who's now a girl—named Elizabeth Eden—and she said that John Wozenkowitz—the bank robber—was eager and willing to tell his story to Truman in case he wanted to write it up, and she mentioned in passing that she was a "transsexual bride," as she called it. She evidently wasn't involved in the robbery.

Truman: She wasn't involved at all.

Andy: She was in Bellevue at the time of the robbery.

Truman: Yes, she was in Bellevue. I don't remember what the reason was.

Andy (laughing): Because he was driving her crazy.

Bob: She sounded very charming on the phone.

Andy: All I can tell you is, don't get involved with drag queens. It's trouble. You're doing a program on them, and they're going to be bothering you for the rest of your life. When you're 60 and the phone rings in the middle of the night, it's going to be a female impersonator.

Bob: A lot of your stars must be in that category. Candy Darling is the most startling thing I've ever seen.

Truman: Candy Darling would make a great mistake to have that operation.

Andy: She doesn't want one.

Truman: Most transvestites are not transsexuals. That's the point we kept trying to make in the thing—that there's no connection.

Andy: But the ones that we have are even something else. You should really write a play for Candy. She's really a great actress, and there's no chance of her even going anywhere unless someone important writes something for her.

Truman: Tennessee should write a play for her. Do you think Candy's talented?

Andy: Yes. She is talented. You should see her at *La Mama* now. She's the best thing. But it's twice as hard for Candy to get a job.

Truman: Why is it twice as hard?

Andy: Because girls are actually prettier. If you're going to use a girl, you might as well use a real girl. But Candy's a great performer. . . .

Truman: She has a certain vulnerability about her that doesn't have anything to do with whether she's pretty or not pretty. She has a certain sort of thing.

Andy: Somebody has to use it.

Truman: She has an aura. We could line up 300 girls who are prettier than Candy in every way, but they just don't have any aura.

Andy: But people wouldn't use Candy in a play because everyone would go to see it because it's a man playing a lady's part.

Truman: Well, that didn't happen to *Small Craft Warnings*. It wasn't really publicized that there was a man playing a woman's part, and of course, with Candy not too many people knew.

Andy: Somebody who saw you on the *Jack Paar Show* said you were great.

Truman: Well, we won't talk about it.

Andy: Why?

Truman: There wasn't anything about it that wasn't a disaster.

Bob: Somebody who I know saw it and said you were terrible.

Truman: I wasn't given much of a chance to be anything but terrible. It was just one of those things. Mr. Paar was so nervous.

Andy: But they're all like that . . . They're all so nervous.

Truman: When Dick Cavett first went on real big-time across the country, I was on his first show and we were on with just one other person. I was ready to go on, leafing through a magazine. I'm set, feeling calm, couldn't care less, and Dick came in shaking—everything going—eyebrows—everything—and I said, "Listen . . . maybe you better take a drink or something." The music starts, the band goes "bo-bo-boom," and "Dick Cavett! From New York!" He walks on the stage, and he's cool as a cucumber.

Andy: And then, during a commercial, they start to shake again . . . It's really strange. You've got to have TV magic to be that nervous and then be that calm. That's the magic some people have. . . .

Truman: Could I have the check, please? . . .

Truman: We can go for a walk and then come back to Trader Vic's. How did you like *Deep Throat*?

Andy: It was a good comedy. I liked it.

Truman: Ahmet Ertegun tells me he's the chief backer of the next movie that the same people—

Andy: Why don't I pay for it and . . . I could just . . . uh . . .

Truman: You could charge it to *Rolling Stone*. [laughs] I wouldn't mind that.

Andy: Yeah.

Truman: On the other hand, I don't mind paying for it, either.

(Leaving the Oak Room. Outside—Central Park South.)

Truman: Why don't we go for a walk in the park? We'll go visit the yak. In *Breakfast at Tiffany's* that's all Holly Golightly ever used to do, every time she got what she used to call "the mean reds." She used to go to visit the yak in the zoo. . . .

(They pass the horse-drawn carriages lined up on the periphery of the park.)

Truman: Somehow, I could never bring myself to ride in one of those because I identify with the horse . . . Do you identify with animals, Andy? I know you identify with cats, because you used to keep 20. . . .

(Truman sees a newspaper.)

Tim Leary's going to Vacaville. Vacaville is maximum security, but it's the best-run prison and the nicest—

Andy: Do you know that I just saw him in St. Moritz?

Truman: —if you can call any prison "nice." Basically, it isn't a prison at all, it's a hospital.

Andy: The zoo's that way. I saw Leary Christmas Eve. Isn't that nutty? . . . The zoo's over there. Isn't that the zoo right over there?

Truman: No, no.

Andy: No, no. The zoo's over there . . . But it was so strange to go to somebody's house and there's Timothy Leary.

Truman: I thought he was on his way to Afghanistan.

Andy: Dig. No. He was with a pretty beautiful girl who's really in love with him.

Truman: Oh, yes. She came back with him on the plane.

Andy: And I asked him when he was coming back—

Truman: Well, what happened to the girl?

Andy: He went to Austria, and they didn't accept him in Austria. And she talked him into coming back, or maybe no country would take him.

Truman: He was just like Meyer Lansky without money. The man did escape from prison in California, rightfully or wrongfully for whatever his offense may have been. But the point is, he really did have a marvelous run for his money. He went through Algeria, he fell out with Eldridge Cleaver . . . Didn't Eldridge Cleaver put him in prison? It'll be interesting to see what happens when they finally catch Eldridge Cleaver. He's going to have to come back because Algeria is absolutely fed up with him. Where can he go?

Bob: He can go to any African country or any Communist country. Cuba would be delighted to have him.

Andy: Well, then why wouldn't Cuba take Tim Leary?

Truman: Well, he applied there. The Algerian government very much wants Cleaver out of there, I understand. They consider him a terrific troublemaker. On top of which—you know that plane they hijacked and sent to Algeria, and they got the $750,000 ransom. It was all done for Eldridge Cleaver.

Andy: Oh.

Truman: And those people were arrested by the Algerian government and they took the money and returned it to the United States, and as I understand it, Cleaver just raised absolute total hell. Well, all he had done was have a plane hijacked, steal $750,000, arrive in the country, expect the money to be turned over to him totally illegally, and the Algerian government refused to do it. The Algerians have been subsidizing Eldridge Cleaver to a considerable extent. But they really would like to get rid of the whole situation.

Andy: Hello, girls. How are you? . . . Hi, Corey. Oh, do you know Corey? . . . You're going to the gorilla? Oh, we're going to the deer. If you ever want your hair done, call Eugene. He's the best hairdresser in town.

Truman: The yak's right along in here—somewhere . . .

Andy: The hippie look is really gone. Everybody's gone back to beautiful clothes. Isn't it great? . . . Did you ever want someone to call you "Daddy"?

Truman: Call me Daddy?

Andy: Yes.

Truman: No. Nor the other way around, either.

Andy: You mean you don't want to call somebody Daddy.

Truman: Oh, no.

Andy: But isn't "Daddy" nice? "Daddy" . . . "Dad" . . . It sounds so nice . . .

Truman: I've always been a highly independent person. Strictly on my own.

Truman: You said something to me that really startled me when you came to the house today.

Andy: What?

Truman: You said that my mother telephoned you. I was absolutely startled. Really startled.

Andy: You were? Why?

Truman: Because my mother really was an alcoholic—

Andy: But I met your mother.

Truman: I know you met my mother. But my mother was a very ill woman, and a total alcoholic.

Andy: Really? When I met her, she wasn't—

Truman: Yes, she was an alcoholic when you met her. She had been an alcoholic since I was 16, so she was an alcoholic when you met her . . .

Andy: I never knew that.

Truman: You didn't realize it?

Andy: No. She was really sweet.

Truman: Well, she had this sort of sweet thing, and then suddenly she'd—Well, you know, she committed suicide.

Andy: She did? Oh, I didn't know that. I thought she just got sick.

Truman: No, no, no, no. She committed suicide. She had this extraordinary sweet quality, but then she was one of those people who would have two drinks . . .

Andy: Did you ever want to be an actor?

Truman: Me?

Andy: Yeah. In movies?

Truman: Lord, no. [laughs]

Andy: Why not?

Truman: Discuss it seriously? . . . In order to be an actor, you have to have absolutely no pride. You see, everybody thinks that to be an actor is a question of . . . well . . . talent . . . and a high level of egoism. My theory is that to be an actor you have to have no ego at all. You have to be a thing. An object. And the less intelligence you have, the better an actor you can be. Because intelligence interferes with the creative process of being an actor.

Andy: But that's the old-fashioned way of acting.

Truman: It's not old-fashioned. It's the *only* fashion. To be an actor at all requires a total immaturity, and takes a total lack of self-respect.

Andy: But being on a talk show is like being an actor.

Truman: Don't be silly. On a talk show, you're just—giving your opinion about something. It has nothing to do with acting. You're being yourself.

Andy: Well I'm talking about the kind of acting in *American Family* where—

Truman: They weren't acting!

Andy: Well, they turn on for the camera. They really do.

Truman: It's a totally different thing. You're talking about a thing in which a person is being himself. I'm talking about acting as an art. Acting as an art is an art.

Andy: Yes, I guess you have to be different to be able to be something else.

Truman: One thing I'll say about Mick Jagger. He's fascinating in the sense that he's one of the most total actors that I've ever seen. He has this remarkable quality of being absolutely able to be totally extroverted. Very few people can be entirely, absolutely, altogether extroverted. It's a rare, delicate, strange thing. Just to pull yourself out and go—*Whamm!* This he can do to a remarkable degree. But what makes it more remarkable is that the moment it's done, it's over. And he reverts to quite a private, sensible, and a more emotionally mature person than most actors and intellectuals are capable of being. He's one of the few people I've seen who's able to do that extrovert thing, and then revert into another person almost instantly. And so, in that sense, he's really an extraordinary actor. And that's exactly what he is because: a) he can't sing; b) he can't dance; c) he doesn't know a damn thing about music. But he does know about coming on and being a great showman. And putting on a fantastic . . . act, of which the vital element is energy. Don't you think?

Tell me what you think. You think he can sing?

Bob: Who are you talking about?

Truman: Mick Jagger. Well, he can't sing compared to, say, Billie Holiday. He can't sing compared to Lee Wiley. He can't sing compared to . . .

Andy: Al Green.

Truman: He can't compared to Frank Sinatra. I know you think we're talking about things in separate categories, but we're not. You know? It's not that it's . . . Sound amplification—rock—is carrying a thing forward. The beat thing. But! It's got nothing to do with the ability of the vocalist actually carrying the thing. Because Mick does not carry the thing. He carries it as a performer with his energy, drive and thrust.

I listen to the records quite a lot. I'm in no way trying to discredit him as a performer, because I think he's an extraordinary performer.

But what I think's amazing about him is that there's no single thing of all the things he does that he's really good at. He's not—he really can't dance, and, in fact, he really can't move. He's moving in the most awkward kind of curious parody between an American majorette girl . . . and Fred Astaire. It's like he got these two weird people combined together. On the one hand, it's the majorette strut, and on the other hand, it's got to be a la Astaire. But, somehow, the combination works. Or at least it works for most people. . . .

Look at that squirrel! He's really got something, and he's going up into the tree to hide it. . . .

Andy: Did you like traveling around with them?

Truman: Oh, I enjoyed it. I just didn't want to write about it, because it didn't interest me creatively. You know? But I enjoyed it as an experience. I thought it was amusing . . . I like the Rolling Stones individually, one by one, but the one thing I didn't like was that they had—and especially the people around them—had such a disrespect for the audience. That used to really gripe me. It was like, "Who the fuck cares about them?" Well, these kids have merely stood in line for 27 hours, you know, and whatnot to go to their concert—they adore them and love them. . . .

Andy: Why don't we go and sit in a bar? Get a drink.

Truman: I found the *real* backstage people nice. The ones who were really doing work. It's those little fakes like the press agent. There's a wretched little press agent whose name . . . something . . . who was a great friend of Charlie Manson's, and who recorded three albums of Charlie Manson's records, and he believed Charlie Manson was Jesus Christ—this was before Charlie Manson was going. *He* was a press agent on the rock & roll tour! I mean they had some beauties . . . Marshall Chess . . .

Andy: Why don't we go to a bar and I can ask you the six questions that *Rolling Stone* wants me to ask.

Truman: OK. My fingers are frozen. There's Dr. Grentreich's office. Now *there's* somebody I must take you to. Haven't you heard about Dr. Grentreich?

Andy: No. What does he do?

Truman: He's a dermatologist. He can take your skin and make you look like . . . I don't know . . . Venus De Milo. Overnight.

Andy: How long would it last?

Truman: Forever. He's not a face lifter or anything. He's the world's greatest dermatologist, but I go to him for quite different reasons . . . He's also the world's greatest hair expert . . . He's a fantastic man. You'd like him, in any event.

Andy: Gee, New York really gets crowded when it's a pretty day.

Truman: Well, it's Sunday, too, you know. It takes about seven months to get an appointment with him.

Andy: Oh.

Truman: . . . He's not there. We'll go around the corner and give him a ring. I'd like for you just to meet him.

Andy: That'd be great. Gee. A dermatologist . . .

Truman: He's a genius.

Andy: Does he live in this building?

Truman: No, he has about four floors in this building, and it's like a hospital.

Andy: Oh.

Truman: He has a townhouse on . . . I don't know . . .

Andy: I get so many pimples, I just don't know how. What does cause pimples?

Truman: Almost every person that you know that has an extraordinary complexion comes right out of that place.

Truman: We're opposite the Carlyle. Do you want to go there?

Andy: OK. How long will you be in California?

Truman (singing): "Dependin' on this/And dependin' on that" . . . I read a sort of fun interview with you in the *Village Voice* where you were all in the Polo Lounge of the Beverly Hills Hotel? And there was some real estate agent there telling all these stories? Does that ring a bell?

Andy: Oh, yes. But it wasn't a real estate agent. It was sort of James Dean's friend. One of his—he owns a lot of houses in California . . .

Here comes the new *paparazzi*.

Truman: What are you doing? Hiding? Don't you like it when people are along the street and they go mm and nudge and mm and turn around? [laughs]

Andy: Well, you're a movie star . . .

Truman: Here we are. The Bad Luck Hotel.

Andy: The Carlyle? Why is it a bad luck hotel?

Truman: Jack Kennedy would never stay anywhere but in that hotel . . . you know? . . . And Bobby would never stay anywhere except in that hotel. He always had to stay in that hotel . . . And we know what happened . . . And David Selznick would never live anywhere except in that hotel . . . Took an apartment . . . moved to California, and in a week dropped dead of a heart attack. . . . And then Ali McGraw and Bob Evans took an apartment there at the height of their romance, and it was right there that it all ended. And also, it was in that hotel more than in any other place that I wrote the script for *The Great Gatsby*.

(Hotel Carlyle Bar.)

Truman: Whose questions are these? Jann Wenner's?

Andy: Yes. The first question is—

Truman: Wait. I want to order something before you do this.

Truman: Do want a sherry flip, Bob?

Bob: What's that?

Truman: Sherry with an egg in it?

Bob: No, thanks. I've had my egg for the day. . . .

Truman: I'll have a J&B on the rocks with a glass of water on the side, please?

Andy: I'll have a Grand Marnier. . . .

Truman: Well, that was a nice walk. I think the nice thing about walking through the zoo in New York is . . . I used to go to school here for two years. I went to a private school here, and I skipped school almost every day. I mean literally, almost every day. At least every other day. I just couldn't bear to go to school. I was about 12 years old. And I used to spend more time walking in that park around the zoo to use up the time between nine o'clock when I was supposed to go to school and two-thirty when I supposed to get out.

Finally, I found three things to do. One was, I'd go for a walk in the park if it was a nice day. Two, I'd go to the New York Society Library. It was there I met Willa Cather, and she became this great friend of mine, when I was, you know . . . only a kid. She took a great interest in me. And the third thing was, believe it or not, going to Radio City Music Hall and sitting through the entire production, starting with the movie at 9:00, and I'd see two stage shows and the movie.

Even so I didn't get the diploma. . . .

Andy: The first question was, "problems."

(Truman laughs.)
Andy: Jann wanted to know your problem. With writing the article.
Truman: Why I couldn't write the article?
Andy: Yes.
Truman: Have you got the thing going?
The reason was—twofold. One: As the thing progressed, I saw more and more trash written about the entire tour, and ordinarily that sort of thing doesn't bother me. I mean, for instance, I could cover a trial that's being covered by 17 or 18 newspapers at the time, and it doesn't faze me in the least becaue I know it has nothing to do with what my own insight is.

But my trouble with this was that especially in journalistic writing . . . *au reportage* . . . there has to be some element of *mystery* to me about it. Something when I start out to do it—whether it's about a trip to Russia, or writing a piece about a person or a place—there has to be something that I can't imagine, before I saw it or even while I'm in it. Something that I'm pursuing, some answer. Like in *In Cold Blood* or like "The Muses Are Heard," the article I wrote about the *Porgy and Bess* tour of Russia. You know? It was like a mechanical rabbit racing ahead of a greyhound on a racetrack and trying to catch the mechanical rabbit. And the problem with me with this piece was that there was no mystery. I mean, I could imagine everything about it.

There was not a thing about it that set some mystery going into my mind as to why this should be or that should be, because it was all so perfectly timed . . . staged—I mean psychologically—I'm not talking about the performance itself. Just the whole combination of the thing was so perfectly obvious. The people were so obvious, and so they really had no dimension beyond their own. I mean, Mick Jagger has a certain mystery to him, but simply because he's a highly trained performer, and on the other hand, he's a businessman *par excellence*. And the whole thing is perfectly obvious, ánd so it had no mystery to it. That was my problem. It couldn't make my imagination expand into trying to find out something. Since there was nothing to "find out," I just couldn't be bothered writing it. Does that make sense to you?

I think that's true of anything in creative work. I mean, I don't think it's just true about a relatively trivial thing such as doing an article about the Rolling Stones. I mean, in theory, it sounded like an amusing idea, something to do, but that's my whole theory about writing in general, or art in particular. I mean, if there is no mystery, for the artist, to solve inside of his art, then there's no point in it. It's nothing. Then it's just mechanical, a mechanical process of repeating and doing something that you know how to do just on a purely technical basis. That's why, I mean for instance, I have actually been characterized as a writer, being so varied. You know? From moving from one subject to another kind of subject to still another. But the whole point of it is quite the opposite. The point of it is that unless there's a mystery to be solved, as to the subject or the style or the presentation, then there's no interest inside me. Why should I do a game that I've already done?

I only move from one thing to another if it's basically totally different from what I've done before. I mean, you can't imagine anything more different, say, from my first book, *Other Voices, Other Rooms,* to *In Cold Blood.* I mean, it's a really biazarre progression. And yet it makes perfect logic. If you follow my particular kind of logic. Each time I'm solving a diffrent stylistic problem, and each thing to me is a mystery. Otherwise, I'm not interested. I can't write something unless it has mystery for me. And the Rolling Stones thing had no mystery. . . .

That's not to say that I disapprove of them or anything at all. I liked them, you know, the whole thing—it's just that for me as an artist it has no mystery. I know what it is. There's nothing to be said about it. There's no comment I could make about it that would be original or fasc . . . I could say, "Oh, I could do a great piece of writing," because I could do a good piece of writing about anything, but that's not the point. I mean, I could write a 60-page thing about sitting here having a drink which would read literally like a dream, in a sentence-by-sentence way, just by the choice and use of the language, you know. . . . In fact, it'd probably be a great deal more fascinating than to do a thing about the Rolling Stones.

For me, every act of art is the act of solving a mystery. They say, "Why is he so inconsistent, moving from one thing to another?" But the reason is, if I don't, then I'm not doing, in a sense, what it is I want to do. Just to solve a stylistic problem. Just to solve a problem that I create for myself. Which is its own mystery. I mean, that's one of the reasons that I like working in television. I like doing this program Bob and I are doing, or doing any documentary, because there's a mystery to be solved. There's a technical mystery to be mastered, and there's a mystery of human nature. Art is a mystery. You know what Henry James says . . . let me see . . . it was in one of the short stories of his . . . It says, "We live in the dark, we do the best we can, and the rest is the madness of art." To me, that's always been my motto.

That's, in fact, the entire difference between art and—just—competence. Or just doing things in a highly professional way. I mean, Neil Simon can write 500 million plays that'll be successes for ever and forever, but he will never write a work of art, you see, because there is no mystery there. It's simply a formula. That he manipulates and maneuvers around one way or another until there's no mystery to it . . . Whereas Tennessee can write a really bad play—and I mean a *really* bad play—and yet it'll have some quality of mystery, some pursuit, something elusive, something that he was searching for. Whether he could catch it or not doesn't matter. it's an artist in pursuit of something, even if he never catches it.

Andy: The second question was, "Terry Southern."

Truman: Terry Southern? Terry Southern was on the tour. I thought he was a very nice person. I never met him before in my life. He was very . . . charming . . . a little bit wasted, as they say. He, uh . . . mmmm . . . One night in Dallas he was, you know, obviously . . . taking a few things . . . and I was standing on the back of the stage with the chief of detectives in Dallas, who was talking to me . . . Mm? And Terry came up and started speaking to me about something, and he pulled something out of his pocket, and it fell on the floor, and out rolled every conceivable kind of pill under the whole sun. And so the chief of detectives of Dallas just looked down at the thing and smiled at me and winked and I said, "Terry, don't you think you'd better pick up your aspirin?" [laughs] But he's a very nice person, Terry. I can't imagine why that was one of Wenner's questions.

Andy: I guess because of the article that Terry wrote. Did you see it?

Truman: In *Saturday Review*?

Andy: Yes.

Truman: Well, what about it?

Andy: Oh, I guess he just wanted to know what you thought about it or something. . . .

Truman: Oh, I thought he was very pleasant and nice to me . . . I mean, it seemed to me that the article was mostly about me and very little about the Rolling Stones [laughs] so the *Saturday Review* didn't get their money's worth. . . .

My particular quality as a reporter is I never ask questions. If you do, it ruins the rapport with the person. I never take notes, I never use a tape recorder, I never . . . mmmm . . . seemingly . . . am particularly interested or occupied by the thing, because if you seem to be, you totally ruin the rapport between you and the person. But if you're really tuned in, you know everything. I mean, if you're really tuned in, you don't have to ask anybody any questions because it just commmmmmmmes to you. You know? I never could have written *In Cold Blood,* for instance, if I had used a tape recorder—if I'd ever taken a note. Ever. If I'd ever produced a pencil. Because that very thing with these parrticular people, these Kansas people, the simple, landscaped, as it were. . . . As it was, I never did, ever.

I kept right "right there," you know, and then would go home and write down a full report about whatever the day's activity was, and conversation . . . But to me that's the whole real art of recording—to never seem to be recording at all. If you seem to be doing it you're tuning into the wrong rapport. That's why, for instance, Marlon Brando was so absolutely startled. Did you ever read the Marlon Brando piece I published in the *New Yorker?* I mean, he simply couldn't believe, you know, what it was that I had done, which was a straight-out understanding.

The *New Yorker* wanted me to do this piece and I was interested in doing it because I said—I had sort of a bet with Bill Shawn, who's the editor of the *New Yorker*—I said, "You know"—this is long before the idea of the New Journalism came in or anything, this is back in 1955—and I said, "You know, I think where people are making a big mistake is that journalism can be one of the highest art forms there is in a certain new genre." And he says, "Well give me an example." "All right. Let's take the very lowest form of journalism that could possibly be: an interview with a movie star. I mean, what could be lower than that?" You know, *Silver Screen, Modern Screen*—as journalism goes, there is no depth that you could go beyond that. He said, "Yes, I quite agree with that." I said, "All right, I'm going to prove to you that you can—I will do an interview with a movie star. You can pick the movie star. Anybody. I don't care who it is, and I'm going to prove to you that it can be a work of art and a very high one." Shawn chose Marlon Brando. Marlon knows what I'm doing. Later, he claims that he really didn't. Well, of course, he knew. He didn't, in a sense. He knew I was doing this interview, but on the other hand, it was done by my own special method, which doesn't seem as though I'm doing anything at all. You know?

When it came out and there were these pages and pages and pages of verbatim quotes in which I hadn't taken a note, but which were so obvious . . . He was just knocked out. And it—it did prove my point: That you could take this thing and actually do in a 40-page piece a psychoanalysis of that boy that I—with no false modesty—will say to you that you see *Last Tango in Paris* lives up to. That thing was a total prediction of his entire life and what happened to him to this very moment. And all done in 40 pages. With no comment by me. No *direct* comment. Just letting a person do it themselves . . .

Truman: Well, what was the next question?

Andy: Backstage people. You sort of talked about it before.

Truman: The only thing I have to say about it is Marshall Chess and all of those people have themselves confused as being one of the Stones. I mean, they're always up on the stage sort of edging nearer and nearer into the spotlight. It's always been conceded that just something *barely* is restraining them from rushing onstage, grabbing the microphone from Mick and starting to really strut . . . Also, they're very cantankerous and jealous of each other, and they're so jealous of their relationship with the Stones, with who's closer, who's nearer, who's more . . . this sort of thing. I mean it's really sort of pathetic. Well, not "sort of." It is pathetic.

Andy: Then the next question was, "The Plane Fuck."

Truman: Oh, yeah. Well, the funny thing is, I actually wrote those things in the notes that Jann Wenner read. He saw those.

Andy: Well, yes. But since this is the interview, I guess he wanted you to talk about it now. Since you're not going to be writing . . . uh . . .

Truman: Well, I don't know. They had this doctor on the plane who was a young doctor from San Francisco, about 28 years old, rather good-looking. He would pass through the plane with a great big plate of pills, every kind you could imagine, everything from vitamin C to vitamin coke . . . I couldn't really quite figure out why. He had just started practice in San Francisco, and this seemed sort of a dramatic thing to be doing, traveling with, uh . . . I mean, especially since he wasn't particularly, as I could figure out, a great fan of theirs.

It developed that he had a super Lolita complex. I mean 13-, 14-year-old kids. He would arrive at whatever city we would arrive at, and there would always be these hordes of kids outside and he would walk around, you know, like a little super-fuck and say, "You know I'm Mick Jagger's personal physician. How would you like to see the show from backstage?" And they'd go "Oooo! Wigawigawigawa!" He would get quite a collection of them. Backstage, you know, he would have them spread out, and every now and then he would bring one back to the plane. Usually someone slightly older.

The one I remember the most was a girl who said she'd come to the Rolling Stones thing to get a story for her high-school newspaper, and wasn't this wonderful how she'd met Dr. Feelgood and got backstage . . . Anyway, she got on the plane, and she sure got a story, all right [laughs], because they fitted up the back of the plane for this. You know Robert Frank? He was on the tour. Robert Frank got out all of his lights, the plane was flying along and there was Dr. Feelgood screwing this girl in every conceivable position while Robert Frank was filming, and as the plane was flying back to Washington it was flying at some really strange angle. And the stewardess kept saying, "Would you please mind moving forward?" [laughs] And then the plane landed and they always brought these authorities on board for check-out, and Dr. Feelgood had a terribly hard time getting his trousers on. And in the end he had to come off the plane holding his trousers in his hand . . . With Robert Frank photographing it all. I mean the whole thing had rather a *Belle Epoque* quality.

Andy: Well, but how long was the fuck?

Truman: It was a very short flight. About 35 minutes. Everybody kept switching and changing camera angles. Robert Frank was photographing for a movie he's making about the tour, and I said, "Well I hope you're going to leave that in."

Andy: Did the girl know that she was being photographed?

Truman: Of course! They had lights up and everything. She was enjoying it! I said to her, "Well, you came to get a story for your high-school newspaper and you're sure getting one." She got off at the next stop. I must say they were always very nice about these kids.

Andy: You mean there were more instances like this?

Truman: Well, it was going on continuously, day and night. And not just girls, but boys. The girls and boys. I mean, there're huge gangs of boys, flocks of them went off with . . . There were, uh . . . mmm . . . a lot of people connected with the tour that used to do that. Um, went off with the boys. Very attractive sort of college kids that showed up, they'd get out there, get involved with everything from an electrician to, mmmm, to—They would go with anybody who was connected with the tour. A carpenter. A lightman. Anyone connected with the tour, no matter who it was. They didn't care. Boys, women, dogs, fire hydrants. I mean, the most extraordinary things you've ever seen.

Andy: But the peculiar things were mostly outside of New York, right? Not in New York. Because I didn't see any of it happening . . .

Truman: Oh, I think in New York less than in Texas.

Andy: Oh.

Truman: The things that went on in Texas . . . That tour of Texas which I was on the entire time was unbelievable. I mean, I've never seen anything equal to it.

Once we were driving, I guess it was in Houston . . . Mmmm, I came up in the limousine . . . I don't know who it was, maybe Mick Jagger and Marshall Chess . . . and there was this bevy of girls all around the stage door, which was interesting because they didn't even know which stage door you were going to go in, there were so many, and so I pointed out the window and I said, "There's a really beautiful girl." And it really was a beautiful girl. And Marshall Chess opened the door, and he went like this, and this girl came forward like a bullet! Out of a cannon! And jumped in the car like that. And then he said something to her, and she said—waved and said something—that she was—and the next thing you knew . . . You know that sort of circus thing where a car drives into the circus and people keep getting out and getting out and getting out? The next thing you know, there were something like 18 people in the car . . . weaving its way . . . So I don't . . .

And then there's sort of all-night partying. One night . . . in Texas—I mean I never did it, because in my own mind I was working at the moment, even though subconsciously I knew I was not going to do it—somewhere in the back of my mind I knew I wasn't going to do it—but nevertheless I was still doing it. You know? But they would come off and be all wagged up, and one night about four o'clock in the morning when I was in bed but wasn't asleep (and I guess in a way this is the key to the first question about why I didn't do it), Keith Richard came and he knocked on my door, and I said, "Yes?" and he said, "It's Keith," and I said, "Yes, Keith." He said, "Oh, come out, we're having a terrific party upstairs."

"I'm tired. I've had a long day and so have you and I think you should go to bed."

"Aw, come out and see what a rock group's really like."

"I know what a rock group's really like, Keith. I don't have to come upstairs to see." And apparently he had a bottle of ketchup in his hand—he had a hamburger and a bottle of ketchup—and he just threw it all over the door of my room. [laughs]

Andy: It sounds like fun. Oh, I've gotten to like ketchup so much! I just can really eat it.

Truman: What?

Andy: Ketchup.

Truman: Oh, ketchup.

Andy: The way you can describe things, there're so many exciting things you could use someday in stories and things like that. Just the stories you're saying now, they're really unusual, and they sound so, you know, interesting. I mean, even just visually—

Truman: But things have to fit in. Everything, after all, is a work of art, not feathers of a fan.

Andy: But it seems like there's just so much material on that trip, and the way you describe things is wonderful.

Truman: Yes, there's material, but it's just that, material. It's just that. It doesn't have any echo. All it is is a little series of anecdotes that amount to a form of gossip, really. You know? Where is the meaning? Where is the art?

Bob: There's something synthetic about the whole thing.

Truman: Well, you always felt that. I did too, basically. Bob said the best thing about it. After the Rolling Stones party, I was sort of stuffed with the idea of doing the piece which I then knew I wasn't really going to do, Bob said, "Oh, it's the sort of thing that you want to forget about two days later." And that's the truth of the matter. It isn't that you want to forget about it because of any unpleasantness; it's just because it doesn't have any echo.

It's like the end of E.M. Forster's novel, *A Passage to India:* She goes to the caves, crawls into them, and says, "Ah, but there's no echo." You know? And when one enters into a work of art, supposedly—and that's what I consider anything I do, I don't care what it is . . . [laughs] fighting a traffic ticket—but as far as I'm concerned—it's a big effort on my part; there's always the question I ask myself, "Ah, but is there an echo? Is there an echo?" Does that make sense to you? When I throw out my voice, do I hear another voice coming back? . . . Does it have some reverberation? Or is it just, you know, a sort of flat, metallic sound . . .

Also, I think it's impossible to write a work . . . mmmm . . . of art in which there is, in no area of it, some quality heroic . . . I mean, when something is totally negative all the way through, I think it's impossible to write a real work of art. There has to be some element of it that's heroic. You simply can't write about . . . uh . . . grubbiness . . . malice . . . greed . . . envy . . . and, you know . . . Nowhere in this whole story of the Rolling Stones could I find anything sympathetic except the naivete of the kids . . . which wasn't—maybe in itself—true, either. Maybe it was just sentimentality.

There was this thing about the Stones that I hated. Which was . . . that . . . the kids would be staying there—they'd end the performance. . . . Chip Monck would say, "Thank you, ladies and gentlemen. The Rolling Stones—" And the lights would go up—or had been up, actually—and the kids are standing there and they're just—breaking their hearts applauding . . . And there they are in this dreary Mobile, Alabama, ghastly—Fort Worth, Texas. I mean, they waited months and months for this thing. They wanted it, you know

. . . for such a long time. And the, the Rolling Stones—Not only have they left, not ony have they no intention of giving an encore, they are already on their airplane up in the sky while the kids are down there applauding and applauding and pleading, saying, "Please come back, please come back!" and everybody knowing that they've long since gone their way . . . Twice I didn't go on the plane because I wanted to watch this phenomenon. It was heartbreaking. I mean, they would stay for half an hour, and nobody would come out and tell them that they aren't going to come back. And then they would finally drift out . . .

That was the one thing in it . . . But, you see, I wrote this thing about these kids in Fort Worth virtually realizing that they weren't going to come back and that the big moment was over and the whole thing, and then they're drifting out into this ghastly July heat, gradually fading away into these dark nights with a street lamp on every other street.

Bob: But Truman, they were all stoned by the time—

Truman: I know, but you see . . . In the entire piece, of everything, it was the only moment I could find in the whole thing that had some sort of moving quality, and it was sentimental! I hate sentimentality for its own sake . . . And it seemed to me here that maybe I'm seeing something altogether wrong . . . I know it's true, but—it would be true in any event about them.

I just couldn't get with it—because the story didn't have any . . . I mean, what else was it? There were admirable people . . . Jo Bergman, who knows all about how you "really put on a good show," how "you're really professional and you really work hard" . . . But where in that is there anything for me? Whereas when I wrote the book about Russia—the company touring Russia—that was full of all kinnnnnds of innuendo and humor and charm and strangeness, and—the Russians never having seen Negroes, and . . . the whole thing. I mean, that was fascinating. I had all kinds of overtones. In this other thing, I couldn't find anything but toughness. . . . Can I have a package of True Blue cigarettes? . . .

The machine doesn't work? . . .

Andy: I'll go get some. . . .

(Andy leaves and returns with the cigarettes.)

Andy: Jann says, "Truman was going to compare the Kansas audience to a painting called, 'It Will Soon Be Here.' "

Truman: There's a famous American primitive painter . . . whose name at the moment . . . He's a famous Illinois painter who painted between 1840 and 1870, and he painted a famous painting of a group of farmers and their wives who were rapidly gathering wheat against an oncoming storm. And you see you can see the storm way off in the distance—there's this great cloud—and they're rushing with the wheat to save it to put it into these barns. And I sort of compared it with how these people in the Midwest, where these concerts were, were actually the descendants of these people, who had been afraid of anything chaotic. And the title of the painting about them was "It Will Soon Be Here." And my title of the piece I was writing was "It Will Soon Be Here." The point being that the very thing their ancestors most feared was this out-of-control, chaotic behavior. It was totally against their idea of just the plan of squirrels putting nuts away against the storm. And there the storm has finally arrived, and they had managed to put the hay away . . .

Well, you've watched the Stones' show over and over . . . The whole thing is sort of like a storm.

Andy: In the end, Mick threw water on everybody.

Truman: Yes. Quite true. Sort of appearing in the distance, vaguely at first, and gradually the audience loses control of itself, and the last thing they're thinking about is gathering hay. They're just ready and waiting and want to be drenched by the storm.

Andy: I guess, actually, the story like this was a little late for you to do.

Truman: It was—I know what you're trying to say, but it was. . . . It was too little and too late. I mean, it was something that I could have done when I was 23 or so, and I could have done it like a zip and it would have been hilarious and full of humor, but I got way beyond that kind of thing. It has to have a whole different—depth—for me . . . I'm only interested in things that have some sort of sociological . . . compassionate . . . interest or quality to them. Otherwise, it doesn't interest me at all.

Andy: But the show could have gotten—Altamont was so tragic, you know, out in California and stuff, and along the way something like that could have happened again or something . . . But I guess they were being really careful and trying to do more entertainment this time. They were more informal before.

Truman: Who? The Rolling Stones?

Andy: Yes. It's now really Entertainment. The kids were really good in the audience in New York, and they didn't you know, yell as much. You actually went to a show where Mick performed, did a really good job, and—

Truman: Oh, of course. They're obviously sensational—

Andy: No, but—

Truman: They're good.

Andy: No, but—

Truman: They know what they're doing—

Andy: Yes, no, but—

Truman: You've seen it. You never saw it when—

Andy: Yes, I know, but—

Truman: You saw it two or three times?

Andy: Yes, but that's what I mean. I'm sure it was the same. They were trying to change their act. Noise wasn't really it. You have to perform now, and people come out to hear the songs and see the songs acted out by the best.

Truman: Well, they're good . . . They're good . . .

Andy: But the new performers are now copying that, their way of working, dyeing their hair and doing more showy stage numbers, so it's all sort of changing . . . And I guess the Stones just had to be a little more careful this time, and they couldn't be informal, because it would be dangerous. But they didn't lose any energy at all. If anything, Mick made up for it by increasing his energy.

Andy: How about Bianca?

Truman: Well . . . you know I like her. I think she has a great deal of style, and they . . . She seems to be a person not too terribly popular with the entourage. I never could figure out why. I mean, you try to pin somebody down, this, that, and the other thing, but the most that I could ever figure out is that it's part of that problem of who's closer to who. And I think that basically they were just jealous of her because she, to me, is an extremely nice girl. A lot of style.

She has extraordinary South American chic. There's a certain kind of South American girl who's unique. At least, I think so. People like Gloria Guiness, or Perla Mattison . . . she's a Brazilian . . . Gloria Guiness is a Mexican . . . Bianca's a Nicaraguan . . . They just have a strange type of special chic . . . Like Madame Arturo Lopez . . . She has some peculiar quality. . . .

There's a certain type of thing that some South American women have, and if they have it, they have it more than anybody. There's another woman called—I'm sure you've met her—Madam Walther Moreira-Salles from Brazil, and these women have an amazing kind of originality and chic, and I think Bianca has that, although her particular quality is very theatrical. I mean theirs is high style. It's what I would really call "high-yellow chic."

Andy: What?

Truman: High-yellow chic.

Andy: What does that mean?

Truman: It's a certain kind of chic that women who've been raised—not that they themselves are Negro, perhaps—but who've been raised in the culture that has a basic element that's from Negro culture into Spanish culture, and it turns into something totally unique. And I think that that's certainly true of Bianca.

Andy: Well, who is like the Number One person. How does it go down there? Is Mick really considered the whole thing?

Truman: Mm. Hmm.

Andy: He is?

Truman: Yes. Mick and Keith Richard. I mean, they are the Rolling Stones. . . .

Andy: But the other kids are really nice. I mean, Charlie Watts is really nice . . .

Truman: Oh, he couldn't be nicer, yes. But that's not the point. When you get right down to it, the people who really are running the show . . .

Bob: She has no tits.

Truman: What? . . . No tits? . . . Well . . . [laughs]

Andy: Oh, but small tits are really special. I think it's better to have small tits when you're young rather than big tits when you're old, and then they just sort of sag. At least, small ones won't sag when you're older. . . .

Truman: I think she's got a lot of style, but no breasts.

Andy: How'd you see her breasts?

Truman (laughs): I didn't. . . . As a matter of fact, I think that if she did have that kind of a figure, she wouldn't have that much style . . . Because the kind of clothes she wears really wouldn't work then. . . .

Andy: Did you run right out and buy their album after touring with them?

Truman: I play the albums. I like them very well.

Andy: Do you dance to them?

Truman: I don't think they're danceable. Do you?

Andy: Oh, the kids dance to them.

Truman: I don't think the Rolling Stones are meant for dancing. . . .

Andy: Well, maybe I could ask you something. How do you like Mick's poetry? The words to the songs. Have you looked at them? Is he any good?

Truman: . . . Well, it's so very hard to differentiate, because most of the lyrics are collaborations between him and Keith Richard.

Andy: They are? Really?

Truman: I don't think the lyrics make much sense. The fact is, if they really made any sense, they wouldn't be any good. The only lyric of theirs that has a real consistency about it that I read—and I read them all—is the one called "Sweet Virginia." But I don't find any of these rock & roll lyricists—for instance, I think Bob Dylan's, on the whole, are absolutely atrocious. I don't think any of these rock & roll lyricists are good as lyricists, compared to people like Larry Hart. Of course, it's a totally different style, and in a way the less sense it makes, the more sense it makes in terms of the sound it's in . . . Because if you really had to follow the lyric of a thing—I mean, I defy anybody, really, to listen to a Rolling Stones record or concert and remember any part of the lyric. I mean, I had a transcription made by an expert—a phonetics expert—who had an absolute hell of a time. And this person is one of the great lip-readers of all times, among other things, and he did for me about 30 lyrics of the Rolling Stones things as actually sung on the records.

One of the few lyrics that does make sense is . . . uhhh, "Midnight Wanderer"—"Rambler"—And yet it doesn't really. It's just a repetition of an evocative phrase that gives you an impressionistic thing, but I find that very true of all of them—that whole new school of lyric writers, all copies of Bob Dylan. Like . . . uh . . . Carole King

... uh ... Carly Simon ... uh ... James Taylor ... You know ... Carole King wrote a really good lyric, I think, for that sort of semi-rock & roll called "You've Got a Friend." The lyrics actually made sense. It wasn't a particularly good lyric ... but it carries some sense to it beyond the simple sound of the thing. But I defy you to listen to, say, Alice Cooper and make any sense at all out of the lyrics. There's nothing there at all. They're just simply batty....

Simon and Garfunkel—Simon, for instance—actually, he's another Bob Dylan derivative—can sometimes write a rather good lyric. But it's always terribly sentimental. Garfunkel, to my knowledge, has never written a word ... I mean, you take something of Simon's like "Me and Julio Down by the Schoolyard." That's a rather fascinating lyric. I've listened to it several times because it doesn't make any sense on the surface, and, in fact, it doesn't make any sense at all, but there is a form of a peculiar psychoanalysis going on inside that lyric, some private thing, some private vision of Paul Simon's about something that happened to him as a ... boy ... at school. My interpretation of that lyric, listening to it, is that it's really all about how Paul Simon was going to school in the Bronx and had a Puerto Rican friend ... And none of this is in the lyric. You have to listen and see whether I'm making this up or not, but I don't think I'm making this up, because it's got to be about how Paul Simon is a boy in the Bronx going to school and in the school he has a friend called Julio who is Puerto Rican. He and Julio are great friends. One day, Julio's parents find out that he, Julio, is having an affair with Paul Simon. Julio's mother gets very upset about this whole thing and sort of laid down a law to Paul Simon, about how he must break up his friendship with Julio. That's what the whole lyric is about. It takes a great deal of analysis about what the thing ... He thinks he's telling you some sort of private joke that's just between himself, and actually he's telling you a lot. Most of these lyrics are meant to be private jokes between themselves, the musicians, and friends. They're not *supposed* to communicate any particular thing. Once in a while, it all comes through [laughs]. Without in the least intending to.

Andy: But have you seen any of the movies Mick has been in?

Truman: Well, I saw two of the most disastrous, in my opinion. I saw three. *Gimme Shelter* ... I saw *Performance*, which I loathed ... and I saw *Ned Kelly*, which—that's Tony Richardson's ...

Andy: But why?

Truman: He never had a good director.

Andy: Is that the only reason? Because—

Truman: Both of those films have lousy scripts. And very bad directors. What can you do with a lousy script? And a bad director?

Andy: Yes, but—

Truman: The boy has talent.

Andy: But—why—

Truman: I know exactly how he could have made a fantastic film debut. Let's suppose nobody had ever made a film of . . . of . . . uh . . . of . . . ohhh . . . What's the one that Albert Finney did and Bob Montgomery did . . . ohhh . . . *Night Must Fall* . . . About the psychopathic killer who chops off women's heads and keeps them.

Now, supposing no one had ever made a film of that . . . it was a very good play. It was a disaster with Albert Finney just a few years ago, a total disaster. Now, if nobody had ever made a film of that, and Mick Jagger was there, and you suddenly said, "listen, this is the perfect thing for you to make a movie of"—he would have been brilliant. He would have come off absolutely *boom!* The perfect part for him.

Andy: But, I mean—

Truman: Because—

Andy: No, no, no! I don't mean that, I mean, with all these people who come to see him, like, and how they stand in line and everything, why didn't those people go to see the bad movies that he did. I mean, they would have kept the movies going . . . They wouldn't know how bad it was until they saw it, but yet they never went in the first place—

Truman: Because they're not interested. Don't you understand? There is no such thing as a *star.* In films. Nobody will go to see a film because somebody is in it.

Andy: But they're going to see Marlon Brando in the nude.

Truman: Ah! But aside from everything else, it's a good film. OK. The film is the feature. It's also a big novelty. It also happens to be a very good film. But that's not the point. The film, itself, is the feature. *It* is the product.

Andy: No, but do you think—

Truman: I mean, Mick Jagger wasn't being Mick Jagger. Mick

Jagger was being a rotten, bad, fifth-rate actor in a second-rate production, with a ninth rate script.

Andy: Yes, but the way things go, it doesn't matter anymore. You know, if you have fans . . .

Truman: No, but they're fans on a different level!

Andy: Well, I don't understand the different fan levels. That's what I don't understand.

Truman: They don't care about going to see Mick Jagger as an "actor." They care about The Rolling Stones! Because they are—don't you realize that with the Rolling Stones, the audience is half the thing?

Andy: Yes.

Truman: So are they getting their kicks watching a bad movie with him up on the screen? No. Of course not. It's two totally different things.

Andy: But then it goes back to your idea when you were saying that you felt sorry for the audience, because when the Stones left them, it was negative stuff. Well, the audience wants that.

Truman: The audience wants to hear the music. The audience wanted to keep on feeling good. The audience wanted to keep on dancing and huggin', shakin', rockin', rollin'. . . .

Andy: But they did it themselves on a stereo while they were gone.

Truman: But it's ridiculous. You can't go on without the stimulus. I think Mick's one of those people who has that peculiar androgynous quality, like Marlon or Garbo, transferred into a rock & roll thing, but it's quite genuine. I mean, there's nothing transvestite about it—it's just an androgynous quality. And it has something that's very sexy and amusing about it, and it appeals to both boys and girls in the audience, aside from just natural talent. It's a very special sort of quality. Brando has it *par excellence.* And Garbo always had it—it was always the secret of her great success. And in his own strange way, I don't know, Montgomery Clift had it . . .

He just has it. I don't know . . . there's something totally asexual about it. But it doesn't offend the boys in the audience or even excite them, to some degree, and it turns on the girls to a great degree, and it's part of the whole unisex syndrome. Don't you think?

Andy: Yes. Does it have morbidity?

Truman: Not for me. I just don't know where it goes from here, because I don't know where the Rolling Stones go from here. I don't know if that particular group and the particular thing that they do can go on for more than a year or two. I think Mick's whole career depends on whether he can do something else. I'm sure he'll go on. I just don't know in what area.

Andy: Well, that's the thing I'm always thinking about: Do you think the product is really more important than the star?

Truman: Oh, definitely.

Andy: Why do you think that?

Truman: Because no-body will go to see a film today just because of who's in it. Let me give you the full proof. No one's going to see Barbra Streisand in *Sandbox*. She's got a big following. It's dead. It's dying in the box office. Nobody's going to see *Judge Roy Bean*. It's got Paul Newman in it, but nobody's going to see it. . . .

Andy: No, but there still are a few people now who can draw them in, whatever their movies . . .

Truman: Nobody.

Andy: Like Steve McQueen. . . .

Truman: Steve McQueen wouldn't draw flies except in something like *Peck*—I mean, look. He just did a film called—what was it? . . . Some racer . . . It didn't even get an opening in New York.

I don't think there's a single Star that by himself or herself could do what Clark Gable could do—what Clark Gable and Spencer Tracy could do together, or Joan Crawford at the height of her career. Bette Davis. They were real stars created by studios for a very specific purpose who were continuously promoted. And you have to remember *television*. Television is the star media today.

Well, the only film I can think of in the last ten years that I can say had influence—of the sort we're talking about—was *Battle of Algiers*.

Andy: It influenced all the Negroes.

Truman: *The Battle of Algiers* really did turn on a whole thing in a certain kind of Negro intellectual mind that infiltrated down into this and that, and in that sense did have true political meaning and influence. And so in that sense, something from a relatively small position can grow to a very volatile and powerful thing. But we're talking about, really, two entirely different things. We're talking about the thing of—

Andy: Well, I want to work in TV. I've always wanted to work for television. That's what I've always wanted to do, but it seems so hard to get in.

Truman: Well, as far as I'm concerned, television is, to me, the thing that interests me most—

Andy: I just think it's great.

Truman: Aside from writing, because writing is my life, it's my particular art. But I do know an awful lot about working in television and it is the only thing that really interests me.

Andy: Why did you go on the tour in the first place?

Truman: I was talked into it . . . ohhh, I don't know . . . Jann Wenner kept sending me these telegrams about it, and I just said, "Oh, well, I don't want to do this." And then I just sort of thought, "Oh, well . . . " And Peter Beard and a lot of people kept telling me, "Oh, you should really do it. It'd be the sort of thing you like to do in a reportage way," and so I thought about it and I said, "Well, there's no harm in going for a little bit." And then I just got kind of caught up in it. And then about halfway through, I knew I wasn't going to do it, and from that point on, it was just sort of gradually phasing it out.

Andy: "What elements of their music does Truman like best?"

Truman: I think they have a fantastic drive and professionality that holds up in its way. I've always liked, basically, rock & roll per se, and of a certain kind of band, they're the best. Now everybody says, "Oh, they're over the hill," and this and that, and I don't agree with that. How much can you say? I like all kinds of music. You know? I play all kinds of music all day long. Especially when I'm working. I always have half a dozen records ranging form Erik Satie to the Rolling Stones. It just rolls on with me, one way or the other. The Rolling Stones are first-rate. I personally prefer them on records to the performances. . . .

Andy: Jann wants to know, "what do you see as the predominant themes running through the recent albums?"

Truman: Well, I don't see any themes running through their songs. It's just like you—taking Polaroid photographs all night long, or . . . I think when they're good, it's really by accident, even though everything about them is rehearsed down to the last degree. The Beatles' songs very often made *some* sense, but I can't think of a single Rolling Stones song that, from beginning to end, made absolutely logical sense. It's all in the sound.

Andy: "Did you have a good time on the tour?"

Truman: Yes, I did. Because I'm a highly curious person. It was a new world—the mechanics of it. The frantic atmosphere in which it was conducted. I really enjoyed it. I wasn't bored. I had a good time.

Andy: Did you feel guilty about not finishing the article?

Truman: Not in the least. When I make up my mind about something, I never feel guilty. That's it. No artist should feel guilty. If you start a painting and you don't like it, you don't finish it. Right?

Andy: No, but with our early movies people seemed to think that I should feel guilty about finishing them. . . .

Truman: I mean, I threw away a whole novel I wrote. I just tore it up.

Andy: When was this?

Truman: 1953. And it was a good novel, but it just wasn't. . . .

Andy: You actually tore it up and threw it out, and you don't have a copy?

Truman: Yes. Because my theory of the thing is that it's like having a toothache and you keep feeling the tooth and thinking, "Does that tooth still bother me?" . . . So, rather than do that, I just take it and tear it up, because then I never think about it. And that's what I dd with the Rolling Stones.

Andy: Why did you take so long to tell him?

Truman: Well, because I hadn't really made up my mind. I had all of the material there, and it was sitting there, and it was bothering me, and I kept thinking, "Well, it would be so easy, really, to do it." Finally, the time came that I just made up my mind that I wasn't going to do it. And I just told him. They voted me Rookie Reporter of the Year [laughs].

I just have my own ideas about things, like anybody else. . . . It wasn't something that I really wanted to do, and there were other things that I really wanted to do, which I really wanted to pull together. Which I have since pulled together, so. . . .

Andy: Did you have anything to do with the cutting of the San Quentin picture? Or did they direct it, or whatever . . . ?

Truman: Mmmmm, well I had the final supervision.
Andy: Oh, you did?
Truman: I thought they did it quite well. But you don't know how well they did it until you see the second half.
Andy: What is the second half about?
Truman: Well, what it's really about is about people. It's basically a real, all-out assault on the prison system by the prisoners themselves, and it took great courage to say what they did, and it's about people who consider themselves, rightly or wrongly—I think 50% wrongly—consider themselves political prisoners. Simply because of race or this, that, or the other thing. But it's really, it's got a real kind of drive to it. Because it's a continuous battle. . . .
Andy: How did you get permission to go in there?
Truman: It takes a lot of time and effort. Six months of total negotiations. . . . We were the only people who had been in San Quentin since George Jackson was killed.
Bob: How many guards were killed in that thing?
Truman: . . . their throats were cut.
Bob: By prisoners who took over or something?
Truman: No, they claimed that George Jackson and two cohorts of his . . . There were five men murdered there. There were three guards whose throats were cut and two prisoners—for reasons that nobody can understand—whose throats were also cut. And they piled them into the cell and then George Jackson escaped into the yard—which is ridiculous—I mean, you can't get out of San Quentin if you could see where you were and whatnot. . . . And he was shot and killed. It's all a very peculiar, curious story, but that's what the whole program is about, and the reactions of the prisoners to it. It's a very bitter, very . . . shaking-up kind of film.
Andy: Couldn't you maybe have helped that man who's accused of all that murder in California?
Truman: Mr. Corona? But he's guilty.
Andy: Why is it, because I always think that people who really insist that they're not guilty are telling the truth. They always are so convincing to me.
Truman: Well, I know the whole Juan Corona case backwards and forwards for different reasons. That was another time the *New York Times* wanted me to do a thing, and I went up there . . . mmm

... I've just got to go to the bathroom for a minute, and then I'll tell you. It's really quite interesting, because the real truth of it—It's never been in the paper at all, what it's really about.

(Truman leaves and returns.)

Truman: Well, anyway. . . . When the whole thing first happened, that was at exactly the same time that the *New York Times* wanted me to do the Manson trial. . . . And after having interviewed all of them, again, for precisely the same reasons that we were talking about before, I didn't want to do it—but . . . it was exactly at that time that the Juan Corona case came up. And Juan Corona was accused of having murdered 25 men. And it was in this town up in Northern California, a small agricultural town and they began discovering these bodies, all of whom had been buried in a peach tree orchard bordering a river. They discovered 25, but they say there are more, because the river was flooded at a certain point at this time, and they say that there were many more missing from this thing and that many of the bodies, because they were in very shallow graves, were carried down the river and lost, but there were 25 actually found. And the 25 that were found, all were itinerant agricultural workers.

Now, Mr. Juan Corona is a Mexican-American, very respectable. He was a person who hired itinerant agricultural workers and he was an extremely respectable, very church-going-type gentleman, not at all—sort of—"Cal-Mex" as they call it. . . . Married to a very attractive woman. . . . And as I remember, three or four children, all extremely well-behaved. . . . And Mr. Corona was always at the church every Sunday with the little girl—Martha, as I remember—who was always in nice little starched dresses and everything. . . . And all the neighbors thought they were just wonderful. And then this extraordinary thing happened: All these people started to be missing over a period of a year. And then the first of the bodies was discovered buried in this peach orchard. And they were all, as I say, itinerant people.

Now they had almost all been hacked to death with machetes . . . but the thing that was consistent in all of the cases was that they had practically no clothes on, and most of them—I won't say all—but most of them were buried without their trousers. Or the trousers were thrown into the grave. . . . So, even the prosecution never attempted to present a motive for the crime, although in several of the cases it was perfectly clear through examination of the bodies that the person had had anal sexual relations with someone quite recently. And this is the real motivation of the whole Corona thing. They've always known it. The prosecution knows it. It's the main reason why Corona never took the defense. He didn't take the stand in his own defense because had he, the prosecution would have then brought it up.

Andy: Why would he keep saying he's not guilty?

Truman: I have seldom met a murderer who didn't tell you that he was innocent. For one reason or another. They may even tell you that they're guilty of killing the person but—Like, for instance, the boy who killed Ramon Navarro? I mean, he *killed* Ramon Navarro. And he says, "Well, I mean, it was sort of an accident. I mean, actually, he strangled on his own blood." And I said, "Well, listen. If you hadn't been to visit Mr. Navarro, he would have been alive today, wouldn't he?" You could say the same thing to Mr. Corona: "If you hadn't decided to do whatever it is, none of these people would be in their graves, would they?"

Andy: Then why should anyone want to defend him?

Truman: There's always somebody who wants to prove somebody innocent. Can I have the check? Do you want to walk down to Trader Vic's? And have some of those little goodies? We don't have to eat a whole meal.

Andy: Oh, sure. We can walk down.

Truman: In that case, we can have another drink here. To fortify us for the walk.

Andy: You were saying that Manson was in love with Bobby Beausoleil.

Truman: That's how it all started. But the whole thing with them all was that everything was interchangeable. For instance, Charlie Manson wanted to get this girl into their group. It was a girl who was the daughter of a minister. He met the girl and she was 14 years old. Her name was Delsie somebody. Charlie Manson seduced the girl. Mmmm, the girl went home and moved out. The father was a Methodist minister in San Jose. The father got private detectives to track down the daughter. Charlie Manson took the father out for a long ride . . . and he seduced the father. The father fell absolutely, madly in love with Charlie Manson—this is all true—and he then became a total disciple of the group, and he ended up being the most incredible drug addict that you've ever known. . . .

Charlie Manson met Bobby Beausoleil at a house they always refer to as The Spiral Staircase. . . . I don't know . . . and Bobby was there playing the guitar. And Charlie just thought Bobby Beausoleil was—You know, Bobby Beausoleil had been the boyfriend of Kenneth Anger, made a movie with Bobby Beausoleil and Kenneth Anger.

Andy: Drugs do make you feel so different.

Truman: I never met anybody connected with the Manson people that wasn't awful.

Bob: How did they find these girls?

Andy: It was drugs.

Truman: It wasn't drugs.

Andy: It was drugs. On drugs, it really is like a movie. Nothing hurts, and you're not the way you used to be or would have been. There were so many crazy little girls who were in love with me, and I never even talked to them! They were all on acid trips and they never came back, and they're still around on acid trips and it damaged their brains. There are so many kids who've just never come back. . . . And these girls were looking for somebody, and Manson picked up on drugs.

Truman: I don't think—No, he—

Andy: He did.

Truman: He was a thug.

Andy: Yes, but he realized that on drugs—

Truman: He was an institutionalized thug who realized that he could take advantage of these—

Andy: On drugs.

Truman: It wasn't really.

Andy: Yes. It was.

Truman: It was a desperate need for affection, and a loneliness that they had, because they wanted to belong to something.

Andy: But without the drugs, what they did would have hurt, but the drugs became a part of them and nothing hurt.

Truman: They needed to belong to something. They needed to belong.

Andy: The drugs became a part of them. On drugs, you're

different. People can hurt you, you don't feel anything, you—you could do S&M, murder—anything. These kids took acid, and they didn't feel the things Manson was doing to them. It was all fun to them.

Truman: But then they wanted to do it in the first place.

Andy: No. They're different.

Truman: No, because even under deep hypnosis, people don't do things that they don't want to do.

Andy: I always think that if drugs change your chemical balance, then the drug users aren't any different from the people who have the same chemical balance in their bodies already, without taking drugs, who do it consciously.

Truman: We're not directly stating anything about what's right or wrong; but on the program I ask Bobby Beausoleil, "You don't think there's anything wrong about going in and killing 14 innocent people?" And he said to me, "No! Not necessarily. I have my own sense of justice—my own sense of right and wrong! Whatever happens is right!"

Truman: The one thing that I *really* dislike about Angela Davis is when she got out and they said, "Well, now does this prove to you that you can have a fair trial in America?" And she said, "The only *fair* trial would have been *no* trial at all." Well, really, for total, incredible arrogance, that takes the super-prize. There is that girl who got away with just absolutely everything, and then she turns around and says, "The only fair trial would have been no trial at all . . . "

Andy: But do you think she really was guilty?

Truman: Of course. All you have to read is George Jackson's letters and Jonathan Jackson's letters. . . . They wouldn't allow the prosecution to bring them in.

Bob: Once you admit a conspiracy theory like that, there's just no end to it. Like J.F.K.

Truman: Oh, the thing that they put out under my name! They sent out this circular of five or six hundred thousand copies, that was written by a professor up in Wisconsin—the F.B.I. traced it back—and it says, "Kennedy Lives by Truman Capote." You heard about that thing. And I was supposed to be the author of this article. This was about five years ago, but for a period there, I was getting two or three hundred letters a week, just on this one subject.

Do you get a lot of poison-pen letters?

Andy: Not so much "poison-pen" as crazy. Nutty people are always writing me. It's like there's some nutty mailing list. . . .

Truman: I wouldn't read them, but this U.U. is so clever about changing his stationery, otherwise I would know enough to just throw it off, but I open it and I'm fascinated by it for a moment. And you don't want to show them to anybody—not that there's any truth to them—but just because they're so unbelievably—like somebody's head opened up and a whole bunch of snakes came out. You don't want anybody to see it just because it's so disgusting that anybody's mind could be that sick.

Andy: The scary thing is that they're thinking about you. That's what's scary.

Truman: Well, it doesn't bother me in the least little bit, but I do get some of the most . . . mmm . . . all-out weird letters that you've ever seen in your life. And phone calls and tapes.

Andy: But your number is really hard to get.

Truman: I keep changing it all the time. But if you're in a hotel, suddenly the telephone rings and people are on the phone saying—well—the most incredible things that you just hardly want to walk down the street. . . . And I've been getting a series of letters that I haven't shown anybody—I keep tearing them up, but I must stop tearing them up.

Andy: What do they say?

Truman: Well, they're increasingly threatening and they're just signed "U.U." Just the letters. They're typed out.

Andy: And what are you doing wrong?

Truman: Oh, anything I do. And they're coming at an increasingly rapid rate—every two or three days. Mailed from New York. And they're not on stationery. They're put in an envelope. On a penny postcard—whatever—you know, from the post office, and they always begin by being . . . terribly critical about something. . . . Sometimes, they're extremely personal, like, "I saw you on the street the other day but you didn't see me. I thought that coat of yours was pretty funny. Where did you get that damn coat, anyway? I would like to see that coat covered with blood. Who the hell do you think you are, anyway?" Signed "U.U. Or, "Saw you on television"—this person obviously follows every move that I do—"Saw you on *Jack*

Paar the other night. Don't you know that gentlemen never wear hats in a room? Who do you think you are, anyway?"

Andy: Do you think it's a lady?

Truman: No, it's a man. From the series I can tell. "Who do you think you are? I'd like to see your head floating in the East River with that hat on." Signed U.U. This has been going on for about six months, but now they're getting more and more . . . I get quite a lot of letters like that, but this person is very persistent. And he has a very clever way of changing the envelopes all the time. Because if I could spot the envelope, I would know and then I wouldn't open it. Different colors and sizes. He must be really maniacal, and he must be somebody who lives within five or six blocks of me. Because he mentions things too often about . . . mmm . . .

Andy: It's weird when someone spends their whole life thinking about you.

Bob: Of course, the classical theory is that this is the way that someone who writes these letters takes out his feelings and he would never do anything. It's the guy who doesn't write letters and broods over it. . . .

Truman: But what kind of a kick are they getting out of it? . . . Some coffee? . . . I could understand it if it were in some small-town situation. But one time I really had such a series of letters that it really was terrifying. It was at least nine or ten years ago. I began to get a series of letters which were, mmm, extremely intelligently written, typed, never signed, but extremely intelligently written. I mean, *very* well written. But filled with total hatred.

At first, it didn't really matter—I'm used to that kind of thing—but then it became more and more interesting, and then they became really threatening, and I told my lawyer at Random House, "I really am becoming upset by this person writing me this series of letters, and they're coming now every day and obviously the person is absolutely batty." They were postmarked from all over Connecticut. No one place, but all over Connecticut. So they got hold of . . . What was his name? . . . Such a nice name . . . He was a police commissioner. . . . And they put the post office on it, and I began saving the letters, and after about two months they caught the person by just carefully working it out. Bit by bit.

Andy: Who was it?

Truman: Well, it turned out to be—this is what's interesting about it—it turned out to be a middle-aged librarian in Connecticut. A woman. A spinster. And the letters, by the way, were all full of sexual fantasies of one kind or another. The problem then was that the woman was very respectable. She came from a very respectable family, nothing like this had ever happened to her, and in theory she was a perfectly normal, sane person. The point was, was I going to bring a case against her? So the woman then wrote me a long, long letter which I saved just because it was a document, in apology, and said, mmmm, that she didn't know why she had done this, but all that she knew was that when she came home at night she would feel all of this anger and frustration and whatnot, and it gave her some great relief, and she said, "I just decided on you. I don't know why, and I'm very sorry, and I'm having psychiatric treatment about it. . . . "

I once had a poison-pen letter situation that was really fascinating. I did that musical, *House of Flowers,* and when we were on the road with it, I began receiving a continuous series of poison-pen letters. The person would only sign it, "A member of the cast." And it had an enormous cast of about 70, and the effect of the letter always was, "You smug little son of a bitch. Who do you think you are? Actually, everybody in this whole company hates you. You think you're so cute. You think everybody just loves you. The truth of the matter is that there's not a single person in the cast that wouldn't like to kill you dead on the stage." Every day. Never found out who it was.

Andy: When did it stop?

Truman: Second week out of town . . . We must tell Andy about our argument with Angela. Angela is one of the transsexuals on the show—the laboratory technician. During our discussion, she said, "You know, the one thing about this that bothers me very much," she said—I mean, she's *very* respectable. [laughs] I mean, she *really* is. . . . She said, "I'm so disturbed by the sort of things that Andy Warhol and his people do with transvestites. I think that's so wrong. It's such an erroneous impression of what it's about. . . . " And I defended you right down the line. I said, "You're making a great mistake."

The point is, after all, that in those films they were not dealing seriously with the problem of transsexualism—they were simply using transvestites who were suitable for a certain kind of part. There's no intention in those films to make fun of a person for being a transvestite. What we're talking about are two different things. You're talking from a totally different point of view, the point of view of a person who wants to be actresses or actors or whatever they are, and in the situation they're in, it's amusing. It's fun. They're just having rather a good time.

I don't know if Angela was convinced.

Andy: Well, it's like Paul always says. For awhile, we were casting a lot of them because they were so dramatic. The real girls we knew couldn't seem to get excited about anything, where as these people could get excited about anything . . . But the girls seem to be getting more energy lately. It's sort of a sophisticated energy, and it's really nice.

Oh, is that Dali? Oh, look at Dali.

Truman: Oh, we see him everywhere.

Andy: Oh, look at all the transsexuals.

Bob: Are those transsexuals?

Andy: Who knows . . .

Truman: Well, Dali's got on a real costume tonight. . . . It's really a tragedy. He was a fantastic technician.

Andy: No, he really is great. Really.

Truman: But he's so unbelievably corny.

Andy: No, he really is a great artist. He's really one of the best artists. . . .

Oh he's coming over to see us.

(Dali comes over, greets Andy and Truman, and returns to his party.)

Andy: He's really a great artist.

Truman: Well, you're really sweet. I don't think Dali's painted a good painting . . . mmm . . . since 1930. At the most. Never in my life have I seen a more disgusting picture than "The Last Supper" in the National Gallery.

Andy: Well, that was his Drunk Period. He's stopped now. He paints very well again. The ones five or six years ago were really painted badly, but now. . . .

Truman: What would a really good Dali painting get on auction now?

Andy: I don't know, because the really good Dalis never come up. And that's good. He gets a lot. He just did a Datsun commercial.

Truman: Everything has its suburbia. Houses are a funny thing. I have five. And I only have a mortgage on one, and I don't even want to have it. I would love to pay it off, but for tax reasons I have to keep it. . . .

Andy: Where are your houses?

Truman: I have two houses in Long Island, an apartment in New York, a house in Switzerland, and a house in Palm Springs. . . .

Andy: A house in Switzerland? When did you think of that?

Truman: I've had it for 14 years. I just happened to like the house. It's right on the Italian frontier. Very pretty.

Andy: That must have been right before they stopped letting people buy houses there.

Truman: Now you can't buy one. I think I was one of the last foreigners who ever bought a house there.

Andy: Switzerland is my favorite place now, because it's so—nothing. There's absolutely nothing to do. We went there for Christmas and New Year's, and everybody's rich. . . .

Truman: I was at one time a Swiss resident.

Andy: You were: And you gave it up? Why?

Truman: It took a great deal of effort to become one. I'll tell you why I gave it up. First of all, I wasn't there for avoiding taxes. There were a lot of restrictions—just so much time here and there to qualify and maintain . . . and I didn't care about being a Swiss resident, and I thought it would be sort of a good thing to do, and then I thought, "Oh, the hell with it. I don't give a damn." And so I gave up my whole Swiss residency and came back here . . . and I just decided I'm going to live here and that's it, and I'm not going to be a victim of any of this sort of nonsense whatsoever. I'm just going to live wherever I want to, even if I only have to live on 25 cents a day. I don't care about any of those taxes. I get mad, but I don't really care. . . .

You've just got one life to live, and if you're going to live it for any other purpose than what you want to live it for, you're doing it all wrong. The people who spend their whole lives moving from country to country to country so as not to pay any taxes, they're so rich they'll never be able to spend all their money if they live to be 70 million years old, so what the hell is it all about? Who cares? You can eat just so many chickens....

Andy: The Rolling Stones are doing that, too.

Truman: Well, their days are numbered. [laughs] I don't mean because of talent, but because they're Fad.

Andy: What is Fad?

Truman: Well, I don't believe in Fad. I only believe in one thing, you see, and that's Classic Style. The one thing I always ask myself is, "Is it timeless?" I mean, just as a subject. "Is it timeless?" Because otherwise I'm not going to put effort into it. I don't care about what's fashionable. If something is good, it's timeless, in any event. There're certain things that you've done, that certainly are totally contemporary, pop, fad, whatnot, but that have a timeless quality about them. They will sort of stay there because of a sort of period quality about them, no matter what happens. Fashions' not going to influence it one way or the other—

Andy: No, but you were talking before about Neil Simon's plays. I think about them, too. They are terrible. Why are they popular?

Truman: Well, this is something I don't mind saying, and I've said it in a thousand interviews and on the *Johnny Carson Show*. The truth of the matter about it is, the entire cultural press, publishing . . . criticism . . . television . . . theater . . . film industry . . . is almost 90% Jewish-oriented. I mean, I can't even count on one hand, five people of any importance—of real importance—in the media who aren't Jewish. I can't.

If those people could have done me in, they would have done me in like nobody's ever been done in. But they couldn't do me in. They would have done me in, because not only wasn't I Jewish and wasn't in the Jewish clique, but I *talked* about not being part of it. I've said it for years: "Here's this god-damned Jewish Mafia working tooth and tong on the *New York Review of Books*, the *New York Times*, whether they're doing it consciously or not." And mostly they're doing it consciously. I'm not in the least bit frightened by them.

Andy: But that's good, too.

Truman: In the sense that it has consistency? It's not a good thing. It's a bad thing.

Andy: But it's funny, because they're the ones that buy your books and go to the plays. . . . They really care. Why don't the other people care?

Bob: Yes, they really don't. Proportionally, they don't.

Truman: You're so wrong. Do you know that as an industry last year the book industry did, by volume, a better business than the film industry did? The book industry last year, $23 billion. They did better, by actual profit, than the television industry. Of course, a huge amount of this money comes from textbooks. I would say 70% of it. Colleges and universities buy textbooks by the absolute carload, and that's why a company like McGraw/Hill—a nothing company—is very rich. That's how they happen to have a million dollars to throw away on Mr. Whatever-His-Name-Is. . . .

All things being equal, I think it's better to be with a company that's got a lot of money. Because of the advertising: If they don't have the money, they won't advertise . . . This subject fascinates me, and I know so much about it I could talk for seven hours. Nonstop. About how publishers work and why you should do this and why you should do that. . . .

Oh, listen, let me pay.

Andy: No. *Rolling Stone* will pay.

Truman: About publishing books, there are three real rules:

One: The book has to be ready at least three months before it's going to be published. I mean, ready in every way. It's got to look, absolutely, the way-it's-got-to-look. It's got to have style. It goes out to, maybe, 300 people, and no more. In a certain way.

Two: All the reviews of the book have to have been arranged—not "arranged" in the sense of whether they're good or bad, but arranged so that they're going to come out within three or four days of the publication date. Wham! At the same time. No spreading out. Everything has to come at the same time. And,

Three: When you get all the reviews together, you get together with an absolutely great layout artist and you layout the reviews just the way you want them. But the simpler the better.

There's no publisher in the entire publishing industry that wouldn't call me up to talk about publishing, because I really know about it. I've been into it since I was 16 years old. . . .

A Lady: Excuse me, Mr. Capote. The next time you have a party, have your friends wear these.
Truman: Oh, aren't you sweet. . . .
Andy: What's that?
Truman: Who knows.
Truman: Why don't you do something on TV with us, Andy?
Andy: All right.
Truman: We've got the best producing unit in television, and we've got the money, too.
(They go to the street and head toward Trader Vic's)
Andy: What is this, your own company?
Truman: No, it's Tomorrow Productions. We have our own unit and our own company inside of it. It's got to be something for network, otherwise it just doesn't work. None of this NET stuff . . . We have to dream up something that'll be real fun to do. But real good, too.
Andy: Reading that article about you was great, because the book you were doing sounds so exciting.
Truman: You're going to really like that book.
Andy: It sounds great.
Truman: It's my life's work, that book.
Andy: And the people you know are so interesting, to combine them together.
Andy: So you think sex means a lot? Or . . .
Truman: To me it does.
Andy: Really? Do you think so?
Truman: Oh, it does to me. It doesn't have anything to do with my liking a person as a friend or anything, but it certainly has a great deal to do with whether I have them as a lover or not. It has *everything* to do with it!
Andy: But what do you mean?
Truman: I certainly could never have a love affair with somone that wasn't sexually exciting to me.
Andy: Well yeah, but—but—after awhile, sex isn't really anything.
Truman: After awhile, nothing's nothing.
Andy: But then, like you say, it isn't timeless . . .
Truman: Oh, I've done it again. Shoot.

Andy: What. You lost something?
Truman: Keys. . . . I've lost still another one.
Truman: I don't understand what you said before about thinking that sex appeal has nothing to do with being in love with somebody. . . .
Andy: It's easier without it.
Truman: But then how can you have a love affair without having some sort of sexual—
Andy: But I think a love affair can get too involved, anyway, and it's not really worth it.
Truman: But then how do you separate the two things?
Andy: You do it like you watch a movie made for television—you don't think about it . . .
Truman: I must say I don't get it. I can have intense, long-sustaining friendship-love-friendships, that eventually don't involve sex . . . but, my God, they did in the beginning!
Andy: I know. Well, it takes a long time. . . . They should have a school for that. Because so many people go through so much pain [laughs] that they should tell you right off the bat what it's all about. Right? The kids nowadays learned how to really not care and do it with boys and girls . . .
Truman: Personally, I must say I always found that true in New Orleans, anyway. Rural Alabama, 30 years ago. . . . [laughs]
Andy: But why didn't they explain it to you a little better, or something?
Truman: (laughs): Nobody ever explained nothing to me.
Andy: I know. Me, either. Learned the hard way. . . . I always think that people who're creative go through these hard love affairs so they can write a book or do a movie or write a poem . . . to get "material."
Truman: I've only had one love affair in my life that I would consider "hard," and that's because the whole thing was a misunderstanding. [laughs] No one was on the same wavelength.
(In Trader Vic's.)
Andy: Last year we met Onassis here.
Truman: I heard all about it. . . . We want ev-er-y hors d'oeuvres. Lots. The entire display. From beginning to end.
Bob: Not the egg roll.

Truman: I'll have the egg roll. Speak for thyself, John. We want all the Polynesian hors d'oeuvres. . . .

Andy: Truman, have you heard about the murders in the Village?

Truman: Oh, yes. It's exactly like the story of that book.

Andy: And he was now living with a very young person, I guess, because they showed both pictures on television and one was really young.

Truman: That was just a friend of his.

Andy: They were just roommates.

Truman: No, I mean they had separate apartments in the building. They were just friends.

Andy: No, but one person went out to cruise, and the roommate went out to cruise, and brought home somebody.

Truman: Well, all I know is that they certainly weren't living in the same apartment. . . . It said in the paper that he had been stabbed 87 times.

Andy: Yes, they were stabbed a lot.

Truman: Eighty-seven times is a lot of times.

Bob: Let's cut this conversation out before dinner, what do you say? We're really touching on them all . . . Corona, Manson . . .

Andy: Oh, but did you know Ed Sanders?

Truman: Yes, I knew Ed. I was at the Manson trial. For awhile. Before I decided not to do it. I thought his book was extremely badly written, but was full of fascinating information. He can't write at all, though.

Andy: Why wasn't it a big seller? Ed's so nice.

Truman: I'll tell you why. It was written in too much of a hippie-slang-in-way. It was written for readers of the *L.A. Free Press*. That's what it was literally written for, and that [laughs] doesn't exactly constitute a wide audience. . . .

Could we have some of that yellow—you know, that sweet sauce? Now this oughta hold us . . . Yes, that's it . . .

Andy: Franco Rosselini really said the best line. He really hit it. He said, "People who are frigid can really make out."

Truman: Because they're never hurt.

Andy: Yes.

Truman: But I'll tell you a corollary to that line which maybe old Franco doesn't know: There is nobody in the world who can put on a more passionate, fantastic act than somebody who's frigid. And it comes as a shock when you find out later. . . .

Andy: Frigid people really make it.

Truman: But I've found that with most "frigid" people, they have one thing that secretly turns them on.

Andy: Really?

Truman: It'll be one rather peculiar thing that you wouldn't even think about. And some people never mature beyond this, that, and the other thing. Thirteen-year-old girls turned this one person I knew on, and I found that out by sheer accident. And it wasn't because of any innocence or purity about him—it was nostalgia. It was a pure question of nostalgia. It was looking and looking back and back.

Andy: But I just got a dog and I think I'm falling in love with him. I think about him all the time, and I know he does, too. I was reading about the two Chinese pandas in Washington, and they won't let just one keeper take care of them because they might fall in love with him and then they wouldn't mate with each other in a couple of years when they're supposed to mate.

Truman: Have you ever read the fantastic book by J.R. Ackerly called *My Dog Tulip*?

Andy: No.

Truman: Well, it's one of the greatest books ever written by anybody in the world, and I'm going to get it for you. It's also by one of my favorite authors that ever lived, named J.R. Ackerly. And if you like to read at all, which I don't know whether you do or not . . . he's dead now. He wrote only four books, and they're all great. They're *all* great. But this one is all about a love affair with a dog, in which it is a totally sexual thing. They don't have sex, but it's . . . the most astonishing book you've ever read, and so beautifully written.

But I find everything understandable. There's nothing that I don't find understandable . . .

Andy: All those people in jail. What about that one on TV?

Truman: Who, Bobby Beausoleil? He's evil.

Andy: Well, being evil is OK if you don't—do anything.

Truman: I know Bobby very well. Bobby's one person. . . . There are very few people in the world that I would ever say this about— but Bobby's one person who could never be turned around. I could talk for hours on that subject. . . . Kenneth Anger was madly in love with Bobby, and when Bobby left, Kenneth Anger had a medallion made: On one side is a picture of Bobby, and on the other side is a picture of a frog. There's a motto on it that says "Bobby Beausoleil" on one side, and on the other side it says, "Turned into a frog by Kenneth Anger."

Andy: How many people did he murder?

Truman: He and Charlie Manson fell in together. And the truth of the matter is that Charlie Manson was in love with Bobby. And the whole setup was bisexual. And Bobby was never terribly under the influence. It was the other way around. . . .

Andy: Oh, here comes Dick Avedon.

(At the coat room.)

Andy: Everybody looks like they're Somebody here. Everyone looks so important.

(Leaving).

(Outside).

Andy: Oh, I have to go home and feed my dog.

Truman: We'll go home, too.

Bob: Can we give you a ride?

Andy: No, that's OK. I go uptown.

Truman: Thank you, Andy.

Andy: Oh, no, thanks, Truman. Talk to you later, 'Bye.

Coda: Another Round with Mr. C.
Jann Wenner/March 1973

From *Rolling Stone,* 12 April 1973, 50, 52, 54.
Reprinted by permission.

The following tape was made in early March when the editor visited Mister Capote at his residence in Palm Springs.

(Saturday evening. Muffled sounds of traffic.)
   TC: Should we go to Don the Beach-comber's?
   JW: I don't like it that much. It's kind of ersatz Trader Vic's. Do you have a personal chopstick holder at Don the Beach. . . . ?
   TC: Well, of course.
   JW: Oh, then—Don the Beachcomber's. Can we have a drink?
   TC: Oh, we will.
   JW: When did you first meet Andy Warhol?
   TC: I don't remember it. He used to write me these letters all the time. They were just admiring letters. He liked my work, etc.
   JW: Did you take any note?
   TC: Well, I got so many of them, of course I remember them.
   JW: What? Every day?
   TC: Yes. For quite a long time. He used to send me lots of pictures and drawings and things. But I don't remember when we first met. I don't have any clear visual memory of it at all. I do remember him sitting in my living room the first time I saw him, and him telling me about his mother and how he lived with his mother downtown and they had 28 cats and he seemed a very shy, pale person, rather like he is today. Only much shyer. That's my first memory of him. I can see him in the room sitting on this pink couch, but I don't remember how he got there. [laughs]
   JW: Well, I was trying to think of a title for it, and I saw on the top of the page—the very first thing on the page said "Sunday."
   TC: Just that all by itself?

JW: Well, with a subtitle like "An Interview Starring Truman Capote by Andy Warhol."

TC: "An Andy Warhol Tape Starring Truman Capote" would be more like it.

JW: Did you have any thoughts for a title?

TC: No, but I'm good at titles. Well, "Sunday"'s nice and simple.

JW: I was thinking about "Sunday with Truman Capote," but that sounds like. . . .

TC: That sounds like a TV program. Um, I know what the subtitle is: "An Audio Documentary by Andy Warhol Starring Truman Capote." 'Cause that's, in effect, what it actually is.

I have a two-way thing, which is really the basic reason why I can do certain things that seem very mysterious to other people. I have both a photographic memory and it's almost 100% reliable, and I also have an audio memory . . . I can focus on two things. Now there are quite a few people who have an audio memory, and there are quite a few people who have a photographic memory. But the two things combined are rather unusual.

JW: Can you re-create a long conversation?

TC: Oh, yes. I can re-create a conversation as long as up to six hours which is over 90% accurate and have done it. You remember I told you how startled Marlon Brando was I hadn't taken a note. I hadn't done a thing. I hadn't even seemed to be interested, and yet I produced six and a half hours of conversation verbatim. . . . A lot of which was used in *Last Tango in Paris*.

JW: Mmhm. What do you think makes people so knocked out about *Last Tango in Paris*?

TC: Most of the reviews that I've seen have missed the whole point. It's about something—and God knows it's been done over and over in literature with Madame Bovary and Anna Karenina, but never really been done in a film before—the way two people create total fantasies about each other on purely sexual terms, and they become involved in a physical enslavement of one another without really knowing anything about the other person or wanting to. The other person is a total creation that you've made up and a symbol of the things that you've most desired and you somehow enslave them and have them enslave you. This happens over and over in life to various degrees. Then gradually the mirage removes itself and there's a rejection, in this case of Brando. It's got extraordinary production values. The photography is wonderfully done. There's all sorts of qualities beyond that, but I haven't seen a single review that said what it was really about.

(Inside Don the Beachcomber's)

JW: Do you see Norman Mailer much?

TC: Norman's a very good friend of mine and always has been. I never had any trouble with him at all because he said, "There's only one person in New York I'm afraid to tangle with, and that's Truman Capote." Somebody asked Norman, "What do you think of Truman Capote?" He said, "Truman's the ballsiest guy I know, and I mean that 100%."

The first time I ever met Norman, we did a television program together in the pioneer days—me and Norman and Dorothy Parker—and Dorothy Parker was scared out of her wits, 'cause this was live television, and she was just afraid to open her mouth, and Norman—I kept tripping him up all the time.

JW: What do you mean tripping him up?

TC: Well, every time he would get led towards some point and then completely—it was like setting an animal trap, leading a person down and then he goes whack. And he really couldn't believe this was happening to him.

A couple of days later he came and rang my doorbell. There was Norman Mailer and he said, "Would you come out and have a drink with me?" And I said all right, sure. So it was later afternoon, and he said, "I just couldn't understand how it happened. I just couldn't figure how you did that." "Did what?" "Well, turn me inside out. I never felt so totally manipulated by anybody. How did you do it?" I said, "I wasn't doing anything. I was just listening. You were listening to yourself, and I was listening to you."

JW: What do you think Mailer's major work was?

TC: I consider his major work, in my own eyes, the work he's done in the last few years in reportage.

JW: The astronaut thing?

TC: No, no, that I didn't like. *Armies of the Night* was very, very good, and I think he's a marvelous critic. And there are portions always in his novels that are good.

JW: Why did you want to trip him up on that TV show?

TC: I didn't. It was just irresistible. If somebody sort of sets himself up for it over and over, what can you do? He was going on about Jack Kerouac, and suddenly I just said, "Oh, Jack Kerouac—that isn't writing, it's typing." And Norman didn't have anything further to say about that, and then somebody asked me who did I think was the finest living writer writing in English. And I said E.M. Forster. And so Norman said, "But you write better than E.M. Forster." Well, of course that was ridiculous. I did not write better than him. I came to write quite differently in my own way, and, in my own opinion, as well. But that wasn't the same thing. Really, mostly Norman falls into it because he's such a good sort of guy, really. Everybody thinks he's rambunctious, looking for a fight, and I suppose in a way he is, but he's always been a very gentlemanly guy in my presence.

JW: He seems to have that quality of talking too much and not listening enough, and sometimes missing . . . but his own reactions are usually quite valid.

TC: I thought your Robert Mitchum interview was very good. The part about the dog was hilarious, the dog who attacked Robert Mitchum's balls. There's a little trick in there that I find all young reporters doing, and I find it quite despicable. I've seen it over and over in *New York Magazine,* but it's everywhere. And the trick is—as in this Mitchum story—the guy standing there says, "I'll tell you something: One day I walked into the room and I banged this chick and suddenly her dog jumped up on the bed and grabbed my balls—but, listen, don't put that in your story. I mean, Jesus Christ, after all, think of his wife." They quote the person saying, "Don't put this in the story." I think it's a sleazy trick.

If I was going to do it, I'd just put it in, but I would leave that remark out. "Don't put that in your story." That's where the sleazy trick comes in, not that you put it in. That's your own judgment. If a person wants to tell you something, OK, that's at their own peril, right?

JW: You think that's cheap sensationalism?

TC: Yes, it's a little trick that all the young reporters follow, and they should stop it. They should be warned. It'll become a real cliché of journalism. 'Tain't no style there.

JW: What was it like to come to New York and be a boy wonder. You had extraordinary, immediate success.

TC: It had been building up for a long time. I was quite ready for it when it finally happened. I was interested in a career, not a success.

I know that I have this one book to write. Everybody says they have one book in them? Well, I've written a lot of books, but basically, I've always had this one book—it was what I was really all about. And I just move slowly, slowly, slowly toward this book and I honestly do think that when I finish it, I'm not going to write again any very, very, ambitious writing.

JW: When were you first cognizant of the idea that you were going to do this one book? Very young?

TC: It just gradually grew on me. I began to really think about it when I was about 17. Maybe earlier than that. I mean, I was completely totally convinced that I was going to be able to write when I was about eight years old, seven or eight years old. I really can remember just like Marjoe can remember his revelation of heaven. [laughs] I was just walking along one day down the road and suddenly this whole book just came into my head. From that point on, I was obsessed with writing, prose style and everything. I never deviated from it for one minute.

JW: What did you do?

TC: Hmm? I just stuck to one thing and I wouldn't do anything else at all. So I got out of school as soon as I could 'cause they had nothing to offer me.

JW: What other books have you got coming out before *Answered Prayers*?

TC: One's called *The Dog's Bark*. It's sort of a geography of my life. It's about places I've lived and people, mostly taken from journals of my own. Diaries and things like that. It's coming out this September. Some of it's been published, but most of it hasn't.

JW: Is there a complete time span covered in the book?

TC: Well, yes, 1948—no, 1945 to 1970. The title comes from something that Andre Gide said to me when I was complaining about some review of a book of mine. He said, "Oh well, as the Arabs say, 'Dogs bark, but the caravan moves on.'"

The next book is called *Then It All Came Down*. It's made up of all the interviews of mine with various criminals and my own opinions of them. And it's my own opinions about what I think makes them work. They're different ones, different people that I've interviewed.

JW: I notice you talk back pretty smartly to a lot of killers and murderers. . . .

TC: Yeah, I sure do. [laughs] For just a punk kid on the corner. [laughs]

JW: Do you think this is an extraordinary prolific pattern to have three books coming out in 18 months? They sound like major works, all of them.

TC: I think it's just coincidence, really. It's just I've been doing them all. Coincidence.

JW: When you write, how much do you write a day?

TC: Oh, I try to work four or five hours a day. Sometimes I'll do it for a couple of months and then I won't write for a month. You know?

JW: How much writing do you do in four or five hours?

TC: Oh, I'd say about—I write very slowly. I like longhand. I'd say I write about three pages of longhand.

JW: Where did the title for your last novel, *Answered Prayers,* come from?

TC: It came from St. Theresa, who said, "More tears are shed over answered prayers than unanswered ones," and I do believe that's true, because I think when you get what you want, and you've really got it, then by the sheer nature of things, something else has to be substituted for what it was that you wanted. So in some way we come to regret . . . And when St. Theresa said that "more tears were shed over answered prayers than unanswered ones," well, it's hell to get rid of an answered prayer. It can be a lover or a career or success of the kind that you've got, but it turned out to be not right. Because always there has to be something else that you want. Otherwise there's really no reason to get up in the morning.

JW: Isn't *Answered Prayers* an answered prayer?

TC: For me? You see, I'm never the least bit satisfied with—can I have some ice with . . . ?

Waiter: Yes.

TC: Wait, wait, wait, wait, wait. We want two more double margaritas, and I want some ice in my drink, and I want a straight jigger of just pure tequila.

I guess it will be—if I finish it the way I want it to be, and just the sheer fact that it occupied my lifestyle for so long. But of course I basically don't really want to finish it. It's just that it's become a way of life. It's like suddenly taking some beautiful animal, say, or a child, some lovely child and you just took it out in the yard and shot it in the head. I mean, that's what it means to me. The moment I give it up it's just like I took it out in the yard and shot it in the head, because then it will never be mine again.

JW: When did you start on it?

TC: Well, I originally started writing it in 1956, and I worked on it for three years. Then I stopped to write *In Cold Blood*, got so trapped into that whole thing that I couldn't write anything except for little short pieces for about a year and a half. I mean, I was really knocked out. It was such a long difficult haul. So I actually didn't start back writing on this book 'til about three and a half, four years ago. It's a very, very, very long, complicated book, but I think that I'll be ready with it—well, I'm planning to publish it a year from September.

JW: What's the status of the book now?

TC: As a book I figure it'll probably be over 800 printed pages. I've got about 480 pages that are really finished.

JW: What's the status of the rest of it? Rough draft?

TC: I wrote the end of the book almost before I wrote the beginning. I always do that. I told Katherine Ann Porter about how I always wrote the last page of a story before I wrote the first page and she said, "You know I've always done that my whole life." And I said, "I bet you do it for the same reason that I do. The reason that I do is because if I write the last page of the story, I always know exactly where I'm going, and I want to know where I'm moving." I wrote the whole end of *Answered Prayers* before I ever wrote the first part of it.

JW: Why do you want to publish it at long last?

TC: I don't want to. I don't want to. But, I mean, I guess there comes a point where you have to give up. . . .

JW: Where you have to give up?

TC: Where you have to give something over. And I don't want to. We'll see. Anyway I have to bring out the other two books. At least it's there, and now quite a number of people have read it. Not "quite a number," half a dozen. My editor at Random House has read it. My friend Jack Dunphy has read it.

JW: You told me once about when Bennett Cerf read it.

TC: That was when he was in the hospital. I knew he was very ill. I first knew him when I was 17. Random House signed me when I was 17, and they published all but one of my books. And he had always been so interested and concerned about this book. I didn't know he was precisely dying, but I wasn't too sure of it one way or the other. So I let him read it.

JW: What did he say?

TC: Well, I won't say what he really said about it, because it's too immodest.

JW: When you first told me about *Answered Prayers* you said that it had a very complicated structure. And you said it begins right after the war and ends in 1965. . . .

TC: It's basically about a woman, and it has five different plots going at the same time, and I mean really plots—not these things that pass for plots—in a sense it's almost medieval, [laughs] and it really has genuine plots.

The main character is a woman who meets a man when she's 19 years old—and he is 42—and she's the roommate in college of this man's daughter. She meets him at a lunch and the father is a highly over-developed swordsman type. He begins an affair with the girl. The girl is absolutely a great, great character, and through the years continues this affair with this man. And she has many, many, many other lovers and many powerful men. But this man won't marry her because he's married and he's content and has a very good reason. He was going to be the next Republican President of the United States. He was convinced of this every four years over a period of 16 years, and each year it doesn't happen, but each year there's every reason to think it will. And there are these enormous wheels spinning around this central situation, which involves dozens and dozens and dozens of people and about 25 other stories all spinning at the same time. It's really about six people who got what they wanted and what happened to them as a result.

I ain't invented a person in the book. [laughs] Oh, a few minor characters, but not really.

JW: Don't you foresee some problems with that? The character who is convinced that he was going to be the President—don't you think that character will be immediately recognizable?

TC: No. I know who the person is, and it's not somebody that anybody would automatically guess. Even playing 20 questions. And anyway, I took one physical-type person quite different from him and just grafted his career onto that other person.

JW: I take it it's based on the people you've known in that period of time especially the beautiful women of New York.

TC: Well not so many of them as people think, although there's a whole section of that that takes place in a restaurant in New York and I go through this whole subject quite thoroughly, what she really is, what she consisted of, what her ambitions were. It's a very long section. If it was published by itself it would be considered a short novel.

JW: If everybody's so recognizable in the book, what kind of reaction do you think that's going to cause?

TC: My theory is the only people that are going to be angry are those that got left out. If they can't find themselves in it then I better cross the street. One person who read it said, "It doesn't matter whether anybody likes it or if they hate it, they're going to love it."

Oh, I'm sure it'll get some of the supreme all-time flat-out attacks. Doesn't bother me because—if something's unmerited it doesn't bother me. And in this case it will not be merited. [laughs]

JW: One of the things that is so intriguing is this idea that you premediatatedly know that this is your life's work. Then what do you see for yourself? A life of ease? You've already got a life of ease.

TC: I don't know.

JW: Are you scared?

TC: No.

JW: Confident?

TC: I'm neither. I guess it's just like you've lived a long, long time in a house, and then for some reason you have to move out of that house.

JW: Can you think of any way in which it will change your life?

TC: My life's already been so changed all the time. How in the world can it change? I know everything there is to know about success, so how can success change your life? I know everything there is to know about failure, too. So nothing can affect me on that score, I mean, professionally. Do you see how it can? If you haven't experienced all of these things, then, of course. I've always been the same. I have been around an awfully long time and not exactly leading the life of obscurity.

JW: Why did you decide not to lead a life of obscurity?

TC: I don't know that that's so true. People say that all the time, but right from the beginning I always attracted a lot of attention, because—well, really—there really isn't anybody else like me. And I've had that wide variety of interests and moved in so many different areas. These things roll along.

JW: Why do you choose to appear so frequently on talk shows?

TC: I can tell you why, and you can take it or leave it. The truth of the matter is that I have a lot of things that amuse and interest me that I like to talk about but I have no time or interest in writing about them. I just like to give my opinion on certain various things. I don't write about it because it's not worth writing about; I just want to talk about it. Really, honestly, that really is the reason. When I started talking with Johnny Carson and Dick Cavett—the first time I really didn't want to. I was reluctant, but then I discovered that I found it sort of easy to get rid of a lot of things, that I enjoyed doing it, and it didn't make me the least bit nervous. I can talk about all kinds of things, my opinions about actors, films, books etc., which I wouldn't do otherwise, and I thoroughly enjoy it.

JW: One thing that seems to have happened is that everywhere I go with you we're stopped by nearly everybody, all *kinds* of people—especially older people.

TC: Actually I think it's about even.

JW: Young people, probably, in general, really love to talk about something you've said rather than stop you as a celebrity.

TC: They've always got something there that they want to grind the axe about. They don't really stop you just because . . . they have some point to make. "I want to know what you really meant by that because I don't agree." That's the big difference between the young people stopping me and the older people.

JW: When you met me at the airport today, you were opening the door for that woman and her husband was yakking away about the *Merv Griffin* show.

TC: I've never been on the *Merv Griffin* show. [laughs] She was just getting a little mixed up.

JW: They always approach you and you're always so kind and responsive, no matter how presuming they are.

TC: I have these great kissers—people that come up and suddenly grab hold of you. I was sitting in 21 having dinner with two people, a man and his wife, and sitting next to us were a very conventional Middle-West couple. The man was a bit loaded, I mean *more* than a bit loaded. Suddenly he leaned over, grabbed hold of me and began kissing me. I just pushed him away. He said, "You don't know. I just love you. I think you're the greatest." And so I said, "Well, if that's the way you feel . . ."

Sure, I'm always polite and nice to them. What are you going to do. If you were unkind to people like that you'd really crush them, unbelievably. That's the worst form of rejection. If you offer somebody your interest or affection and the person treats you like you were a madman . . . I despise rejection in all forms.

JW: I wonder why you feel so strongly about rejection?

TC: I do think rejection is the unkindest thing people do, and maybe it stems from my childhood when I was shoo'ed from one family to another for different reasons. I certainly didn't feel as though I had any very sturdy foundation to stand on. I never exactly felt rejected, but maybe that's what it stems from to some degree.

What could be crueler than to reject somebody? I think the only unforgivable sin is deliberate cruelty. When you sit down and really think up something deliberately cruel, I think that's unforgivable. Everything else is forgivable. I mean, rejection of course is forgivable, under various circumstances, because there may be something inevitable about it, say a divorce or a love affair. It's a very powerful trauma, rejection, or to be the recipient of any kind of deliberate cruelty.

JW: You go well beyond saying "thank you." You give these people who you just don't know really remarkable chunks of your time.

TC: I do one thing that is rude, and I feel guilty about it all the time. I get an enormous amount of mail, and I simply can't answer it. There is no way; it would take three-quarters of my day, every day just to answer them. I read them, even very, very intelligent and very wise letters, but I just can't answer them—and the few times I did, I found myself in the incredible situation where the person writes another letter then another letter and you don't answer, and the next thing you know they appear on your doorstep.

JW: At Trader Vic's there was that one woman who sat right down and talked with you for 20 minutes. By looks, by mannerism and by voice, you've become so recognizable.

TC: Telephone operators always say, "Is this Truman Capote?" And I say, "Yes." And they say, "I thought so!" [laughs] I've never understood really what it is, because all interviews—I can always tell when an interview is going to be just ordinary. They begin with some sort of thing about how small I am, you know, physically small, and there's something edging into it that's not particularly—I couldn't care less about it, I'm perfectly delighted with my appearance—and it seems right away that they get into this thing about my voice. This terribly distinctive, strange voice that I have. "It sounds lisping, like, an adolescent child who never went through puberty," etc. Now, I've made a lot of phonograph records for RCA and Columbia and whatnot and I listen to them. Well, I know that I have an unusual voice in many ways, but I don't—can't for the life of me find anything in which the words aren't very distinctly pronounced. I mean, I think it's something that they get into their heads that they think should be there, a lisp, that ought to be there, though it isn't. So they just put it there.

Anyway, none of that bothers me.

JW: Do you like the idea of "Sunday" for the title? With that subtitle?

TC: I think it's good.

JW: It does imply the idea of a whole day in the life.

TC: How are you going to fit this part of it in?

JW: I thought I'd say that Jann Wenner hadn't prepared very well, but came to finish up the missing parts. I especially wanted to know more about *Answered Prayers*.

TC: Well, I've got an idea how you can do it. Finish the one interview. Then have, Jann Wenner, unprepared, decided to visit Mister C. in Palm Springs, and do the whole thing and then, instead of Andy, it'll be you. Like a coda.

Truman Capote Talks About His Crowd
Richard Zoerink/1975

From *Playgirl*, 3 (September 1975), 50-51, 54, 80-81, 128. Copyright © 1986 by Playgirl Magazine. Reprinted by permission of Playgirl Magazine.

"He knows what he wants and he keeps himself straight. And if it's not the way he likes it, he'll arrange it so it is."
—HARPER LEE

"Never rent a house in Cozumel sight unseen," Truman Capote intoned, punctuating the warning with a giggle as he sat slumped on a dark leather banquette in the crowded smoke-filled cocktail lounge of the Hotel Carlyle in New York. Capote was tired. He had just returned from Cozumel, an island off the coast of Yucatan, where he paid his first visit to the house he had rented for the summer with close friend and almost constant companion Lee Radziwill and her sister Jackie Kennedy Onassis.

"They said the house was secluded," Capote continued, straightening in his seat, sipping his screwdriver and peering at me from behind rose-tinted lenses. "Oh, was it everrrrr secluded all rrrrright!" Capote, growing more animated, made his mouth go rubbery, like a hand puppet's, and dragged the guttural stresses from the corner of his lips. His famous laugh began, in short staccato bursts. "So is Devil's Island secluded! The house is on this, kind of, you know, on this bluff that overlooked the ocean. Annnnnd, there was this clump of palm trees at the edge of this bluff. And, *welllll* . . ." Capote paused to swallow his laughter. Composed again, he took another sip of his drink, twirled an open palm in the air and continued. "And so Lee and I got there just before it was dark. We got out of the car and there was this . . . this dark cloud, like some poisonous fog, just kind of hovering in the tops of these trees. And *thennnnn*, it started to move toward us! And . . . and Lee grabbed my arm and she said, 'Truman! What's that?' "

Laughing harder now, Capote fought for breath and then began to wheeze. He wadded a handkerchief in his palm and shoved a part of the fabric up under each rose-tinted lens, drying his cheeks and eyes. "The cloud was *mosquitoes!*" He jerked his fistful of handkerchief in the direction of my glass, at the two soggy cocktail onions in the bottom of my Vodka Gibson. "Mosquitoes as *big* as those *onions!*"

Capote collapsed against the back of the banquette, his laughter erupting above the din in the crowded lounge. His laughter was contagious, and soon we were both laughing as others in the room stared at our table.

We were in the lounge of Bemelmans' Bar, where Capote had suggested that we meet. The bar is named for the author/artist Ludwig Bemelmans, who, in the 1940s, painted the many small murals which decorate its walls. Bemelmans also did covers for the *New Yorker* about the time Truman Capote was working at the magazine as a writer for the Talk of the Town column. Over the years the bar has become a popular five o'clock watering hole for many prominent Manhattan editors and publishers.

Capote cleared his throat and delicately lifted his dark glasses slightly up the bridge of his small nose. "I haven't been here in years. I used to come here a lot with Jackie Kennedy. She liked to come here, when she worked at *Vogue*. That was nineteen fifty-two."

He paused and glanced around the room at the murals, faded now, retouched by other artists over the years and faded again. In the room's late dusk light, they resembled bouquets of pressed, dried flowers unfolding on the charcoal brown walls. Capote sipped his drink, his mood subdued.

"Jackie's changed a lot since then,. though," he said.

"How do you mean?"

"Oh, I don't mean for the worse," he said, "I mean, well . . . when I first met Jackie I thought she was very bright, charming, well-read. We used to see a lot of each other. She was always very much in the background. And then, after she married Jack and went to the White House, she seemed to survive by sheer publicity alone. She just developed this peculiar star quality. It happens to people. You never know quite what it is. It's like this . . . this candle has been lighted inside them. They never again quite look like anybody else. And then, too, it all made Jackie quite cynical where she hadn't been before."

Capote spoke, slower, more softly now. He took off his glasses and laid them on the table, wiping the back of his hand across his eyes. He was difficult to hear, his voice low as he continued.

"Jackie disliked politics. She disliked politicians. She didn't like watching them, didn't like the manipulations of power. But there she was. By the time of the assassination she had become a personality in her own right. And after, that became quite a cross to bear. I mean it was really awful, because she was hounded and hounded and hounded. Jackie said to me once, 'I guess the worst part of it is I just can't walk out the door any time I want to. Because I know one of those *buzzards* will be lurking around and run after me and take pictures. And so I find myself standing there in front of the mirror combing my hair. I guess it must be some sort of innate vanity, Truman, because you know people are going to be staring at you.' "

Capote paused a moment. "And then the other thing Jackie said was, 'Oh, let's face it. I'm just a *freak*! Because of an accident of history, I'll always be an object of curiosity, like something you go to see in a freak show.' And I said, 'Jackie, don't you think that's a very hard way of looking at it?' And she said, 'It may be hard, but it's true.'

"Well, you know," he went on, a wan smile on his face, "She's had many, many more reasons than that to feel bitter. There was the assassination. I mean, she had bitterness because her husband was assassinated and all. But she knew that it was the work of some psychopath."

"You mean, she does not believe in the conspiracy theories about the President's murder?"

"No, no, no. Not at all. She and Jack were always taking into account that it was something that might happen. But she never talks about it anymore. At first she used to talk about it a lot, but never from that point of view. I mean, not about who did it or anything, but about how badly some people behaved right after the assassination. And some people behaved *very* badly."

"Who, for instance?" I was intrigued by Capote's report on Mrs.

Kennedy's feelings at that time because she has never spoken them publicly.

"She told me that Governor John Connolly, who was in the seat in front of her and got hit by one of the bullets, was just screaming and hollering and carrying on like he was the biggest coward there ever was!" Capote curled his lip and with a wave of his hand he dismissed the memory. He sipped his drink.

"And then when she was in Washington, after the funeral, she wrote the Connollys saying how sorry she was about what had happened and that she hoped John Connolly was feeling better. And neither Mrs. Connolly nor John Connolly ever sent her a letter or even a note of condolence. I must say, though, you have to give Jackie credit. She's never complained publicly about that sort of thing. She's not that kind of person. But, you know, it was little things like that. If some people had been more thoughtful, it would have helped, made things easier for her . . . And then when she married Daddy O.—I mean, people wanted to believe she was a little saint. They wanted her to go through the rest of her life as the President's widow. And then she married this man Onassis. For reasons of her own, reasons that were *not* greedy. There never was a marriage agreement. She never got anymore out of it than a free ticket on Olympic Airways. I mean, she was *alone*. She had two children to think of, take care of. Why shouldn't a woman who's alone, a widow . . . ?" He trailed off.

"Do you think her marriage to Onassis was a good one? A happy one?"

He looked at me a moment, and then looked away. "I once told Jackie that she should marry a nice college professor, and then pretty soon people would forget her and leave her alone. And Jackie said, 'Where would I find a college professor who would want to marry Jackie Kennedy?' An ordinary person would just *drown*. Onassis was *not* ordinary."

He drained his glass, and set it loudly down on the table. He looked at his Cartier tank watch. "Well," he said, slapping his knees and rocking forward to his feet, "I have to go now."

He was on his way to dinner at Lee Radziwill's Fifth Avenue apartment. I asked him if I could accompany him to her door.

We walked the four or five blocks up the avenue, Capote nattily dressed in a tweedy jacket, blue suit trousers that had a scholarly rumpledness about them, and a vaguely patterned tie knotted and twisted above the V-neck of his blue sweater. He walked quickly, with all the sober purposefulness of a country priest off on a visit of the parish. The night air was chilly and invigorating.

"I mean, all those articles Gore Vidal wrote about the Kennedys, especially about Bobby, were so *cruel*," he said as we walked.

"Why did Vidal resent the Kennedys so terribly?" The feud between Vidal and the family was well-known, although somewhat one-sided because the only one who made a public issue of it was Vidal. The reasons behind it had never been stated.

"*Welllll*, I think it goes back to when Bobby had Gore thrown out of the White House. It was the only time he had ever been invited to the White House and he got drunk. *Annnnnd* . . . he insulted Jackie's mother, whom he had never met before in his *life*! But I mean insulted her. He said something to the effect that he had always hated her. But he'd never even met the woman. And she just went into something like total shock. And Bobby and Arthur Schlesinger, I believe it was, and one of the guards just picked Gore up and carried him to the door and threw him out into Pennsylvania Avenue. That's when he began to write all those cruel pieces about the Kennedys."

We paused in front of the side entrance to Radziwill's apartment building. A cool breeze was blowing across Central Park, mussing Capote's hair. He self-consciously smoothed the thin wisps back into place.

"Are you still on friendly terms with Vidal?"

"Well, I think the situation can be described now as something of a détente," Capote laughed. "We knew each other quite well when we were about eighteen, nineteen, twenty or so. Then we had this big fight. I can't even remember what it was about. But you know, the thing about Gore Vidal is . . . I remember once, a long time ago, we were just kids and we were sitting in the Oak Room at the Plaza and both Gore and I had already published our first books. And Gore turned to me and said, 'You know, Truman, I want this and this and this. And you have to be *very hard* to get it. You have to be hard.' He said that, telling me what he wanted from life, in terms of career, sex, money, fame. He always wanted to be very famous and rich. I don't know, a house on the Riviera, that sort of thing. And you know, he got *everything* he said he wanted all those many, many years ago. Everything. And he became hard so he could get it. And no one can be close to him anymore."

Capote went inside the apartment house and stopped in the lobby, calling out to remind me that I was to see him on Sunday at his house in Bridgehampton, Long Island.

Like Gore Vidal, Truman Capote has, in a way, everything he set out to get, but he has done it without bitterness and without the sacrifice of friendship. In fact, there is perhaps no other writer in the world who knows as many people of such wide social and political backgrounds. He numbers prisoners and princes, the obscure and the famous among his friends. And, more important, some think he is among the greatest prose writers ever produced by America.

Truman Capote spent much of his early childhood in a small Alabama town, a rural region dependent on local cotton and lumber industries. There was no library, and education was not highly valued. But Capote, before he was old enough to enter school, taught himself to read by collecting old farm magazines and meeting the Trailways bus every day at the depot at six p.m. to collect the two newspapers it delivered, *The Mobile Register* and the *Montgomery Advertiser*. But his precociousness at reading and his exceptional intelligence put him at a disadvantage with his classmates once he began school. "They thought there was something freaky about it."

When he was about seven, Truman Capote began writing short stories in Red Chief school tablets as a means of combating his isolation from his peers, his sense of being a pariah. And he wrote to relieve the boredom of life in a small southern town during the Depression.

"My stories were totally different from what I read in the newspapers and magazines I was able to obtain. They were about things around me. They were real and there was nothing childish about them. I never thought of them as being good or bad. But gradually I realized there was a door beyond which I could not go."

That impasse was breached when a group of WPA child psychologists, who were touring the south and administering tests to school children, discovered in the young Capote a special intelligence and talent. As a result Capote was given a scholarship to the Horace Mann School in New York City.

It was about that time, when he arrived to attend school in New York, that he began submitting short stories and articles to various magazines. One of his submissions caught the eye of Harold Ross, editor of the *New Yorker*. That was in the beginning days of World War II and the magazine was short of staff. So Capote, then only seventeen, was asked to come to the *New Yorker* offices to be interviewed for a job as a staff writer.

"I looked maybe eleven years old then," Capote recalls. "So I was tucked into some small office after I was hired and for two years I wasn't allowed to be seen very often. It was at this juncture that I had to make my first real decision in terms of my writing. I considered the *New Yorker* representative of popular culture in a way that I didn't think at that moment I wanted my writing to be. And so after a great deal of hemming and hawing I went off by myself to write my first novel."

The book was *Other Voices, Other Rooms*, and it made him famous. Still, Capote wasn't happy.

"It had a curious success. Some said it was successful because it had a certain notorious quality. Others said it was successful because of all of the publicity that surrounded it, mainly due to a rather exotic photograph of me that appeared on the jacket. Whatever the reason, I felt very guilty about the book. I didn't feel I could be a very good writer if I was so successful. Like most intellectual snobs, there was in my mind—at that time—a conflict between the ideas of elitist and popular culture. It took me years to rid myself of that initial paranoia."

However intense that personal conflict was for Capote, it didn't stop him from writing, nor did it prevent him from enjoying—as few authors have—both commercial and critical success. He followed *Other Voices, Other Rooms* with two more novels, volumes of short stories and essays, a musical (*The House of Flowers*, with Harold Arlen), numerous TV and film scripts and, in 1965, secured his place in the front ranks of American writers with the publication of *In Cold Blood*, a book that has been hailed by some as the most important literary event of this century.

Despite this coup, Capote continues to work strenuously, often driving himself precariously close to the edge of physical and emotional exhaustion. He has published a new story, "Mojave," and is currently at work on a collection of short stories and a four-volume fictionalized autobiography, the first volume, Answered Prayers, due for publication late this fall.

On Sunday I drove out to Long Island to visit Capote as planned. His house is a large two-story modern building, a sea-gray cube of weathered wood sitting in a clump of pines at the end of a long, tree-lined gravel road that winds toward the ocean. It sits among the dunes, not far from the ocean, like an enormous clamshell dropped in the scrub trees. It is isolated yet serene.

Inside, half the area of the house is taken up by a two-story living room. An antique wooden spiral staircase winds to the second floor, which is divided into a loft area (an open study overlooking the room) and a guest room and bath. Downstairs is another bedroom and bath, and a kitchen. The living room is done in a kind of turquoise enamel color, furnished to reflect Capote's eclectic but comfortable tastes and scattered with the *objets d'art* and memorabilia he has collected over the years.

"I had this house built exactly the way I wanted," Capote said, making an expansive gesture as he led me through the kitchen and into the living room. The far wall of the room was a floor-to-ceiling window looking out on a rolling expanse of sand dunes, prickled with dune grass and dropping dramatically to the surf some two hundred yards from the house.

Capote sunk into a yellow velvet easy chair facing the window. The chair was squat and fuzzy, like a collapsed tennis ball, its upholstery blotched white in places by the sun.

Somewhere, lost among the dunes and the roar of the surf, was a barking dog.

"That's Maggie," Capote said fondly.

"Maggie?"

'My doggy. Maggie." Straining, Capote reaches behind him, his hand rummaging through the *tzaskes* and small silver-framed photographs on the bookshelves behind his chair.

He handed me a picture of Maggie and himself standing among drifts of snow in front of his house in the Alps, Capote holding the

English bull in his arms, their heads pressed together as he tried to imitate the expression on the dog's face.

"Maggie's the terrorrrrrrr of the dunes," he growled, and laughed, looking at the picture before he replaced it on the shelf. "She hides out in the dunes and raids the picnic baskets when people go into the water."

Capote laughed again. Then his mood suddenly shifted. He was silent for a time and it was difficult to tell if his eyes were open behind the blue-tinted prescription lenses he wore. Suddenly he straightened, turning his head toward me, his elbow propped on the arm of the chair as he cupped his chin in his palm.

"You know, you're one of only about a half dozen people who have seen this house," he said. "I don't really ever have people over."

It seemed odd, given Capote's literally thousands of friends, so I asked why.

He sighed again. "Oh, I don't know. I sort of like to come here and work alone sometimes."

"You were alone a lot as a child, weren't you?"

"Yes, most of the time. But when I was a kid I really didn't have much choice. My mother was always running off to do something or other. She was what you might call a southern belle, always doing things, always interested in improving her mind. Although I loved her very much I never really saw her. I never really saw very much of my father either, although *that* I didn't mind so much. Oh, he was always good to me, would come and visit me in New Orleans, where I had been sent to live with this woman because my parents had more or less decided to lead separate lives. I never really cared if he would come or if he didn't come at all. I had a very good friend by then though, so I really wasn't totally alone all the time. This little girl, Harper Lee—you know, she wrote *To Kill a Mockingbird*—she and I would play . . . you know, just pretend games all the time. She's still my closest friend."

Capote seemed to be sinking further into himself as he spoke about friendship and the many people who have moved in and out of his life over the years.

"You know," he said, a slight quaver in his voice. "The only way people can ever hurt me is if I let them get close to me. That's because I'm very loyal. I stick by people no matter what. And sometimes I meet people who aren't what they make themselves out to be. Then I get hurt. But I'm very careful about that now, about who I get close to."

In the three decades Capote has been on the celebrity circuit he has been the intimate of many beautiful and talented people who eventually met with tragic ends. I asked if that hurt as much as betrayal by a friend, mentioning specifically Marilyn Monroe, with whom he'd been close right up to the time of the star's death.

"Oh, I don't know," he said, his voice seeming to curl in on itself, almost self-protectively. "Sometimes these things, sometimes it all just seems so inevitable. I became very close to Marilyn right from our very first meeting. I met her in New York when Paramount was making the movie *Breakfast at Tiffany's.* Marilyn was my first choice to play the girl, Holly Golightly. I had seen her in a film and thought she would be perfect for the part. Holly had to have something touching about her . . . unfinished. Marilyn had that. But Paramount doublecrossed me and gave the part to Audrey Hepburn. Audrey was not what I had in mind when I wrote that part, although she did a terrific job. But Marilyn was what I wanted—at that age she was exactly right for the part."

I asked Capote what Monroe was like then, and whether the rumor that Monroe was having an affair with Robert Kennedy at the time of her death had any basis in fact.

"Well, you know . . . funny thing about Marilyn," Capote cocked his head to the side, averting his eyes toward the corner of the ceiling and readjusting his glasses, "she was really very, very shy, very insecure. But she was also very, very bright. People would humor her, thinking she was a dumb blonde; but Marilyn was *very* perceptive. She wasn't fooled by many people, and they thought they were fooling her all the time. But, you know, Marilyn was such a little girl."

"How do you mean?"

"Well, I mean she was emotionally about eleven years old. Like that affair with Bobby Kennedy. It was such a *little* affair. But Marilyn always took things like that so seriously. I think he only saw her two or three times. Bobby had many, many affairs. All the Kennedy boys were like that. Bobby. Teddy. Jack. I have a line about the Kennedy boys that I once wrote: 'The Kennedy boys are like dogs. They can't pass a fire hydrant without pissing on it.'"

Capote glanced at me, grinning mischievously. "Did that get you in trouble?" I asked. He said nothing, shrugging and continuing to smile. I changed the subject.

"What do you suppose it is about women like Marilyn Monroe, who have such enormous success in everything but their personal lives?"

"*Welllll*," he drawled after a moment's thought, "I think it has to do with sheer careerism. It's very difficult to be a very big star, a *woman* star, and have any really successful relationship with a man. I can't think of any big woman star who's ever had a long, successful relationship with a man. Or with another woman, for that matter. I mean, Garbo's had lots of lovers just devoted to her. Mercedes Acosta who lasted the longest just lived her *life* for Greta. But Greta could never sustain a relationship with anybody. Look at Bette Davis! Her relationship with Gary Merrill was absolute *misery* because he was so jealous of her career. Look at Lana Turner. Elizabeth Taylor, when asked if she was going to marry that car salesman, said that she didn't think that she would ever marry again because she didn't want to be another Lana Turner. I think Elizabeth sees that man just because she's confused and unhappy. And, he's attentive, but . . . well, I think obviously on the make. Elizabeth has had vulgar men in her life before, but at least they had talent. Mike Todd knew how to handle himself—maybe he pushed too hard, but . . . Eddie Fisher too, she got along all right with him. But, I mean, he was just a *slave*. We all used to call him the busboy! And then one day she overheard me ask someone, Where's the busboy? and she roared with laughter and afterward started calling Eddie that too. I mean, not to his face . . ."

We sat and talked a few more minutes about his writing and about the new novel he was working on. More than friends or money, work seemed to be at the center of his life.

"That was why I had to sell the house in Palm Springs; because, from the point of view of my work, I associated it with this dreadful period in my life. I was working on *Answered Prayers* there and I suddenly discovered I had made this dreadful mistake in terms of the book's narrator. I was just *devastated*. It took me months to recover after I realized I would have to redo years of work. And then, too, I had an unhappy love affair there."

Capote's voice trailed off. He slumped sideways in his chair, an arm over its side and his hand nearly dragging on the floor. The sun had moved in the sky and its chill brightness of earlier in the afternoon now had a milky softness as it poured through the window and through the green glass of a Tiffany shade. Maggie's barking had grown closer and was now right outside the screen door in the kitchen.

"I'd better let Maggie in," Capote said, struggling to his feet. I had to drive back to New York so I walked with him to the door. We said good-bye and, as he threw open the door to let me out and Maggie in, he stepped back, laughing uncontrollably. I looked down and there was Maggie, sitting on her haunches, her raised front feet pawing the air, a drumstick dangling from her mouth.

The Literary Aquarium of Truman Capote
Beverly Grunwald/1975

From *W*, 14-21 November 1975, 26. Copyright © 1975 by Beverly Grunwald/W. Reprinted by permission.

Truman Capote cries easily. Like all great writers, he is hypersensitive and has been known to cry—when The Colony closed, when the two killers of his epic *In Cold Blood* were electrocuted, at the TV presentation of "A Christmas Memory"—a short story based on his lonely childhood. His novel-in-progress, *Answered Prayers,* gets its title from Saint Theresa's statement that more tears are shed about answered prayers than unanswered ones.

One might predict that a lot of tears will be shed (and a great deal of laughter) when and if Truman Capote actually finishes his 15-year-old roman a clef. There's been so much contemplation, conjecture and anticipation in literary circles and other places where friends and enemies meet, that it is reassuring to encounter a flesh-and-blood chapter in the current *Esquire*. And what flesh and blood: the scene is set in La Cote Basque in 1965 where no ordinary lunch bunch congregated. Under the poreine eye of M. Soule, Lady Ina Coolbirth (your guess may be better than mine) and Jonesy (a good part Capote) gossip more than they eat. Choice morsels make for delectable reading.

The author invites us to play the game of guessing who is really whosis. And, indeed, he does name some names. Lee Radziwill and Jackie O have a walk-on as "a pair of Western Geisha girls; they know how to keep a man's secrets and how to make him feel important." Gloria Vanderbilt di Cicco Stokowski Lumet Cooper and her friend, Carol Marcus Saroyan Saroyan (twice because she married him twice) Matthau play a larger scene from a closely located banquette. In one of the most biting and titillating snatches of eavesdropping since Clare Boothe Luce's *The Women*, Carol and

Gloria chat chummily about Walter Mathau's roving eye for other women, Oona Chaplin and her destiny to marry an old, rich genius which led Gloria in turn to marry Stokowski, and Carol, after that, to wed Saroyan. When an exciting customer stops at their table, he is greeted by both women, although Gloria Cooper cannot quite place him. Who is he? she asks Carol Matthau:

> "Once upon a time you thought very highly of him. You cooked his meals and washed his socks—" Cooper's eyes enlarged, shifted, "and when he was in the army you followed him from camp to camp, living in dreary furnished rooms—"
> "No!"
> "Yes!"
> "No."
> "Yes, Gloria. Your first husband.
> "That . . . man . . . was . . . Pat di Cicco?

Readers will be equally intrigued by the "governor's wife" and her extra-marital bed-play of "Sidney Dillon," adviser to presidents, "Ann Hopkins," the ex-floozy turned socialite who murders her husband and doesn't go to jail, and assorted other "fish" with real or fictitious names. For, in Truman Capote's vision, his book is like an aquarium.

"These same characters don't reappear in the book, except for the narrator—P.B. Jones—Jonesy," says Capote. "Well, maybe you could say that they sort of splash by for a moment against the background. When you read the book itself, it's really as though you walked through an aquarium. You know how it is when you walk through and see those great, round windows and each has a different exhibit and yet there are certain fish who swim all the way behind, from one window to the next? Well, that's really the technique of the book, and you, the reader, move from one climate to the other, pictorially and mentally."

How much is left to do? "It's like I was making big, stained glass windows and what I have to do now is put them all in place." The stained glass fish tanks need to be connected, some corrections have to be made, some additional building. More chapters will be published from time to time—like a cliff-hanging serial.

His last nonfiction "novel," *In Cold Blood*, took the 51-year-old Capote six years of work and succeeded because it was a masterpiece of reportage about two killers and their mass crime in

Kansas. ("I should have won the American Book Award and the Pulitzer," Truman says.) He takes great pride in his accuracy as "a reporter who probes behind the actions of his characters."

"Norman Mailer was scornful of this form until my success—and then he copied me," he claims vehemently—although he admires Mailer. Combined with what his late publisher, Bennet Cerf, called Truman's favorite pastime—gossip—*Answered Prayers* is undeniably the writer's most ambitious and lustiest effort. For 15 years he's filled enormous black notebooks with "things." For the curious he says, EVERYTHING in the book is either observed, heard or overheard by myself. This book is the result of my own experience as a witness."

Just back from a lecture tour of five colleges, which he sandwiched between an acting assignment in Hollywood, Capote has barely had time to read the letters and telegrams and press reports about this excerpt. I wondered about libel suits and wasn't he worried? Truman chuckled with gusto. He enjoys his chuckles. "Do you think the 'governor's wife' is going to sue me?" True, she may not choose to reveal herself—but how about the people he named? "I let Carol Matthau read it. I let Oona Chaplin read it when I visited in Switzerland. I let Lee Radziwill read it and anyone else I had access to." None of these ladies had any objections, which may be a tribute to his friendship or their respect for him as a writer. Or both.

I asked Henriette Soule of La Cote Basque for her reaction. Her late husband has been remembered as "pink and glazed as a marzipan pig." "Oui, I hear all the people talking about it," she said, "but I am too sick to read. I have laryngitis and sinus and I'm going home to bed." It will be Christmas, at least, before Truman Capote returns from California and tests his welcome at her restaurant.

Currently, he has turned actor for Neil Simon's *Murder by Death*, a film which stars Peter Falk, Alec Guinness and Elsa Lanchester. He's delighted with his comfortable, trailer on the set where he goes when they don't need him—which he says is often.

"It's quiet and no one disturbs me. I can write and relax and there's no telephone. I'm enjoying the part. I don't know how much I would if I had to do it really—I mean as a living. It's an escape. But it's a great comedy script. I play an eccentric billionaire—it's impossible to describe. He's built a strange, haunted house filled with every kind of odd device to frighten people. In any event, I have a house party and invite all of these people and I lock them all in the house for the weekend. After that, it's sheer madness. I'm really having a good time with it."

Truman Capote manages to have a good time whether it's reading a book a day, going to frequent movies (he walks out on 50 percent of them), or preparing his favorite dish: baked potato with a quarter pound of fresh caviar and a dash of sour cream. He enjoys talking to college students: "Why do they put them down? All these kids are very bright. It's really impressive. I think television has homogenized the regional differences between people." He revisits the South often and sees a "miracle" of difference. "In my own family, I see how their minds and attitudes have changed—people I thought would never be dragged into the 20th Century."

I accused Truman Capote of sounding happy. He wasn't complaining about anything. "I don't like to complain," he says. How about the far-fetched story that he and Lee Radziwill tried an experiment in sex in New Orleans? "Not true. It was made up by the hotel manager for publicity."

As a shrewd people-watcher, what does jar him these days? "I'm not really jarred by anything except a certain kind of middle-class pretentiousness. I've always said I can go first class or third. But I could never go second." A writer like Truman Capote will never have to.

Truman Capote, the Movie Star?
Josh Greenfeld/1975

From *The New York Times*, 29 December 1975, II, 1, 17. Copyright © 1975 by The New York Times Company. Reprinted by permission.

I liked Truman Capote a lot the moment I met him. He's a cute, little guy—jockey height, with a freckled pink face, thinning blond hair and thickening mid-section. He was wearing white striped maroon jogging pants and a purple sweat shirt. At 51, he looks like a Buddha who's been around the track more than once. Very charming and hospitable, too. When I rang the door of his rented Coldwater Canyon home he greeted me warmly. "Come in my dear," he said, immediately offering me something to drink. I took him up on a glass of Soave Bretone. He poured some grapefruit juice for himself and lay back on the couch and watched me nurse my wine.

On an end table near him was an opened copy of the screenplay, *Murder by Death*, a Neil Simon spoof on whodunits which is scheduled for release next summer and in which Capote, who until now has been known chiefly as a novelist, journalist, raconteur and party giver, is making his acting debut. Capote plays an eccentric millionaire who invites a slew of famous sleuths to his mansion to solve an as-yet-uncommitted murder. On the floor were the trades—*Daily Variety* and *The Hollywood Reporter*. Next to the telephone was a copy of something by Dorothy Parker. Wasn't she the smart aleck who said Hollywood money had a way of evaporating?

I asked him if he was getting a lot of money for his acting debut?

"Oh Lord no," he said.

So why was he doing it?

"Well," he answered, licking his teeth, "I'd been offered parts in films before. But I was just never amused by the idea. Or had the time. But last spring I was out here in California and I had just finished a good long section of my novel, *Answered Prayers*. And I was in the mood to take four or five months off, take a trip or something like that, when the producer, Ray Stark, sent me the script. And I found it amusing. I thought it would be fun. One should do everything one thinks might be fun." He turned his palms up like an ingenue making an entrance.

"So here I am. I mean, I'd been on the other side of the camera enough. I did the screenplay for *Beat the Devil* and *The Innocents* way back. And I did the first screenplay for the last remake of *The Great Gatsby*. But they didn't like it."

He sipped his grapefruit juice. "I don't even know who they were: David Merick, Frank Yablans, Robert Evans or Peter Bart. All I know is after I handed it in there was silence. Total dead silence. I tried to get someone to tell me something. And finally, someone did say—and I don't remember which of the four—'The real trouble with your script, Truman, is it is *The Great Gatsby*. It is the book.' And I said, 'But that's what you gave me. The book.' And he said: 'But we wanted something more.' "

The telephone rang and Capote reached for it. "Hello. . . . uh huh . . . I'll consider it for about a million dollars a week," he said with a giggle. Then he giggled some more and hung up.

"Oh yes," he resumed. "So I've become an actor. In the movie I play someone named Lionel Twain. Get it. Evidently, when they were casting they decided they wanted someone like Truman Capote. And then someone had the brilliant idea of asking me to play like Truman Capote. But I don't care what they expect. I'm playing Mr. Twain. I believe in Lionel Twain. The original intent may have been for me to parody myself. But that's not how it's going to work out."

How was it working out?

"So far I've just been in the picture bit by bit. My blue eyes in one scene. My tongue in another. That's all: my tongue. Just think, I could get an award for the best supporting tongue."

Hadn't Capote once put down acting?

"Oh," he said, sitting up, "people keep bringing that up now. I didn't put down acting. I was talking of the difference between a primary art and an interpretative art, the difference between the psychology of sensibility. My point being that an interpretative art such as acting depends on sensibility, not intelligence.

"Most people think an actor must be intelligent. But to be an actor you must have sensibility, that tremendous talent to be in touch with your inner self. In that respect, Marlon Brando, for example, is all talent. He's all sensibility. But he's completely confused outside of his art. Full of rhetoric and nonsense. Which has very little to do with what he is as an interpretative artist.

"Oh, God knows, Brando thinks he's intelligent. Marlon looks at you with his Oh-poor-you eyes, as if he knows something you don't know. But the truth is you know something he doesn't know: he's not very intelligent."

But aren't there writers too who depend primarily on sensibility?

"Oh, yes," Capote said, rolling his eyes. "Tennessee Williams, for example, is total sensibility. Absolutely no intelligence. For a writer, sensibility is like capital in the bank and intelligence is interest. And there's poor Tennessee, always spending his sensibility. One shouldn't dissipate one's sensibilities. Unless one is an actor. That's why I've always thought an intelligent person couldn't be just an actor. Acting couldn't be a very fulfilling occupation for an intelligent person. Writing is obviously more fulfilling. You have something more permanent, you're dealing with a primary art."

If intelligence is the hallmark of writing, whom does he consider a writer of intelligence?

"Saul Bellow," said Capote, "writes with intelligence."

I asked him what he thought of Bellow's latest book.

"Oh, I never read Bellow," he answered, licking his lips. "He's much too intelligent."

Who does he read then?

"I've reached the point in life where I don't read so much as reread. I may not be a compulsive writer, but I am a compulsive reader. I read 20 to 30 magazines a week, three or four newspapers a day, and I'm always reading a book. Or rather, as I say, rereading: Jane Austen, Dickens, Proust, Turgenev, Flaubert. I used to like Henry James a lot, but I don't any more."

Why not?

"I just find—well, Stein said a great thing about Glenway Westcott: 'He has a certain sorrow, but it doesn't pour.' Henry James, I've decided, has a certain cream but it coagulates."

Has he received any feedback from fellow novelists in regard to his acting career?

"They're all jealous, I'm sure. Norman Mailer used his own money to star in three films, but I'm getting paid. And Jimmy Jones and Irwin Shaw told me they were jealous. And Gore Vidal," he paused deliciously, "must be dying. But then I always said that Gore was the only person who could possibly have played Myra Breckenridge."

He turned serious. "Anyway, it really doesn't matter what one does to amuse oneself as long as one is true to one's art. My art is prose writing and my real range is fairly narrow. Narrative writing, factual or fiction, involving the ear and the eye."

But wouldn't bad reviews as an actor upset him?

"Oh no. If they say I'm a lousy actor, who cares? Whoever said I was a good actor? That isn't the area where my vanity lies. Anyway, I really have no vanity. I'm probably the least vain person I know. I have pride. But pride is different. Pride touches inner things, important things. Pride involves a sense of honesty, courage, truth. Vanity is sitting at the right table. Vanity has to do with status."

What about his famous Plaza Hotel party, in 1966, for Kay Graham, publisher of the *Washington Post?* Didn't that involve status?

"Maybe it was status for the people who came. But not for me. I just wanted to go to a pretty party. So I gave it. I spent $75,000 without one penny I.R.S. write-off. It was probably the only private party given in this country during this century. But it was a beautiful party. I don't regret it. I had such a good time."

It's not hard to have a good time for $75,000, I suggested.

"It's very hard," said Capote, "if you're paying for it."

I drove out to the Burbank Studios a week and a half later to watch them shoot Capote's first big scene. There were potted palms and ferns, marble fireplaces and tapestried walls, and a huge chandelier hung over the long dining-room table that dominated a drafty set. There were takes and rehearsals galore of the scene in which the world's master detectives—Peter Falk playing Sam Diamond, Elsa Lanchester as Miss Marbles, James Coco as Milo Perrier, Peter Sellers as Sidney Wang and David Niven and Maggie Smith as Dick and Dora Charleston—were being welcomed by a 76-year-old-detective-faddist Capote played by—well, Truman Capote.

While the professionals gave the exact same readings over and over again, Capote's seemed to vary, the energy levels fluctuating. He mopped his brow frequently, a pudgy picture of dejected gray and pink: a gray fedora over his pink sun-glassed face, a gray fur-lined dinner jacket, a gray bow tie riding on a pink collar, even gray dancing shoes with pink pom poms. I asked the suave David Niven how he thought Capote was doing. "I think he'll be fine," Niven smiled, "until he finds out how really difficult it all is."

After the next take, director Robert Moore called, "Print it!" and draped an arm around Capote's shoulder. "That was fine, Truman," he said. "Very good. Now the next time Peter asks you how you look so young, enjoy your answer a little more: 'I eat only vegetables. I sleep 12 hours a night. And I use lots and lots of make-up!' Understand?"

Capote nodded weakly.

"But that was a very good take," said Moore, and wandered away.

"If it was so good," Capote wondered to James Coco, who was sitting beside him, "why do we have to do it again?"

"They have to shift the camera a little to catch the other end of the table," Coco explained.

"Are you having a good time, Truman?" I asked.

"No," he said, rolling his eyes.

Scriptwriter Neil Simon stopped by. "How did it feel, Truman?"

"Fine," Truman replied.

An assistant director came over. "I've been looking at your script, Truman, and I see you've never put in the new cues. The same speeches, but new cues."

Capote looked over the changes. "All right. Thanks a lot. What are we going to do next?"

"The same thing," said the assistant director, "only closer to the people on the other side of the table."

"Oh, that's right," Capote said, taking off his fedora and fanning himself with it. "I forgot. My God," he turned to me, "I've been here since 8 this morning and I'll be here until 8 tonight."

"Do you have any second thoughts about acting?" I asked.

"I'm afraid I never had first thoughts," he said, giggling. "I was just kind of moving on impulses."

There was a call for places. And Capote put on the fedora and leaned back in his chair at the head of the table. He seemed to have aged 25 years in the 10 days since I had first met him. But then his role did call for a 76-year-old man. I just hoped, for his sake, that he was really using "lots and lots of make-up!"

Tiny, Yes, but a Terror?
Do Not Be Fooled by Truman Capote in Repose
Patricia Burstein/1976

From *People Weekly*, 5 (10 May 1976), 12-17. Copyright © 1976 by Time Inc. Reprinted by permission.

"I like Holiday Inns," says Truman Capote as he waddles into the lobby. "They're fundamentally, deeply mediocre. You get a bed, an air conditioner, bad service and anonymity. Everybody who works for them is soooo dumb. I mean, they wouldn't recognize Chiang Kai-shek if he walked in the door."

Almost on cue a desk clerk at the Virginia motel stares vacantly at his impish little customer and inquires, "Mr. Capote, what firm are you with?" Instantly, Capote flashes a "see-what-I-told-you" look. Then, rolling his eyes and savoring the possibility of the late Chiang Kai-shek trying to check in, Truman repairs to his room for an afternoon nap.

Clearly, anonymity is a rare commodity in the life of 51-year-old author Truman Capote. For the last several months he has been reviled publicly for his latest work, *Answered Prayers*, three installments of which have run in *Esquire*. It is a thinly disguised fiction which rattles the skeletons of the *beau monde*. Capote's intimate revelations about jet setters, writers, entertainers and sexual acrobats—most of whom confidently regarded themselves as Truman's friends—have earned him the nickname "the Tiny Terror."

"The reason why these people are so upset is that almost without exception they struggled like galley slaves to get where they are, which is nowhere," he says of critics of his novel. "Then somebody who was absolutely at the center of all of it comes along and says, 'Oh, well, I think this is a lot of bullshit, the emperor has no clothes.' "

Patricia Burstein/1976

The author of *In Cold Blood* and *Breakfast at Tiffany's*, Capote intrigues people who haven't even cracked his books. In his trademark tinted glasses and extravagant Panama hats, he titillates millions of viewers with naughty chatter on the talk shows. Recently he broadened his arena, playing a portly eccentric in Neil Simon's forthcoming movie, *Murder by Death*. Even in Hollywood, where he rented the house of actress Diane Keaton (close friend of Woody Allen), Capote persisted as Peck's Bad Boy: "She never bothered to change her number. I had the most intimate conversations with people who called her. 'Well, Diane's not here just now. Would you like to leave a message?' Then the person would go into a deep psychoanalysis of Woody Allen. Ho, ho, ho."

Waking at 6:30 p.m. from his nap, Capote slips into a 1928 black Lanvin suit, white suspenders and a black La Coste tennis shirt and sips his fifth vodka-and-orange juice of the day. Two students arrive to escort him to Washington and Lee University, where he will lecture on writing. Of his campus appearances—he gets $3,500 plus expenses—Capote says: "My favorite place was the University of Montana at Mahzooooola. There was something very special about the students. Removed from television and other urban nonsense, they're sort of pure. They really read and they're very bright." He also enjoyed the University of Florida where a question-and-answer session turned free-for-all. Asked pointblank if he was a homosexual, Capote replied: "Is that a proposition?"

The college dates appeal to his sense of drama. Offstage at Washington and Lee with more than a thousand students awaiting him, Capote asks a student organizer for a pitch-black house. "Now when I count to 20," he instructs, "you turn on the spotlight." Truman counts and suddenly jumps onstage, popping into view like a mad genie. He pirouettes, bows, tips his hat and wildly waves his hands. The hall rocks with laughter, then falls silent. Capote begins reading *A Christmas Memory*, a tender story from his childhood. The voice is nasal and simpering, the plump figure almost ludicrous, and yet he has captivated the young audience. "Oh, I'm great at disarming people," Truman says. "As a child other children sensed that I was different. There was a certain fear and fascination about me."

Born Truman Streckfus Persons in New Orleans, he was the only child of a marriage that ended before he was 5. His alcoholic mother ("very beautiful, a Southern Ava Gardner who wanted to forget she had this life with my father") eventually remarried a wealthy businessman named Capote. In 1953 she killed herself with sleeping pills. Of his father, a steamship manager who later went into the vending machine business, Capote says: "I don't have any sort of feeling about him. He was a completely strange person I never knew. But he writes me very sweet, affectionate letters."

At 3, Truman was sent to live with his mother's relatives in Monroeville, Ala. Out of his love for one of the spinster cousins in the house, he wrote *A Christmas Memory.* "She was the only stable person in my life," he says. Though her literary taste was limited to the comic strips, she taught him to read. Saturdays she would give him a dime to go to the movies and Truman would later tell her the story. "I really think this explains my interest in narrative prose writing," he says. "You should have seen me do King Kong: 'Fay Wray, why do you want to be in movies?' " Truman growls, " 'Because,' he squeaks, 'it's FAME, it's FUN, it's MONEY!' "

His neighbor in Alabama was Nell Harper Lee, author of *To Kill a Mockingbird.* One of its characters, Dill, is Capote. Today the two old friends remain close—she has an apartment in New York. "We are bound by a common anguish," Harper says without further explanation. She recalls how the kindergarten teacher whacked Truman on the hands with a ruler because he read too well. "It's true," Capote wails, and Lee, glancing protectively at her friend, winces and says, "It was traumatic for him."

At 10, Capote left for New York to live with his mother and stepfather. Shortly thereafter he began to shuttle between schools, eventually dropping out to write. "I was pretty and bright," he remembers, "and I stood apart from the other kids."

When he was 16, Capote, who has never received a rejection slip, published his first story, "My Side of the Matter." It deals with the grievances of a young Southerner against his bride's family. Two years later "Miriam," a bizarre story about a waif inflicting her disquieting presence on a middle-aged widow, won him an O. Henry Memorial Award and a contract from Random House. "I was unusual," he says with self-disparagement. "Like a musical prodigy, blah, blah, blah."

Today Capote maintains an apartment in Manhattan, plus homes in Malibu, California (where a male companion is installed), Vevey, Switzerland and East Hampton, Long Island (a male writer lives there). Capote's bulldog, Maggie, spent the winter in Switzerland "romping in the snow" and "stopping off in Paris for the collections."

"To be a somebody," says Capote, "you have to work hard." He skims through 12 papers and magazines each day and reads five books a week. Though he writes only four months a year, five hours a day, he never takes a complete break. "The writing is completely in my head," he says, patting his brow like a treasure chest. "I never stop thinking about it for one minute, thinking, thinking." Once a bit of gossip enters his Humpty-Dumpty head, it instantly becomes a story. Capote frets about writing. "I want my writing to be as pure as a distilled glass of water. I want it to be precise, easy and maintain a high level of artistry."

Of his controversial *Answered Prayers*, he says: "I was born to write that particular book. It is the only true thing I know about a certain level of American society. Nobody else could have written it—not one of them would have had the pure guts. I lived through it, backwards and forwards. This book means a lot to me. It means everything!"

Though his body aches from bursitis and his left eye is hemorrhaging from an infection, Capote shows up at a post-lecture reception at the Washington and Lee gym. He sits in a corner and patiently autographs his books. At 10 p.m., too exhausted to sleep or eat, he creeps back to the motel.

Collapsing on the bed with his trousers and shirt still on, Capote admits he is conscience-stricken about Babe Paley, a friend who has been ill. A society beauty and wife of CBS chairman William Paley, she was greatly disturbed by some of his portrayals in *Answered Prayers*. Tears streaming down his chubby cheeks, Capote says, "I love Barbara more than anybody in the world. She's really special. And now she's sick." He holds a vodka-and-orange juice in one hand, massages his temples with the other and dismisses the rest of the chic crowd. "Really rich people are the most pathetic, so frightened, so insular. A yacht and five houses are what they have in common. They don't even like each other. My book will be the definitive work on a whole kind of ambience."

A room-service roast beef sandwich arrives and is limp. He gives it a melancholy glance. "I could write a book about my book which would be amusing," he chuckles. "People call and ask me, 'Truman, am I in your book?' 'Not yet,' I say, 'but we're saving space for you—like we say at Forest Lawn. We'll fit you all in, coffins to measure.' Ho, ho, ho."

After Hours: Books
Beverly Gary Kempton/1976

From *Playboy*, 23 (December 1976), 47, 50. Copyright © 1976 by Playboy. Reprinted by special permission of Playboy Magazine.

Truman Capote has been called many things—from literary gadfly to serious writer—and his long-awaited novel *Answered Prayers* isn't going to set the record straight if the reaction to the three chapters previewed in *Esquire* is any indication of what's to come. The media went crazy speculating about the real identities of his characters—which Capote says isn't the point of the novel at all. So *Playboy* sent writer Beverly Gary Kempton to talk with him in an attempt to untangle media event from literary event.

Playboy: The media have probably spent more time trying to figure out who the characters in your book are than remarking on how it works as a novel. What is your reaction to all this?
Capote: Amazement. I've published only three chapters, after all.
Playboy: How long will the finished book be?
Capote: It will print out to about 600 pages of good-sized type. But at this point, I don't think people understand what it is I am doing.
Playboy: What *are* you doing?
Capote: I'm just carrying my ideas about nonfiction writing one step further. *In Cold Blood* was pure journalism; every word of it was true. But the logical extension of that was to write a novel that was really a novel—and yet everything in it was true. A *roman à clef* is something that's disguised very vaguely, but I'm not bothering to disguise anything. I'm laying it right on the line and, to me, it is a literary experiment.
Playboy: Why did you want to combine the two forms?
Capote: Because I've never seen it done before and it's a

challenge. My book is in no way modeled after Proust, although it has certain elements that are the same. It's very American and very contemporary, written in a language that is of the moment. But I've always had the theory that Proust's books would have been better if he hadn't spent all that time disguising things and transposing sexes.

Playboy: When did the idea for this book come to you?

Capote: About 20 years ago. I wrote the last 250 pages first, so I would always know exactly where I was going. It's such a complicated book, like a series of Chinese boxes that keep opening and opening.

Playboy: What are you trying to cover in the book?

Capote: Just about everything. It's not about the jet set per se; that's just part of it. The book is really about the narrator, and even very intelligent people seem to think the narrator is me.

Playboy: Well, isn't he?

Capote: That has been the difficulty. Sometimes the narrator is me—for example, in a scene with Colette. But I took another person—his background and his particular personality—and grafted the two together. Otherwise, the book wouldn't work. There are certain things about the narrator that could never have happened to me, but there are also things about the narrator that could never have happened to the other person. It's necessary to the story that the narrator be a failed person.

Playboy: The main scene to which people are reacting is the one in the New York restaurant La Côte Basque. The narrator is lunching with the ladies of the jet set, some of whom, like Walter Matthau's wife, Carol, are called by their real names, others of whom are called by fictional ones. Who is the narrator in this excerpt?

Capote: Obviously, I am.

Playboy: The narrator in another excerpt, "Unspoiled Monsters," says he'd like to be a grownup. What does being a grownup mean to you?

Capote: I mean I wanted to have some mature feelings and mature judgments and not be so subjective and erratic in my behavior and opinions. And I wanted to be less fearful.

Playboy: Is it possible to be grown-up?

Capote: No. Maybe on your deathbed.

Playboy: You've been in and out of the Côte Basque world for years. Why has it attracted you, when you've said repeatedly that much of what goes on there is a waste of time?

Capote: Because I wanted to write this book.

Playboy: Really?

Capote: Basically, yes. Actually, there were four or five people in that world I really liked a lot, and still like very much.

Playboy: Who?

Capote: Well, Barbara Paley, Lee Radziwill . . . oh, I don't know, a half-dozen people.

Playboy: Are the rich different?

Capote: Of course they are different. They have extraordinary freedom. They live in a dimension beyond that of most other people. They have a strange way of hanging together all the time, but they don't really like one another at all. It's as if they were afraid to go outside their little enclave.

Playboy: What do *you* represent to them?

Capote: I don't know, really. I'm a very good conversationalist, very amusing.

Playboy: You never felt they were using you?

Capote: Oh, no.

Playboy: But you've been conscious, as the years went by, of the extent to which you were using them?

Capote: But I *wasn't* using them. I mean, it was a fair exchange.

Playboy: Is gossip literature?

Capote: Of course it is—and, in fact, my entire book is gossip. I don't deny that for an instant. What I say is that *all* literature is gossip, certainly all prose-narrative literature. What in God's green earth is *Anna Karenina* or *War and Peace* or *Madame Bovary* if not gossip? Or Jane Austen? Or Proust? Gossip is the absolute exchange of human communication. It can be two ladies at the back fence or Tolstoy writing *War and Peace*.

Playboy: Do people confide in you?

Capote: Oh, yes, they tell me, they write to me. I think it's because I have a totally noncritical attitude; people feel they can tell me anything at all. I can see things from two angles. I have an extremely strong, masculine mind and a feminine sensibility level, which is kind of an unusual combination. Both men and women tell me things and I can relate on two levels simultaneously.

Playboy: Do you care what other people think about you or your work?

Capote: I don't give a damn, really. I know what I think about myself as a writer. The fact is I'm very good. But I do want to prove to myself that I can do something as complicated as this book.

Playboy: And are you proving it to yourself?

Capote: So far. So far.

Truman Capote: An Interview
Cathleen Medwick/1979

From *Vogue*, 169 (December 1979), 263, 311-312. Copyright © 1979 by Condé Nast Publications Inc. Reprinted by permission.

Truman Capote knows how to make an entrance. He has always known. In 1948, when he published his first book—a slim siren of a novel called *Other Voices, Other Rooms*—he quite simply created a sensation. It was not just the lush beauty of his prose, his precocious mastery. It was also that the book's jacket displayed a photograph of the unknown young author: a delicately pale young man reclining on a chaise longue, his eyes leveled provocatively at the camera. They were the eyes of a lover, or a murderer. A tough faun, as a friend has said. Truman Capote at twenty-three was the New Orleans country boy who came to the big city and, with cool country know-how, seduced it. That was an artful seduction: as though Truman, a boy fishing at an enormous pond, spotted a great, elusive fish and knew just how to get it: camouflaged his hook with gleaming bait (himself) and waited with the patience of saints. When he caught that fish, fame, he caught it suddenly, and for keeps. His talent, was, of course, the hook. Without that, he could never have joined the front ranks of contemporary Southern writers—Porter, Welty, McCullers—and stayed there, as one of America's foremost literary talents, for over thirty years.

Since the boy on the book jacket, we have seen many Capotes. Like a wizard, he is always assuming new shapes, new disguises. A small, dapper Capote in a grey pinstripe suit and black-rimmed glasses, leading a gelatinous Marilyn Monroe in a dance at El Morocco in 1954. A beaming, black-tie Capote in a black mask (Capote the social butterfly), the darling of the jet set, ushering newspaper heiress Katharine Graham into the $75,000 ball he threw for her in 1966—threw it, he said then, in order to go to a party where he could *really* have a good time. A thinner, dowdier Capote (one of his friends said that his pants always looked baggy, like he'd been whacked in the ass with a shovel) being frisked at San Quentin, where he was interviewing murderers in 1972—several years after his mercilessly detailed account of a Kansas murder, *In Cold Blood*, established him as a major force in American writing (Capote the serious author). A plump, porcine Capote wearing shades and playing in the 1976 movie *Murder by Death* (Capote the movie star). A betrayed and belligerent Capote, after chapters from his still forthcoming book *Answered Prayers*, a thinly disguised tale about his jet-set friends, were published in *Esquire*, and the Beautiful People closed their doors on him. Finally (it seemed then), a down-and-out Capote confessing his addictions to drugs and drink on the Stanley Siegel talk show, and expressing quivery intentions of overcoming his addictions—if he didn't accidentally kill himself first.

These were the images the press eagerly fed the public over the years. Or, rather, the images that Capote fed the press. But no matter how many masks he assumed, how much each new Capote shocked and titillated the public, there was always a backbone of achievement that made Capote more than fodder for gossip columnists, or his erstwhile friends. There was always a new work, and it was always good. Capote's writing, like his public imaage, seemed capable of endless transformations. Out of the haunting prose-style of *The Grass Harp* and the early stories he distilled a new literary genre—a kind of reporting that revealed reality to be even more freakish, more fabulous than fiction. *In Cold Blood* was (like its author) vivid, shocking, and impossible to ignore. As Capote's own life became more of a fable than ever, as the "tiny terror" sharpened his claws on Gore Vidal and other opponents, as his social status plummeted, the public's appetite for Capote's prose became even keener. Today, more than ten years after it was first promised to them, prospective readers of *Answered Prayers* are still licking their chops with anticipation. Fame and notoriety have always mirrored each other in Capote's life, and still do, like the Siamese twins he uses nowadays as his literary personae: Capote, meet Capote. Janus faces, the killer and the saint.

To his enemies, Capote is, almost literally, the spitting image of the person they have attacked: he can caricature himself better than they can and, in so doing, become a kind of avenging demon. To his friends (and his lovers), Truman is a childhood fantasy—a Dutch uncle, a bosom companion. These are also masks, mirror-images; but they are not lies. Inside the fiction hides the truth. Inside the mask, another mask.

There is a Truman Capote that few people have ever seen: the artist who is continually taking the measure of himself and his work. Talking about his career, Capote assesses himself minutely, as a saint would do; he details, with an objectivity that can be chilling, the progress he has made toward his goal.

"It has nothing to do with ego. It certainly doesn't in my case because I honestly don't have very much ego. I have a tremendous feeling about the importance of my writing. I mean, I owe it to God, if you want to put it that way, to achieve what I know I can. I can't stop here, you know, because there is this other level, the ultimate state of grace—and *I have to get there.*"

The Truman Capote who speaks is, at fifty-five, a wisp of a man— only ninety-three pounds—wearing, nevertheless, a big, flamboyant straw hat ("Do you like my hat?" is what he asks as he makes his entrance into the room). In fact, the hat makes his face look longer, paler, a kind of underlying apparition. But the eyes are burning bright—the eyes of someone who has seen and fought demons, is still seeing and fighting them. As if to flick the demons out of sight, Truman finds things to entice him in far corners. He drifts—is wafted—into a chair; but, instead of resting in it, he seems to be buffeted by some mean, childish wind that ruffles the loose skin on his neck and makes his hands float in the air, his body flutter. He is like some angular bird that might, at any moment, fly out of the room and escape into the noon sky.

When he talks, it seems at first as if his voice, too, is weightless— that mewing whine of his, but fading or (his kind of word) perishing. Until he speaks about himself, his reputation: then his voice concentrates into a glassy, sharp-edged ping; he flies at you, even pounds his fist on the table, wanting you to know about him, who (he says) he really is.

"I consider that I have a career as an artist. I'm fifty-five years old and I've been writing professionally for almost forty years. That's a very long time. Most people—you know, famous people, personalities, usually they're entertainers—have very short careers. A writer *can* have a long career, but very few of them actually do. Because it's so nerve-shattering. It's this continuous, constant gamble. I mean, if you're really a good artist. If you're not a good artist, well, it doesn't matter, because your conscience isn't affected. You're not continuously striving and reaching and being miserable and happy and taking drugs and drinking and doing something to try to get out of this ghastly tension. Because what you're doing is gambling with your life" (a strident ping here). "It isn't reputation, this is your life, these are the years gone by, and am I wasting them? Have I totally wasted it?"

Capote is leaning forward now, his eyes shooting blue lasers as he speaks, his fist pounding the table, punctuating his words.

"I mean, I think I have a really great gift, and I owe it somehow to *get it out!* But I have to get it out the best possible way, and that is what makes an artist have a career: it is this integrity of holding on, holding on, holding on no matter what."

Like Proust, when he shocked the elite of Paris by publishing their secrets, in *Remembrance of Things Past?*

"Well, Proust really had a relatively short career. It was monumental, but it was short. And when he first began to publish his books, he was not a famous writer. So when he was attacked, he was attacked in a very limited circle by people who knew him. But the big difference is that when I started to publish I was a very famous writer. And person, period. The attack on me was monumental! I mean, from all sides—you'd think I'd killed Lindbergh's baby! That it wasn't Hauptmann at all, no, it was Truman Capote who had stolen the child and strangled him."

Capote is in his element now. In control of his tale.

"And they didn't let it go at that. I mean, everything in my personal life, you know. So, I had an alcoholic problem. Well, my God, they turned that into the war of the worlds or something. I survived it. I overcame it. It was a tremendous struggle, but God knows nobody was helping me. I mean, I thought it was a very small reward for having devoted so much of your life to contributing, you know. . . . But that's how things go. They build you up and they knock you down. Build you up and they knock you down."

Why, in Capote's mind, do people turn against him?

"It's a kind of human nature thing, I suppose. It happens to everybody. It happens to everybody who has a career that lasts long enough, I can assure you. At some point they're going to turn against you. I mean, I've been turned against several times. When my first book came out, *Other Voices, Other Rooms*, I was overnight an incredibly notorious person. Well, I would call it turning against me, wanting to destroy the book and the reputation I achieved by attacking my personal character."

Superimposed: the image of the sultry, smoky-eyed young man, challenging from his chaise lounge. . . .

"Well, the photograph was simply an image of something else they wanted to attack. They wanted to attack my entire nerve, the gall of me to be what I was."

And when people attack him that way, does he think they really want him to go on being what he is?

"Basically, they do. . . . I no longer pay any attention to any kind of an attack at all. Believe me, I don't. They can accuse me of mass murder and it wouldn't make my pulse skip a beat. I don't care about anything, I . . . but what was the question?"

Does he think people . . .

"I think," (his voice like a schoolmarm's, like a ruler rapping the knuckles) "that if you back down from something when you're attacked, they will then scent fear and blood and come after you, wham. And I knew that full well and so I never backed down. Well, I didn't feel like backing down. Why should I? I was right! I was doing the right thing! They were wrong! They were stupid! And so, I wouldn't back down, I didn't back down, that's what you should do.

"Just go on doing what you're doing. And even if it's wrong, go on doing it. You shouldn't ever let them sense a weakness in you, because then they'll go for you like sharks go for somebody with his blood in the water."

In a world of predators, it is either eat or be eaten. And an artist faces one more danger, that he will consume himself.

"It's really totally incredible the state of tension that a person like me lives in. And most people don't realize it. First of all, I am receiving about fifteen more impressions per minute than most people. You know, that's a big strain in itself."

Truman receives impressions as if they were telegrams, secrets that no one else knows. Like the way a lizard moves, liquidly, and the way it turns a dreamily disturbing color under water. The way a cottonmouth rears up, winding, hypnotizing with its eyes, until there is no place to run.

"And people say, well, why do so many painters and writers drink, why do they take drugs? Well, I understand it perfectly, because I went that route. I got out of it because if I hadn't got out of it I would have eventually killed myself."

Does he ever feel he is working against time?

"Yes, that phrase has crossed my mind, but I don't feel it in the sense that Proust felt it, since he was dying. I feel that I have to achieve a certain thing by a certain time in order to relax enough to go on to the ultimate fulfillment of my gift. I feel that I have to, within a year, have achieved something in my new phase that will give me a certain sense of relaxation and confidence so that I can catch my breath before, you know, taking that tremendous leap."

He writes now for many hours at a stretch, in a room he has acquired just for the purpose. The room is all white, with just some photos taped to the walls. A view of the river. Truman writes standing up, facing the view.

"For the last year or so, I really have been doing nothing but work work work work work. I work at writing ten, eleven hours a day. I mean, I've never done that in my life. And I know it's going to go on that way. I long for some sort of break in the thing, an end to it. . . ."

He says he does not go out anymore—except to the gym, where "I go swim in the damn pool every day for an hour and I hate it; it bores me out of my mind. And I don't want to eat, because I have a mild anorexia, I don't know why. But I force myself to eat just because I've got to stay in top condition."

There is this feeling he has, really always has had in public, that he is there but not there. Recently, he had to leave a Broadway show in the middle because he couldn't concentrate. And he has come to hate going out for lunch or dinner because, frankly, it makes him extremely nervous.

"I have a distinct feeling that my whole life has been, since I was seventeen years old—that I've been living inside an electric light bulb, and that it's all a play. People come in and take various parts in the play, and then they depart and they come back, or they sit down, but it's like a continuous, ongoing play with a large audience watching it.

"Somebody asked me about a year ago what am I famous for, and I said 'I'm famous for being famous.' You know? That's one way people can be destroyed. I've always been famous for being famous; but, at the same time, I was *aware* of it. So therefore it didn't affect me, and it wasn't the poisonous thing that it is. It's a subtle kind of poison, and people don't realize when it starts."

When the cottonmouth is posed to strike, Capote does something. He writes. So that always, however venomous the attack, there is a substance that is indestructible, a body of work. Writing is Capote's most potent kind of wizardry, his antidote for snakebite. With it, he can charm the beast and protect the most vital part of his own being.

That is how Truman Capote has survived—drugs, alcohol, serious physical illness, betrayal of friends—and that is why his literary reputation is his life's blood. His survival is, as he readily admits, a miracle. Still, it was no surprise to see his gremlin face grinning from the pages of *Interview* this past year, with the running question, "Is Truman Human?" (Not even *Interview* dared to answer that.) It is no surprise that *Esquire*, which heralded his fall from grace with tidbits from *Answered Prayers*, is publishing this month a new piece called "Dazzle." A miraculous kind of comeback—but Truman never really went away. He is a fighter, after all, red in tooth and claw—and perhaps it is just that killer instinct that saves him.

20 Questions: Truman Capote
Nancy Collins/1980

From *Playboy*, 27 (December 1980), 259, 270. Copyright © 1980 by Playboy. Reprinted by special permission of Playboy Magazine.

Each of Truman Capote's books has generated strong opinion—most (but not all) of it enthusiastic. *Music for Chameleons*, his latest, is no exception, so we dispatched syndicated television reporter Nancy Collins to discuss that and other subjects with him at his New York apartment. "He had a terrible cold," she told us, "but that didn't muffle any of *his* opinions."

1.

Playboy: Americans seem obsessed with other people's opinions—especially yours. Why?

Capote: My *own* opinion is that people don't have good opinions. Everybody borrows his opinions from other people, who have already borrowed theirs from somebody else. That's why conversation is so difficult.

2.

Playboy: Do you think your opinions are the basis of your appeal?

Capote: I don't have any appeal. I just arouse curiosity. Actually, that's about 70 percent true. I do think I have a largish following of people who really just like my writing.

3.

Playboy: What is the state of man/woman relationships today?

Capote: The same as it has been and always will be; I don't think anything is ever going to change between men and women. The real difference between men and women is nature. There's something in the nature of a woman that makes her want to be dominated by a man, at least in some sexual sense. And that's something that can't be eradicated.

4.

Playboy: Hasn't the women's movement changed that?

Capote: Women's liberation has gone a long way and it's done a terrific lot, economically speaking. Actually, inflation has more to do with women's liberation than anything else—you know, the need for a second income. The old husband is glad to push the old wife out to work nowadays. Before, he would have said, "Oh, honey, I wouldn't have you soiling your hands down at the garage." Now he has her pushing an 18-ton truck.

5.

Playboy: What have women lost because of the women's movement?

Capote: I don't think they've lost a thing, or at least, they've gained a lot more than they've lost. They gained economic independence. What they lost—if they lost it—is what their actual role *is* in relation to a man. That particular seesaw, balancing a successful career and a successful marriage—well, I've never seen it work. I've never known a career woman who didn't essentially dominate her husband.

6.

Playboy: But isn't power in a woman sexy?

Capote: I think power in a man is sexy, but I don't think power in a woman is sexy. I think power in a woman turns men off. It's too intimidating.

7.

Playboy: Then you wouldn't find, say, Barbara Walters sexy?

Capote: I don't consider Barbara Walters powerful in that sense. She's a television personality. Her power can go like that [*snaps his fingers*]. It's hanging on a very thin string. By tomorrow, ABC could fire her and she'd be selling lingerie at Bloomingdale's.

8.

Playboy: Who are the sexiest women you know?

Capote: I think Kay Graham is extremely sexy. Her figure and make-up are great; she has extraordinary eyes and one of the most seductive voices you ever heard—when, that is, she's being seductive. She makes any man she's with totally forget all about Kay Graham, Tycoon. I don't think she's always had this quality; she didn't when I first knew her.

Very few men are attracted to women because of their minds, although for my next candidate that might seem to be the only reason: Lillian Hellman. Lillian is not at all what we would normally call a particularly attractive woman. However, she has this amazing thing—if women have it, they can put themselves over, no matter what they look like. Lillian Hellman simply believes she is the sexiest, most alluring woman in any room. She moves that way; she acts that way; she looks at men that way. The *last* thing on Hellman's mind is literature or art. Her whole manner is strictly below the belt—the way she moves her hips, her arms, her hands, the whole thing. The funny thing about it is it works; I know innumerable men who have been in love with her.

The next woman is Maria Theresa Caen, the wife of columnist Herb Caen. She is from Louisiana, is small and Spanish. She's not exactly beautiful at all—she's always well-groomed—but you always notice that men gravitate toward her. There's something in her voice, her laugh. She's got this real merriment about her. She's also extremely intelligent.

Also, Gloria Guinness is an extraordinarily sexy woman. She has great allure and mystery. She's a self-creation—that's why I like her. All the women I really like are self-creations.

9.

Playboy: What makes rich women more interesting than poor ones? Or are they?

Capote: I don't think rich women are interesting at all. My idea of joy is not to sit next to Blanchette Rockefeller at dinner, you know.

The only rich women who ever interested me, the only ones who were ever my friends, were adventuresses—people who were total self-creations. Gloria Guinness is a prime example. And Jackie Onassis and Lee Radziwill are not far off the mark. They started out with money, so they weren't entirely self-made. And, of course, there was Babe Paley. She came from a very distinguished background, but, indeed, she was a total self-creation. She made herself look that way; it was her taste, her style, her total invention.

10.

Playboy: Is the age of the adventuress over?

Capote: A top-class adventuress is in a category all by herself. But she's a rare creature, so when one comes along, there's always a big market for her.

I would advise a lot of women who have brains, good looks, style, and so forth, and set out to make a career as an actress or a model, to forget it. Pretend you never heard of the theater or the movies. Say all that interests you is leading a very subdued, settled, high-society life and you'll make it. I don't know if you'll get what you want, but you'll get more than you would the other way. Unless she's got fantastic drive, a woman shouldn't be too career-oriented. It's OK up to a point, but you have to have inhuman drive.

11.

Playboy: In *Breakfast at Tiffany's*, Holly Golightly says she has taught herself to like older men because she thinks it's good for her. Is this still good advice for a woman?

Capote: Indeed it is. Older men are a passport that'll carry you across all frontiers.

12.

Playboy: Why are older men better?

Capote: Well, first of all, there's so much more security attached to an older man. And with an older man, a woman is just as—probably more—agreeably active sexually. You're not going to get your brains pounded out morning and afternoon, as—I read in *Ann Landers*—many women are. In fact, to hear *Dear Abby* tell it, the women in this country are in hysterics over getting fucked to death.

13.

Playboy: Are the rich really different from you and me?

Capote: Yes, they're more disloyal. In the long run, the rich run together, no matter what. They will cling until they feel it's safe to be disloyal, then no one can be more so. They also serve better vegetables.

14.

Playboy: It seems as if the rich—that is, the old rich—have lost some of their allure. What was it in the first place and what happened to it?

Capote: I think the thing about the rich is their great terror. You see, their only identification is their money. They have this real fear about money, because if they lose it, they lose their identity. What they have lost—what you call allure—is their stability, because no one is really rich anymore. Being rich is like the Presidency—it just doesn't have the cachet it used to. On the whole, I don't think young people are interested in rich people today. I mean, who the hell wants a 180-foot yacht and 25 servants? That sort of thing had to do with money being the only thing that gave a person identity, so you had to spend more and more to get more and more identity.

15.

Playboy: Define decadence—once and for all.

Capote: Decadence is deliberate cruelty. It is any act you perpetrate against another person that you know is going to hurt him—and you do it on purpose, with full knowledge that you are doing it.

16.

Playboy: Who is America's most unattractive public couple?

Capote: Hands down, Julie and David Eisenhower. No competition.

17.

Playboy: Who is the person most responsible for pushing America down the tubes?

Capote: Sammy Davis, Jr.—if you're referring to television. You simply cannot turn on the damn set without seeing that ugly, hideous face, with his million dollars' worth of jewelry, jingling and jangling, hugging and kissing *somebody*. Yuuuch! God!

18.

Playboy: What is the future of democracy?

Capote: The same as Broadway's. Everything seems to be picking up. Theaters last year made more money than ever. Yes, it's like Broadway—everybody always says it's dead, it's gone—but it always comes back.

19.

Playboy: What is your idea of a fun date?

Capote: Miss Piggy or Anita Bryant.

20.

Playboy: In a movie about your life, who would you like to play you?

Capote: Greta Garbo. It'll be her great comeback part.

Nocturnel Turnings, or How Siamese Twins Have Sex
Truman Capote/1980

From *Music for Chameleons* (New York: Random House, 1980), 243-262. Copyright © 1980 by Random House, Inc. Reprinted by permission.

TC: Shucks! Wide awake! Lawsamercy, we ain't been dozed off a minute. How long we been dozed off, honey?

TC: It's two now. We tried to go to sleep around midnight, but we were too tense. So you said why don't we jack off, and I said yes, that ought to relax us, it usually does, so we jacked off and went right to sleep. Sometimes I wonder: Whatever would we do without Mother Fist and her Five Daughters? They've certainly been a friendly bunch to us through the years. Real pals.

TC: A lousy two hours. Lawd knows when we'll shut our eyes agin. An' cain't do nothin' 'bout it. Cain't haf a lil old sip of sompin 'cause dats a naw-naw. Nor none of dem snoozy pills, dat bein' also a naw-naw.

TC: Come on. Knock off the Amos 'n' Andy stuff. I'm not in the mood tonight.

TC: You're never in the mood. You didn't even want to jack off.

TC: Be fair. Have I ever denied you that? When you want to jack off, I always lie back and let you.

TC: Y'all ain't got de choice, dat's why.

TC: I much prefer solitary satisfaction to some of the duds you've forced me to endure.

TC: 'Twas up to you, we'd never have sex with anybody except each other.

TC: Yes, and think of all the misery *that* would have saved us.

TC: But then, we would never have been in love with people other than each other.

TC: Ha ha ha ha ha. Ho ho ho ho ho. "Is it an earthquake, or only a shock? Is it the real turtle soup, or merely the mock? Is it the Lido I see, or Asbury Park?" Or is it at long last shit?

TC: You never could sing. Not even in the bathtub.

TC: You really are bitchy tonight. Maybe we could pass some time by working on your Bitch List.

TC: I wouldn't call it a *Bitch* List. It's more sort of what you might say is a Strong Dislike List.

TC: Well, who are we strongly disliking tonight? Alive. It's not interesting if they're not alive.

TC: Billy Graham
Princess Margaret
Billy Graham
Princess Anne
The Reverend Ike
Ralph Nader
Supreme Court Justice Byron "Whizzer" White
Princess Z
Werner Erhard
The Princess Royal
Billy Graham
Madame Gandhi
Masters and Johnson
Princess Z
Billy Graham
CBSABCNBCNET
Sammy Davis, Jr.
Jerry Brown, Esq.
Billy Graham
Princess Z
J. Edgar Hoover
Werner Erhard

TC: One minute! J. Edgar Hoover is dead.

TC: No, he's not. They cloned old Johnny, and he's everywhere. They cloned Clyde Tolson, too, just so they could go on goin' steady. Cardinal Spellman, cloned version, occasionally joins them for a partouze.

TC: Why harp on Billy Graham?

TC: Billy Graham, Werner Erhard, Masters and Johnson, Princess

Z—they're all full of horse manure. But the Reverend Billy is just *so* full of it.

TC: The fullest of anybody thus far?

TC: No, Princess Z is more fully packed.

TC: How so?

TC: Well, after all, she *is* a horse. It's only natural that a horse can hold more horse manure than a human, however great his capacity. Don't you remember Princess Z, that filly that ran in the fifth at Belmont? We bet on her and lost a bundle, practically our last dollar. And you said: "It's just like Uncle Bud used to say—'Never put your money on a horse named Princess.' "

TC: Uncle Bud was smart. Not like our old cousin Sook, but smart. Anyway, who do we Strongly Like? Tonight, at least.

TC: Nobody. They're all dead. Some recently, some for centuries. Lots of them are in *Père-Lachaise*. Rimbaud isn't there; but it's amazing who is. Gertrude and Alice. Proust. Sarah Bernhardt. Oscar Wilde. I wonder where Agatha Christie is buried—

TC: Sorry to interrupt, but surely there is someone alive we Strongly Like?

TC: Very difficult. A real toughie. Okay. Mrs. Richard Nixon. The Empress of Iran. Mr. William "Billy" Carter. Three victims, three saints. If Billy Graham was Billy Carter, then Billy Graham would be Billy Graham.

TC: That reminds me of a woman I sat next to at dinner the other night. She said: "Los Angeles is the perfect place to live—if you're Mexican."

TC: Heard any other good jokes lately?

TC: That wasn't a joke. That was an accurate social observation. The Mexicans in Los Angeles have their own culture, and a genuine one; the rest have zero. A city of suntanned Uriah Heeps.

However, I *was* told something that made me chuckle. Something D.D. Ryan said to Greta Garbo.

TC: Oh, yes. They live in the same building.

TC: And have for more than twenty years. Too bad they're not good friends, they'd like each other. They both have humor and conviction, but only *en passant* pleasantries have been exchanged, nothing more. A few weeks ago D.D. stepped into the elevator and found herself alone with Garbo. D.D. was costumed in her usual striking manner, and Garbo, as though she'd never truly noticed her before, said: "Why, Mrs. Ryan, you're *beautiful.*" And D.D., amused but really touched, said: "Look who's talkin'."

TC: That's all?

TC: *C'est tout.*

TC: It seems sort of pointless to me.

TC: Look, forget it. It's not important. Let's turn on the lights and get out the pens and paper. Start that magazine article. No use lying here gabbing with an oaf like you. May as well try to make a nickel.

TC: You mean that Self-Interview article where you're supposed to interview yourself? Ask your own questions and answer them?

TC: Uh-huh. But why don't you just lie there quiet while I do this? I need a rest from your evil frivolity.

TC: Okay, scumbag.

TC: Well, here goes.

Q: What frightens you?

A: Real toads in imaginary gardens.

Q: No, but in real life—

A: I'm talking about real life.

Q: Let me put it another way. What, of your own experiences, have been the most frightening?

A: Betrayals. Abandonments.

But you want something more specific? Well, my very earliest childhood memory was on the scary side. I was probably three years old, perhaps a little younger, and I was on a visit to the St. Louis Zoo, accompanied by a large black woman my mother had hired to take me there. Suddenly there was pandemonium. Children, women, grown-up men were shouting and hurrying in every direction. Two lions had escaped from their cages! Two bloodthirsty beasts were on the prowl in the park. My nurse panicked. She simply turned and ran, leaving me alone on the path. That's all I remember about it.

When I was nine years old I was bitten by a cottonmouth water moccasin. Together with some cousins, I'd gone exploring in a lonesome forest about six miles from the rural Alabama town where we lived. There was a narrow, shallow crystal river that ran through this forest. There was a huge fallen log that lay across it from bank to bank like a bridge. My cousins, balancing themselves, ran across the log, but I decided to wade the little river. Just as I was about to reach the farther bank, I saw an enormous cottonmouth moccasin swimming, slithering on the water's shadowy surface. My own mouth went dry as cotton; I was paralyzed, numb, as though my whole body had been needled with Novocaine. The snake kept sliding, winding toward me. When it was within inches of me, I spun around, and slipped on a bed of slippery creek pebbles. The cottonmouth bit me on the knee.

Turmoil. My cousins took turns carrying me piggyback until we reached a farmhouse. While the farmer hitched up his mule-drawn wagon, his only vehicle, his wife caught a number of chickens, ripped them apart alive, and applied the hot bleeding birds to my knee. "It draws out the poison," she said, and indeed the flesh of the chickens turned green. All the way into town, my cousins kept killing chickens and applying them to the wound. Once we were home, my family telephoned a hospital in Montgomery, a hundred miles away, and five hours later a doctor arrived with a snake serum. I was one sick boy, and the only good thing about it was I missed two months of school.

Once, on my way to Japan, I stayed overnight in Hawaii with Doris Duke in the extraordinary, somewhat Persian palace she had built on a cliff at Diamond Head. It was scarcely daylight when I woke up and decided to go exploring. The room in which I slept had French doors leading into a garden overlooking the ocean. I'd been strolling in the garden perhaps half a minute when a terrifying herd of Dobermans appeared, seemingly out of nowhere; they surrounded and kept me captive within the snarling circle they made. No one had warned me that each night after Miss Duke and her guests had retired, this crowd of homicidal canines was let loose to deter, and possibly punish, unwelcome intruders.

The dogs did not attempt to touch me; they just stood there, coldly staring at me and quivering in controlled rage. I was afraid to breathe; I felt if I moved my foot one scintilla, the beasts would spring forward to rip me apart. My hands were trembling; my legs, too. My hair was as wet as if I'd just stepped out of the ocean. There is nothing more exhausting than standing perfectly still, yet I managed to do it for over an hour. Rescue arrived in the form of a gardener, who, when he saw what was happening, merely whistled and clapped his hands, and all the demon dogs rushed to greet him with friendly wagging tails.

Those are instances of specific terror. Still, our real fears are the sounds of footsteps walking in the corridors of our minds, and the anxieties, the phantom floatings, they create.

Q: What are some of the things you can do?

A: I can ice-skate. I can ski. I can read upside down. I can ride a skateboard. I can hit a tossed can with a .38 revolver. I have driven a Maserati (at dawn, on a flat, lonely Texas road) at 170 mph. I can make a soufflé Furstenberg (quite a stunt: it's a cheese-and-spinach concoction that involves sinking six poached eggs into the batter before cooking; the trick is to have the egg yolks remain soft and runny when the soufflé is served). I can tap-dance. I can type sixty words a minute.

Q: And what are some of the things you can't do?

A: I can't recite the alphabet, at least not correctly or all the way through (not even under hypnosis; it's an impediment that has fascinated several psychotherapists). I am a mathematical imbecile—I can add, more or less, but I can't subtract, and I failed first-year algebra three times, even with the help of a private tutor. I can read without glasses, but I can't drive without them. I can't speak Italian, even though I lived in Italy a total of nine years. I can't make a prepared speech—it has to be spontaneous, "on the wing."

Q: Do you have a "motto"?

A: Sort of. I jotted it down in a schoolboy diary: *I aspire.* I don't know why I chose those particular words; they're odd, and I like the ambiguity—do I aspire to heaven or hell? Whatever the case, they have an undeniably noble ring.

Last winter I was wandering in a seacoast cemetery near Mendocino—a New England village in far Northern California, a rough place where the water is too cold to swim and where the whales go piping past. It was a lovely little cemetery, and the dates on the sea-grey-green tombstones were mostly nineteenth century; almost all of them had an inscription of some sort, something that revealed the tenant's philosophy. One read: NO COMMENT.

So I began to think what I would have inscribed on my tombstone—except that I shall never have one, because two very gifted fortunetellers, one Haitian, the other an Indian revolutionary who lives in Moscow, have told me I will be lost at sea, though I don't know whether by accident or by choice (*comme ça*, Hart Crane). Anyway, the first inscription I thought of was: AGAINST MY BETTER JUDGMENT. Then I thought of something far more characteristic. An excuse, a phrase I use about almost any commitment: I TRIED TO GET OUT OF IT, BUT I COULDN'T.

Q: Some time ago you made your debut as a film actor (in *Murder by Death*). And?

A: I'm not an actor; I have no desire to be one. I did it as a lark; I thought it would be amusing, and it was fun, more or less, but it was also hard work: up at six and never out of the studio before seven or eight. For the most part, the critics gave me a bouquet of garlic. But I expected that; everyone did—it was what you might call an obligatory reaction. Actually, I was adequate.

Q: How do you handle the "recognition factor"?

A: It doesn't bother me a bit, and it's very useful when you want to cash a check in some strange locale. Also, it can occasionally have amusing consequences. For instance, one night I was sitting with friends at a table in a crowded Key West bar. At a nearby table, there was a mildly drunk woman with a very drunk husband. Presently, the woman approached me and asked me to sign a paper napkin. All this seemed to anger her husband; he staggered over to the table, and after unzipping his trousers and hauling out his equipment, said: "Since you're autographing things, why don't you autograph this?" The tables surrounding us had grown silent, so a great many people heard my reply, which was: "I don't know if I can autograph it, but perhaps I can *initial* it."

Ordinarily, I don't mind giving autographs. But there *is* one thing that gets my goat: without exception, every grown man who has ever asked me for an autograph in a restaurant or on an airplane has always been careful to say that he wanted it for his wife or his daughter or his girl friend, but never, *never* just for himself.

I have a friend with whom I often take long walks on city streets. Frequently, some fellow stroller will pass us, hesitate, produce a sort of is-it-or-isn't it frown, then stop me and ask, "Are you Truman Capote?" And I'll say. "Yes, I'm Truman Capote." Whereupon my friend will scowl and shake me and shout, "For Christ's sake, George—when are you going to stop this? Some day you're going to get into serious trouble!"

Q: Do you consider conversation an art?

A: A dying one, yes. Most of the renowned conversationalists—Samuel Johnson, Oscar Wilde, Whistler, Jean Cocteau, Lady Astor, Lady Cunard, Alice Roosevelt Longworth—are monologists, not conversationalists. A conversation is a dialogue, not a monologue. That's why there are so few good conversations: due to scarcity, two intelligent talkers seldom meet. Of the list just provided, the only two I've known personally are Cocteau and Mrs. Longworth. (As for her, I take it back—she is not a solo performer; she lets you share the air.)

Among the best conversationalists I've talked with are Gore Vidal (if you're not the victim of his couth, sometimes uncouth, wit), Cecil Beaton (who, not surprisingly, expresses himself almost entirely in visual images—some very beautiful and *some* sublimely wicked). The late Danish genius, the Baroness Blixen, who wrote under the pseudonym Isak Dinesen, was, despite her withered though distinguished appearance, a true seductress, a *conversational* seductress. Ah, how fascinating she was, sitting by the fire in her beautiful house in a Danish seaside village, chain-smoking black cigarettes with silver tips, cooling her lively tongue with draughts of champagne, and luring one from this topic to that—her years as a farmer in Africa (be certain to read, if you haven't already, her autobiographical *Out of Africa*, one of this century's finest books), life under the Nazis in occupied Denmark ("They adored me. We argued, but they didn't care what I said; they didn't care what *any* woman said—it was a completely masculine society. Besides, they had no idea I was hiding Jews in my cellar, along with winter apples and cases of champagne").

Just skimming off the top of my head, other conversationalists I'd rate highly are Christopher Isherwood (no one surpasses him for total but lightly expressed candor) and the felinelike Colette. Marilyn Monroe was very amusing when she felt sufficiently relaxed and had had enough to drink. The same might be said of the lamented screen-scenarist Harry Kurnitz, an exceedingly homely gentleman who conquered men, women, and children of all classes with his verbal flights. Diana Vreeland, the eccentric Abbess of High Fashion and one-time, long-time editor of *Vogue*, is a charmer of a talker, a snake charmer.

When I was eighteen I met the person whose conversation has impressed me the most perhaps because the person in question is the one who has most impressed me. It happened as follows:

In New York, on East Seventy-ninth Street, there is a very pleasant shelter known as the New York Society Library, and during 1942 I spent many afternoons there researching a book I intended writing but never did. Occasionally, I saw a woman there whose appearance rather mesmerized me—her eyes especially: blue, the pale brilliant cloudless blue of prairie skies. But even without this singular feature, her face was interesting—firm-jawed, handsome, a bit androgynous. Pepper-salt hair parted in the middle. Sixty-five, thereabouts. A lesbian? Well, yes.

One January day I emerged from the library into the twilight to find a heavy snowfall in progress. The lady with the blue eyes, wearing a nicely cut black coat with a sable collar, was waiting at the curb. A gloved, taxi-summoning hand was poised in the air, but there were no taxis. She looked at me and smiled and said: "Do you think a cup of hot chocolate would help? There's a Longchamps around the corner."

She ordered hot chocolate; I asked for a "very" dry martini. Half seriously, she said, "Are you old enough?"

"I've been drinking since I was fourteen. Smoking, too."

"You don't look more than fourteen now."

"I'll be nineteen next September." Then I told her a few things: that I was from New Orleans, that I'd published several short stories, that I wanted to be a writer and was working on a novel. And she wanted to know what American writers I liked. "Hawthorne, Henry James, Emily Dickinson . . ." "No, living." Ah, well, hmm, let's see: how difficult, the rivalry factor being what it is, for one contemporary author, or would-be author, to confess admiration for another. At last I said, "Not Hemingway—a really dishonest man, the closet-everything. Not Thomas Wolfe—all that purple upchuck; of course, he isn't living. Faulkner, sometimes: *Light in August*. Fitzgerald, sometimes: *Diamond as Big as the Ritz, Tender Is the Night*. I really like Willa Cather. Have you read *My Mortal Enemy*?"

With no particular expression, she said, "Actually, I wrote it."

I had seen photographs of Willa Cather—long-ago ones, made perhaps in the early twenties. Softer, homelier, less elegant than my companion. Yet I knew instantly that she *was* Willa Cather, and it was one of the *frissons* of my life. I began to babble about her books like a schoolboy—my favorites: *A Lost Lady, The Professor's House, My Ántonia*. It wasn't that I had anything in common with her as a writer. I would never have chosen for myself her sort of subject matter, or tried to emulate her style. It was just that I considered her a great artist. As good as Flaubert.

We became friends; she read my work and was always a fair and helpful judge. She was full of surprises. For one thing, she and her lifelong friend, Miss Lewis, lived in a spacious, charmingly furnished Park Avenue apartment—somehow, the notion of Miss Cather living in an apartment on Park Avenue seemed incongruous with her Nebraska upbringing, with the simple, rather elegiac nature of her novels. Secondly, her principal interest was not literature, but music. She went to concerts constantly, and almost all her closest friends were musical personalities, particularly Yehudi Menuhin and his sister Hepzibah.

Like all authentic conversationalists, she was an excellent listener, and when it was her turn to talk, she was never garrulous, but crisply pointed. Once she told me I was overly sensitive to criticism. The truth was that she was more sensitive to critical slights than I; any disparaging reference to her work caused a decline in spirits. When I pointed this out to her, she said: "Yes, but aren't we always seeking out our own vices in others and reprimanding them for such possessions? I'm alive. I have clay feet. Very definitely."

Q: Do you have any favorite spectator sport?

A: Fireworks. Myriad-colored sprays of evanescent designs glittering the night skies. The very best I've seen were in Japan—these Japanese masters can create fiery creatures in the air: slithering dragons, exploding cats, faces of pagan deities. Italians, Venetians especially, can explode masterworks above the Grand Canal.

Q: Do you have many sexual fantasies?

A: When I do have a sexual fantasy, usually I try to transfer it into reality—sometimes successfully. However, I do often find myself drifting into erotic daydreams that remain just that: daydreams.

I remember once having a conversation on this subject with the late E. M. Forster, to my mind the finest English novelist of this century. He said that as a schoolboy sexual thoughts dominated his mind. He said: "I felt as I grew older this fever would lessen, even leave me. But that was not the case; it raged on through my twenties, and I thought: Well, surely by the time I'm forty, I will receive some release from this torment, this constant search for the perfect love object. But it was not to be; all through my forties, lust was always lurking inside my head. And then I was fifty, and then I was sixty, and nothing changed: sexual images continued to spin around my brain like figures on a carrousel. Now here I am in my *seventies*, and I'm still a prisoner of my sexual imagination. I'm stuck with it, just at an age when I can no longer do anything about it."

Q: Have you ever considered suicide?

A: Certainly. And so has everyone else, except possibly the village idiot. Soon after the suicide of the esteemed Japanese writer Yukio Mishima, whom I knew well, a biography about him was published, and to my dismay, the author quotes him as saying: "Oh, yes, I think of suicide a great deal. And I know a number of people I'm certain will kill themselves. Truman Capote, for instance." I couldn't imagine what had brought him to this conclusion. My visits with Mishima had always been jolly, very cordial. But Mishima was a sensitive, extremely intuitive man, not someone to be taken lightly. But in this matter, I think his intuition failed him; I would never have the courage to do what he did (he had a friend decapitate him with a sword). Anyway, as I've said somewhere before, most people who take their own lives do so because they really want to kill someone else—a philandering husband, an unfaithful lover, a treacherous friend—but they haven't the guts to do it, so they kill themselves instead. Not me; anyone who had worked me into that kind of a position would find himself looking down the barrel of a shotgun.

Q: Do you believe in God, or at any rate, some higher power?

A: I believe in an afterlife. That is to say, I'm sympathetic to the notion of reincarnation.

Q: In your own afterlife, how would you like to be reincarnated?

A: As a bird—preferably a buzzard. A buzzard doesn't have to bother about his appearance or ability to beguile and please; he doesn't have to put on airs. Nobody's going to like him anyway; he is ugly, unwanted, unwelcome everywhere. There's a lot to be said for the sort of freedom that allows. On the other hand, I wouldn't mind being a sea turtle. They can roam the land, and they know the secrets of the ocean's depths. Also, they're long-lived, and their hooded eyes accumulate much wisdom.

Q: If you could be granted one wish, what would it be?

A: To wake up one morning and feel that I was at last a grown-up person, emptied of resentment, vengeful thoughts, and other wasteful, childish emotions. To find myself, in other words, an adult.

TC: Are you still awake?

TC: Somewhat bored, but still awake. How can I sleep when you're not asleep?

TC: And what do you think of what I've written here? So far?

TC: Wellll . . . since you *ask*. I'd say Billy Grahamcrackers isn't the only one familiar with horse manure.

TC: Bitch, bitch, bitch. Moan and bitch. That's all you ever do. Never a kind word.

TC: Oh, I didn't mean there's anything *very* wrong. Just a few things here and there. Trifles. I mean, perhaps you're not as honest as you pretend to me.

TC: I don't pretend to be honest. I *am* honest.

TC: Sorry. I didn't mean to fart. It wasn't a comment, just an accident.

TC: It was a diversionary tactic. You call me dishonest, compare me to Billy Graham, for Christ's sake, and now you're trying to weasel out of it. Speak up. What have I written here that's dishonest?

TC: Nothing. Trifles. Like that business about the movie. Did it for a lark, eh? You did it for the moola—and to satisfy that clown side of you that's so exasperating. Get rid of that guy. He's a jerk.

TC: Oh, I don't know. He's unpredictable, but I've got a soft spot for him. He's part of me—same as you. And what are some of these other trifles?

TC: The next thing—well, it's not a trifle. It's how you answered the question: Do you believe in God? And you skipped right by it. Said something about an afterlife, reincarnation, coming back as a buzzard. I've got news for you, buddy, you won't have to wait for reincarnation to be treated like a buzzard; plenty of folks are doing it already. Multitudes. But that's not what's so phony about your answer. It's the fact that you don't come right out and say that you *do* believe in God. I've heard you, cool as a cucumber, confess things that would make a baboon blush blue, and yet you won't admit that you believe in God. What is it? Are you afraid of being called a Reborn Christian, a Jesus Freak?

TC: It's not that simple. I did believe in God. And then I didn't. Remember when we were very little and used to go way out in the woods with our dog Queenie and old Cousin Sook? We hunted for wildflowers, wild asparagus. We caught butterflies and let them loose. We caught perch and threw them back in the creek. Sometimes we found giant toadstools, and Sook told us that was where the elves lived, under the beautiful toadstools. She told us the Lord had arranged for them to live there just as He had arranged for everything we saw. The good and the bad. The ants and the mosquitoes and the rattlesnakes, every leaf, the sun in the sky, the old moon and the new moon, rainy days. And we believed her.

But then things happened to spoil that faith. First it was church and itching all over listening to some ignorant redneck preacher shoot his mouth off; then it was all those boarding schools and going to chapel every damn morning. And the Bible itself—nobody with any sense could believe what it asked you to believe. Where were the toadstools? Where were the moons? And at last life, plain living, took away the memories of whatever faith still lingered. I'm not the worst person that's crossed my path, not by a considerable distance, but I've committed some serious sins, deliberate cruelty among them; and it didn't bother me one whit, I never gave it a thought. Until I had to. When the rain started to fall, it was a hard black rain, and it just kept on falling. So I started to think about God again.

I thought about St. Julian. About Flaubert's story *St. Julien, L'Hospitalier*. It had been so long since I'd read that story, and where I was, in a sanitarium far distant from libraries, I couldn't get a copy. But I remembered (at least I thought this was more or less the way it went) that as a child Julian loved to wander in the forests and loved all animals and living things. He lived on a great estate, and his parents worshipped him; they wanted him to have everything in the world. His father bought him the finest horses, bows and arrows, and taught him to hunt. To kill the very animals he had loved so much. And that was too bad, because Julian discovered that he liked to kill.

He was only happy after a day of the bloodiest slaughter. The murdering of beasts and birds became a mania, and after first admiring his skill, his neighbors loathed and feared him for his bloodlust.

Now there's a part of the story that was pretty vague in my head. Anyway, somehow or other Julian killed his mother and father. A hunting accident? Something like that, something terrible. He became a pariah and a penitent. He wandered the world barefoot and in rags, seeking forgiveness. He grew old and ill. One cold night he was waiting by a river for a boatman to row him across. Maybe it was the River Styx? Because Julian was dying. While he waited, a hideous old man appeared. He was a leper, and his eyes were running sores, his mouth rotting and foul. Julian didn't know it, but this repulsive evil-looking old man was God. And God tested him to see if all his sufferings had truly changed Julian's savage heart. He told Julian He was cold, and asked to share his blanket, and Julian did; then the leper wanted Julian to embrace Him, and Julian did; then He made a final request—He asked Julian to kiss His diseased and rotting lips. Julian did. Whereupon Julian and the old leper, who was suddenly transformed into a radiant shining vision, ascended together to heaven. And so it was that Julian became St. Julian.

So there I was in the rain, and the harder it fell the more I thought about Julian. I prayed that I would have the luck to hold a leper in my arms. And that's when I began to believe in God again, and understand that Sook was right: that everything was His design, the old moon and the new moon, the hard rain falling, and if only I would ask Him to help me, He would.

TC: And has He?

TC: Yes. More and more. But I'm not a saint yet. I'm an alcoholic. I'm a drug addict. I'm homosexual. I'm a genius. Of course, I could be all four of these dubious things and still be a saint. But I shonuf ain't no saint yet, nawsuh.

TC: Well, Rome wasn't built in a day. Now let's knock it off and try for some shut-eye.

TC: But first let's say a prayer. Let's say our *old* prayer. The one we used to say when we were real little and slept in the same bed with Sook and Queenie, with the quilts piled on top of us because the house was so big and cold.

TC: Our old prayer? Okay.

TC and TC: Now I lay me down to sleep, I pray the Lord my soul to keep. And if I should die before I wake, I pray the Lord my soul to take. Amen.

TC: Goodnight.

TC: Goodnight.

TC: I love you.

TC: I love you, too.

TC: You'd better. Because when you get right down to it, all we've got is each other. Alone. To the grave. And that's the tragedy, isn't it?

TC: You forget. We have God, too.

TC: Yes. We have God.

TC: *Zzzzzzz*

TC: *Zzzzzzzz*

TC and TC: *Zzzzzzzzzz*

Index

A

Acapulco, 58, 71, 78, 86, 197
Acosta, Mercedes, 318
Ackerley, J.R., 294; *My Dog Tulip*, 294
Agee, James, 27, 37
Agnelli, Gianni, 113
Agnelli, Marella, 245
Agnew, Spiro, 233
Albany, 167
Albee, Edward, 157, 166
Algren, Nelson, 198, 228; *The Man with the Golden Arm*, 198–99, 228
Allegro, John, 219
Allen, Woody, 331
American Family, 240–41, 254–55
Amos 'n' Andy, 351
Andrews, Lee, 61–62, 63
Anger, Kenneth, 282, 294–95
Antonioni, Michelangelo, 106
Arvin, Newton, 139–40
Astaire, Fred, 256
Astor, Lady, 358
Aswell, Mary Louise, 4, 15–16, 24
Atlantic Monthly, 14
Austen, Jane, 27, 42, 107–08, 117, 169, 187, 198, 326
Avedon, Evelyn, 187
Avedon, Richard, 295

B

Bacall, Lauren, 202
Backstage Wife, 34, 93
Baker, Carlos, 229
Baldwin, Billy, 189
Baldwin, James, 157, 158, 187
Bart, Peter, 325
Bassett, 131
Battle of Algiers, 276
Beard, Peter, 237, 277
Beardsley, Aubrey, 96, 114
Beatles, 278
Beaton, Cecil, 358
Beattie, Ann, 171–72
Beausoleil, Bobby, 237, 281–83, 294–95
Beauvoir, Simon de, 144
Beck, Martha, 23, 210, 212
Bell, Arthur, 249
Bell, Michael John, 127–28
Bell, Mr., 53, 60
Bellow, Saul, 158, 199, 326
Bemelmans, Ludwig, 309
Bergman, Jo, 268
Bernhardt, Sarah, 353
Bible, 138
Birch, John, 143–44
Blake, Robert, 167
Bogart, Humphrey, 92–93
Bonnie and Clyde, 129, 166
Bourjaily, Vance, 158
Bowie, David, 241
Bowles, Jane, 158
Brando, Marlon, 40–41, 192, 210, 227–28, 262–63, 274–75, 297, 326
Breen, Bobby, 94
Breit, Harvey, 17–19
Breslin, James, 50
Brian, Denis, 210–35
Brice, Fanny, 188
Bridgehampton (Long Island), 106, 114
Bronte, Emily, 118, 172
Brooks, Richard, 79, 106, 160
Brown, H. Rap, 155
Brown, Jerry, 352
Bryant, Anita, 350
Buchwald, Art, 115
Buckley, William, 152–53, 169, 216–17, 224 227, 234
Bundy, McGeorge, 107
Burden, Amanda, 187
Burroughs, William, 83, 122

Burstein, Patricia, 330–34
Bussman, Barbara, 171–72

C

Caen, Herb, 348
Caen, Maria Theresa, 348
Camus, Albert, 144, 194
Cantwell, Mary, 179–84
Capote, Joseph Garcia, 39, 111–12, 117, 205, 332
Capote, Nina Faulk, 38–39, 111–12, 116–17, 204, 240–41, 253–54, 316, 332
Capote, Truman, "Among the Paths to Eden," 91, 105, 189; *Answered Prayers*, 79, 84, 90, 161, 165, 190, 199–201, 291, 300, 301–4, 307, 315, 318–19, 320–22, 324, 330, 333, 335–38, 340, 345; *Beat the Devil*, 27, 73, 92–93, 325; *Breakfast at Tiffany's*, 13, 45–46, 73, 79, 92, 113, 119, 141–43, 160, 190, 196, 228, 251–52, 317, 331, 349; "Children on Their Birthdays," 24, 74; *A Christmas Memory*, 43, 73, 74, 79, 84, 87, 91, 93, 106, 116–17, 118, 179, 184, 189, 191, 204, 219, 320, 331, 332; "Dazzle," 345; *Dead Loss*, 239; *Death Row U.S.A.*, 189–90; *The Dogs Bark*, 300; *The Grass Harp*, 18, 24, 26, 30, 35, 38, 73, 79, 113, 160, 244, 340; *The Great Gatsby* (script), 190, 246, 258, 325; "Headless Hawk," 13; "Hilda," 11; House of Flowers, 73, 92, 106, 113, 160, 286, 314; *In Cold Blood*, 41–42, 47–68, 69–72, 73–74, 77–81, 83–84, 86, 88, 90, 91–92, 100–2, 105, 106, 107, 110–11, 113, 118, 119–34, 160, 175, 189, 190, 200, 201, 203, 206, 210–11, 212–20, 227, 259, 260, 262, 302, 314, 320, 321, 331, 335, 340; *In Cold Blood* (film), 83, 91–92, 105, 106, 107, 111, 160, 165, 166–67; *The Innocents*, 325; *Local Color*, 49, 73, 113; "Master Misery," 24; "Miss Belle Rankin," 11; "Miriam," 3, 14, 24, 35, 91, 112, 189, 332; "Mojave," 315; *Monday's Folly* see *Breakfast at Tiffany's*; *The Muses Are Heard*, 25, 40–41, 49, 70, 73, 113, 118, 119, 222, 232, 259; *Music for Chameleons*, 346; "My Side of the Matter," 8, 35, 332; "Old Mr. Busybody," 8–9, 21, 34–35, 112; *Other Voices, Other Rooms*, 3–7, 12–13, 15, 24, 30, 33, 35, 38, 39–40, 43, 69, 73, 74, 78, 80, 83, 88, 103, 108, 112–13, 114, 115–16, 169, 191, 196, 205, 260, 314, 339, 343; "Portrait of Myself," 203; *Selected Writings*, 69, 113; "Shut a Final Door," 13, 24, 74; "Swamp Terror," 11; *The Thanksgiving Visitor*, 86, 189, 191; *Then It All Came Down*, 300–1; "A Tree of Night," 13; *A Tree of Night and Other Stories*, 13, 24, 38, 73, 113; *Trilogy*, 189; "Unspoiled Monsters," 336
Carmichael, Stokeley, 155
Carson, Johnny, 114, 196, 208, 289, 305
Carter, Billy, 353
Cash, Johnny, 238
Castro, Fidel, 143, 144–45
Cather, Willa, 27, 29, 96–97, 198, 258, 359–60; *A Lost Lady*, 97, 360; *My Ántonia*, 360; *My Mortal Enemy*, 97, 359; *The Professor's House*, 360
Cavett, Dick, 225, 251, 305
Cerf, Bennett, 81, 302–3, 322
Cerf, Phyllis, 187
Chandler, Raymond, 109, 187, 198
Chaplin, Oona, 187, 321, 322
Chekhov, Anton, 12, 23, 27, 96
Chess, Marshall, 242, 256, 263, 265
Chessman, Caryl, 128
Chester, Alfred, 74
Chiang Kaishek, 330
Chicago, 35, 82, 84, 86
Christie, Agatha, 353
Cicco, Pat di, 321
Clarke, Gerald, 196–209
Clayton, Jack, 106
Cleaver, Eldridge, 233, 252–53
Cleveland, 154
Clift, Montgomery, 243–44, 275
Clutter, Herbert W., 41, 50–51, 110, 129
Clutter, Nancy, 58–59, 62–63
Cockettes, 243
Coco, James, 327, 328
Cocteau, Jean, 358
Colette, 29, 336, 358
Collins, Nancy, 346–50
Columbia University, 95, 117
Como, Perry, 169
Connolly, Cyril, 3
Connolly, John, 311
Coogan, Jackie, 94
Cooper, Alice, 273
Cooper, Gloria, 187, 320–21
Cooper, Jackie, 94
Cooper, Wyatt, 201, 209
Corona, Juan, 279–81, 293
Cosmopolitan, 201, 203
Coward, Noel, 173
Cowley, Malcolm, 215

Crane, Hart, 357
Crawford, Joan, 276
Crespi, Rudi, 113
Crump, Paul, 128
Cullivan, Donald, 211
Cunard, Lady, 358

D

Daily Variety, 324
Dali, Salvador, 287–88
Daniels, Margaret Truman, 113
Darling, Candy, 250
d'Arenberg, Princess, 113
Davis, Angela, 193, 283
Davis, Bette, 276, 318
Davis, George, 112–13
Davis, Sammy, 350, 352
Dean, James, 257
Deep Throat, 251
de la Mare, Walter, 18
DeMott, Benjamin, 223
Desperate Hours, 107, 217
Detroit, 189
Deutsch, Laurie, 171–72
Dewey, Alvin, 61, 66, 67–68, 81, 213, 215
Dickens, Charles, 25, 27, 117, 187, 198, 326
Dickinson, Emily, 359
Dietrich, Marlene, 191
Dinesen, Isak, 29, 358; *Out of Africa,* 358
di Sica, Vittorio, 28
Doors, 153, 165
Dostoevski, Feodor, 74; *Crime and Punishment,* 74; *Notes from the Underground,* 74
Douglas, William O., 139
Dreiser, Theodore, 29
Duke, Doris, 355
Dunphy, Jack, 158, 206, 302
Dylan, Bob, 192, 272, 273

E

Eden, Elizabeth, 249–50
Eisenhower, David and Julie, 350
Eisenhower, Dwight D., 41–42, 51, 110
Eli, Nathan, 238
Epstein, Edward, 151
Epstein, Jason, 206–7
Erhard, Werner, 352
Ertegun, Ahmet, 251
Esquire, 215, 234, 320, 330, 335, 340, 345
Evans, Bob, 258, 325

F

Falk, Peter, 322, 327
Fallaci, Oriana, 228
Faulk, Sook, 87, 93, 103, 191, 195, 219, 332, 353, 363, 364
Faulkner, William, 12, 27, 29, 36, 37, 198, 359; *As I Lay Dying,* 12; *Light in August,* 12, 359
Finney, Albert, 274
Firbank, Ronald, 28, 29
Fisher, Eddie, 318
Fitzgerald, F. Scott, 109, 119, 190, 198, 359; *The Great Gatsby,* 190, 246, 258, 325
Flaubert, Gustave, 23, 26, 27, 29, 35, 91, 96, 97, 108, 117, 187, 326, 360, 363; "A Simple Heart," 26, 91; "The Legend of St. Julian the Hospitaler," 35, 363–64; *Madame Bovary,* 108, 297, 337
Ford II, Henry, 113
Forster, E. M., 12, 27, 28–29, 68, 118, 198, 267, 299, 361; *A Passage to India,* 267
Fort Worth (Texas), 267
Fosburgh, James Whitney, 76
Frances, Arlene, 81
Frank, Robert, 264–65
Frankel, Haskell, 69–72
Freeman, Barry, 217
Freeman, Jeannace, 216
Frost, David, 173–78, 224
Frost, Leslie, 211
Frost, Robert, 36, 191, 205, 211, 228, 229–230
Fulbright, J. William, 145

G

Gable, Clark, 276
Gandhi, Indira, 352
Garbo, Greta, 187, 275, 318, 350, 353–54
Garden City (Kansas), 41–42, 51–52, 56, 66, 81, 85, 214
Gardner, Ava, 332
Garfunkel, Art, 273
Garrison, Jim, 151–52
Genovese, Kitty, 134–35
Gide, Andre, 14, 18, 300
Gielgud, John, 192
Gimbel, Mary Bailey, 217
Gimme Shelter, 273
Ginzburg, Ralph, 139, 140
Gold, Herbert, 111
Goldwater, Barry, 147
Golightly, Bonnie, 141

Index   369

Gortner, Marjoe, 240, 300
Goyen, William, 29, 158
Graduate, 166
Graham, Billy, 352, 353, 362
Graham, Katherine, 162, 187, 327, 339, 347
Great Gatsby, 190, 246, 258, 325
Green, Al, 255
Green Witch, 11–12
Greene, Graham, 29
Greenfeld, Josh, 324–29
Greenwich (Conn.), 7, 10, 16, 35, 96, 205
Grentreich, Dr., 256–57
Griffin, Merv, 224–25, 305
Grunwald, Beverly, 320–23
Guess Who's Coming to Dinner, 166
Guevara, Ernesto, 145
Guinness, Alec, 322
Guinness, Gloria, 78, 187, 200, 270, 348

H

Hanoi, 103, 146
Hardy, Thomas, 169; *Return of the Native,* 169
Harper's Bazaar, 4, 14, 24, 78
Harriman, Pamela, 187
Hart, Larry, 272
Hawkes, John, 158
Hawthorne, Nathaniel, 29, 117, 359
Heard, Gerald, 34; *A Taste for Honey,* 34
Heine, Sonja, 93, 164
Helen Trent, 93
Hellman, Lillian, 348
Hemingway, Ernest, 22, 29, 31, 89, 115, 165, 166, 198–99, 225, 228–29, 359
Hemingway, Mary, 228–29
Hepburn, Audrey, 113, 160, 317
Herlihy, James Leo, 158
Hersey, John, 29, 40, 49; *Hiroshima,* 49
Hickock, Richard, 52, 53, 56–68, 71, 80, 88, 110, 124, 128–34, 160, 162, 212–16, 220
Hicks, Granville, 118
Hill, Pati, 20–32
Hillsman, Roger, 147
Hoffa, James, 148
Hoge, Alice Albright, 82–85
Holcomb (Kansas), 105, 110
Holiday, Billie, 194, 225
Hollywood, 160
Hollywood Reporter, 324
Hoover, J. Edgar, 352
Horizon, 3
Hotchner, A.E., 229
Houston, 265

Howard, Jane, 211
Huston, John, 27, 92–93
Hutchens, John K., 112
Hyman, Stanley Edgar, 88

I

Interview, 345
In the Heat of the Night, 166
Isherwood, Christopher, 358
Ives, Marion, 14

J

Jackson, George, 279, 283
Jackson, Jonathan, 283
Jacksonville (Florida), 107
Jagger, Bianca, 270–72
Jagger, Mick, 242, 255–56, 259, 264, 265, 269–76
James, Henry, 22, 27, 35, 36, 109, 117, 165, 188, 198, 261, 326, 359
Javits, Jacob, 152–53, 193
Jefferson Airplane, 84, 153, 155, 166
Jennings, C. Robert, 164–70
Jewett, Sarah Orne, 118, 198, 199; *The Country of the Pointed Firs,* 198
Johnson, Dr., 71
Johnson, Lynda Bird, 113
Johnson, Lyndon, 146–47, 148
Johnson, Samuel, 33, 358
Johnson, Virginia, 352–53
Jones, James, 327
Jones, LeRoi, 157
Jones, Mrs. Acey, 4, 5
Jones, Quincy, 165
Joyce, James, 22
Judge Roy Bean, 276
Junior Bazaar, 14

K

Kafka, Franz, 36
Kansas State University, 51, 110
Katzenbach, Nicholas, 113
Kauffmann, Stanley, 111
Keaton, Diane, 331
Keith, Slim, 187
Kempton, Beverly Gary, 335–38
Kennedy, Ethel, 221
Kennedy, Jacqueline, 77, 81, 149–50, 152,

167, 208, 221, 231–32, 234, 308–12, 320, 348
Kennedy, John F., 149–52, 193, 232, 233–34, 258, 283, 310–11
Kennedy, Robert F., 87, 114, 148–52, 166, 190, 193, 225, 232, 234, 258, 312, 317–18
Kennedy, Rose, 113
Kerouac, Jack, 299
Key West, 357
Kidwell, Sue, 68
King, Carol, 272–73
King Kong, 332
Kinsey, Alfred C., 140
Knickerbocker, Susy, 114
Knowles, John, 158, 202, 206, 207; *A Separate Peace*, 202, 206
Kurnitz, Harry, 169, 358

L

Lafayette, 86
Lanchester, Elsa, 322, 327
Lane, Mark, 151
Lansky, Meyer, 252
Lasky, Victor, 148
Last Tango in Paris, 263, 274, 297–98
Las Vegas, 58, 59, 61
La Touche, John, 142
Lazar, Irving, 79, 165
Leary, Timothy, 153–54, 252–53
Lee, Harper, 51, 52, 71, 76, 94, 103, 158, 204–5, 210, 308, 316, 332; *To Kill a Mockingbird*, 51, 71, 94, 204–5, 210, 316, 332
Leigh, Vivian, 17
Leningrad, 182–83
Lerner, Max, 135
Levin, Meyer, 5; *Compulsion*, 50
Lewis, Oscar, 49; *Children of Sanchez*, 49
Life, 111, 203, 211
Lilienthal, David, 227
Lincoln, Abraham, 147
Linscott, Robert N., 14–15, 24, 109
Little Orphan Annie, 93, 152
Loewy, Viola, 187
Look, 150
London, 185
Long, Barbara, 223–24
Long, Edward, 140
Long, Huey, 152
Longworth, Alice Roosevelt, 358
Lopez, Madame Arturo, 271
Lord, Walter, 50; *A Night to Remember*, 50
Lorre, Peter, 74, 75
Los Angeles, 241, 353
Los Angeles Free Press, 293
Los Angeles Magazine, 166
Loud, Lance, 240–41

M

MacBride, Robert, 238–95; *Dead Loss*, 235
MacDonald Dwight, 159
Machiavelli, Niccolo, 202
Mademoiselle, 14, 24, 35
Mailer, Norman, 108–9, 112, 158, 187, 198, 199, 222, 232–33, 298–99, 322, 327; *Armies of the Night*, 298
Malamud, Bernard, 158
Malcolm X, 155, 233
Malibu, 333
Maloff, Saul, 89
Malraux, Andre, 144
Manchester, William, 149–51; *Death of a President*, 149–51
Manhattan (Kansas), 51
Mansfield, Katherine, 23, 96
Manson, Charles, 256, 281–83, 293
Marat/Sade, 107
Marquand, J.P., 29
Marx, Groucho, 208
Masters, William H., 352–53
Matthau, Walter, 321, 336
Mattison, Perla, 270
Maugham, Somerset, 29, 36, 109, 163
Maupassant, Guy de, 23, 27, 96, 117
Maxwell, Elsa, 113
McCarthy, Eugene, 146
McCarthy, Joseph, 148
McCarthy, Mary, 89, 111, 159, 167; *The Group*, 89
McClain, James, 51
McCullers, Carson, 14, 27, 35, 37, 158, 181, 205, 339
McGraw, Ali, 258
McNamara, Robert S., 147
McQueen, Steve, 276
Meagher, Sylvia, 151
Medwick, Cathleen, 339–45
Meehan, Kay, 187
Melhado, Louise, 187
Melville, Herman, 36, 74, 198; *Moby Dick*, 74, 198; *Pierre*, 74
Mendocino, 356
Menuhin, Yehudi, 360
Merick, David, 325
Merrill, Gary, 318

Index

Merrill, James, 29
Mexico City, 58, 59, 130
Miami Beach, 58, 78
Millbrook (Conn.), 10
Miller, Arthur, 146
Mishima, Yokio, 361
Mitchell, Joseph, 47
Mitchum, Robert, 299
Mitford, Nancy, 164
Mobile (Alabama), 8, 21, 33, 34, 174, 267
Mobile Press Register, 21, 34, 313
Modern Screen, 263
Monck, Chip, 267
Monroe (Louisiana), 5
Monroe, Marilyn, 317–18, 339, 358
Monroeville (Alabama), 38–39, 95, 112, 204, 332
Montgomery Advertiser, 313
Montgomery, Robert, 274
Moore, Robert, 328
Moreira-Salles, Madam Walther, 271
Moscow, 146
Murder by Death, 322–23, 324–29, 331, 340, 357
Myrt and Marge, 34, 93

N

Nabokov, Vladimir, 199; *Laughter in the Dark*, 199; *Lolita*, 199
Nader, Ralph, 352
Nance, William, 222–23; *The Worlds of Truman Capote*, 222–23
National Review, 153
Navarro, Ramon, 238, 281
Ned Kelly, 273
Newby, P.H., 29
Newman, Paul, 276
New Orleans, 4, 5, 7, 34, 38, 69, 75, 116, 152, 173, 238, 292, 332, 339, 359
Newquist, Roy, 38–46
New Republic, 111
Newsweek, 78, 147, 203
New York City, 3, 7, 10, 11, 13, 39, 76, 78, 81, 86, 95, 108, 110, 112, 114, 117, 118, 135, 144, 158, 160, 173–74, 181, 194, 198, 208, 257, 258, 265, 288, 304, 308, 314, 319, 336, 346, 359
New York Daily News, 205
New Yorker, 4, 5, 39, 40–41, 49, 69–70, 73, 96–97, 108, 112, 118, 153, 173, 181, 191, 205, 210, 226, 227, 228, 230, 262–63, 309, 314
New York Herald Tribune, 4, 45, 49, 112

New York Magazine, 299
New York Post, 217, 227
New York Review of Books, 45, 111, 289
New York Times, 3, 41, 45, 50, 70, 110, 111, 122, 144, 208–9, 211, 216, 226, 230, 279–80, 289
Niarchos, Mrs. Stavros, 113
Nicolson, Harold, 227
Night Must Fall, 274
Nixon, Mrs. Richard, 353
Norden, Eric, 110–63
Northampton (Massachusetts), 139

O

O'Connor, Flannery, 29, 109, 158, 187
Olivier, Laurence, 17
Omaha (Nebraska), 53
Onassis, Aristotle, 311
O'Neill, Eugene, 29
Orwell, George, 94
Oswald, Lee Harvey, 151
Our Gal Sunday, 93

P

Paar, Jack, 251, 284–85
Packard, Vance, 140
Packer, Barbara, 171–72
Paganini, Nicole, 165
Page, Geraldine, 106, 191
Paley, Barbara, 81, 167, 169, 187, 200, 204, 333, 337, 348
Paley, William S., 333
Palm Beach, 78, 197
Palm Springs, 114, 164, 170, 197, 237, 288, 296, 318
Paris, 185, 194, 195, 209
Paris Review, 222
Parker, Dorothy, 298, 324
Parker, Thomas Andrew, 165
Pearson, Drew, 162
Peck, 276
Peking, 110
Performance, 273
Persons, Joseph, 8, 38
Persons, Nina Faulk, see Nina Faulk Capote.
Persons, Truman Streckfus, see Truman Capote.
Photoplay, 41
Pierce, Marjorie, 10
Pierce, Phoebe, 11, 16
Playboy, 107, 114, 225, 335

Plimpton, George, 47–68, 200–1, 202, 226
Poe, Edgar Allan, 27, 34, 117
Porgy and Bess, 25, 40–41, 49, 73, 113, 118, 232, 259
Porter, Cole, 187
Porter, Katherine Anne, 27, 29, 44, 89, 109, 158, 187, 302, 339; *Noon Wine,* 26; *Ship of Fools,* 44, 89
Portis, Charles, 169; *True Grit,* 169
Preminger, Otto, 79
Presley, Elvis, 165–66
Price, Reynolds, 158
Proust, Marcel, 12, 23, 27, 29, 35, 36, 118, 169, 187, 198, 326, 336, 337, 342, 344, 353; *Remembrance of Things Past,* 342
Purcell, Mrs. M. K., 107
Purdy, James, 158

R

Radziwill, Lee, 77, 83, 85, 86, 113, 165, 166, 208, 231–32, 308–12, 320, 322, 323, 337, 348
Reagan, Nancy, 170, 193
Reagan, Ronald, 148, 193
Rebecca of Sunnybrook Farm, 138
Reed, Rex, 223, 224
Richard, Keith, 242, 266, 271, 272
Richardson, Tony, 273
Righter, Carroll, 98
Rilke, Rainer Maria, 27
Rimbaud, Jean, 353
Roa, Raulito, 145
Roberts, Charles, 147
Robinson, Selma, 3–16
Rockefeller, Blanchette, 348
Rockefeller, Nelson, 148
Rolling Stone, 251, 256, 290
Rolling Stones, 207, 208, 238, 241–43, 256, 259–61, 262–78, 289
Rome, 185
Ross, Harold, 191, 205, 314
Ross, Lillian, 47, 228; *Picture,* 47, 49
Rosselini, Franco, 293
Roth, Philip, 158, 199, 207; *Our Gang,* 199
Russell, Bertrand, 146
Ryan, D.D., 187, 353–54

S

Sagan, Francoise, 29
St. Louis, 51, 354
Salinger, J.D., 29, 37, 74, 75, 187; *Catcher in the Rye,* 74; *Seymour,* 74
Sandbox, 276
Sanders, Ed, 293
San Francisco, 3, 243
Santayana, George, 65, 127; *The Last Puritan,* 65
Sartre, Jean Paul, 14, 29, 144
Satie, Eric, 277
Satten, Joseph, 55, 132
Saturday Review, 203, 261
Sauvage, Leo, 151
Sayonara, 227
Schaap, Dick, 227
Schlesinger, Arthur, 150, 312
Scottsdale (Arizona), 165
Sellers, Peter, 327
Selver, Charlotte, 209
Selznick, David O., 258
Shakespeare, William, 159
Shaw, Clay, 152
Shaw, George Bernard, 27
Shaw, Irwin, 112, 159, 327
Shawn, William, 262
Siegel, Stanley, 340
Silverman, Judi, 171–72
Silver Screen, 263
Simon, Neil, 261, 289, 322, 324, 328, 331
Simon, Paul, 273
Simenon, Georges, 34; *Act of Passion,* 34
Sinatra, Frank, 255
Singer, Isaac Bashevis, 158
Smith College, 139–40
Smith, Edgar, 216–17; *Brief Against Death,* 216
Smith, Maggie, 327
Smith, Margarita, 14, 24, 181
Smith, Perry, 52, 53, 55, 56–68, 71, 75, 80–81, 88, 110, 124, 126–34, 160, 162, 195, 211, 212–16, 220
Smith, Robert Benjamin, 129
Soule, Henriette, 320, 322
Southern, Terry, 261–62
Speck, Richard, 132–33, 239
Spellman, Cardinal, 352
Stapleton, Maureen, 105
Stark, Ray, 325
Stein, Gertrude, 326, 353
Steinem, Gloria, 73–81, 86–104
Stevenson, Adlai, 192–93
Stevenson, Robert Louis, 27
Stewart, Rod, 239
Story, 8
Streisand, Barbra, 276
Styron, William, 29, 108–9, 158, 167, 187, 199; *Confessions of Nat Turner,* 109
Sunday Express (London), 111

Index

Supremes, 79

T

Talese, Gay, 226; *The Kingdom and the Power*, 226
Tallmer, Jerry, 105–9, 217, 225
Taylor, Elizabeth, 188, 318
Taylor, James, 273
Temple, Shirley, 93–94
Terkel, Studs, 224, 226; *Hard Times*, 224
Thackeray, William Makepeace, 169; *Vanity Fair*, 169, 170
Theresa, Saint, 90, 161, 165, 190, 199, 301, 320
Thompson, Josiah, 151
Thompson, Lawrance, 230
Thoreau, Henry David, 65, 66, 127
Thurber, James, 29, 37
Time, 36, 153
Tiny Tim, 240
Todd, Mike, 318
Toklas, Alice B., 353
Toledano, Ralph de, 148
Tolson, Clyde, 352
Tolstoy, Leo, *Anna Karenina*, 297, 337; *War and Peace*, 337
Tompkins, Phillip K., 215
Toscanini, Arturo, 165
Tracy, Spenser, 276
Tree, Penelope, 187
Trilling, Lionel, 139
Turgenev, Ivan, 27, 96, 97, 118, 326
Turner, Lana, 318
TV Guide, 217, 226
Twain, Mark, 29, 117
Tweedle, John, 82
Tynan, Kenneth, 174–75, 215, 220–21, 225

U

Ullanova, Galina, 160
Undset, Sigrid, 10
University of Florida, 331
University of Montana, 331
Updike, John, 44, 158, 198, 199; *Rabbit Run*, 199

V

Vanderbilt, Alfred Gwynne, 113
Van Gogh, Vincent, 206
Venice, 181, 360
Verbier (Switzerland), 114, 197
Vevey (Switzerland), 333
Vidal, Gore, 112, 167, 187, 197–98, 199, 202, 205–6, 234–35, 312–13, 327, 340, 358; *Myra Breckenridge*, 167, 327
Village Voice, 224, 249, 257
Vogue, 153, 241, 244, 309, 359
Vonnegut, Kurt, 199
Vreeland, Diana, 358–59
Vuillard, Edouard, 77

W

Wainscott (Long Island), 106, 197
Wallace, Mike, 224
Walter, Eugene, 33–37
Walters, Barbara, 347
Warhol, Andy, 83, 236–95, 296–97, 307; *Heat*, 246
Warwick, Dionne, 79
Washington (D.C.), 103, 144, 146, 294, 311
Washington, George, 86
Washington and Lee University, 331, 333
Washington Post, 162, 327
Watts, Charlie, 271
Waugh, Evelyn, 222
Weisberg, Harold, 151
Wells, Floyd, 59
Welty, Eudora, 27, 109, 187, 205, 339
Wenner, Jann, 258–59, 261, 263, 268, 277, 296–307
Wertham, Fredric, 212
Wescott, Glenway, 158, 326
West, Duane, 211, 215
West, Rebecca, 40, 47, 50, 78
Westmoreland, William C., 170
Weymouth, Lally, 187
Wharton, Edith, 12; *Custom of the County*, 12
White, Byron, 352
Whitman, Charles, 129
Whitman, Walt, 36
Whitney, Dwight, 217, 226–27
Wilde, Oscar, 96, 117, 165, 195, 209, 353, 358
Wilder, Thornton, 29
Wiley, Lee, 255
Williams, Tennessee, 76, 99, 157, 176, 197–98, 205–6, 224, 233, 250, 261, 326
Willingham, Calder, 158
Wilson, Colin, 29
Wilson, Edmund, 139
Wilson, Scott, 166–67

Windham, Donald, 158, 201
Windsor, Duke and Duchess, 86
Wolfe, Thomas, 23, 27, 96, 359
Wolfe, Tom, 50
Wood, Catharine R., 10–11, 24, 35, 90, 96
Woolf, Virginia, 12, 22
Women's Wear Daily, 167
Wozenkowitz, John, 249–50
Wray, Fay, 332

Y

Yablans, Frank, 325

Z

Zavattini, Cesare, 28
Zoerink, Richard, 308–19